COMMENTARY ON ACTS 2

COMMENTARY ON ACTS 2

STEPHEN MANLEY

COMMENTARY ON ACTS 2
© 2015 by Stephen Manley

Published by Cross Style Press
Lebanon, Tennessee
CrossStyle.org

All rights reserved. No part of this book may be reproduced in any form without prior permission from the publisher, except for brief quotations.

Scripture taken from the New King James Version®. Copyright © 1982 by Thomas Nelson, Inc. Used by permission. All rights reserved.

First Edition 2012
Second Edition 2015

Edited by Delphine Manley

ISBN-10: 0692454969
ISBN-13: 978-0692454961

Printed in the United States of America.

CrossStyle.org

CONTENTS

A New Level – Acts 2:1-4

Acts 2:1	What a Day!	3
Acts 2:1	The Joy of the Law	12
Acts 2:1	Avenues of Unity	21
Acts 2:2	The Sound from Heaven	30
Acts 2:2	The Filling	38
Acts 2:3	To Be Seated	46
Acts 2:4	Filled with What?	55
Acts 2:4	The Spirit's Mouthpiece	64

The Wonder of Dispersion – Acts 2:5-13

Acts 2:5	The Dispersion	75
Acts 2:6	The Occurring Sound	83
Acts 2:6	Necessary Amazement	91
Acts 2:11	The Language of Praise	100
Acts 2:12-13	What Does This Wish To Be?	108
Acts 2:5-13	The Reversal	116

In My Eye – Acts 2:14-28

Acts 2:14	Listen to Me	127
Acts 2:15	God or the Devil?	136
Acts 2:16-39	Peter's Explanation	144
Acts 2:16-21	The Text of Pentecost	152
Acts 2:22	The Proof	161
Acts 2:22	The Proof – His Life	170
Acts 2:23	The Proof – His Death: A Divine Plan	179
Acts 2:23	The Proof – His Death: Man's Action	187
Acts 2:24	The Proof – His Resurrection	195
Acts 2:24	The Proof – Death is Conquered	205
Acts 2:25	A Man's Concentration	214
Acts 2:26	A Man's Celebration	223
Acts 2:27	A Man's Communion	231
Acts 2:28	A Man's Communication	240
Acts 2:28	The Ultimate Goal	250

David's Message – Acts 2:29-35

Acts 2:29-30	Going Beyond	261
Acts 2:29	A Patriarch	270
Acts 2:29-30	The Patriarch Approach	278
Acts 2:29-30	The Prophetic Approach	284

Acts 2:30	The Prophetic Promise	290
Acts 2:31-32	Resurrected Life	300
Acts 2:33-35	Ascension – Decension	310

I Promise You – Acts 2:36-39

Acts 2:36	The Wrong Conclusion	321
Acts 2:36	LORD and Christ	329
Acts 2:36	Know and Knowing?	337
Acts 2:36	Lord and CHRIST	345
Acts 2:36	Power and Authority	354
Acts 2:37	Hearing	363
Acts 2:37	What Shall We Do?	371
Acts 2:38	Context of Responding	379
Acts 2:38	Content of Responding	387
Acts 2:38-39	The Promise	396

Early Church Mathematics – Acts 2:40-47

Acts 2:40-47	Early Church Mathematics	407
Acts 2:41	A Change in Location	415
Acts 2:42	Apostles' Doctrine	423
Acts 2:42	Business with Jesus	431
Acts 2:42	Eating at the Cross	440

Acts 2:42	Beseeching God	449
Acts 2:43	Fear / Awe	457
Acts 2:43	Minor / Major	465
Acts 2:44	Being Together	473
Acts 2:44-45	A Religion of Having	481
Acts 2:46	Unity of the Believers	490
Acts 2:46-47	The Lord's Addition	498

About the Author   507

PART ONE
ACTS 2:1-4

A NEW LEVEL

Acts 2:1

WHAT A DAY!

The celebrations of the Jewish nation were always focused on God Jehovah. These celebrations commemorated the significant things their God had done. God had not only delivered them from their enemies, but He had also given great provisions for their living.

The Feast of the Passover was an exciting celebration which actually continued into the Feast of Pentecost. The Jews called Pentecost "the concluding assembly of the Passover." What took place in the Passover was so powerful and long reaching it flowed into the Feast of Pentecost. There was a combination of things being celebrated during these Feasts. It started out with the offering of a Lamb. The entire ceremony was family oriented. Each family, numbering at least ten, would tell the story of how God delivered them from Egyptian bondage. They would highlight how the Death Angel passed over (Passover) their homes because the blood of the sacrificed lamb had been placed on their doorposts. This happened on the fourteenth day of the first month, which was always a Friday.

On Saturday, the fifteenth, which was the Sabbath Day, they celebrated the Feast of Unleavened Bread. During the next seven days they ate only unleavened bread. This was a remembrance of the march out of Egypt land. The next day, the sixteenth, was the first day of the week. It was the Feast of the Firstfruits, and it was the beginning of the great harvest. The

Part One: A New Level

people of Israel were to bring a sheaf of the firstfruits of the harvest to the priest, marking the beginning of the offering of the firstfruits. Fifty days later the harvest was completed. Two leavened loaves of the finest of flour were baked and brought to the priest as the firstfruits of the completed harvest. So the first sheaf offered at the Passover and the two leavened loaves at Pentecost marked the beginning and the end of the grain harvest, and sanctified the interval between as the whole harvest or Pentecostal season.

Do you see that God was ushering in the New Covenant? The Passover lamb was the symbol and means of Israel's deliverance from Egypt. It marked the beginning of everything good God had promised the Israelites. The only reason they had a land of plenty and a great harvest was the blood of the lamb. On that very day of the Passover celebration, at that very moment when the High Priest offered the official Passover lamb, hanging on a cross, Christ gave up His right to live. The veil of the temple was ripped from top to bottom. All that the Passover pointed to and symbolized was now fulfilled.

The day following the crucifixion was the Sabbath Day and the Feast of the Unleavened Bread. This was referred to as the "bread of affliction." The yeast, which in time would permeate the bread, was eliminated. The Israelites were to remember the haste of the journey from Egypt. It was a symbol of the journey of our Lord as He made His way in death to the full payment of sin. Here was the clash of good and evil in the greatest of battles. Everything would rise and fall on the outcome of this journey. Would the Savior emerge victorious? Even if He escaped, would the foe actually be defeated and redemption for mankind be grasped?

The next day was the first day of the week. It was the Feast of the Firstfruits. The harvest had begun and the first sheaf was brought to the priest. What a day this was! It is the very day God raised Jesus from the dead! Paul wrote, **But now Christ is risen** *from the dead, and has become the firstfruits of those who have fallen asleep* (1 Corinthians 15:20). The resurrected Lord is the Firstfruit of a great harvest which was be completed on Pentecost.

This is all one great event from the Biblical view. In our society we segment and departmentalize, but in the Jewish culture it was not so. The writers of the Bible viewed the crucifixion, resurrection, ascension and Pentecost as God's one redemptive movement. It was all connected. God did something very big in the crucifixion. It would manifest its firstfruits in the resurrection, but would come to the full harvest on the Day of the Feast of Pentecost.

Therefore it is absolutely impossible to understand the impact of the Day of Pentecost without looking at the many elements of the "firstfruits" and embracing their concept.

First in Sequence

The Greek word translated "firstfruits" is the combination of a prefix and a basic root word. The prefix is a primary particle which denotes "from." The root word means "to begin." It denotes the first point of time according to the context. It may have to do with creation (Hebrews 1:10; Matthew 19:4, 8), the first appearing of Jesus (Luke 1:2; John 15:27), or the ministry of Christ (Acts 1:2).

Our basic interest is with the firstfruit of the crucifixion. We have discovered the Day of the Feast of the Passover focused on the offering of the sacrificial lamb, enabling Israel's deliverance from the Death Angel. On that day as the High Priest was in the Holy Place with the official sacrifice lamb, Jesus was hanging on the cross. At the exact same moment the priest's knife touched the throat of the lamb, *Jesus cried out again with a loud voice, and yielded up His spirit* (Matthew 27:50). Could this have been an accident or coincidence? Was not God bringing to pass all

Part One: A New Level

He had promised?

The next day was the Sabbath Day. We are given details of the activities of man during that day. The **chief priests and Pharisees gathered together to Pilate** (Matthew 27:62). They broke their law by traveling beyond a Sabbath Day's journey. They also broke their defilement law by going into Pilate's palace. What was so important to them? They were anxious to seal the tomb with a Roman seal and prevent the disciples from stealing the body of Christ. However, we have very little knowledge of what took place in the spiritual realm during this time. What was Jesus doing? The mystery of the tremendous invasion into the demonic territory is beyond us. Jesus paid the equivalent of our entire eternity in hell. Yet, hell could not contain Him. This day was the Feast Day of Unleavened Bread. It was the celebration of the march out of Egypt and was surrounded by the miracles of God. Jesus experienced His own Feast Day of Unleavened Bread for us.

The next day was Sunday, the Lord's Day. It was the Feast Day of Firstfruits. It was on this day Israel presented to the priest the sheaf of grain from the beginning of the harvest. It was a symbol of all that was to come as the harvest was completed. It was a promise of hope concerning the provision of God for His people. What a celebration it must have been! Christ, the Lamb, had been crucified and brought forth firstfruits. He made the journey into death and hell. Now the firstfruit, the resurrection, was given.

Jesus was the first sheaf of grain. Let me remind you what Paul wrote, **But now Christ is risen from the dead, and has become the firstfruits of those who have fallen asleep** (1 Corinthians 15:20). He is the first in the sequence. He is the first One to appear in the full potential of all the crucifixion would produce. If you were wondering, what would be the full and complete product of the crucifixion, you need no longer wonder. Jesus is the Firstfruit.

Paul went on to state, **And He is the head of the body, the** *church, who is the beginning, the firstborn from the dead, that in all things He may have the preeminence* (Colossians 1:18). In this sense He is the first, the *firstborn*, the **beginning** (root word of **Firstfruits**) from which all creation has received its norm. The average has been established again. It is Jesus!

First in Substance

This is the second element. The root word in *firstfruits* has a philosophical application. It denotes the original material from which something has evolved. This "something" is determined by the context of the source. When the sheaf of grain was presented to the priest, it was the substance of the source. It represented the original material of the grain plant which entered into death that the sheaf might be produced. The rest of the harvest was to be of this same original matter.

Jesus spoke forcibly on this issue. Several Greeks came to Jerusalem to worship at the feast. They confronted Philip, desiring to speak to Jesus. We are not absolutely sure as to their intentions. However, it seems reasonable they were interested in securing Him as a new leader among the Greeks. Perhaps they wanted Him to start a new college in Athens. He would be the greatest teacher the world had ever known. He could spend His time writing books and influence the world forever. Jesus did not even need to pray about such a proposition. *But Jesus answered them, saying, "The hour has come that the Son of Man should be glorified,"* (John 12:23). In John's Gospel account this is always a reference to the crucifixion of Christ. Jesus confronts the Greeks with the crucifixion.

He gave a physical illustration with His description. He said, *"Most assuredly, I say to you, unless a grain of wheat falls into the ground and dies, it remains alone; but if it dies, it produces much grain,"* (John 12:24). It is an illustration from nature highlighting the firstfruits. One grain of wheat dies to produce a harvest of the original material in many grains.

Jesus is the first in the sequence. He represents the quality of the complete harvest which is to come. He is the representative of the rich grain, the golden kernels which will flow as the harvest is completed. We are again forced to use "prototype" language. Everything produced from this point on will be compared with Jesus. Is it the same material? Does it come from the same source? Is it the same texture, fiber and substance?

Do you realize we are surrounded by a lot of religious plastic? If you simply drive by the churches of our day, you would not recognize anything is different. The buildings are shaped the same. The songs have the same words and express the same theme. There are many of the same rules and activities. But when you stop the car and actually get close, it is not the same substance. It is synthetic in nature. It does not have the aroma of Christ. The texture is radically different. The material of the grain of wheat is not present. Its death did not produce the harvest. It came from another source and is not acceptable. The Firstfruit of the crucifixion is the standard. It is far beyond imitating Jesus; it requires participation in the material until we are the same. What would Jesus do (WWJD)? This is not the question. At best it is a beginning question. We cannot simply attempt to be like Jesus. The issue is not that we try to be like Him, but we are to be sourced by Him. The substance, the original material, from which He is made, is now to be ours. We are to be **partakers of the divine nature, having escaped the corruption that is in the world through lust** (2 Peter 1:4).

What exactly is this original material? How can I experience it? Where can we find it? We must go back to the Prototype. He is the Firstfruit of the crucifixion. What is the source which has brought this to pass? It is the fullness of the Holy Spirit!

First in Surety

Before we look at this third element, we want to review the pattern which God has been following. The Feast of the Passover focuses on the sacrificial lamb. It is fulfilled in the crucifixion of Jesus. *The next day John saw Jesus coming toward him, and said, "Behold! The Lamb of God who takes away the sin of the world!"* (John 1:29). Our crucified Christ is the fulfillment of the Feast of the Passover.

Following the Good Friday fulfillment was the Sabbath Day. It was the celebration of the Feast of Unleavened Bread which symbolized the haste, hardship, and miracles connected with the flight out of Egypt land. This was fulfilled in the burial and mystical activity of Christ during His death.

This was followed by the Feast of Firstfruits, taking place on Sunday, the Lord's Day. It marked the beginning of the harvest which would continue to be completed on the Day of the Feast of Pentecost. Israel was to bring to the priest the first sheaf of grain from the harvest. It contained the substance or material characteristic of the remaining harvest. The resurrected Lord is the Firstfruit of the harvest. Paul stated it this way, *But now Christ is risen from the dead, and has become the firstfruits of those who have fallen asleep* (1 Corinthians 15:20). He is the norm, the prototype, of all who are to follow.

The harvest continued for fifty days. It climaxed on the Day of the Feast of Pentecost. The actual word Pentecost means fifty. This feast was called The Festival of Weeks because it was celebrated for seven complete weeks, or fifty days, after the Feast of the Passover (Exodus 34:22). It was also called the Festival of the Harvest because it concluded the harvest of the later grains (Exodus 23:16).

The sheaf of grains (firstfruits) was offered to the priest on the first day of the week (Sunday) after the Day of the Feast of the Passover. Again, it marked the day of the harvest's beginning. Fifty days later the harvest was completed. On this Day of the Feast of Pentecost, two leavened loaves with the finest flour were baked and brought to the priest as the firstfruits of the completed harvest. So the first sheaf offered at the Passover marked the beginning of the grain harvest, and the two unleavened loaves at Pentecost marked its end.

These two fresh baked loaves brought at the completion of the harvest symbolized the Holy Spirit given to us. The outpouring of the Holy Spirit on the Day of the Feast of Pentecost is the completion of the harvest or crucifixion. This is what God planned all the time. This is the goal, dream and vision of God for you. If the crucifixion had ended the life of Christ there would have been no harvest. The firstfruits of the resurrection would never have been presented. We would have been forgiven through the shedding of blood, but this was not the complete dream of God for us. God's dream was not completely fulfilled with the crucifixion and resurrection. There was something more He wanted to accomplish than forgiving us and allowing us to live forever.

Even though the crucifixion, resurrection, and ascension took place, God still had not accomplished His goal. He forgave us, gave us eternal life, and crowned Jesus King, but our destiny as determined by God was still undone. The completion of the harvest, the two baked leavened loaves, is none other than God living within us. We can now be possessed by the very nature of God. He will not settle for anything less than this. Do you see how big this is?

It is bigger than you have ever dreamed! In speaking of this the Apostle Paul wrote, **Now He who has prepared us for this very thing is God, who also has given us the Spirit as a** guarantee, (2 Corinthians 5:5). The Greek word translated **guarantee** means "a pledge or earnest." It is part of the purchase money on property given in advance as security for the rest of what is due. Do you see what this means? The two fully baked loaves given at Pentecost are simply a down payment. What we experience in the fullness of the Holy Spirit now is only a surety. It is not that God has something new and different for us. No! It is the same material and original substance found in Christ. What we experience in the nature of God now is only a fraction of what He is going to continue to do in and through us. He will source our daily living as we are in intimate relationship with Him.

You do not want to miss this! You must be filled with the Spirit. Whatever obstacles are in your way, allow God to remove them. Experience the cross that you might experience His life.

Acts 2:1

THE JOY OF THE LAW

In this passage, Luke distinctly pinpoints the exact day in which God fulfills His promise. The disciples have been waiting in Jerusalem for the "Promise of the Father." They are minus the full details of this eminent outpouring of the Holy Spirit, but they are following God's instructions to wait. The Holy Spirit comes and pours Himself on these open seekers on **the Day of Pentecost** (Acts 2:1). It is very important to understand how the Old Testament patterns were simply *shadows* of the realities of God's plan for His people.

We need to consider these verses. In speaking of the priests, the author refers to them as those **who serve the copy and shadow of the heavenly things, as Moses was divinely instructed when he was about to make the tabernacle. For He said, "See that you make all things according to the pattern shown you on the mountain,"** (Hebrews 8:5). **For the law, having a shadow of the good things to come, and not the very image of the things, can never with these same sacrifices, which they offer continually year by year, make those who approach perfect,** (Hebrews 10:1). In referring to the requirements of the Old Covenant, Paul wrote that these **are a shadow of things to come, but the substance of Christ** (Colossians 2:17).

It is for this reason we are investigating **the Day of Pentecost** in light of the Jewish celebrations. Let me remind you the Day of the Feast of the Passover took place on Friday. It was a remembrance of the day when the Death Angel passed over the Hebrew people who were enslaved in Egypt. The blood of the sacrificial lamb was used for the deliverance of their firstborn sons. This lamb was a constant reminder of the promise of the Messiah. Jesus surrendered His life on the cross at the very moment the high priest offered the official Passover lamb on that Good Friday.

The next day was the Sabbath Day. It was the celebration of the Feast of Unleavened Bread, commemorating the difficult journey out of Egypt. This was the symbol of the journey of Christ in His burial experience. All of the unknown portions of this involvement remain a mystery to us. However, the next day was the first day of the week. It was the celebration of the Day of the Feast of Firstfruits. The beginning of the harvest was acknowledged as the people presented a sheaf of grain to the priest. This is the shadow of the resurrection of our Lord. He is the firstfruits of the great harvest to come (1 Corinthians 15:20).

The harvest continued for a period of fifty days. It climaxed on the Day of the Feast of Pentecost. Two baked loaves of bread made from the finest flour and yeast were presented to the High Priest. It was the symbol of the fulfillment of the harvest and the provision of God for His people. During those fifty days Jesus ascended to the right hand of the Father. We are given only brief insight into the activities in the heavenly realms. He serves as the great High Priest who offers His sacrifice once and for all. He receives the Promise of the Father in order to pour the blessing upon us. The completion of the dream of God for His people takes place. It is the climax of the harvest.

However, in the Jewish celebration of the great Day of the Feast of Pentecost, there was an additional element. It was the celebration of the law. The Day of the Feast of Pentecost not only celebrated the completion of the physical harvest, but also commemorated the giving of the law, the spiritual harvest. The time period from the passing over of the Death Angel in Egypt to the experience on Mount Sinai when Moses received the law from God was fifty days. The Day of the Feast of Pentecost was sometimes called by the Jews, "The Joy of the Law."

I would like for you to think of the tremendous parallel of all of this. In the Old Testament the fulfillment of the great harvest in the spiritual sense was the giving of the law of God. In the New Testament the fulfillment of the great harvest was the indwelling of God. In the Old Testament, the Day of Pentecost was the writing of the law of God on tablets of stone. In the New Testament the Day of Pentecost was the writing of the law of God on the hearts of men. In the Old Testament the climax of the movement of God was the establishment of the nation of Israel, the organization of the government, and the giving of the law. In the New Testament the climax of God's dream is the Kingdom of God, the crowning of its King, and the empowering of its rule. The Kingdom of God is within you (Luke 17:21). God and man have moved into such intimacy that the empowering, sourcing flow of the nature of God has indwelt man. It is the fulfillment of the dreams of God for us!

There are distinctions between the Old Covenant Pentecost and the New Testament Pentecost. It is the law contrasted with the indwelling of the Spirit of Christ. We need to consider these distinctions together.

Concentration

We do not have the time or space to investigate the entire Old Testament concerning this issue. From the days of the Judges, down through the experiences of captivity, a central issue was the backslidden condition of the people of Israel. It was always focused on breaking the law of God. But something happened to the people of the Kingdom of Judah during the last captivity. They came back to Jerusalem and rebuilt the temple and the

The Joy of the Law | Acts 2:1

walls of the city. They rediscovered the law of God. There was a re-dedication of their lives to God's law from which they would never again stray.

This was the time period in which the group called Pharisees began. They concentrated on the law of God. They interpreted the law of God by their oral traditions. This accelerated during the four hundred years that God was silent, the period of time between the Old and the New Testaments. They had nothing left but their law. It became their only focus. The Day of the Feast of Pentecost was a celebration of their focus.

The law had become their light in the dark hours. It was their guide through difficult circumstances. The only measurement they had of right and wrong was contained in the law. The highest position in their social status was an interpreter of the law. These people outranked all other political positions. All rights and wrongs were determined by the law. Judgments in the Jewish courts were decided by the interpretation of the law. All actions were measured by the law. The very basis of their security in relationship to the favor of God was the law. To remove the focus of the law would be to leave them with nothing. Their focus was the law, the law, and the law!

The outpouring of the Spirit of Jesus came on the very day when they were celebrating their focus on the law. How radical it was! God Himself was breaking through all of the structure, ceremonies, and doing, in order to present Himself. It was a total focus on the Person. The Book of Acts is an account of a people who are absolutely captivated with the Person of Christ. What they knew in the external has become internal. The fellowship they experienced in the flesh has moved to the Spirit. He became the center of everything happening in their lives.

The intensity of the Jew's focus was on the law. Think of how their lives must have been filled with it. It was the measure and judge of everything they did. If the law was lost, then everything they held close was gone. The law was their total focus. NOW shift that intense focus to the person of Christ. He has come to indwell them. Everything is being determined by Him. How do I know I am righteous? He is my righteousness. How do I know I am doing the right thing? I respond to the "poieo-ing" of His presence. How do I know I love properly? His love is flowing through me.

As I once argued for the law, now I embrace Him. As once theology was the great issue of my life, now He is my supreme love. As once I was filled with religious doing, now I respond to His movement. As once I ministered for Him, now He ministers through me. I used to serve Him, now He serves through me! The greatest example in the Scriptures of this shift is the Apostle Paul. He wrote, **And I advanced in Judaism beyond many of my contemporaries in my own nation, being more exceedingly zealous for the traditions of my fathers** (Galatians 1:14). Can you see him on his horse riding to Damascus? He has papers in his hands giving him the right to destroy men, women, and children who are called Christians. But his testimony continues, **But when it pleased God, who separated me from my mother's womb and called me through His grace, to reveal His Son to me,** (Galatians 1:15-16). It was a shift from the law to the Person. As he had been focused on the law, now he was focused on Jesus.

The Day of Pentecost is now a great celebration of our focus. We are centered on Jesus. We have nothing else if He is not our concentration. We are left lifeless and empty without Him. We have no way to measure where we are or to sense security without Him. He is our all in all!

Circumference

There is a second contrast between the Old Covenant Pentecost and the New Testament Pentecost. The circumference which established the limits of the lives of the people of Israel was contained within the law. We must go back to "boundary language." The boundary which established the fences beyond which the children of Israel were not to go was the law. This was the constant cycle in the Old Covenant. Israel was not willing to live within the boundaries of the law and experienced the consequences of it.

The message of the Old Testament is one of relationship. God's dream for mankind from creation, to the fall, to the redemption, is all about relationship. In the Old Testament it is highlighted as "Covenant." The basic Hebrew word translated "covenant" in the Old Testament appears two hundred and eighty times. There is some debate among scholars as to the origin of this word. Some have said it comes from a custom of eating together (Genesis 26:30; 31:54). Others have suggested the idea of cutting an animal (Genesis 15:18). The preferred meaning of this Old Testament word is "bond." A covenant is two or more parties bound together.

The Old Testament presents many covenants between two equal parties; this means that the covenant relationship is bilateral. Both parties sealed the bond by vowing, often by oath. They had equal privileges and responsibilities within the covenant. But the covenant between God and Israel is different. It is unilateral. This basically means that the covenant only involves or is affected on one side, or it is performed or undertaken by only one side. It obligates only one of two parties. God initiates the covenant. Israel is the recipient not a contributor. Israel is not expected to offer elements to the bond or covenant; Israel simply accepts it as offered. Israel is to keep its demands and to receive the results that God, by oath, assures them He will not withhold.

The law is the boundary within which Israel is to abide and receives the benefits of this relationship. We see the picture of what took place when they stepped outside the law. The benefits of the covenant protection and provision were immediately removed. They had gone beyond the circumference of the relationship.

Part One: A New Level

The Day of Pentecost in the New Testament was a shift in the boundaries of the covenant. God was moving His people to a new level of relationship. The covenant was going to take on an exciting new aspect. The Old Covenant Pentecost celebrated the law. But through the years the law had taught the reality of sin. The law was a schoolmaster. *Therefore the law was our tutor to bring us to Christ, that we might be justified by faith. But after faith has come, we are no longer under the tutor* (Galatians 3:24-25). Romans chapter seven is Paul's description of a person who is living in the Old Covenant, celebrating "the joy of the law." It could not be done. Mankind, who lived out of his own resource, was incapable of staying within the boundaries of the law, thus the provisions of the covenant were lost.

But now the boundary of the law of the Old Covenant has moved from external to the internal (Hebrews 10:16). It is no longer on tablets of stone but in the hearts of men. We are no longer motivated by provisions or benefits of a covenant, but by relationship. *For the love of Christ compels us, because we judge thus: that if One died for all, then all died; and He died for all, that those who live should live no longer for themselves, but for Him who died for them and rose again* (2 Corinthians 5:14-15). Therefore the actual boundary of the covenant has shifted from law (doing) to Christ.

Jesus said, *"Do not think that I came to destroy the Law or the Prophets. I did not come to destroy but to fulfill* (Matthew 5:17). The boundary of the covenant is no longer keeping a list of rules (doing), but embracing the Person. God has initiated the covenant; it is unilateral. I bring nothing to the covenant. It is not my part and His part. It is all His part! In embracing Christ, I am sourced with life to live. The law brought nothing but death (Romans 7:10). Christ brings nothing but life! The single source of God's dreams for me is in the embrace of the Spirit of Christ. I am to live within the boundaries of His Person. I am constantly responding to His provision in me.

Communication

We come now to the third contrast between the Old Covenant Pentecost and the New Testament Pentecost. It is communication. It is amazing how in the Pentecost of the New Covenant a new language was formed and a new vocabulary emerged. It was an absolute necessity that this would take place. This new level of experience and intimacy with Christ demands new expression. There will have to be new imagery to picture the relationship. The Old Testament law language will no longer be adequate.

Jesus introduced this idea in the great manifesto of the Kingdom of God, the Sermon on the Mount (Matthew 5, 6 & 7). He used a contrast in the middle of the sermon. It was a contrast between, **You have heard that it was said to those of old** and **But I say to you.** The old was about not committing murder; but the new is about not being angry (Matthew 5:2-22). The old was about not committing adultery while the new is about lust in the heart (Matthew 5:27-28). The old was about no divorce in the family; the new is about faithfulness (Matthew 5:31-32). The old was about not getting even with your brother; the new is about not resisting (Matthew 5:38-39). The old was about not hating your enemy; loving everyone is the new (Matthew 5:43-44). The language has changed!

The old language was about Hebrews, Jews, Israelites, chosen ones, children of Abraham and isolation. It was about Gentiles, Samaritans, and defilement. The new language is explosive. New language like "the body of Christ" began to give a new picture of intimacy with each other and Him. The language of the Church was born. We became the bride of Christ (Ephesians 5:25-32), born from above, sons of God, and joint heirs with Christ. We are the temple of the Holy Spirit which is made up of living stones (Ephesians 2:22; 1 Corinthians 3:16; 1 Peter 2:5). We moved from not being allowed to even pronounce the name

Part One: A New Level

of God Jehovah to the constant use of the name of Jesus. We went from God isolated in the Holy of Holies to living in His presence. He was inaccessible; but now we embrace Him. It is a whole new language.

Do you recognize that all of the new language is related to the person of Christ? It is absolutely impossible to have this language when the focus is on the law. Now we are the bride of Christ, joint heirs with Christ, and the temple of the Spirit of Christ. Let us live in intimacy with Him!

Acts 2:1

AVENUES OF UNITY

They were all with one accord in one place. All the commentaries focus on these two phrases as meaning they were all assembled together in a single location. The commentators attempt to reveal where this place might have been, although there is often disagreement. They argue about whether it was the one hundred and twenty disciples present, or whether it was only experienced by the twelve apostles. It amazes me that no one seems to deal with the real issue. Why would Luke go to so much trouble to double state what would have been otherwise very obvious to any one reading the passage?

To further complicate the issue there is the Greek word which is translated *with one accord.* In verse fourteen of chapter one this same translation is used for one Greek word. The issue is whether it is the same Greek word in both verses. Most Bible scholars believe they are not the same in the original Greek text, and the word used in verse one of chapter two should be changed to a translation reading, *together.* It appears the earliest Greek manuscripts have two different Greek words for these verses. The Greek word translated *with one accord* (Acts 1:14) has the idea of likeminded. They were thinking and feeling the same way. The Greek word translated *together* (Acts 2:1) is more of an emphasis on the fact they were physically together in one location.

Our consideration is whether this really changes anything.

Part One: A New Level

Something has already happened to these disciples as a group. The resurrected Jesus has captivated them and their new focus has elevated them above all strife and differences. We cannot forget how often, before the crucifixion, there was strife and division among them. Jesus was faced with not only strife from outside the group, but from within. They were divided over issues of position in the coming Kingdom (Matthew 18:1). They were competitive when others outside the group were successfully ministering (Luke 9:49). There was a major upset when two disciples who were brothers sought to secure the right and left hand positions for themselves (Matthew 20:24). Racial division rose to the forefront when a Samaritan village refused to give them lodging (Luke 9:52). It was such a heated issue, they wanted to **command fire to come down from heaven and consume them** (Luke 9:54). They all disagreed with Jesus over the cross style (Matthew 16:22). Mighty arguments were staged concerning this proposal. On and on it goes! Now things are very different. What has happened to the disciples to cause such a radical change?

In chapter one Luke highlights the disciple's new focus. It is the Resurrected Lord. They spend forty days with Him (Acts 1:3). His person, heart and vision capture them. He becomes so large in their eyes that everything else diminishes. This sets the stage for the outpouring of the Spirit of Jesus, and the New Covenant is established. All contention ceases. They are **with one accord** and then Pentecost happens.

Now let us return to our passage (Acts 2:1). The Greek word which is translated **with one accord** is used ten times in the Book of Acts. It is only used one other place in the New Testament (Romans 15:6). The gathering of the disciples **in one place** (Acts 2:1) is not one of the ten usages of this Greek word. However, this gathering is certainly surrounded by the Greek word translated **with one accord**. It is used to describe the waiting period in Jerusalem before the Day of Pentecost.

Avenues of Unity | **Acts 2:1**

These all continued with one accord in prayer and supplication, with the women and Mary the mother of Jesus, and with His brothers (Acts 1:14). Luke gives us a summary description of the one hundred and twenty disciples during the seven to ten day period between the ascension of Christ and the Day of Pentecost.

When the Day of Pentecost happened, Peter preached a powerful sermon (Acts 2:14-40). About three thousand converts were added to the group of one hundred and twenty (Acts 2:41). In the summary description of what was taking place among this enlarged group, Luke uses this same Greek word. *So continuing daily with one accord in the temple, and breaking bread from house to house, they ate their food with gladness and simplicity of heart* (Acts 2:46). Luke emphasizes this concerning the disciples both before and after Pentecost.

There is an event recorded by Luke immediately after Pentecost. A lame man *whom they laid daily at the gate of the temple which is called Beautiful* (Acts 3:2) was healed. This great miracle created a platform for Peter to deliver a message about Jesus, and hundreds of people responded (five thousand men, Acts 4:4). The leaders of Israel were greatly distressed and put the apostles in jail for the night. The next day they gave them a hearing. After warning and threatening them *not to speak at all or teach in the name of Jesus* (Acts 4:18), they released them. Immediately the apostles returned to the gathering of the early church and reported all that had been said to them. Here is how the early church responded to the report of the threats: *they raised their voice to God with one accord and said: "Lord, You are God, who made heaven and earth and the sea, and all that is in them,"* (Acts 4:24). Again Luke emphasizes the linkage of the believers even as it expanded to a larger group.

Should we not interpret our passage in light of this fact? The actual text says, *When the Day of Pentecost had fully come, they were all with one accord* (together) *in one place* (Acts 2:1). Again, notice the double emphasis! Luke states they were *together.*

Part One: A New Level

In addition he adds *in one place.* In light of what Luke has already told us (Acts 1:14) and what he will tell us (Acts 2:46; 4:24), we must understand the content of *together in one place* to mean *with one accord.*

It is also important to note the Greek word translated *with one accord* is a combination of two Greek words. The first word is the Greek word translated *together* as in our passage (Acts 2:1). The second Greek word has to do with passion as if breathing hard. So the Greek word used in our passage (Acts 2:1) is the basis of *with one accord* used in the other passage. This combination of two words is very expressive. It signifies that all their minds, affections, desires, and wishes were concentrated on one object; every man's focus had the same end in view. They had but one desire. There was no person uninterested, none unconcerned, none lukewarm; all were in earnest; and the Spirit of God came down to meet their united faith. This kind of uniting gives to the Holy Spirit a powerful platform for Divine action in our world!

There is nothing to indicate that this removed their differences. The experience of *one accord* is not the absence of strife over differences but the concentration on one object which brings the passion of the individuals into unity. They did not all suddenly like the same color, crave the same dessert or drive the same make of car. Nothing had changed among them except their overwhelming passion for one object. In our previous studies we discovered the object of their affections. The resurrected Lord had captivated them. He spent forty days sharing with them about the dreams of the Kingdom of God (Acts 1:3). He became so large in their vision that nothing else seemed to matter. Other things were still there, but these things diminished in their eyes. Their love for Christ overtook all other concerns.

Being in *one accord* demonstrated itself in various areas. Their absolute obsession with the resurrected Christ began to reveal itself in the essential spiritual avenues for the flow of the Holy Spirit. Their unity manifested itself not in liking the same music or enjoying the same hobbies, but in the areas where the Holy Spirit needed to affect their world. What are these areas?

Prayer

One specific area of flow is prayer. This was utilized by the Holy Spirit prior to the outpouring on the Day of Pentecost. The unity manifested in this area seems to have been a key factor in releasing the hand of God for the outpouring. Luke describes the one hundred and twenty disciples in the "waiting" time in Jerusalem. This is not a retreat setting where they were isolated from conflict. They were in the heart of Jerusalem spending their time in the temple with the leadership of Israel (Luke 24:53). They were dwelling in the very seat of the movement which crucified Christ. It was here ***these all continued WITH ONE ACCORD in prayer and supplication, with the women and Mary the mother of Jesus, and with His brothers*** (Acts 1:14).

The flow of the Holy Spirit through the avenue of prayer was not something only experienced in preparation for Pentecost. Prayer is emphasized repeatedly among this group throughout the Book of Acts. The Greek word translated *prayer* is used nine times as a noun and sixteen times as a verb in the Book of Acts. What is really revealing is that this word is used eight times in the Gospel accounts as a noun and forty-seven times as a verb. It is startling to realize in the Gospel accounts the disciples are never seen doing this word. The only One who actually experiences this word *prayer* in the Gospels is Jesus. He is either talking about it or doing it.

Can you imagine the first time the disciples get together in the upper room and experience *prayer?* Even before Pentecost through Christ there was a new access to the spiritual realm. The Old Testament, old covenant, had never provided anything like this. Then as they experienced Pentecost, *prayer* was widened and deepened in their lives. But understand it was not getting on their knees and reading a list of requests to God. It was not the rehashing of memorized phrases repeatedly. There was actually fellowship and living in the presence of God. **Prayer** had become "practicing His presence." They were living in a new God awareness!

These early disciples were **with one accord** in the realm of **prayer.** This did not mean they were all praying for the same thing, but they were all in intimate fellowship with Jesus. The awareness of His presence had become such a focus they were elevated above all their differences. If there is strife among us, is it not evident that we do not have the awareness of His presence? Unity in this area releases the power of God as it did in the Book of Acts. Strife destroys intimacy with Jesus in the individual and also in the corporate body of Christ. The moment we are not in intimacy with Him we are left to our own devices. We become man produced rather than God sourced. We cannot afford strife!

Partnership

Another area utilized by the Holy Spirit to flow His influence through them was the unity experienced in partnership. What an experience it must have been to see hundreds of people in the temple giving their lives to Christ and being filled with the Holy Spirit. After the outpouring of the Holy Spirit, Peter confronted those in the temple area with an explanation of this great event. The disciple group suddenly was enlarged to over three thousand individuals. ***Then fear came upon every soul, and many wonders and signs were done through the apostles*** (Acts 2:43).

While these happenings must have been wondrous, what took place afterward was beyond comprehension. They were ***continuing daily WITH ONE ACCORD in the temple, and breaking bread from house to house, they ate their food with*** *gladness and simplicity of heart* (Acts 2:46). There was a unity that possessed them which can only be expressed in the full understanding of the Greek word ***koinonia*** (partnership).

The content of **with one accord** in this setting is explained by the proceeding verses. The disciples (enlarged group) **had all things in common** (Acts 2:44). Again this was not about liking the same kind of music or the same athletic competition. Luke gives us the details. He writes, **and sold their possessions and goods, and divided them among all, as anyone had need** (Acts 2:45). Think of the kind of unity which would remove all materialistic barriers. What could possibly take place within an individual or group of people that would bring them to this level?

This is a strong example of partnership (***koinonia***). This Greek word comes from the root word meaning "to do business." It is far beyond fellowship or even companionship. This word includes those ideas along with linking together in an enterprise. The disciples had been pulled into the heart of Christ. They were all in a single business; it was Christ. The Kingdom of God, Christ within you had become so huge in their lives there was nothing else. All other concerns diminished in light of this one great enterprise. Christ received their entire energy, desires, passion and obviously materialism. They were in unity in the flow of the Holy Spirit through the enterprise of the heart of God.

Is this not the key element to how they won their entire world in seventy years to Christ? This kind of unity brought the flow of the Holy Spirit which empowered and sourced an evangelism which swept people into the Kingdom. Nothing could stop such evangelism. The power of the Holy Spirit flowed through this unity with signs and wonders. Everything needed to convince their world of Christ was available to them. In the midst of the lack of organization, education, money and buildings, they simply swept their world into the Kingdom of God.

What could stop such a thing from happening among us? The great hindrance to such a movement is strife. Strife is produced by a focus on minor issues. When we argue about methodology, style of worship, even theology, we destroy the avenue through which the Holy Spirit can release His power. We are again back to our own abilities. Strife is the evidence that we have lost focus on Him. The sin of our world has never stopped or hindered the church. Persecution has only increased the effectiveness of the church. Outside threats have never destroyed the body of Christ. It is from within we are ruined. The moment we are no longer totally His we find ourselves belonging to minor issues which always produce division.

Praise

There is a third avenue of unity which became an avenue for the Holy Spirit's flow. It is the avenue of praise. A tremendous evangelistic gathering occurred from the miracle which happened at the gate of the temple called Beautiful (Acts 3:2). At the hour of prayer, Peter and John went to the temple and were encountered by a lame man. The power of God healed the man astounding everyone. Peter used this as an opportunity to share Jesus with the gathering. There was an additional five thousand men who believed in Christ (Acts 4:4). The leaders of Israel arrested the disciples and left them in jail for the night. The next day they threatened them regarding preaching in the name of Jesus (Acts 4:18).

Upon their release the apostles made their way to the expanded group of believers. They ***reported all that the chief priests and elders had said to them*** (Acts 4:23). What a terrible position in which to be! These are the same leaders of Israel who crucified Christ. This is a life threatening situation. How will the early church respond? ***So when they heard that, they raised their voice to God WITH ONE ACCORD and said: "Lord, You are God, who made heaven and earth and the sea, and all that*** *is in them,"* (Acts 4:24). They responded in praise and worship to their great God! Did you notice the unity in this worship?

As the passage develops, it is clear this expanded group of disciples is focused on the greatness of God. They are absolutely convinced of Jesus (Acts 4:27). They believe the life of Christ was a fulfillment of the plan of God which is now going to continue through them (Acts 4:28-30). As they spoke these declarations in unity, *they were all filled with the Holy Spirit, and they spoke the word of God with boldness* (Acts 4:31). It was through this kind of unity in praise and worship to God that the Holy Spirit was able to move!

Exactly what was their level of unity? *Now the multitude of those who believed were of one heart and one soul; neither did anyone say that any of the things he possessed was his own, but they had all things in common* (Acts 4:32). They were *with one accord* in their focus on Christ and the fulfillment of the plan of redemption in spite of any obstacles. Their praise and worship was not focused on music, beat, or environment, but was captured by Him. All styles of worship faded in importance. There was no manipulation of the crowds but a unity of focus on Him.

This avenue of worship and focus was so strongly used by the Holy Spirit that all who did not join in this focus were struck dead (Acts 5:1-10). *And believers were increasingly added to the Lord, multitudes of both men and women,* (Acts 5:14). Do you see how central unity was in the flow of the Spirit? All strife is destructive to the flow of the Spirit of God and must be eliminated. There is no chance of revival when we are divided. Walls and barriers are the supreme hindrance to the movement of the Spirit both in our individual lives and the corporate body of Christ. God give us unity!

Acts 2:2

THE SOUND FROM HEAVEN

Is there any way to describe God's awesome gift to the world? God had been speaking through the generations of time, but now He chooses to climax it all in a new dynamic movement. The Spirit of Jesus moves within the lives of human beings. The Day of Pentecost has *fully come.* It is time to reveal it to mankind. Are there any adequate words?

Luke uses naturally familiar and physical elements to give us a feel for the occasion. He speaks of the wind and the fire (Acts 2:2-3). Wind and fire always emit excitement, but we must resist the temptation to become enthralled with these occurrences. Luke specifically writes, *And suddenly there came a sound from heaven, AS OF a rushing mighty wind, and it filled the whole house where they were sitting* (Acts 2:2). There was no *rushing mighty wind,* but only what sounded like wind. *Then there appeared to them divided tongues, AS OF fire, and one sat upon each of them* (Acts 2:3). There was no *fire,* only that which appeared as fire.

In my attempt to go past the physical representations which illustrate what is happening, I was astounded to find that both wind and fire point to the issue of "communication." In Luke's second illustration, there were *divided tongues* which focus on communication of speech. As demonstrated in the next verse, Luke writes, *And they were all filled with the Holy Spirit and began to speak with other tongues, as the Spirit gave them utterance* (Acts 2:4). The obvious result of the fullness of the Holy Spirit is that of communication.

Luke's first illustration of the event is the phrase; ***there came a sound*** (Acts 2:2). To hear this sound was to think of a roaring, blasting wind. However, as the sound fills the room, it is connected to communication and the speaking which is happening. ***And when this sound occurred, the multitude came together and were confused, because everyone heard them speak in his own language*** (Acts 2:6).

This revelation forced me to a definite conclusion. In every movement of God His motivation is communication. I am unable to find an event in God's actions or presence where communication is not predominate. ***There came a sound,*** but it was not for the mere sake of noise. God is making known a startling and amazing truth.

I investigated the Book of Acts to discover the places where the fullness of the Holy Spirit takes place without communication. Such an occasion does not occur. The Book of Acts is about the coming of the Holy Spirit, communicating truth to us! Let me list a few of these references for our study.

But you shall receive power when the Holy Spirit has come upon you; and you shall be WITNESSES to Me in Jerusalem, and in all Judea and Samaria, and to the end of the earth (Acts 1:8).

And they were all filled with the Holy Spirit and began to SPEAK with other tongues, as the Spirit gave them UTTERANCE (Acts 2:4).

Therefore being exalted to the right hand of God, and having received from the Father the promise of the Holy Spirit, He poured out this which you now see and HEAR (Acts 2:33).

Then Peter, filled with the Holy Spirit, SAID to them… (Acts 4:8).

When they had prayed, the place where they were assembled together was shaken; and they were all filled with the

Holy Spirit, and they SPOKE the word of God with boldness (Acts 4:31).

And those of the circumcision who believed were astonished, as many as came with Peter, because the gift of the Holy Spirit had been poured out on the Gentiles also. For they heard them SPEAK with tongues and magnify God (Acts 10:45-46).

There are many more Scriptures we could add to the list, but space does not allow. Communication of truth always surrounds the fullness of the Holy Spirit. Repeatedly, as the apostles speak the truth of God, the Holy Spirit comes upon others. **Sound** seems to be a consistent element in the movement of the Spirit of Jesus.

Having established this premise, let us investigate the *sound from heaven, as of a rushing mighty wind* (Acts 2:2). Let me remind you of the great occasion when God instituted the law for His people. He made an appearance before Israel on Mount Sinai. As the people gathered at the base of the mountain, here is what took place. **Then it came to pass on the third day, in the morning, that there were thunderings and lightnings, and a thick cloud on the mountain; and the sound of the trumpet was very loud, so that all the people who were in the camp trembled** (Exodus 19:16). All of this was a prelude to the speaking of God as He gave His law to Moses! It is not about noise; it is all about communication.

One is immediately drawn to remember that when God came in the flesh, He is referred to as the "Word." **And the Word became flesh and dwelt among us, and we beheld His glory, the glory as of the only begotten of the Father, full of grace and truth** (John 1:14). The incarnation was definitely about communication. Jesus was and is the speaking of God. His coming is God's attempt to tell us something. Communication from God has now arrived at a new level. We have moved from thunderings and lightnings, accompanied by trumpets, to God becoming flesh. What a revelation!

But there is more. God takes us to an even higher level. He re-establishes His indwelt presence within! What He has intended for man from the beginning is now coming to pass. It is not about emotional feelings, nor power to do miracles. God raises His communication with man higher still. *"I will put My law in their minds, and write it on their hearts; and I will be their God, and they shall be My people,"* (Jeremiah 31:33). This is definitely a new level of communication. And how astounding is it that the very first description of this happening is *sound*? God indwells man with communication!

We need to carefully note that this is a *sound FROM heaven*. Its primary meaning is "out of" or "from." It is the little Greek word "ek." It is used to speak of objects which were in another time before this time. If the object was simply on, by, or with another, but not in it, then the Greek word "apo" is used. The *sound* which was heard was not by or around heaven; it was actually in heaven. What was heard on the Day of Pentecost is the same communication which is present in heaven itself! The communication of the Holy Spirit has its origin in heaven. The music of heaven is now being heard on earth! The message shared in heaven is now being communicated on earth! The attitude which is a part of the *sound* of heaven is now being felt on earth!

You need to carefully think through what this means. The *sound* taking place on the Day of Pentecost is not on the circumference of God's existence. It is not outside the person of God and adjusted by Him for us. This sound comes from the interior of the heart of God. This is what His dwelling place sounds like. It is not a watered down version or an anemic substitute of His communication. God opened up the heart of His being to us. In the fullness of the Spirit we experience the inner thoughts of God. The beloved music of God now plays within us. His wisdom runs through our lives. God is communicating with us!

But here is what is so startling about the word *sound*. It

is only used four times in the New Testament. It is the Greek word "eechos." From it we get our English word "echo." While the actual Greek word is not used, it is connected with Paul's trip to Rome. In the midst of the storm *they took soundings and found it to be twenty fathoms; and when they had gone a little farther, they took soundings again and found it to be fifteen fathoms* (Acts 27:28). The sailors suspected they were getting close to land. The Greek word translated *soundings* means that the sailors suspected that there was an echo coming from the land.

The author of the Book of Hebrews uses the Greek word "eechos" one of the four times. He discusses the giving of the law on Mount Sinai. He compares the old covenant with the new covenant. He tells us that we have not come to the *mountain that may be touched and that burned with fire, and to blackness and darkness and tempest* (Hebrews 12:18). He goes on to describe the scene of Mount Sinai; *and the sound of a trumpet and the voice of words, so that those who heard it begged that the word should not be spoken to them anymore* (Hebrews 12:19). The echo coming from Mount Sinai was a communication so powerful that the people of Israel could not tolerate it. They requested Moses to go and get the message and bring it back to them. The giving of the law was an echo of the holiness of God. God reflects Himself in the law He communicates.

You remember the great "love chapter" of Paul's writings (1 Corinthians 13). He begins by saying, *Though I speak with the tongues of men and of angels, but have not love, I have become sounding brass or a clanging cymbal* (1 Corinthians 13:1). If one speaks without love, there is no communication. He is not echoing the heart of God, but the sound of a gong banging in the temple. The communication of the Gospel is far beyond the speaking of certain words. It must be the echo of God's heart. The Gospel is not communicated through doctrine or theology, but through those individuals who have become a reflective echo of God's heart, for God is love. This is what happened on the Day of Pentecost.

Another place this same Greek word is used is in connection with Jesus. The ministry of Jesus had expanded throughout Galilee. Luke states, ***And the report about Him went out into every place in the surrounding region*** (Luke 4:37). Here our Greek word "eechos" is translated ***report.*** What was being spoken on the streets about Jesus was an echo of the activities and message He had been sharing with them. The report being given was a reflection of the real life of Christ.

One of the delights of childhood is the echo of the mountains. In certain places sound reverberates between two mountains. If we yell at the top of our lungs in these unique places we will hear our words repeated back to us. It is as if the mountains are talking to us! But the mountains only repeat what we say. They do not produce the sound, nor form the statements. They simply echo our words!

Luke attempts to describe the indwelling of the Spirit of Christ within us by use of this physical illustration. The fundamental purpose for which God created mankind is now being fulfilled. Man is to be an echo of the very essence of God. Mankind is not to produce or mimic the sound. He is not to be an imitation of the sound. God created mankind to be a sounding board from which the nature of His person could be reflected and heard. The actual voice of God is to echo from within our being.

Do you grasp how essential this is? A life lived less than this is a forgery. Whatever is produced by us is phony regardless of how good and great it may appear. Ministry sourced by our talents, developed skills, and personality types is counterfeit. It may attract people and produce church growth, but it does not grow the Kingdom. Any expression of our personality and discipline is a fake! We are to be an expression of the Divine Love, a display of God's very nature. We do not love for His sake; He must come and love through us. We are to be an echo of His heart!

Oh, to be filled with the *sound* of His presence! I am repulsed by how often I have been a fraud, an impostor, or a replica. I have filled my life with excuses as to why this is my lot. Christianity is not about right and wrong. Christianity is about Him. If one could discover the right thing to do, go and do it, he would still go to hell. Christianity is not about doing the right thing. God calls each of us to be an echo of His person.

Christians witnessing as described in the Book of Acts won their world in a matter of seventy years. They were filled with the *sound* which was the essence of heaven. They became an echo of the voice and heart of God. Jesus forcibly demonstrated this before them. He did not call them to do what He did, only to be what He was. He was the echo of the Father. Anyone who viewed Him was viewing the Father. He did not produce His own life nor walk His own path. He was the reflection of the face of the Father. For the first time in history we discover what God sounds like. We hear the echo of His voice through the life of Christ.

Now we see the purpose of the crucifixion, resurrection, and ascension events. The ultimate purpose is not to get us into heaven or to forgive our sins. God wants to restore us until we properly echo His being. All that echoes through Jesus now echoes through us. It is the fullness of the Spirit of Christ.

One can quickly see the kind of surrender this demands. It requires a complete crucifixion of all self-will. There can be no mixing of my part and His part. This is not about my doing and His helping. This is not even about my repeating what He says and does. This is death to all that spills from me. I must cease to be the source of the echo. This is difficult for all of us. Most of us have spent years developing and cultivating our skills, talents and abilities. We have been shaping our lives so we can be acceptable. We take great pride in our wise accomplishments, and we acknowledge that God has certainly helped us. But what Luke describes is far beyond this. He calls us to renounce all self-reliance. Everything that comes from us must cease. Who will become available to God in such a manner? Remember everything but this is simply a replica, a forgery, a phony, a fake, a fraud, and an impostor. Who will be an ECHO?

Acts 2:2

THE FILLING

Luke establishes a contrast between chapters one and two of the Books of Acts. He uses It is in this contrast to highlight the turning point in the history of the Kingdom of God. Many believe the birthday of the Church is contained within this new phase of His redemptive plan. In chapter one the disciples are reminded of the promise of the Father; in chapter two they are actually receiving the fulfilled promise! In chapter one, they are waiting for the coming of the Holy Spirit; in chapter two He comes. In chapter one the disciples were equipped by Jesus; in chapter two they are empowered by the Spirit of Christ. In chapter one the resurrected Savior ascended; in chapter two the Spirit descends. In chapter one the disciples are being spoken to; in chapter two they are speaking in languages they do not even know. Something is being birthed in this great event! The Kingdom of God has come to a new level of life!

It seems to be significant that Luke is using three different Greek words for "filled" in the first four verses of chapter two. The first two are closely related to each other, thus forming a presentation of two major ideas. Our study will be filled with the comparison of these two concepts.

In Luke's opening statement he writes, **when the Day of Pentecost had fully come** (Acts 2:1). As he continues his description of this great event, he speaks of a **sound from heaven** which **filled the whole house where they were sitting** (Acts 2:2). The Greek word translated *fully come* and *filled* are formed from the same basic Greek word. It has the meaning of "to fill a vessel." The focus of the word is on a container being filled with content. It focuses on something outside coming to be inside. In the Greek translation of the Old Testament, the authors speak of God filling the heavens and the earth (Jeremiah 23:24). This term is used consistently by Matthew with prophecy. He describes an event taking place *that it might be fulfilled which was spoken by the prophets* (Matthew 2:23). Here the idea is one of completion or being filled to the brim. The recorded event has been placed into the prophecy and fills this container full with the proper content.

This is the impact of Luke's statement in our passage. *And suddenly there came a sound from heaven, as of a rushing mighty wind, and it filled the whole house where they were sitting* (Acts 2:2). In the grammar structure of the sentence there is no choice but to relate the filling with the *sound*. This is more startling than it may appear upon the first reading. If there had been an actual tempest, it would have been frightening. If there had been a blasting, furious wind, there would have been destruction. But this would have been understandable because such storms often happened. But there was no storm, no wind, no rain, nor thunder. The entire attention of the disciples was focused on the *sound*. Visible objects looking like *divided tongues* (Acts 2:3) came upon each person. They appeared as fire, but there was no fire. Thus, the descent of the Holy Spirit was not only heard but also seen. The initial descent of the Holy Spirit ushers in the life of the Kingdom of God.

Jesus described this to His disciples as being *baptized with the Holy Spirit* (Acts 1:5). Peter was present at the Jerusalem Council when the issue of the Gentiles and Christianity was discussed. Peter related his personal involvement in the outpouring of the Holy Spirit upon the Gentiles. He said, *"And as I began to speak, the Holy Spirit fell upon them, as upon us at the beginning. Then I remembered the word of the Lord, how*

He said, 'John indeed baptized with water, but you shall be baptized with the Holy Spirit,' (Acts 11:15-16).

The concept of ***baptized*** was not new to the disciples or the Jewish culture. There is a strong distinction between the root Greek word (bapto) and the expanded Greek word for ***baptized*** (baptidzo). The basic idea is to dip repeatedly, to immerse or submerge. However, to illustrate the difference between the two words, the Greek lexicons give a recipe for making pickles. In order to make a pickle, the vegetable should first be dipped (bapto) into boiling water and then ***baptized*** (baptidzo) in the vinegar solution. Both verbs involve immersing the vegetable. But the first (bapto) is temporary while the second (baptidzo) produces a permanent change.

This is the reality of Luke's intent in verses two and three. This was the initial baptism of the Holy Spirit upon the believers. It brought about a permanent change in the structure of the Kingdom of God as well as in the lives of individual believers. It is the official announcement of the shift from the old covenant to the new covenant. God is no longer going to walk with man; He is going to walk in man! A permanent change takes place in how God is going to relate to mankind. The church is born!

However, this is not only true in a general, corporate sense, but also on the individual basis. Each individual believer received his own personal baptism of the Holy Spirit. Luke describes this as ***and one sat upon each of them*** (Acts 2:3). Paul discovered some disciples in Ephesus. He inquired of them, ***"Did you receive the Holy Spirit when you believed?"*** (Acts 19:2). They answered that they had not even as much as heard of the Holy Spirit. Paul continued to question them. He asked, ***"Into what then were you baptized?"*** So they said, ***"Into John's baptism,"*** (Acts 19:3). He immediately led them into a baptism in the name of the Lord Jesus, ***and when Paul had laid hands on them, the Holy Spirit came upon them*** (Acts 19:6). Paul expressed this by writing, ***for by one Spirit we were all baptized into one*** *body – whether Jews or Greeks, whether slaves or free – and have all been made to drink into one Spirit* (1 Corinthians 12:13). A permanent change (not meaning eternal security) has taken place in the individual life of a believer through this baptism.

Again Luke describes this as, *and suddenly there came a sound from heaven, as of a rushing mighty wind, and it filled the whole house where they were sitting* (Acts 2:2). This filling of the Holy Spirit expressed in the verse relates to the baptism of the Holy Spirit. It has to do with that which was outside coming to be inside. What an overwhelming experience it is to be filled with the Spirit of Jesus in a moment of time. There is no salvation outside of the infilling. We find a permanent change (baptidzo) in the embrace of this Person.

It is important to note the Greek word for *filled* in this verse is in the active voice. The subject is responsible for the action of the filling. It is the *sound* (Spirit of Jesus) who is responsible for the infilling during this baptism of the Holy Spirit. There is absolutely no self-effort that contributes to this. We have done nothing to accomplish this. If God ever comes to live within us, it will be exclusively a result of His action toward us. Will we allow Him to act upon us?

This brings us to the second major Greek word for *filled* (Acts 2:4). It gives us something of a contrasting picture to that described in the previous paragraphs. *And they were all filled with the Holy Spirit and began to speak with other tongues, as the spirit gave them utterance* (Acts 2:4). The Greek word Luke uses in this verse is distinctly different from the word in verse two. In verse two the idea expressed is that something outside was coming inside. The focus was on "to fill with content." However, now Luke shifts to a Greek word which focuses on the content which is already present coming to an end or permeating the whole. It is used to describe what takes place in a sponge. *Immediately one of them ran and took a sponge, filled it with sour wine and put it on a reed, and offered it to*

Him to drink (Matthew 27:48). This presents the concept of saturation, soaking, flow, or permeating.

The Greek word for ***filled*** implies a purposed plan which is now coming to an end. The gift of languages in this passage did not come to the disciples. It was the Holy Spirit who was already within them who began to flow in this method of ministry. This was an expression of the already present Spirit of Christ who was permeating their lives to accomplish and fill up this new purpose of proclamation. Another example of this is found in the life of Peter. He, along with others, has been put in jail for the night. They are being interrogated by the leaders of Israel. Something takes place in his life as he addresses the group. ***Then Peter, filled with the Holy Spirit, said to them, "Rulers of the people and elders of Israel:"*** (Acts 4:8). Luke is not saying that the Spirit of preaching came and filled Peter for this occasion. This is not something outside of him that came to be inside. Peter had already received the Holy Spirit who now began to fill him with the ability to minister in this method.

It must be understood this is the Greek word which is consistently connected to the movement of the Holy Spirit in the disciples throughout the Book of Acts. What a picture this paints for us! God wants to actually come to be within us. We are to be the temple of the Holy Spirit. It is in this receiving of the Spirit of Christ (baptism) that the most intimate relationship is established. The Holy Spirit is then on a moment by moment basis filling the purpose He wants to accomplish. We become an instrument of the expression of the Spirit of Jesus! He has a plan; we are the means by which He is filling that plan to completion.

What would happen if you saw the circumstances of your life from this view? Look at Peter again. He has just been used to bring five thousand men into the Kingdom of God (Acts 4:4). What should be an occasion of great joy became a circumstance of great pressure. The leaders of Israel are offended and order the capture of those involved in this evangelistic endeavor. It is evening when they are taken into custody. This required that they spend the night in jail before having a proper hearing. Think of how you would feel if this happened to you. You tried to do the right thing and it has become a tragic mess! You know what these very same leaders of Israel are capable of doing when threatened. They are the ones who crucified Christ. What should you do? How should you respond? Peter is our example. He relaxed in the Spirit of God who had come to be within him. He refused to own the situation as his. He allowed the Spirit of Christ to fill his circumstance. Peter realized the Holy Spirit had a purposed plan and would fill that plan with the accomplished end by His power.

This is exactly the situation in our passage (Acts 2:4). The disciples have received the Holy Spirit (Acts 2:2). No doubt they are in the temple at this time. They spend most of their time during this waiting period in the temple. They are rejoicing and praising God over what He has done in the resurrection and what He is going to do in the days ahead. This is where the large crowd has gathered (Acts 2:9-11). The Spirit of Christ has an agenda. He could simply fill the one hundred and twenty disciples and later make plans for church planting. However, there is a multitude to which communication of truth is needed. The disciples who receive the Holy Spirit now are instruments through which the Spirit can accomplish His purposed plan. He fills them, brings His immediate purpose to a completion as they speak in languages they do not know. This is not the outside Spirit of tongues which comes to be inside of them, but the Holy Spirit who is already indwelling them permeating their lives to fill up His purposed plan!

The Book of Acts demonstrates the very essence of Christian living. Do you grasp the consistent, moment by moment surrender to the control of the Spirit of Christ this requires? The very baptism of the Holy Spirit requires a dying which must continue. This is not just an experience to remember, but a life to be lived. The depth of surrender, the crucifixion achieved in the fullness of the Spirit of Christ must be maintained in living or all is lost. The dream of God was not just to give you His life, but to manifest His life through you in every circumstance. It is a "filling," to bring to an end His accomplished purpose. This is a call to a "living dying."

There is one other major idea which is connected to this Greek word *filled.* In the Greek language, the basic root word used in *they were all filled* is sometimes used with the prefix "in." It means "to fill" therefore "to satisfy." In a sermon preached in Lystra, Barnabas and Paul defend the greatness of God. The people thought they were gods who had come down to earth. Barnabas and Paul declared, ***"Nevertheless He did not leave Himself without witness, in that He did good, gave us rain from heaven and fruitful seasons, filling our hearts with food and gladness,"*** (Acts 14:17). It is a testimony that God has indeed satisfied our desires. It is interesting that this Greek word is used only in relation to food. It is used in the story of the feeding of the five thousand. ***So when they were filled, He said to His disciples, "Gather up the fragments that remain, so that nothing is lost,"*** (John 6:12). However, this Greek word is never used in connection with the filling of the Holy Spirit.

The emphasis of the fullness of the Holy Spirit is not on being completed in terms of satisfaction, enough, ended or finished. There is a continual flow to the movement of the Spirit of God. The picture of the filling of the Holy Spirit is not the gluttonous, satisfied, holding his belling, eating too much, overweight, overfed and spoiled Christian. It is the picture of the Christian on the edge of his seat anticipating the action of the Holy Spirit who is already with him. What will the Spirit of Christ do through me in the midst of this crisis? What attitudes will the Spirit of Christ flow through me?

This is so strongly emphasized in the New Testament that the satisfied, gluttonous, holding his belly Christian is viewed as not experiencing the filling of the Holy Spirit. It is a contradiction in terms. It simply cannot be! There is no filling of the Holy Spirit for satisfaction. Other words which bespeak this same condition might be; comfortable, arrival, finished, ingrown and completed. The filling of the Holy Spirit is characterized by such words as: seeking, expecting, desiring, hungering, thirsting, yielding, surrendering, depending and openness.

The purpose of the baptism of the Spirit of Christ is the filling of the Spirit of Christ. Christ comes to live within us for the purpose of flowing through us to accomplish a purposed plan. This is the sourcing of the Spirit which Jesus proposed to His disciples. *"But you shall receive power when the Holy Spirit has come upon you; and you shall be witnesses to Me in Jerusalem, and in Judea and Samaria, and to the end of the earth,"* (Acts 1:8). The baptism of the Holy Spirit was to bring to death all self-sourcing. As Jesus constantly lived in the filling of the Father, so we are to constantly live in the filling of the Spirit of Christ. As Jesus was consistently sourced by the Father, so we are to be sourced by the Spirit of Christ. Think of the life that could be lived in the power and sourcing of God! It would be the Christ life!

Acts 2:3

TO BE SEATED

In verse one, Luke pin-points the exact time the Promise of the Father was fulfilled. It was on the Day of the Feast of Pentecost. It marked the fulfillment of the dreams of God to restore us to the full purpose for which He made us. We have again become the container of the Spirit of God. He has come! In verse two, Luke attempts to discuss the wonder of this coming. There was a sound (echo) which was like a great and mighty wind. The disciples heard this. There was also that which they saw in verse three. It was like a tongue appearing as fire. It separated and came upon each one of the believers individually. The process is described as **sat upon each of them** (Acts 2:3).

The Greek word translated *sat* is most unique. It is used forty-eight times in the New Testament, but it always has a particular slant or tone to it. One must realize that the author had a multitude of choices. There were numerous words available to describe the coming of this object which looked like a tongue of fire. He might have used a word which would have stated the Holy Spirit was "coming upon" the disciples. If he wanted to emphasize the permanent remaining of the Holy Spirit upon the believers, he could have used the Greek word meaning "resting upon." Even if his desire was to simply tell us that the Holy Spirit "sat" upon the disciples, the normal Greek word for "sat" could have been used.

However, Luke chose a Greek word which is uniquely

used for authority. This Greek word is used exclusively for someone sitting down in the place of authority. A King does not simply sit down; he does whatever this word projects! Let me give you some examples of the usage of this Greek word. After choosing His disciples, Jesus went to a mountain and "sat down" to proclaim the manifesto of the Kingdom of God in the Sermon on the Mount (Matthew 5:1). Two disciples who were brothers enlisted their mother in a request. They wanted the right and left hand positions in the coming Kingdom of God. The word used throughout the passage to describe their achieving these positions is this Greek word (Matthew 20:21). Jesus is preaching His final public message to the multitude. In describing the scribes and the Pharisees, He says, **"The scribes and the Pharisees SIT in Moses' seat,"** (Matthew 23:2). This was the place of authority when one spoke the Law of God. Paul was on trial and found himself before Festus. Festus was intrigued with Paul, **and the next day, SITTING on the judgment seat, he commanded Paul to be brought** (Acts 25:6).

It is amazing the number of times this word is used in the Book of Acts. Luke highlights this word nine times. We just referred to one of them. He also writes, **So on a set day Herod, arrayed in royal apparel, SAT on his throne and gave an oration to them** (Acts 12:21). In Peter's sermon on Pentecost Day, he reminded them of the promise God made to King David. He said, **"Therefore, being a prophet and knowing that God had sworn with an oath to him that of the fruit of his body, according to the flesh, He would raise up the Christ to SIT on his throne,"** (Acts 2:30).

This word is used consistently to describe the enthroning of Jesus as King of the Kingdom. Matthew quotes Jesus as saying, **"Assuredly I say to you, that in the regeneration, when the Son of Man SITS on the throne of His glory, you who have followed Me will also SIT on twelve thrones, judging the twelve tribes of Israel,"** (Matthew 19:28). Paul describes the great power of God *which He worked in Christ when He raised Him from the dead and SEATED Him at His right hand in the heavenly places* (Ephesians 1:20). The writer of the Book of Hebrews uses this word several times to express the authority of Christ. In describing Jesus, he writes, *who being the brightness of His glory and the express image of His person, and upholding all things by the word of His power, when He had by Himself purged our sins, SAT down at the right hand of the Majesty on high* (Hebrews 1:3). In summarizing the first seven chapters, he says, *Now this is the main point of the things we are saying: We have such a High Priest, who is SEATED at the right hand of the throne of the Majesty in the heavens,* (Hebrews 8:1). He contrasted the greatness of the sacrifice of Christ with the Old Testament sacrifices. *But this Man, after He had offered one sacrifice for sins forever, SAT down at the right hand of God* (Hebrews 10:12). The promises of Christ spill forth from the Book of Revelation. The ascended Lord promises *"To him who overcomes I will grant to SIT with Me on My throne, as I also overcame and SAT down with My Father on His throne,"* (Revelation 3:21). John saw something overwhelming in the future of the saints. *And I saw thrones, and they SAT on them, and judgment was committed to them. Then I saw the souls of those who had been beheaded for their witness to Jesus and for the word of God, who had not worshiped the beast or his image, and had not received his mark on their foreheads or on their hands. And they lived and reigned with Christ for a thousand years* (Revelation 20:4).

    If you have grasped the tone of this great word, I would like to suggest a radical concept. Dare we take for granted the use of this Greek word in relation to the Day of Pentecost? As this word is forcibly used to describe the enthroning of Christ, it is now used to describe the enthroning of the Holy Spirit in our lives. As the word depicts who Jesus is as King of the Kingdom, now it depicts who the Holy Spirit is within us. What is happening in the heavenly realms is in like manner taking place in the earthly realms. Christ enthroned at the right hand of the Father as King of the Kingdom is parallel to the Spirit of Jesus now enthroned as King of the Kingdom within you!

Would this not be the complete fulfillment of the prayer of Jesus?

"In this manner, therefore pray:
Our Father in heaven,
Hallowed be Your name.
Your kingdom come,
Your will be done
On earth as it is in heaven," (Matt 6:9-10).

Jesus gives us pointed teaching about this concept. He began to use "church" language with His disciples. He describes the church and a group of people who have linked with what is taking place in heaven (Matthew 18:18). In turn they have reached out to link with each other (Matthew 18:19). With one arm embracing all that is in heaven and one arm embracing each other there begins to be a flow from heaven to earth. In this connection and flow the image of Christ is produced in their world (Matthew 18:20). What a progression this is! The foundation of it all is linking with heaven. What is happening there must begin to happen here within us.

Again, consider carefully this truth! Is the Day of Pentecost, the outpouring of the Holy Spirit upon the believers, a duplication of what is taking place in the ascension of Christ? As Christ ascended to the heavenly realm and was seated at the right hand of the Father, did the Spirit of Jesus descend to the earthly realm and "sit" upon the believer? Is this what the fullness of the Holy Spirit is?

I must confess this is a change in focus and emphasis regarding the baptism of the Holy Spirit. Perhaps the real focus of the

Part One: A New Level

Holy Spirit is not about empowering but about reigning. Perhaps His real purpose is not about miracles, but about ruling. The Biblical concept of the Kingdom of God is completely opposite from the concept of the kingdom of the world. In our world, we consider a kingdom in terms of space, acres, population, budgets, power, size, etc., and in the Bible the Kingdom of God is always about God reigning. Where ever God reigns, there is the Kingdom! In answering the Pharisees, Jesus said, *"The kingdom of God does not come with observation; nor will they say, 'See here!' or 'See there!' For indeed, the kingdom of God is within you,"* (Luke 17:20-21). If the Kingdom of God is within us, it requires the presence and reigning of the King. Is the fullness of the Holy Spirit in the life of the believer the coronation of Christ as King of the Kingdom of God? The Spirit of Christ is SITTING on His throne here in the exact same manner that Christ is SITTING on His throne there!

While this may all sound great theologically, what does it mean in practical life experience? This is what really matters to most of us. How does this affect my life on a daily basis? We must come back to the text. **Then there appeared to them divided tongues, as of fire, and one sat upon each of them** (Acts 2:3). The Greek word which is translated **divided** is actually a verb in the form of a participle. In this case it acts like an adjective modifying the word **tongues**. The emphasis of the word is on separation (to separate into parts or divide up). It gives you the idea that the tongues were divided out to each person from one common source. This gives you the picture of a fire-like appearance coming into the room corresponding with the hearing of the sound. At first it appeared as a single unit, but suddenly it parted in every direction. A portion of it **sat** on each of those who were present.

The Greek word translated **tongues** is definitely plural. The passive, participle **divided** gives a description of what happens with these **tongues**. They were together as if a whole unit, but then began to divide. The Greek word translated *sat* describes what happens to each person. The outpouring of the Holy Spirit was upon each person individually. It is a personal experience. The Holy Spirit *sat* upon each individual disciple! Does God want to do this in my life?

However, to grasp the significance of this we must see it through the understanding of the word *sat*. The Spirit of Christ is coming to SIT upon the individual believer in the same way the ascended Lord went to SIT at the right hand of the Father. We must see the outpouring of the Holy Spirit in light of this parallel. The emphasis is not upon the Spirit of Christ reigning over you. This is not the Holy Spirit coming to be your King. He did not come to indwell us so He could be our boss. In light of the word *sat* we must see that He has come in order to reign FROM us not over us. We are the actual platform of His authority.

Picture with me the heavenly realm and the great throne of God, the Father. At His right hand is the throne of authority which belongs to the King of the Kingdom. It belongs to the one to whom the Father gives it. At the base of the mountain, the resurrected Lord said to His disciples. ***"All authority has been given to Me in heaven and on earth,"*** (Matthew 28:18). What does this throne look like? Is it gold plated? Do not let your focus be on the physical aspect (if there actually is one) of the throne. Let your attention be upon the throne as the platform from which He reigns. Now transfer that picture into the descending of the Holy Spirit who has come to sit upon you as a believer! You are the throne which has nothing to do with shape or gold, but platform for authority. Your life is to be the throne from which the authority of the Spirit of Christ, who is the King of the Kingdom is distributed. He is not just reigning over you but from you!

One scholar says this about the Greek word translated *sat*. "In the New Testament this highest human concept is used to express the inexpressible." This tells you the dilemma in which we find ourselves. What is the difference between Christ reigning OVER us and reigning FROM us? I am afraid the difference is inexpressible! But do we not have to attempt to grasp the great concept?

When He reigns OVER us, we are told what to do and are expected to be obedient. However, when He reigns FROM us, we become an avenue through which He demonstrates His Kingship and authority. We will most likely be totally unaware of what He is accomplishing. But the authority of Christ is accomplishing a great plan! When He reigns OVER us, we must discipline ourselves to come under His authority. Spiritual disciplines are necessary to bend our rebellious tendencies to His purposes. When He reigns FROM us, we find self-control as a fruit of the Spirit (Galatians 5:22-23). What we are experiencing is completely beyond self-contribution. When He reigns OVER us, we find ourselves obligated because He has done so much for us. When He reigns FROM us, we experience the thrill of being a part of the very heart of God being displayed in our world.

Surely you must recognize this is far beyond and on a higher plane than surrender. All my life I have heard "total surrender" taught and preached. I have sung the favorite song, "I Surrender All." Total surrender is always focused on things or items. I am never sure I have surrendered everything to Christ because I am always finding new things or areas of my life which I have not faced. Christ is constantly revealing new aspects of His greatness which I have not experienced. These may be areas of which I am not aware. When these things are revealed I must surrender them. I wonder if I am capable of surrendering all things to Christ. The conclusion is I must continually surrender everything to Christ. It is going to be a life time experience of always surrendering.

When He comes to reign FROM me, I am moved to another realm. This is far beyond surrender. Every aspect of my life becomes a platform upon which He can display Himself to my world. I become a dispenser from which He distributes His authority and power. I am the stage upon which He manifests His greatness. It is the fulfillment of Paul's statement, **But we have this treasure in earthen vessels, that the excellence of the power may be of God and not of us** (2 Corinthians 4:7). The *earthen vessel* is the clay "cracked" flower pot. Its total purpose of existence is to contain something. The beauty of the flower it holds so masters the viewer that the clay pot is unnoticed. God has designed us to be used like the clay pot. Our purpose is ***that the excellence of the power may be of God and not of us.*** He is reigning FROM us.

It is amazing to embrace this concept and read the Book of Acts with this distinction. One hundred and twenty individuals have just received the Spirit of Christ reigning FROM them. They are in a crowded place where at least seventeen different nationalities and languages are represented. Suddenly the Gospel message is being proclaimed in each of these languages. The crowd is confused. They are not confused with the message but the deliverance of the message. How can these uneducated Galileans know all of these languages? This does not have anything to do with these unlearned Galileans. They have become a platform upon which the dynamic of the Spirit of Christ is reigning. The Truth (Christ is the Truth) must be communicated. It is definitely the fulfillment of the promise that they will become His witnesses. Therefore, witnessing must be defined as the demonstration of the authority of Christ reigning FROM the believer without the contribution of his knowledge, skill, or talent. It is not the product of seminars or training. It is Him reigning from the believer.

You and I need to radically apply this to our lives. It appears that the average evangelical believer of this generation has a Christianity which he has mastered. Perhaps he has received some kind of touch from God, but has proceeded to live his life as a product of his training. Even in our discipleship programs we are strong on the emphasis of developing our Christian patterns. We develop follow-up material which teaches the new convert to do the right things and have the right disciplines. Do you understand how far beneath Christ ruling FROM us this is? Have we developed a Christianity which is a product of ourselves? We reap meager results and have little affect on our world. We spend our time developing programs. We busy ourselves with our buildings and maintenance. But the action of the Holy Spirit as in the Book of Acts is missing. We allow the Spirit of Christ to reign OVER us. He dictates our actions and practices. No one can accuse us of being unchristian in deed or word. But the Holy Spirit reigning FROM us is missing.

Do I need the sound of His presence to come again? Do I need what looks like a tongue of fire to separate itself and come and *sit* on me?

Acts 2:4

FILLED WITH WHAT?

Luke confronts us repeatedly with the reality of the "fullness of the Holy Spirit" in the Book of Acts. This is not a minor issue that can be easily dismissed. This is the central focus of the book and all the historical information concerning the spread of the church is a testimony to it. To miss this would be to miss it all!

We must restate the distinction of this book. It is the baptism of the Spirit and the filling of the Spirit. This distinction is found in the contrast between the two Greek words translated *filled* in verses two and four (Acts 2:2 & 4). In verse two, the Greek word refers to content which is placed in a container. It is something outside coming inside. The Holy Spirit, both heard in the sound and seen in the tongue as of fire, has come! While He was present in Old Testament days, He has now come to fill the container in a new way. It is both a corporate and individual filling. The Church was born in the initial outpouring of the Promise of the Father. But the tongues as of fire separated and rested on each individual believer (Acts 2:3). Each person experienced this baptism of the Holy Spirit. Paul describes it as *for by one Spirit we were all baptized into one body – whether Jews or Greeks, whether slaves or free – and have all been made to drink into one Spirit* (1 Corinthians 12:13).

In verse four the Greek word translated *filled* describes a flow of something which is already present. It is not outside coming inside, but inside permeating and saturating. The baptism of the Holy Spirit is equaled with initial sanctification. It is the new birth! The very life of Christ has come to be within the believer. Justification (forgiveness) has taken place and the believer has been invaded by the Spirit of Christ. The fullness of the Holy Spirit is equated with entire sanctification. It is not something different, but a continuation of what has already happened. The Holy Spirit already present within moves to fill the entire being. This requires crucifixion of self-will. The carnal mind must be put to death.

In the baptism of the Spirit, I belong to His body (1 Corinthians 12:13). The fullness of the Spirit means that my body now belongs to Him. The baptism of the Spirit of Christ does not need to take place again. The fullness of the Spirit of Christ is repeated again and again as I die daily to the patterns of my established self-will. The Holy Spirit will constantly fill me in new demonstrations of His being. I will grow in the embrace of Christ. The baptism of the Holy Spirit links me with other believers (Ephesians 4:1-6). The fullness of the Spirit is personal and individual.

Paul commands us to be filled with the Spirit. ***And do not be drunk with wine, in which is dissipation; but be filled with the Spirit*** (Ephesians 5:18). The grammar of this verb be *filled* is the present, passive, imperative. This indicates that the Spirit is to be continuously filling the believer. Paul then begins to list the results of being filled with the Spirit (Ephesians 5:19-33). He restates this list in the Book of Colossians (3:16-25), and he says these things are a result of having a mind saturated with the Word of God! He says, **"Let the word of Christ dwell in you richly,"** (Colossians 3:16). To let the Word of Christ richly dwell in you is identical to being filled with the Spirit. These two are the same spiritual reality viewed from two sides. To be filled with the Spirit is to be controlled by His Word. To have the Word dwelling richly in you is to be controlled by His Spirit.

Filled With What? | Acts 2:4

Since the Holy Spirit is the author and the power of the Word, the expressions are interchangeable. Therefore, Paul gives the same results for each one!

Let us examine these two parallel statements: ***Let the word of Christ dwell in you richly*** (Colossians 3:16). ***But be filled with the Spirit*** (Ephesians 5:18). Is there a difference between ***dwell in you richly*** and ***be filled?*** The Greek word translated ***dwell*** means to dwell within, live in or among. It is fascinating to contrast the use of this Greek word in the Greek translation of the Old Testament (Septuagint) and the Greek New Testament. It is used in the Septuagint for human dwelling and settling on earth. This takes place in the land, on mountains, or in cities. This Greek word is used to refer to the human possession of these places. Thus, this word becomes a fixed term for "inhabitants." God is never the subject of this Greek word. In the Old Testament, man is constantly indwelling (land, mountains, cities, etc.) but God never indwells. In the Old Testament God is never an inhabitant!

In the New Testament it is completely the opposite. Mankind is never the subject of this word. Man becomes the object or the dwelling place. Man is indwelt by sin. Paul stated it, ***But now, it is no longer I who do it, but sin that dwells in me*** (Romans 7:17). Mankind can definitely be indwelt by the Holy Spirit. Again Paul states, ***that good thing which was committed to you, keep by the Holy Spirit who dwells in us*** (2 Timothy 1:14). Another way of saying this is that God indwells you. Paul said,

and what agreement has the temple of God with idols? For you are the temple of the living God. As God has said:
"I will dwell in them
And walk among them.
I will be their God,
And they shall be my people," (2 Corinthians 6:16).

Part One: A New Level

Human beings can even be indwelt by faith. Paul wrote, **When I call to remembrance the genuine faith that is in you, which dwelt first in your grandmother Lois and your mother Eunice, and I am persuaded is in you also** (2 Timothy 1:5). In the same manner man can be indwelt by God's Word. **Let the Word of God dwell in you richly** (Colossians 3:16).

A shift is made between the Old and New Testament. Man has moved from being the inhabitant to being the habitat. The New Testament view is that an individual is actually indwelt by an external Being of power. This Being actually comes within the human being to live. This Being is able to dominate that individual. The person's body becomes a "house" or "temple" of this Being. Obviously there are only two possibilities by which a person can be indwelt. There is God and the devil. Romans chapter seven would convince us that the devil continuously takes possession of a person, dominates that person, and has him or her in his power. Sin not only controls the actions of the person (Romans 7:7) but also acts in place of that person (Romans 7:18). It forces the person to do what he or she does not want to do and drives the person to destruction.

The opposite picture of this is a person being indwelt by the Spirit of Christ. It is only the Spirit of Christ who can break the power of the one who has possessed us. Paul cries out, **But if the Spirit of Him who raised Jesus from the dead dwells in you, He who raised Christ from the dead will also give life to your mortal bodies through the Spirit who dwells in you** (Romans 8:11). We are considering the passage in Colossians. **Let the word of Christ dwell in you richly** (Colossians 3:16). Paul states this in the imperative; so this is a command. We are ordered to allow the Word of Christ to be at home in us **richly.** This Greek word can also be translated abundantly or extravagantly rich. In this verse, the word can be used in two ways. It can be an adjective of the **word of Christ.** Who could possibly dispute the richness, abundance, and extravagant wealth of the Scriptures? Who can dismiss the Gospel account and the depth of the movement of God in our behalf as if it is a cheap issue? The **word of Christ** must be taken in the full expanse of its abundance. However, this word *richly* can also apply to how the **word of Christ** indwells the believer. Every area of the believer's life must be dominated and richly possessed by the Word. This is not one aspect or ingredient within him; this is the abundance, the completeness of the indwelling.

Now, how does this compare with the use of the word *filled?* In Ephesians (5:18) the believer is commanded (imperative) to **be filled with the Spirit!** The Greek word which is translated *filled* is the same as Luke's description of the sound filling the whole house (Acts 2:2). It has the idea of something outside coming to be inside, but it definitely has completeness about it. The concept of abundantly, extravagantly rich is ingrained within the word. There is no difference between the "filling" and the "indwelling."

Let us now consider the comparison of **the Spirit** and **the word of Christ.** Is there a difference? Obviously **the Spirit** is a reference to the Holy Spirit who came in an outpouring on the Day of Pentecost (Acts 2:1-4). The Holy Spirit is not an "it" but a person! He is so closely linked and united with Christ that we refer to Him as the Spirit of Christ. To be *filled* with the Holy Spirit is to be filled with Christ. Paul refers to being *filled with the Spirit* (Ephesians 5:18) and **Christ in you** (Colossians 1:27). In the upper room before His death, Jesus spent time relating the promise of the Father to His disciples. He said, *"And I will pray the Father, and He will give you another Helper, that He may abide with you forever – the Spirit of truth, whom the world cannot receive, because it neither sees Him nor knows Him; but you know Him, for He dwells with you and will be in you. I will not leave you orphans; I will come to you,"* (John 14:16-18). Jesus refers to the Holy Spirit with you as Himself!

The Biblical concept of **the word of Christ** is never a story narrative, doctrinal statement, or theology. ***The word of Christ*** is always linked with the person of Christ. It is impossible to separate them. While the communication may come from Christ, the communication is always considered Christ. This is why Jesus could say, ***"I am the way, the truth, and the life,"*** (John 14:6). The Living Word is speaking the Written Word. It is an extension of His very being and is considered Him. It is impossible for His Word to be other than He is!

God gives us a tremendous opportunity in the Gospel. He calls us to the rich, full and complete filling of His Person within our very beings. This very Person speaks to us in His Word. He is not writing it down and later we are to study it on our own. No! The interaction of the Word in our lives is God Himself speaking His Word to us as we saturate in it. Is this not a call to saturate, feed upon, live in and completely immerse ourselves in the Scriptures, His Word? The fullness of His Spirit requires the saturation in His Word. Saturation in His Word requires the fullness of His Spirit. No wonder the Apostle Paul says they are the same.

Here are two statements which are so interlocked that to say one is to speak the other. They are the same. ***Let the word of Christ dwell in you richly*** (Colossians 3:16). ***But be filled with the Spirit*** (Ephesians 5:18). From these two (same) statements Paul gives a list of results. The list is virtually the same for both. It contains three strong elements which are fundamental to all of Christian experience; they hardly need to be explained. What does need explanation is their focus! These three elements must not be seen as the cause, only as the result. One does not do these three things and then have the fullness of the Holy Spirit and the Word of Christ indwelt. These are the natural byproduct of the presence of Christ. To state it stronger – these are always present when the Holy Spirit is filling the individual.

Singing

Paul says we are to be *speaking to one another in psalms and hymns and spiritual songs, singing and making melody in your heart to the Lord* (Ephesians 5:19). This is a result of being filled with the Spirit. He also says, *Let the word of Christ dwell in you richly in all wisdom, teaching and admonishing one another in psalms and hymns and spiritual songs, singing with grace in your hearts to the Lord* (Colossians 3:16). These are very specific statements. Notice the idea of *psalms and hymns and spiritual songs* in both passages. The content of the singing is a total focus on the Word of Christ. From a Biblical view there is no song outside of this content. I am not sure what this does to secular music, but it is a fake, fraud, and an attempt to duplicate the greatness of our God. The song is not to be an expression of personal feelings or experiences but a *word of Christ.* If the preacher is obligated to base his sermon on Scripture, how much more the singer! If every sermon is to be an explanation and exposing of the Scripture, how much more the song! Therefore the basis of worship is always the Word. The melody, beat, and rhythm is unimportant to the worshipper. The reason the believer can worship is because of the truth. Style of worship becomes insignificant. It is the expression of truth which inspires worship within the believer.

Both of Paul's statements contain a focus on *in your heart.* One dare not say, "I am not a musical person. I have no musical ability and therefore do not sing." What about the music produced by the Holy Spirit within you? The expression of it may be quite sad, but it must be expressed. The *heart* is the seat of all life. If there is music in the heart, how can it not be expressed? Should it not be on your face, in your eyes, and dominate your talk?

Supper of the Lord

Paul continues by saying, we are *giving thanks always for all things to God the Father in the name of our Lord Jesus Christ,* (Ephesians 5:20). In his parallel passage he says, *And whatever you do in word or deed, do all in the name of the Lord Jesus, giving thanks to God the Father through Him* (Colossians 3:17). Do you see the strong parallel between *for all things* and *do all?* There is something all inclusive in these statements. This powerful gratitude within the believer affects everything!

How can Paul be so bold as to make such a broad statement? The Greek word for *giving thanks* is the same root word for Eucharist. All of life is an act of coming to the table of our Lord. Remember our study of the Day of the Feast of Pentecost. They called it the "concluding assembly of the Passover." It was the celebration of the conclusion of the harvest. Israel saw the harvest as a result of the Passover, the blood of the lamb. The reason they had the land, established a home, had a family, and planted a crop was because of the lamb. If everything is seen in light of the blood of Christ, would we not live in constant gratitude? Where do griping, complaining, and dismay fit into this?

Submit

Paul continues, *submitting to one another in the fear of God* (Ephesians 5:20). In his parallel passage he says, *Wives, submit...* (Colossians 3:18); *Husbands, love...* (Colossians 3:19); *Children, obey...* (Colossians 3:20); *Bondservants, obey...* (Colossians 3:22); *And whatever you do, do it heartily, as to the Lord and not to men* (Colossians 3:23). It is very significant that the material in both passages on this subject is lengthy. Perhaps it is here that we have our major problem. He seems compelled to give illustrations and break it down into our every day relationships.

It must be recognized that submission is not an "act" but an "attitude." It is a spontaneous result of being filled with the Spirit of the Word. It does not come from obligation. It is not the result of power, fear, or intimidation. It is the natural flow of the Spirit of Jesus.

These three elements are results not criteria for being filled with the Sprit of God. One does not do these things and then become filled with the Spirit and indwelt by the Word. It is because the Word richly indwells the believer that these three things happen. If they are not present, it is an immediate warning for concern. Their absence tells us of our lack. Examine your life through the eyes of Christ.

Acts 2:4

THE SPIRIT'S MOUTHPIECE

The Word of God has much to say about the tongue. The tongue is described as wicked, deceitful, perverse, filthy, corrupt, flattering, slanderous, gossiping, blasphemous, foolish, boasting, complaining, cursing, contentious, sensual, and vile. No wonder God put the tongue in a cage behind the teeth, walled in by the mouth! Someone observed that because the tongue is in a wet place, it can easily slip.

Some sins are not committed because there isn't an opportunity. However, the tongue is always available, ready, and anxious. There are no limits or built-in restraints. Scientists propose that once a sound wave produced by the tongue is set in motion, it continues on a never-ending journey. If we had sophisticated enough instruments, each wave could be captured and reproduced at any time. This would mean that every word spoken by any person who has ever lived could be retrieved! Could that be the judgment day review? God simply does a replay of every word you and I have spoken. We judge ourselves by our own tongue. No wonder Jesus said, *"For by your words you will be justified, and by your words you will be condemned,"* (Matthew 12:37).

James writes very pointedly about this issue in his epistle. He mentions the tongue in every chapter of his epistle (James 1:19 & 26; 2:12; 3:5, 6 &8; 4:11; 5:12). He describes the controlling power of the tongue with various illustrations. *Indeed,*

The Spirit's Mouthpiece | **Acts 2:4**

we put bits in horses' mouths that they may obey us, and we turn their whole body (James 3:3). His analogy is strong. So our entire life or body will be controlled by our tongue. He goes on to speak of large sail boats which are controlled by a small rudder (James 3:4). The tongue is the rudder of our life determining the direction in which we go. The tongue is an indicator of a person's spirit; it reveals what is in the heart!

Do you not find it fascinating that Luke describes the first expression of the filling of the Holy Spirit as that of the tongue! Those filled with the Spirit become the Spirit's mouthpiece. In the language of James, the Spirit of Jesus has harnessed the very heart of the believer's life. He has taken control of the rudder of man's ship. However, Luke takes this concept one step further. The Holy Spirit does not just control what is being said, He is actually saying it. The Holy Spirit does not tell the believer His message and the believer delivers it. This implies separation from the Holy Spirit. There is a merging of the life of the Spirit and the believer. The mind of the Spirit becomes the mind of the believer. The believer's tongue now becomes the Spirit's tongue!

In studying our passage (Acts 2:4) we will begin with the conclusion and then work through the passage to be sure it is verified. The Spirit of Jesus desires to permeate our faculties in order to produce through our tongue His message to our world. He is not asking us to speak in His behalf. He wants to speak through us. He is not holding seminars for our training in proper spiritual communication. He is merging with the believer in an intimate union which will produce one mind, one voice, and one message! Now let us view the passage.

The opening statement of verse four is **They were all filled with the Holy Spirit** (Acts 2:4). One Biblical scholar states, "To be filled with anything is a phrase denoting that all the faculties are pervaded by it, engaged in it, or under its influence." Let your mind grasp the reality of such an invasion of the Spirit of Christ in your life. Remember the emphasis of the Greek word translated *filled* in this verse (Acts 2:4). It is contrasted with a different Greek word translated *filled* in verse two. Verse two refers to content actually coming into a container. It is the picture of the outside God coming to be inside. Now in verse four the emphasis shifts to that of permeating and saturating. It is something already present which is now moving into the whole being.

This is demonstrated in what is taking place in the lives of the disciples. There is only one explanation of the sudden ability to speak in languages they do not know. They have been invaded by the presence of another Being that is controlling and using them for the purposed plan of His design. Is this not a complete verification of our conclusion?

In his Gospel, Matthew records a discussion between Jesus and His disciples. It is at the close of His Galilean ministry. A summary statement of Jesus' feeling about this ministry is given. He has seen the great multitudes **like sheep having no shepherd** (Matthew 9:36). He calls upon His disciples to pray for laborers for the harvest (Matthew 9:37-38). As they end their prayer, Jesus calls them as the answer to their prayer. He gives them power and they become apostles (Matthew 10:1-2). Before He releases them to minister, He gives them lengthy instructions. One part of that instruction is: **"But when they deliver you up, do not worry about how or what you should speak. For it will be given to you in that hour what you should speak; for it is not you who speak but the Spirit of your Father who speaks in you,"** (Matthew 10:19-20). If that was true in the early ministry of the apostles, how much more it is true now in the filling of the Holy Spirit! Can He become the source of my communication? Can he pervade my mind and spirit until nothing can be said with my tongue that will not be sourced by Him?

Luke continues in the verse by saying, **and began to speak** (Acts 2:4). The focus of the Greek word translated *speak* is not on the content of the speaking. It is the idea that the disciples uttered sounds which the hearers heard. This word is used in the sense of "to talk at random" contrasted with a speaking which involves the intellectual reason of man. Often this is used of children who talk and talk, but say nothing. Do you see this word strikes a blow at the foundation of the wisdom of man? My concern is not on the speaking, but on the content. What will I say? Will it make sense? Did I speak it correctly? How will it be received? This means I must be in control of what I am saying. I must figure it out and understand it thoroughly.

Something is happening to the tongues of the disciples which is completely beyond their reasoning and understanding. They are not in control of the content of their speaking. They are speaking in languages they do not know and therefore do not understand. A shift is being made in the lives of the disciples. The direction of the rudder determines their lives are changing sources. They will no longer be in control of their tongues, but the Spirit of Christ has invaded the deepest area of their lives. He will source even their speaking.

I want to be very plain about how strong I believe Luke is making this! Some one may say, "Well, my problem is I speak without thinking." Let me boldly say that this is not anyone's problem. That is not what is being advocated in this passage. Our speaking is not to be a product of our own thinking. There will be no difficulty in speaking if the Spirit of Christ pervades the depth of your mind and is in control of the rudder of your life. Listen closely again to the words of Jesus to His disciples. ***"But when they deliver you up, do not worry about how or what you should speak. For it will be given to you in that hour what you should speak, for it is not you who speak but the Spirit of your Father who speaks in you,"*** (Matthew 10:19-20).

Is it possible to be filled with the Spirit of Christ like this? Can I become so intimate with Him that my tongue is under His control? Is it possible for Him to pervade my mind and heart so even my tongue is sourced by Him? Is your Christianity "guarding, protecting, disciplining, and controlling," or is it, "relaxing, yielding, surrendering and dying? Is Christianity about doing it right and speaking correctly? Or is it about the filling of the Holy Spirit who becomes the controlling agent of my being? Does not this statement verify our conclusion? The Spirit of Jesus desires to permeate our faculties to produce through our tongue His message to our world. Will we let Him?

Let us return to our basic text. *And they were all filled with the Holy Spirit and began to speak with other tongues...* (Acts 2:4). The Greek word translated *tongues* is used at least fifty times in the New Testament. What is so interesting is the variety of usages it seems to have. It is used to refer to an organ of the body (Revelation 16:10). It is used in regard to taste (Luke 16:24). The tongue is often connected to the idea of speaking or the ability of speech (Mark 7:33-35). It is often personified (Romans 14:11; Philippians 2:11). It is used metaphorically to mean speech or language. This is the usage in our passage. This seems to be the area of controversy. It can refer to a particular language or dialect as spoken by a particular people (Acts 2:11; 1 Corinthians 13:1). But it can also refer to an "unknown" tongue (1 Corinthians 14:14).

It is clear from the study of the New Testament that there were two distinct uses of the word *tongue* in this regard. One was the promised gift of languages other than one's own native language. This was experienced by those who were filled with the Spirit of Pentecost. They affirm the Gospel among at least seventeen dialects on this great Day. However, this same word when used in the singular with a singular subject is translated "unknown tongue." It refers to the Corinthian practice of speaking in an unknown tongue not comprehended by anyone, and therefore, not an ordinary spoken language.

It is very clear which of these tongues is happening on the Day of Pentecost. The great crowds which heard the speaking *were all amazed and marveled, saying to one another, "Look,*

The Spirit's Mouthpiece | Acts 2:4

are not all these who speak Galileans? And how is it that we hear, each in our own language in which we were born?" (Acts 2:7-8). The great concern of this Day of Pentecost was not in speaking in an unknown tongue, but in a known language.

Does this not verify our conclusion? The Spirit of Jesus desires to permeate our faculties in order to produce through our tongue His message to our world. Certainly this was accomplished in the first event of the filling of the Holy Spirit. Do we not see it continuing to be done throughout the book of Acts? Do we see it in our personal lives?

And they were all filled with the Holy Spirit and began to speak with other tongues, as the Spirit gave... (Acts 2:4). Luke is so concerned about the source of the speaking; he goes beyond the normal statement to emphasize the Holy Spirit who **gave**. The Greek word translated *gave* is used to speak of a person who does anything to or for another. It is one from whom anything is received, the source, author or cause. There is a definite emphasis on the "source." This word is often used in connection with God or of Christ as the author or source of what one has or receives. The Spirit of Christ furnished them with the content as well as with the language.

This Greek word is used four hundred and sixteen times in the New Testament. It is the ninth most frequently used verb. It is the most common expression for the procedure whereby a subject deliberately transfers something to someone or something so that it becomes available to the recipient. So you can see how strong Luke is in his emphasis of the Holy Spirit as the source! Luke gives no other explanation for what is taking place. There is not even a slight emphasis upon the disciples, but a total focus on the Spirit of Christ. Everything which is happening is a gift from Him.

We have already understood this concept from the example of Christ. The life Jesus lived was by God's gift. The Father gave Him His works (John 5:36). It was the Father who gave

Him His disciples (John 6:37). Even His name was given by the Father (John 17:11). All things have been given into His hands (John 3:35). This strongly verifies our conclusion. The Spirit of Jesus desires to permeate our faculties in order to produce through our tongue His message to our world. There is no lack of resource or ability. There is no excuse! It is of Him and not of us.

We now come to the concluding part of our verse. *And they were all filled with the Holy Spirit and began to speak with other tongues, as the Spirit gave them utterance* (Acts 2:4). The Greek word which is translated *utterance* is in the infinitive mood. It is a verbal noun. In the English it is usually introduced with the word "to." It could be translated *as the Spirit gave them* "to utter." The purpose of this verbal noun is to fill out and give content to the main verb. Luke gives us a double emphasis to be sure we understand exactly what is happening. He tells us that *the Spirit gave* and *the Spirit ... uttered.* Again he highlights the unity between the Spirit of Christ and the believer. The Spirit did not give to the believer and then the believer uttered. This would indicate division or separation between them. The Spirit acted through the believer.

This Greek word is two words put together. It is the Greek word "apo" which is translated "from" and the Greek word meaning "to enunciate plainly or declare." This word is only used three times in the New Testament. All of these usages are in the Book of Acts. Luke uses this word to introduce Peter's sermon on the Day of Pentecost. *But Peter, standing up with the eleven, raised his voice and said* (uttered) *to them,* (Acts 2:14). Obviously Luke is using this word to indicate the clarity of Peter's message as he explains what is happening from the Book of Joel.

Luke uses this word in reference to the speaking of Paul. Festus was present when Paul defended himself before King Agrippa. Festus was so moved by Paul's defense that he cried out,

"Paul, you are beside yourself! Much learning is driving you mad!" But he (Paul) *said, "I am not mad, most noble Festus,*

The Spirit's Mouthpiece | **Acts 2:4**

but speak (utter) *the words of truth and reason,"* (Acts 26:24-25). On both of these occasions Luke specifically uses this word to emphasize clarity, and plainness of speaking. He stresses the issue of intelligible and meaningful words which we heard. This is also the meaning found in our verse (Acts 2:4). Our conclusion is verified once again. The Spirit of Jesus desires to permeate our faculties to produce through our tongue His message to our world. His message is plain and forceful. He will not leave our world in confusion. Will we become His mouth piece?

Is it possible to be so intimate with the Spirit of Jesus that even our tongue is under His control? He does not call us to speak in His behalf. He does not give us the message and we deliver it. This is not about obedience in that sense. He wants to unite with us in such a merging of beings that our tongue becomes His tongue. His mind becomes our mind. His will becomes our will. He is allowed to live His life through us. His life becomes our life. Oh, to be one with Him!

PART TWO
ACTS 2:5-13

THE WONDER OF DISPERSION

Acts 2:5

THE DISPERSION

You may or may not be familiar with the term "Dispersion." It only appears three times in the New Testament. Each place is worthy of our attention. In the Gospel of John, Jesus says something very mysterious to the leaders of Israel. They are desperately seeking ways to take Him and kill Him. Yet, He says, *"I shall be with you a little while longer, and then I go to Him who sent Me. You will seek Me and not find Me, and where I am you cannot come,"* (John 7:33-34). This confused the Jews who raised several questions among themselves. They asked, *"Where does He intend to go that we shall not find Him? Does He intend to go to the Dispersion among the Greeks and teach the Greeks?"* (John 7:35). At that time there were at least one hundred and fifty places outside of Palestine where Jews had settled. The Jews called all of their people who did not live in Palestine "The Dispersion."

This term "Dispersion" is used in two of the opening statements of the epistles. One is found in James. He writes, *James, a bondservant of God and of the Lord Jesus Christ. To the twelve tribes which are scattered abroad; Greetings* (James 1:1). Peter opens his first epistle with this word as well. He says, *Peter, an apostle of Jesus Christ, to the pilgrims of the Dispersion in Pontus, Galatia, Cappadocia, Asia, and Bithynia* (1 Peter 1:1).

The total Jewish population of the Dispersion considerably exceeded the Jewish population of Palestine. Historians often

Part Two: The Wonder of Dispersion

suggest that five to six million Jews were living in the Dispersion in the first century, but these figures are only estimates. We do know for certain that the Jews of the Dispersion constituted a group of significant size. On his missionary journeys, Paul established a pattern of always preaching at the Jewish synagogue upon arrival in any city. It appears every city he visited had a group of dispersed Jews who had built and established a synagogue. James made reference to this factor in his statements at the conclusion of the Jerusalem Council. He said, ***"For Moses has had throughout many generations those who preach him in every city, being read in the synagogues every Sabbath,"*** (Acts 15:21). Everyone seemed to recognize that Jewish settlements were in all the major cities worldwide.

There are obvious historical reasons for the Dispersion. According to the Old Testament prophets, the ultimate cause for the Dispersion was that Israel had sinned. The Lord spoke through the prophet Jeremiah, ***"I will scatter them also among the Gentiles, whom neither they nor their fathers have known,"*** (Jeremiah 9:16). The ten northern tribes of Israel were first in exile and later the two remaining tribes were later exiled to Babylon. Under the leadership of Nehemiah and Ezra a remnant returned to Palestine. However, many Jews being born and raised in exile, married inhabitants of the land, and established homes and businesses. They did not return to Palestine. The spread of the Roman Empire and the domination of the Greek language brought a surge of trade and business from all over the world. Many Jews saw business opportunities in the great cities of the world.

This brings us to the first verse of a new paragraph in Acts chapter two. It is the first statement after the description of the great outpouring of the Holy Spirit upon the believers. Luke writes, ***And there were dwelling in Jerusalem Jews, devout men, from every nation under heaven*** (Acts 2:5). This is a direct reference to the Jews of the Dispersion. Luke distinctly states

The Dispersion | Acts 2:5

they were *from every nation under heaven.* He proceeds to list those nations in verses nine through eleven. He gives additional insight into exactly who they were by the words *dwelling* and *devout.* There must have been a significant reason for his interest in identifying this group. They experienced the believers being enveloped by the Holy Spirit and heard the powerful sermon preached by Peter which was to follow (Acts 2:14-36). The three thousand souls added to the church that day came from this group (Acts 2:41).

To properly understand this group we need to analyze Luke's description of them. He was definite that these Jews were *dwelling in Jerusalem.* The same Greek word (katoikountes) is used to describe those who had knowledge of Judas (Acts 1:19). The Greek word is translated "reside." It refers to a certain, fixed and durable dwelling, as distinguished from sojourning or dwelling in a place temporarily. There is another Greek word (paroikountes) which means to have a temporary and transient residence in a place. However, as Luke continues his description he makes note that they are from *every nation under heaven.* He even proceeds to list those nationalities *in which we* (they) *were born* (Acts 2:8). He distinguishes this group from those who are the permanent, born and raised, dwellers in Jerusalem.

During this time in history there were many foreign Jews of great wealth who had a permanent residence in Jerusalem for the convenience of being near the temple. Some did so with the expectation of the coming Messiah. Others would come and stay in Jerusalem for the Feast Day of the Passover and remain there until the Feast Day of Pentecost which was celebrated fifty days later. These may have formed the large majority of those present at the outpouring of the Holy Spirit.

Luke also adds to this description that they were *devout men.* This Greek word literally means men of cautious and circumspect lives. These were men who lived in a prudent manner. It is a general expression to denote pious or religious individuals. Luke uses it to describe ***devout men carried Stephen to his burial, and made great lamentation over him*** (Acts 8:2). Luke also uses this word to describe Simeon who ***was just and devout, waiting for the Consolation of Israel, and the Holy Spirit was upon him*** (Luke 2:25). According to Webster's Dictionary, ***devout*** means "yielding a solemn and reverential attention to God in religious exercises, particularly in prayer, pious, sincere, and solemn." This kind of religious commitment is expressed in the fact that these men left their home lands and established residence in Jerusalem (either permanently or for several months a year) to be near the temple and religious activities.

Luke highlights this group of people as those who were the most affected by the outpouring of the Holy Spirit. But there were hundreds of other Jews dwelling in Jerusalem who went untouched by this great event. Why were those of the Dispersion more open and responsive to the message? Why would the Holy Spirit choose to give to them this special message and invitation? They all heard the Gospel in their own native language. How did they arrive at this point? Whatever they had, I also want!

It seems to be all about attitude. There was an attitude present in the lives of those of the Dispersion that was not present in the Jews of Palestine. The more I understand this attitude or the lack there of, the more frightened I become. I would identify my life with the stable, always been there, never left Palestine group. I started attending church before I was born. I have always been involved in ministry. I have never been involved in the binding habits of worldly sin. I am in line for the highest Pharisaical award. This seems to produce something within the heart and attitude of an individual which hinders him from responding in openness to the new revelation of God. Those who have been around the church for a long time respond by saying, "Your message is too deep and goes over our heads." However, the new people who have no religious background sit on the edge of their seats absorbing every word we speak and rejoice in the simplicity of the truth. Those of the Palestine group seem to be stale and unenthused while those of the Dispersion seek and are zealous for each new truth. How can this be explained?

An investigation of the mindset of those people of the Dispersion would be very helpful at this point in our study. Understand that not all of this group would have this attitude, but the Dispersion seemed to bring them to a new understanding of their relationship to God. Also understand that many of the things which have affected their lives are a product of their heritage. Their forefathers, living in a foreign land were more directly impacted, which helped to formulate the attitudes of this present group. Are all of these truths a part of your life? Our search now leads us into a progression of ideas.

Directed Events

God has been directing the events of your past! Notice the difference between directing and causing. If God causes the events, then all is lost. He is a mean God that I cannot trust and all human responsibility is gone. Can you imagine at the heart of the universe a fickle, whimsical, moody God who is constantly playing tricks on us? Can you imagine a universe where the consequences of the events of your past cannot be altered? There are no second chances and no way back. I cannot accept either alternative and remain sane.

Biblically, the Dispersion was all started by the disobedience of the Israelites. The people of God were taken into exile from their home land as a direct result of their own sin (Jeremiah 9:16). No one can be blamed except them. It was a tragic scene. The foreign armies killed many of them. The rest were herded like cattle and brought into captivity in a foreign land. One might simply state that it was a punishment from the hand of God. The Old Testament would seem to verify this fact. However, as you view the Old Testament through the eyes of Christ it becomes evident that the seed of destruction and exile was contained within the sin and disobedience of Israel. Israel was simply reaping the results of what they had sown through their disobedience. In this sense God did not cause their exile but was directing it. They must bare the responsibility for their exile.

I must come to terms with this concept in my own life. It is easy to blame every one else, including God, for my problems. I developed this in my earliest childhood, establishing a pattern. The explanation to my parents concerning the bruise on my sister's shoulder was, "Well, she hit me!" It really was not my fault. This reasoning continued to adulthood. The reason my life is in such a maze of complication is God. How could I have caused such things to happen? God must be punishing me; although I really do not deserve such severity.

The first step in developing the attitude of those of the Dispersion is to admit my responsibility. This is very difficult to do. The only way I can recognize my responsibility is to embrace the fact that God has been involved. The consequences of all my disobedience have not been void of the love of God. He has not abandoned me! He has been carefully directing even the results of my sin.

Directed Events for Good

If God has been directing all of the events of my life without causing them, what is the purpose? The purpose is intimately connected to the character of God. He is good! Therefore, God has been directing, not causing, the events of my life for good! It is almost too good to be true.

It is the fundamental truth about the Dispersion. The Jewish people were scattered abroad through the terrible captivities. Exile is a horrific thing! Indeed it is; but it becomes bearable when seen through the compassionate eyes of Christ. God took the deplorable tragedy of the consequences of the disobedience of Israel and prepared a way for the missionary activity of the Church in the Book of Acts.

About two hundred years before the birth of Christ an amazing thing took place. The Septuagint was produced. The Septuagint is the Greek translation of the Old Testament which was written in Hebrew. This was a direct result of the Dispersion. Large numbers of Jews found themselves in lands where the dominant language, at least of commerce, was Greek. The Hebrew language was lost to those of the Dispersion. Thus, the Dispersion produced the great need for a Greek translation of the Old Testament. This never would have happened if it had not been for the exile of Israel which was a result of the consequences of disobedience. The actual translation of the Septuagint was a product of non-Palestinian Judaism, since it was done in Alexandria. The Septuagint is the source of the great majority of quotations from the Old Testament by writers of the New Testament. This reveals that though they may have known the Old Testament Hebrew, the New Testament writers were quite familiar with the language of the Septuagint.

Long before the missionaries of the New Testament church came to the communities of the world, the ground had been thoroughly cultivated by Jews who had distributed the translation of the Old Testament in the common tongue of the people. The Dispersion was the divinely ordained means which provided a beachhead for the spread of the Gospel in alien territory.

Who could have orchestrated such a plan? A God of anger, wrath, and punishment could not! God is so good He took the heartbreaking disobedience of the people of Israel and directed it. He is so redemptive that by the time He was finished with it, He produced good. What an amazing God we have!

Part Two: The Wonder of Dispersion

Directed Events for Personal Good

Even if you accept the premise already stated, there is one other factor. It is such a deciding factor that all is lost without it. Perhaps there is a good God who takes all the evil consequences of sin and directs them toward goodness. But what does that have to do with me? Even if there is a kind, benevolent God at the heart of the universe, I seem to have my own universe of destruction. God may be directing the flow of world history toward goodness, but how does that relate to my personal tragic history?

Could you by faith embrace the possibility that God directed the events of the exile of Israel for the purpose of your personal goodness? Was it true for the individuals who were present at the outpouring of the Spirit of Jesus? It was not masses of people, but each individual of the three thousand who responded to the message preached by Peter. Is God willing to manipulate the history of mankind in order to reach one individual person?

How can I translate this into my personal life? I can easily see the consequences of my evil disobedience and that of others which are imposed upon me. But the hand of God has directed all of those consequences without causing them. He is not mad at me; He is not even punishing me! He flows redemption into the midst of every circumstance producing goodness for my personal life.

If this is true, nothing can defeat me! I must respond to a God like this. I can trust Him with my entire life. Where else can I go and to whom can I respond? He is the only One! I find life in Him!

Acts 2:6

THE OCCURRING SOUND

The re-occurrence of truth in every section of the Bible is a validation of the Scriptures as God's Word. This has become my reality as I have studied a paragraph in Matthew and then in Acts over these last several years. Matthew leaps from the Christmas narratives to the full adult ministry of John the Baptist. He continues with the emphasis on prophecy by basing John's ministry on the prophecy of truth. He quotes him as saying:

> *"The voice of one crying in the wilderness:*
> *Prepare the way of the Lord;*
> *Make His paths straight,"* (Matthew 3:3).

Matthew establishes linkage between John the Baptist and Jesus Christ. John the Baptist is **the voice.** This word is a translation of the Greek word "phone." This is the Greek word from which we get our word "telephone." John the Baptist is not the originator of the message. He did not invent, start, or imagine any of this. God sourced him from his birth through his death. The Spirit of God acted upon and through Him for a great purpose. He was simply **the voice.**

Matthew contrasts John the Baptist with Jesus, who is the **Word** (John 1:1). This is a translation of the Greek word "logos." It is a rational expression of the mind. It is equivalent to reason and can only be an attribute of one who can think. Therefore,

Part Two: The Wonder of Dispersion

Jesus is not the "phone," but "Logos." We can actually embrace the mind of God in Christ!

John the Baptist is a translational example of the intimate relationship we can experience in the New Covenant. The fullness of the Spirit of Christ is to flow through the believer much like the message flows through a phone. The phone does not originate the message. Jesus is the message who enables the believer to demonstrate the truth about God. We have the opportunity to become the display of Christ!

While this study came from the Book of Matthew, it is amazing to see the same truth coming from the Book of Acts. The Jews of the Dispersion are strongly highlighted at the great event of Pentecost (Acts 2:5). Luke contracts the Jews who were born and raised in Jerusalem with the Jews who had been dispersed outside the area of Palestine. The leadership of Israel were those who had been born and raised in Jerusalem and were closed and stale, while the Jews of the Dispersion were seeking the fresh and the new. God seems to go overboard to give them the message of the Gospel through this great event. They are the group to whom the miracle of languages communicates the truth. Peter preaches his great sermon to them because of their confusion and questioning (Acts 2:12-13). Three thousand of this group become converts and form the base for the early church (Acts 2:41).

It started when they heard the sound of the coming of the Holy Spirit. Luke records, **And when this sound occurred, the multitude came together, and were confused, because everyone heard them speak in his own language** (Acts 2:6). The grammar and words of the beginning of this verse are very revealing. The first Greek word in the sentence is translated *occurred*. It is a translation of the Greek word "ginomai." We have highlighted this word in several of our past studies. It means "to become" or "begin." It is contrasted with the Greek word "een" which emphasizes the eternal aspect. The sound came into being while the Holy Spirit who produces the sound has always been.

The Occurring Sound | **Acts 2:6**

Something was brought into being which originated with and from the Holy Spirit. It is not the *sound* which occupies our interest. It is not the *sound* which we seek. To know the eternal One from which the *sound* flows is our desire.

The second Greek word in the sentence is translated, *and when.* The primary translation of this word is the conjunction "but." It establishes the contrast. On the one hand are the Jews of the Dispersion who are confused and amazed by what they are hearing, and on the other hand are one hundred and twenty disciples who are rejoicing in the fullness of the Holy Spirit and experience the miracles of God in their lives.

The third and fourth words in the Greek text are *the sound.* There is a definite article just prior to the main word. Luke gives distinction to the *sound* and earmarks it so we will not confuse it with other noises which may have occurred. There is no question he is relating back to *and suddenly there came a sound from heaven* (Acts 2:2). These two ideas are linked. The reason this is important to note is the Greek word for *sound* in verse six is different than in verse two. Luke does not want us to think he is referring to two different sounds in verses two and six because he uses different Greek words. To insure that we grasp the concept he gives us one idea and paints the picture with as many different word pictures as possible.

The Greek word for *sound* in verse two is "echooes" from which we get our English word "echo." You may want to review our previous study on this subject ("The Sound from Heaven" in the book **A New Level**, 2005). This Greek word is only used four times in the New Testament. Luke makes a great statement concerning the coming of the Spirit of Jesus. God is depositing His heart and nature within the life of the believer. It originates from heaven itself. We do not manufacture it nor add to it. We become the vessel for the life of God to reproduce the life of Jesus in our day. The Spirit of Christ wants to echo through our lives. Our sole involvement is to focus on Him! He will be the

Part Two: The Wonder of Dispersion

source of everything in our lives. We are not living our lives for Christ; rather He is living His life through us. We experience the echo of His presence.

Now Luke guards this concept. He restates it for us in different words just to be sure we understand. In verse six he changes the Greek word for *sound.* He does not change concepts, only illustrations. The Greek word he now uses is "phone." He gives a word picture for the fullness of the Holy Spirit. Here is the essence of the Christian faith. God and man merge together, display or communicate that which neither can give without the other. God can give this display without man, but He has decided to limit Himself to this merger. He is the message to be heard through the phone of our lives. We do not originate nor source it. There is even something natural about it. It is as if we have been created for this purpose. It is simply who we are! Our difficulty is found in wanting to add to or adjust the message which is who He is. The moment we think we can improve what He is doing through us, chaos is created. We disfigure the shape of His person. We must allow Him to be who He is through us. We are only the phone.

This concept is used consistently in the New Testament. There was a man who was a ruler of the Jews who came to Jesus one night. His questions were sincere, but his understanding was extremely limited. Jesus used the word picture of "birthing" to help him grasp the new sourcing of the Spirit of God. ***Jesus answered and said to him, "Most assuredly, I say to you, unless one is born again, he cannot see the kingdom of God,"*** (John 3:3). Nicodemus could not conceive in his mind how he could live in such an experience. He had sourced his own life for so long; he could not grasp how he could accomplish a new birth. ***Nicodemus said to Him, "How can a man be born when he is old? Can he enter a second time into his mother's womb and be born?"*** (John 3:4). Do you see how his confusion comes from his own self-sourcing? He must figure it out and accomplish it. How could he possibly do it? It is completely beyond his best attempt!

Jesus begins again to describe the life that comes from the birthing of the Spirit. *"That which is born of the flesh is flesh, and that which is born of the Spirit is spirit. Do not marvel that I said to you, 'You must be born again.' The wind blow where it wishes, and you hear the sound of it, but cannot tell where it comes from and where it goes. So is everyone who is born of the Spirit,"* (John 3:6-8). This is Jesus' description of a person who is sourced by the Spirit of God. One experiences nothing but the results of the flesh when he is sourced by the flesh. But the results are entirely different when one is sourced by the Spirit of God. When the life one is living is sourced or born of the Spirit, it is Spirit.

I am not sure you and I, nor the translations of the New Testament, have grasped the picture Jesus paints. Look closely at your translation of this verse (John 3:6). Jesus compares the birth of the flesh with the birth of the Spirit. He establishes a parallel. One who is born of **the flesh is flesh** while the one who is born of **the Spirit is spirit.** Notice the first **Spirit** is capitalized as it refers to the Holy Spirit. The second *spirit* is not because it refers to our spirit. This is not a translation of the original text, but an interpretation. In the original Greek language there was neither capital nor small case letters. Therefore, the translators interpreted the passage in order to decide if Jesus is referring to the Holy Spirit or our spirit.

What if both times the word *Spirit* should be capitalized? This would mean that Jesus is referring both times to the Holy Spirit. **That which is born of the Spirit** (Holy Spirit) **is Spirit** (Holy Spirit). What else could He possibly mean? When the Holy Spirit produces something it is a reproduction of Himself. One who is sourced by flesh is experiencing the life of the flesh. But one who is sourced by the Holy Spirit is experiencing the life of the Holy Spirit.

Part Two: The Wonder of Dispersion

This is further verified as we read on into verse eight. *"The wind blows where it wishes, and you hear the sound* (phone) *of it, but cannot tell where it comes from or where it goes. So is everyone who is born of the Spirit,"* (John 3:8). Jesus parallels the life of the Holy Spirit with the wind. When the wind blows you definitely hear the *sound* (phone) of it. The *sound* (phone) is the effect of the wind, but not the wind itself. It is the demonstration of what you cannot see. *So is everyone who is born of the Spirit.* The life of the one who is sourced by the Holy Spirit is the visible demonstration of the essence of the Holy Spirit. Yet, it is the practical demonstration of the essence of the life of the Spirit. In a sense it is not the demonstration of the Spirit by itself, yet if it is produced by the Spirit it is certainly of the Spirit. The life which is lived is of the same texture and fabric of the Spirit, because it is the Spirit or at least an extension of the Spirit. We are the vessel of His demonstration.

Notice the word which Jesus chooses to describe this life! He uses the word *sound* which is a translation of the Greek word "phone." Our lives are to be the "phone" of the Spirit of Christ. We do not originate the message, nor do we simply repeat it. We do not mimic, reproduce, or duplicate it. Our flesh becomes the instrument through which His demonstration takes place. The wind of the Spirit is blowing; He is speaking. However, He will not be heard unless it is through our lives.

Paul does something of the same thing in an attempt to clear up the confusion caused by speaking in an unknown tongue. It was one of the difficult situations the Church at Corinth was facing. This problem seems to persist even into our day. Paul's approach to the problem is interesting. He does not play the role of a judge and simply gives a ruling. He does not lecture the law and speak a commandment. He takes them back to Christ who is presented as the only answer for every problem confronted in this epistle. Jesus flows and sources their lives to produce the right things.

As part of that answer, Paul writes, ***But now, brethren, if I come to you speaking with tongues, what shall I profit you unless I speak to you either by revelation, by knowledge, by prophesying, or by teaching?*** (1 Corinthians 14:6). Then he immediately begins to illustrate his point. ***Even things without life, whether flute or harp, when they make a sound*** (phone), ***unless they make a distinction in the sounds, how will it be known what is piped or played?*** (1 Corinthians 14:7). A musical instrument is a wondrous thing. Obviously the shape and length of the instrument will influence the sound which is produced. There is a purpose for the instrument or it would be discarded. It is of value for the clear sounding of the notes. However, the instrument does not originate anything, but is carefully used by the artist who is communicating his own heart and soul in his music.

The Greek word translated ***sound*** at the beginning of the verse is "phone." However, the Greek word translated ***sounds*** later in the verse is a different Greek word used exclusively for musical instruments. Why would Paul not have used this second word in both cases? He is giving us insight into the fullness of the Holy Spirit. The analogy is definitely an instrument which does not originate the sound. The sound heard does not even belong to the instrument, yet again it is certainly influenced by the size and shape of the instrument. This is the picture of one who has become the phone of Christ. We do not originate what takes place through us and yet we are intimately attached to it, and we influence how it is displayed. What an awesome thought! God has made each personality different. He has not done so for variety but with distinct purpose. The Spirit of God wants to use the instrument of your personality to display a demonstration of the nature of God which will reveal tones and notes of extreme beauty. You become the phone through which He originates this unique display of Himself.

We now have adequate insight to come back to our passage

Part Two: The Wonder of Dispersion

in Acts (2:6). In this verse Luke definitely refers to the *sound* which was heard as a result of the descending of the Holy Spirit (Acts 2:2). However, to further illustrate the outside God coming to be inside the believer, he changes the Greek word. He uses the Greek word "phone." God wants to do something very special. He created mankind for the purpose of being an instrument through which this special thing could be done. However, the destructive element of sin destroyed the ability of the instrument to fulfill its function. God unleashed His full power and nature in redemption. This movement would not stop until a complete restoration of man had taken place. This event of the indwelling of the Spirit of Christ within the believer is the fulfillment of that dream. It is why this instrument of mankind was created. Man was made by God to be the phone through which the message of His person could be heard!

Is your life allowing the message of God to be heard? This is not an appeal for you to live your life for Christ; but for you to allow Christ to live His life through you! This is not a call for you to live a life responding to the question, "What would Jesus do?" Rather we cry for you to live a life responding to the question, "What will Jesus do?" He is the source of the action. We do not originate or even maintain this display. He is adequate to flow His life in the unfolding demonstration of His greatness. What an opportunity we have to manifest His life in the midst of our world.

Acts 2:6

NECESSARY AMAZEMENT

The Greek language is very significant in our study. It is a picturesque language and was necessary to give expression to the great revelation of the Gospel. Luke, the historian, exhausts his vocabulary of terms found in the Greek language to express the reaction of the Jews of the Dispersion to the event of Pentecost.

God uses extreme measures to reach this group because of their openness and seeking. He has attracted them to the outpouring of the Holy Spirit by the great ***sound from heaven*** (Acts 2:2). He causes the disciples to speak in the native dialects of each of the fifteen nationalities represented in this group. Obviously this was not necessary for them to understand the message. They all spoke the common language of Jerusalem and understood Peter's sermon which followed. But God did an overwhelming miracle to amaze them! This all set the foundation for God to inspire a message through Peter which brought great concern to them (Acts 2:37). Three thousand converts came from this group of Jews.

There seems to have been one great element in their reaction. Luke highlights this response five times. He states it repeatedly from verse six through verse twelve. He exhausts his vocabulary of terms with which to express this. He uses four different Greek words to say the same thing. His repetition in so many different ways is bound to strike the truth for a seeker. He uses one Greek term twice in order to give a double emphasis.

Part Two: The Wonder of Dispersion

He highlights their reaction a total of five times.

He begins with, *And when this sound occurred the multitude came together, and were confused because everyone heard them speak in his own language* (Acts 2:6). The word translated *confused* may not present a proper picture of their response. The New International Version translates this with the word *bewildered.* Astonished and confounded are descriptions found in other translations. The Greek word is formed by two words, the word "together" and the word meaning "to pour." It is the idea to thoroughly mix. We discover this reaction often in discussion groups. New information will be shared. The immediate response is an expression, "I am confused." I am convinced they are not confused at all. New information has been placed into the equation. As this new information mixes with what they have always thought, they are not immediately able to make sense of it. They are in the process of taking new truth and bringing it into the old framework of thought process. They call it confusion. This takes place in our verse of study (Acts 2:6).

The word *amazed* is used two different times in this paragraph (Acts 2:7-12). The word denotes overwhelming surprise. The Greek verb is literally "to put out of place," hence, "out of one's senses." This word is used when the brothers of Christ heard about His ministry and miracles. They came to get Him. *For they said, "He is out of His mind,"* (Mark 3:21). In our passage each time this word is used it is linked with another word. *Then they were all amazed and marveled,* (Acts 2:7). *So they were all amazed and perplexed,* (Acts 2:12). In the Greek the use of the two verbs is essentially a device to indicate intensity. The second verb does not really introduce any additional components which are not already suggested in the first verb.

Amazed and marveled (Acts 2:7) describes the reaction to Galilean disciples speaking in languages they could not know. The Greek word translated *marveled* denotes the continuing wonder or amazement. It suggests the beginning of speculating on the matter. It is in the imperfect tense which means something in the past is continuing into the present. This was not a fleeting reaction but would continue.

Amazed and perplexed (Acts 2:12) is a result of continued thought. They could not unravel what this could possibly mean. They have moved from being shocked by what is happening to why it is happening. The Greek word translated *perplexed* is two words put together. The word "through" and "to be perplexed" form the idea of thoroughly perplexed, to be in much doubt, or hesitate greatly.

There seems to be a tremendous pattern established in this first effort of evangelism. I have been in many seminars and conferences on evangelism. One of the leaders is bound to present the Book of Acts to discuss church growth strategies. How did the early church do it? What was the methodology most effective? What techniques can we adopt as truly Biblical? I am afraid these questions all miss the point of the writing of this great book. This is not a "how to do evangelism" instruction manual.

The sole purpose of this book is to reveal Jesus. Luke states this boldly in the "Prologue," (Acts 1:1-3). His highlighting is thoroughly on Jesus in this section. The revelation of His person will dominate everything that happens in the lives of the disciples. Even the fullness of the Holy Spirit is going to be a fuller revelation of the nature and person of Christ. All of the sermons preached in this great book are about Jesus. He must be revealed to the world. Evangelism is a natural by-product of the revelation of Christ. As we move into the first event where evangelism takes place, look for the natural pattern.

Inspiration of the Amazement

The Jews of the Dispersion represented fifteen different nationalities and are the target group. They have come to

Part Two: The Wonder of Dispersion

Jerusalem for an extended period to be near the temple and experience the feast days. It is during the Day of the Feast of Pentecost that the Promise of the Father is experienced by the one hundred and twenty disciples. The Jews of the Dispersion definitely witnessed the disciples' filling of the Holy Spirit. According to the passage it was the ***sound from heaven*** (Acts 2:2) which initiated the gathering together of this group.

In order to adequately understand what is happening we must grasp the strength of the gathering. And when this sound occurred, ***the multitude came together,*** (Acts 2:6). The verb ***came together*** is two Greek words combined. It begins with the Greek word translated "together with." This is combined with the Greek word translated, "to come." The Greek word flows with the idea of "to go or come with someone, to meet together." The word does not describe just a group of various individuals who happen to be in the same place. There is the idea of purpose of involvement in the gathering and also the idea of relationship. What they are experiencing has brought them together until they are acting as a unit.

Further investigation of the word reveals an interesting usage. This word is used to suggest the most intimate relationship expressed in marriage. ***Now the birth of Jesus Christ was as follows: After His mother Mary was betrothed to Joseph, before they came together, she was found with child of the Holy Spirit*** (Matthew 1:18). Again, this Greek word carries with it more than just two people in a group of people who happen to be in the same place. There is definite connection between the people who have assembled.

Something happened which was so captivating and riveting that this group began to think as one person. They were confused (Acts 2:6), thoroughly mixed. It appears Luke is establishing a parallel between two groups. The one hundred and twenty believers were with one accord (Acts 1:14; 2:46). With one accord is also used eight other times in the book. This is a translation of two Greek words which are combined. It is the idea of together and passion (heavy breathing). It was the forty day revelation of the physically raised from the dead Jesus who accomplished this! Now it appears this is happening again with a group of unbelievers. God has caught their attention with the ***sound from heaven*** and has continued to amaze them with the Gospel being preached in their own native languages (Acts 2:6). This caused them to be drawn together until the whole group was thoroughly mixed, confused. They have been brought to a whole new level of focus on the movement of the Spirit of Christ in the lives of the believers.

Let us never fall into the trap of thinking that we must produce this. Unbelievers are never captured on this level by our marketing strategies. Church growth programs and techniques will never bring this to pass. It is clearly stated in the passage that God alone is the source of the attraction. The ***sound from heaven*** is what drew them. Remember the details of our previous study on this subject. The Greek word for ***from*** means "something which was previously inside another object." This sound represents that which is inside the very heart of God. The Greek word for ***sound*** is where we get our English word "echo." What attracted the Jews of the Dispersion was the echo of the heart of God. God initiated this! The disciples did not advertise, promote, or market this gathered crowd.

This picture of evangelism is not that we have a product that no one wants and we develop a market for it. We are not salesmen manipulating someone into something they could really do without. God has gone before us. The hunger and need has permeated the entire being of the individual before we get there. This is the prevenient grace of God. It is the love that goes before. God has aggressively done this in the heart and life of every single individual.

Part Two: The Wonder of Dispersion

Instrument of the Amazement

If God is the author of the amazement, why do we have to be involved? Why did God not limit evangelism to His own actions? He certainly got their attention on His own. Let us never fall into the trap of thinking that God does not want to use us. Through the *sound from heaven* God initiated the gathering of the Jews of the Dispersion; however the amazement which drew them into listening to the message of Peter happened through the disciples. The disciples were actually the instruments of the amazement.

It must be understood that the disciples did not initiate the activity which amazed the group. They were simply the "instrument" through which God stimulated their interest. God chose to do something through the disciples which amazed their immediate world. More specifically in our passage, it was the act of speaking in the fifteen different dialects which produced the amazement. *And when the sound occurred, the multitude came together, and were confused, because everyone heard them speak in his own language* (Acts 2:6).

What is really startling about the disciples being an instrument of the amazement is that it always seems to be produced through their weakness. Amazement always seems to happen when something takes place in or through the disciples which they are totally incapable of producing. Luke says this in our passage. *Then they were all amazed and marveled, saying to one another, "Look, are not all these who speak Galileans? And how is it that we hear each in our own language in which we were born?"* (Acts 2:7-8). They understood that it was impossible for these uneducated Galileans to produce such an amazing feat.

This is not only true in our passage but is consistent throughout the entire Book of Acts. Evangelism seems to take place when the world is amazed at what is happening in the framework of the weakness or inability of believers. This is illustrated again in the next chapter. **Peter and John went up together to the temple for the hour of prayer** (Acts 3:1). As they approached the temple, they were confronted by a lame man begging for alms. A miracle takes place which astonishes the crowd. **Now as the lame man who was healed held on to Peter and John, all the people ran together to them in the porch which is called Solomon's, greatly amazed** (Acts 3:11). The crowd seems to attribute the miracle to Peter and John. Peter immediately **responded to the people: "Men of Israel, who do you marvel at this? Or why look so intently at us, as though by our own power or godliness we have made this man walk?"** (Acts 3:12). This becomes the opportunity for the preaching of the message of explanation and the conversion of five thousand men (Acts 4:4).

Notice the pattern of evangelism! God initiates an amazing happening through the instrument of the disciples. He uses their weakness and inability to cause this miracle. This was neither about their training nor their personal skills. This was about God doing something through them which they were incapable of doing. They were the instrument of God amazing the world!

There was another group of people who are not easily amazed. They are the leadership of Israel. They are overseers of the entire operation of the temple which is the core of Judaism. People from Galilee are far inferior to them both in education and culture. This leadership group was greatly disturbed that these uneducated men taught the people and preached that Jesus was resurrected from the dead (Acts 4:2). They put the disciples in jail for the night. The next morning during the interrogation, **Peter, filled with the Holy Spirit, said to them...** (Acts 4:8). He proceeded to preach a powerful message of insight and wisdom. **Now when they saw the boldness of Peter and John, and perceived that they were uneducated and untrained men, they marveled. And they realized that they had been with Jesus** (Acts 4:13). While this did not result in conversion, the pattern of evangelism is maintained. God used the weakness and lack in the disciples to display His greatness which produced amazement in the lives of the leadership of Israel. Truth was proclaimed and had its affect upon the leadership of Israel.

I have been deeply concerned about our concept of spiritual gifts. In the evangelical church our problem does not seem to be in whether we believe in spiritual gifts, but in what we believe about them. In the spiritual gift test, you give expression of your belief. If you have never taken a spiritual gift test, you may not understand. The test is designed to help you discover what your strong abilities are. It is assumed that this is what God will use in service to His Kingdom. The Book of Acts seems to emphasize the exact opposite. God consistently amazes our world with His greatness by demonstrating Himself through our weakness and lack.

Paul proposed this idea. **Therefore I take pleasure in infirmities, in reproaches, in needs, in persecutions, in distresses, for Christ's sake. For when I am weak, then I am strong** (2 Corinthians 12:10). He illustrated this truth when he said, **but we have this treasure in earthen vessels, that the excellence of the power may be of God and not of us** (2 Corinthians 4:7). Paul was advocating the principle that God purposely chooses the weakness and inabilities of our beings in order to demonstrate His greatness. Is this not what is so amazing to our world?

Intention of the Amazement

One must understand that God is not doing this without purpose. Let us again review the sequences of what is happening. God begins by creating within the life of an individual a hunger for Himself. We see this in the lives of the Jews of the Dispersion. They have bought homes in Jerusalem for the purpose of being near the temple. They anticipate that God is going to do something great and new in their time. They are open and seeking. This hunger has come to them by the prevenient grace of God. This is further demonstrated by their attraction to the ***sound from heaven.*** God has initiated something which has gathered the Jews of the Dispersion together.

The movement of God continues as God uses the believer's weaknesses to do something amazing. Out of the life of the believer something miraculous takes place. It astonishes the unbelievers around him. It is something which cannot be attributed to talent or skill. It is not something which is due to training or education. It comes not from the believer's strengths but from his weaknesses. The only explanation is God is displaying Himself to the believer's world. In the case of our passage, the disciples begin to speak in languages of the Jews of the Dispersion. They speak with an uneducated Galilean accent and yet are articulating the dialects of fifteen different nationalities. It is amazing!

Finally, God fills the believer in order to communicate an explanation of the spiritual reality being witnessed. In our passage this happens as Peter gives a powerful sermon which explains and calls the Jews to Christ (Acts 2:14-40). The amazement of the unbeliever extends the opportunity for the believer to reveal the Word of God to him. Peter experienced this in the temple (Acts 3). When God heals a crippled man through Peter and John, the crowd is amazed. Peter immediately begins to explain to them the power of the resurrected Christ which is active in this situation (Acts 3:12+). Five thousand men were converted (Acts 4:4).

Do you and I dare compare our lives to this pattern? Have our lives become the platform for the amazing activities of God in our day? Is anything happening in and through us by the power of Christ which would attract our world? Are we living out of our strength and self-resources, or are we living out of our weaknesses which are filled with the power of Christ? Oh, to be crucified with Christ until His life is manifested through me!

Acts 2:11

THE LANGUAGE OF PRAISE

There has certainly been a renewed emphasis in praise and worship in the last decade. I am grateful for the contribution this has made in my own spiritual life. This new emphasis has caused the development of new styles of music as well as the use of new methodologies to stimulate praise within the congregation. Who would want to criticize such an awakening?

There is, however, a danger within this new approach which raises its head in every Christian endeavor. It is the most fundamental concern raised in the Book of Acts. It is the question of "sourcing." Everyone's attention is drawn to this one factor. The resurrected Christ is seen as the One Source. The prologue (Acts 1:1-3) sets the boundaries of the Book of Acts. It is the infallible proofs of His resurrected Being. His indwelt presence is the source of everything happening in the book. The only explanation for each miracle, all converts, and every message preached is the Spirit of Christ who has come to reside within the believer. Nothing happens that He does not source.

I fear we have approached praise with our normal activity oriented thought process. We consider it a new program or activity to be preformed. This is the way we have led our congregations. Our praise director announces when we will move into moments of praise. The "praise service" is listed in the church bulletin. When the lively activity of praise and worship happens on Sunday there are comments made from one to another about it.

The Language of Praise | Acts 2:11

The Book of Acts gives us a new view of praise. It focuses on the person of Christ who gives us His nature and Spirit. How does this relate to praise? Might I boldly state that praise is a "feeling?" You may be hesitant about linking feelings and praise. A part of the definition for "feeling" in Webster's Dictionary is "an affective state of consciousness, such as that resulting from emotions, sentiments, or desires." It is "awareness or impression" or "an emotional state or disposition, an emotion." Praise is always a response to the sourcing of the Spirit of Jesus within the believer which affects his emotions. Praise is not an activity I do regardless of how I feel; it is a feeling which is a response to the revelation of Christ within me! Other words might be used to express this concept. Praise is a state of awe and wonder, or a thrill which is generated by the sourcing of Christ within my life. This is not an activity which I do but a state in which we live. It is the emotion of praise.

If you follow the trail of your time, energy, money, affections, and allegiance, you will find a throne. Whatever is on that throne is what you value most. This is what brings joy to your life. Here is what supplies the constant challenge and thrill for your loving. This is what produces the "wow" of your heart. It makes your face light up and brings a spring to your walk. It alone produces the emotion of praise in your life. Is the person of Jesus on your throne? This is the issue of the Book of Acts.

It is impossible to praise without the Spirit of Christ! You and I must be filled with the presence of the Holy Spirit or we find it impossible to live in this constant state of praise. This means the Holy Spirit is the source of all praise. Does He simply indwell the believer and then praise Himself through the believer. No, this is not the procedure.

It is the Spirit of Jesus who is the source of all revelation. Our response to revelation is an emotion. That emotion is praise. What is revealed is not data or information. Those things are simply facts. The revelation which comes is truth. Jesus said it clearly, *"I am the way, the truth, and the life,"* (John 14:6). Truth is the revelation of the reality of His person. It is the way things really are as they are seen in Him. He takes the facts to a new level called truth. This understanding can only come from Him. A person may know hundreds of facts about history, but not understand the reality of who directs the events and where things going. They may never see that history is His story. One may study the Scriptures and know Biblical information but not see the reality of truth as found in Christ.

Praise is a byproduct of the believer responding to a revelation sourced by the Spirit of Christ. This response to revelation immediately affects his emotions. This emotional feeling is called praise. Because one knows what he cannot know and sees what he cannot see, he lives in a state of awe and wonder. It is a condition of praise.

This is not an activity the believer has to initiate. He does not need to check a list to see if he spends an adequate amount of time praising. Praise is an automatic; it is a byproduct of the revelation of the Holy Spirit within the believer. Jesus reveals truth and praise is the result. Look carefully at what Jesus taught His disciples.

"And I will pray the Father, and He will give you another Helper, that He may abide with you forever – the Spirit of truth, whom the world cannot receive, because it neither sees Him nor knows Him; but you know Him, for He dwells with you and will be in you" (John 14:16-17).

"But the Helper, the Holy Spirit, whom the Father will send in My name, He will teach you all things, and bring you remembrance all things that I said to you" (John 14:26).

"But when the Helper comes, whom I shall send to you from the Father, the Spirit of truth who proceeds from the Father, He will testify of Me" (John 15:26).

*"I still have many things to say to you, but you cannot bear them now. However, when He, the Spirit of truth, has come, He

will guide you into all truth; for He will not speak on his own authority, but whatever He hears He will speak; for He will tell you things to come" (John 16:12-13). In this verse, Jesus expresses the desire to reveal truth to His disciples but they are inadequate to grasp or see it. He uses the word *bear*. This is translated from a Greek word which means "base or foundation." It has the idea of to carry or pick up. Jesus says that the disciples have no foundation for truth or even the strength to pick up the truth until the Holy Spirit comes to fill them. They have no foundation for revelation; therefore there is no praise until He comes.

This removes praise from certain personality types or from praise leaders who can manipulate crowds for "praise response." This is not about how the inward emotional feelings of praise are expressed. The expression of praise has to do with style which will be determined by culture and personality. The real issue of concern is the inward revelation of truth which stimulates the response of praise.

We can see this clearly in the contrast of the Old and New Testament covenants. In the Old Testament a call of praise was placed upon the people of God. The Book of Psalms repeatedly commands the people to express praise (66:1 and 100:1). In the Hebrew grammar these imperative verbs are in the Hiphil-Stem. This means that the subject causes the direct object of the verb to participate in the action of the verb as a "secondary subject." In the sentence "Bob caused the car to crash," the direct object (car) participates in the action that the subject (Bob) caused. In the Old Testament God is outside of man and commands him to praise. When man praises, God responds to man and participates with him.

However, in the new covenant of the fullness of the Spirit of Christ within the believer, things change. Praise is not what man does and God responds; rather God moves and man responds. God moves upon the inward being of man by bringing revelation of truth. Upon seeing this truth of who He is, man feels and

Part Two: The Wonder of Dispersion

expresses this great emotion of awe, wonder and praise. Praise is a response to Jesus within your life.

With this as a background, let us go to our passage in the Book of Acts (2:5-13). The Jews of the Dispersion are being introduced to us. The rest of chapter two is going to be about them. They are different from the Jews who have been born and raised in Judea. The Jews of the Dispersion are open and seeking. With great sacrifice, they have come to Jerusalem, bought homes, and are seeking a new movement of God in their midst. God goes overboard to communicate to this group. They are the ones who hear the *sound from heaven.* This brings them together in a unit. When they hear the disciples speak in their native dialects, they are thoroughly amazed.

What are the disciples saying to the Jews of the Dispersion? It is significant that the content is downplayed. The focus is on the hearing and speaking and not upon the content. However, the last part of verse eleven does give us some insight into the content. **We hear them speaking in our own tongues the wonderful works of God** (Acts 2:11).

The content was not a Gospel message focused on evangelizing this group. This was to come later as Peter preached the first sermon after Pentecost (Acts 2:24-40). The disciples were not even addressing the Jews of the Dispersion. They were simply praying. The Holy Spirit had just filled them; they broke forth in great praise as a new revelation came to them. The Greek word which is translated **wonderful works** is only used two times in the New Testament. Both times it is used by Luke. He uses it only when God is moving to bring His people to a new level of revelation.

As Luke relates the details of the birth of Christ, he is drawn to this Greek word. The angel has made the announcement to Mary of her privilege. The angel also speaks to Elizabeth who carries John the Baptist in her womb. It is a miraculous birth. Mary runs to the home of Elizabeth knowing she will understand.

As they greet each other they break forth in great praise. In the midst of Mary's praise, she says: *"For He who is mighty has done great things for me,"* (Luke 1:49). *Great things* is a translation of the same Greek word found in our passage in the Book of Acts.

There are significant parallels between these two occasions. In both cases God brings new revelation of Himself to His world. In Luke there is the birth of Christ; in Acts there is the birth of the Church. In Luke there is the descent of the second member of the Trinity to our world; in Acts there is the descent of the third member of the Trinity to our world. In Luke Mary is indwelt by Christ; in Acts the one hundred and twenty are indwelt by the Spirit of Christ. In Luke the revelation of God is outward; in Acts the revelation of God is inward. In all instances God brings revelation of Himself stimulating the emotion of praise.

There are several other things which we need to note about this kind of praise as found in Acts.

Evangelism

God moved upon the believers with the *sound from heaven.* This startling event brings the Jews of the Dispersion together with great focus. In this setting the believers break forth in great praise. This praise is communicated to every nationality in their own dialect. This forms the basis which opens the door for Peter's explanation and evangelism takes place. This setting of praise attracts Jews of the Dispersion to what God is doing.

Praise, as described above, has natural qualities which creates evangelism. Praise is positive and draws people into focus. Praise does not highlight itself as a technique or method, but hides itself in His presence allowing only Jesus to be seen. Genuine praise communicates in all languages. The unbeliever who does not understand the language of theology can understand praise. The father who desperately wants to speak to his teen aged child discovers he does not know the teenager's language. Praise speaks the language of every teenager. The husband and wife who do not speak the same language find new understanding through praise.

There are a few words which are universal in every language. In every country and in every setting these words are recognized. Everyone understands. One of those words is "coca cola." There is a word of praise which is understood by all languages. It is "hallelujah." Praise bridges all barriers, crosses all cultural lines, and communicates to every heart. Let us not stifle praise in our lives.

Expression

Do not surmise from the above paragraphs that praise is a method of evangelism. It is not a methodology or technique. Praise is not to be your focus. Do not commit yourself to praise. We are not proposing praise as the solution to church growth. Praise is a byproduct of the continual, growing revelation of Jesus through the indwelt Holy Spirit. Jesus must be your focus. As He reveals Himself in you, the awesomeness of who He is will grip your life. The expansion of His person in your life will initiate praise from your being.

Can you imagine a lowly peasant girl being visited by an angel of the most high God? A revelation of the person of Christ is given to her. A new relationship with Jesus is established which grows throughout her life. As God reveals the various aspects of this embrace, she breaks forth in praise. She can not contain it.

The focus is not upon the praise or the expression of such. Those aspects will naturally happen. Do not concern yourself about praising. Seek only the revelation of His being within you. Let Him be your passion and drive. Let Jesus consume your entire being and instill a hunger for Himself within you. All other things will be a byproduct of His revealed heart.

Explanation

As this unfolds in our passage (Acts 2:5-13), we see that praise raises issues in the minds of the crowd. They are thoroughly intrigued and greatly amazed by what is happening. They find themselves attempting to give explanation to the praise. They approach the issue from their normal fleshly, self-sourced position. They explain it by drunkenness (Acts 2:13).

Praise demands explanation. God moves in the scene and provides a Biblical explanation through the witness of Peter (Acts 2:14-40). The result of praise is explained by three thousand converts (Acts 2:41). As the Holy Spirit reveals Jesus in your life, praise will be the natural result. It will be so noticeable to your world that you will be required to give an explanation. Everyone will want to know your technique. What is your method? How do you manage to discipline yourself? What is your secret? How do you do it?

Let it be known that you will also have to explain the absence of praise. In your heart and life you must rationalize the absence of the "feeling" of awe brought about through the revelation of His face. Why are you not praising? What is the blockage? The absence or presence of praise in your life becomes a measuring rod of your focus on Christ. If praise is not present, the only adequate explanation is that you are not experiencing the revelation of His person within you. If you are absent of praise, you are absent of the Holy Spirit and you do not have the "wow" factor in your life. It is time to ask yourself, "What are people seeing in me? Am I speaking the universal language of praise, notifying my world that Jesus lives in me?" If praise is absent in your life you must find relationship with Him and allow Him to create His praise within you.

Acts 2:12-13

WHAT DOES THIS WISH TO BE?

It is hard to mature! One of the most difficult aspects of this process is moving from what I have always been taught to what I actually believe. My father trained me with his personal beliefs. I accepted them because my father taught them, not because they were personally mine. I eventually came to a serious period of questioning. What was I willing to die for? What was I convinced was the truth?

My only option at this point was to push aside all I had been taught and come to the Bible fresh. It was difficult to become a blank page and ask the Word of God to fill me. The most important part of this is not data or information but thought process and perspective. Theological conclusions come as a result of a distinct thought process or point of view. This is why saturation Bible study is so important. To saturate in the Book of Acts is to attempt to get into the mind of Luke, the author, in order to take on his perspective. Once the proper mind set is acquired, the conclusions will automatically fall into place. Thus the conclusions are not a result of a proof text from one Scripture verse, but I draw my conclusions from the flow of the entire Scriptures.

This takes on even more importance when we realize the Holy Spirit is the true author, having inspired Luke to pen the words. We want to know the mind of the Spirit of Christ. Therefore we do not come to the Scriptures with our theological bias and bend them to our thought process. Rather we come to the Scriptures to be shaped by the flow of His thought. We do not handle the Scriptures; rather the Scriptures handle us. We do not draw our conclusions and come to the Scriptures to prove them. We come to the Scriptures to get into the flow of His thoughts and receive His conclusions. This brings radical change in our lives if we are open and seeking.

This is true for us, just as it was true for those who are lived in Scriptural times. In the Book of Acts, chapter two, there is a significant contrast between two groups of people. We have discussed this contrast in earlier lessons. Luke brings us face to face with its reality as we move into the last few verses of information concerning these groups. The contrast is so dominate it forces us to consider ourselves in one group or the other. The distinctive characteristic of each group is not cultural, educational, or economical. If it were we could avoid any association with either of them. However, it has to do with the spiritual, which is attitude. This is why it spans the element of time and brings each of us into an active role within the group. The Word of God consistently reveals our hearts and lives. Let us look into the mirror of His Word.

Two Assemblies

In our previous studies we have detailed the two groups represented in our passage. However, they were not as clearly delineated as they are in the verses under present saturation. The two groups are the Jews of the Dispersion and the Jews of Palestine. There were more Jews living outside of the Holy Land (Palestine) than were living inside. The actual numbers are questionable, but they go as high as five to six million Jews scattered throughout the world. This was promoted by the exiles in the Old Testament brought about by the disobedience of

Part Two: The Wonder of Dispersion

the people of God. Ten tribes of Israel had gone into exile and never returned. However, they maintained their Jewish identity and culture.

There are two significant factors to remember. It seems that every major city in the world had a Jewish synagogue where the teachings of Moses were preached and practiced (Acts 15:21). Everywhere the Apostle Paul went on his missionary journey, he would first preach in a Jewish synagogue. This formulated a beach head for the great missionary thrust of the early church. Secondly, the Old Testament was originally written in Hebrew. The Jews of the Dispersion instigated the translation of the Old Testament into Greek, the dominate language of the world in their day. It was called the Septuagint and was translated in Alexandria, Egypt, which is outside the Holy Land. It became very popular, so much so that the New Testament writers often quoted the Old Testament from the Septuagint.

The Jews of the Dispersion are those described in verse five. ***And there were dwelling in Jerusalem Jews, devout men, from every nation under heaven*** (Acts 2:5). These Jews of the Dispersion were seeking and anticipating that God was going to do something new. These very devout and religious Jews actually lived outside of Palestine but spent months at a time in Jerusalem, especially during the feast days. They bought second homes in Jerusalem to stay in the place where they thought God would move. Luke highlights this group when he focuses on them and the movement of God in chapter two. It is amazing the lengths to which God was willing to go to bring them to Him. This group became aware of the movement of God on Pentecost Day. ***The sound*** attracted them to the one hundred and twenty disciples (Acts 2:6). The disciples began to speak in the fifteen different dialects represented in this large group of dispersed Jews. This was not necessary for them to understand the message. It was a miracle of God meant especially for this seeking group. It so amazed them that it demanded explanation.

What Does This Wish To Be? | Acts 2:12-13

Peter proceeded to be used by the Spirit to preach a sermon which brought conviction to them. There were three thousand converts from this group which helped form the basis of the early church movement (Acts 2:41).

This group is again delineated clearly in the Greek grammar of this passage (Acts 2:12). There is a phrase in the Greek language which consists of three Greek words. It is translated *to one another*. The order of the words in the Greek language places the word *one* first. There is then added the words *to another*. This phrase is an idiom for the Greek language of that day. It is equivalent to the Greek reciprocal pronoun "allelon" which can be translated "to one another." Luke has been describing this group since verse five and now he distinctly highlights them. This group was *amazed, perplexed, confused, and marveled.* Now in verse twelve he actually puts their attitude into words, *"Whatever could this mean?"*

Luke contrasts this group with the Jews that were born and raised in Palestine. They have spent their entire lives within the borders of this holy place. Included in this group are the Pharisees and Sadducees, the leadership of Israel. They speak with the proper accent. They have a sense of superiority because of their status. They believe they are superior to the Jews of the Dispersion because these outsiders have undoubtedly been defiled in some way by the influence of their worldly culture. They picture themselves as those who have remained true and faithful to the heritage of Israel.oHHoly

This group is clearly described in our passage (Acts 2:13). Luke writes, *Others mocking said, "They are full of new wine."* The Greek word translated *others* is not a synonym for the idiom used in the previous verse. It is a pronoun which relates to a group of people who are entirely different from those described as the Jews of the Dispersion. It is not hard to discover those to whom he refers. The mockers are identified for us (Matthew 27:41; Mark 15:31, 10:34; Luke 18:32). They are the Jews of Palestine.

They have been born and raised in the protective environment of the religious surroundings of Jerusalem. They have kept the laws of Israel and know the ceremonies well. They observe the feast days and have a genealogy traceable through the remnant which returned from the exile. They have never left.

Two Attitudes

These two groups would not be so delineated if they did not have two distinct attitudes, though there certainly were exceptions within each group. Perhaps their environment and cultural training opened a door for these attitudes, but they are still not without responsibility. Truth, not data or information, is greater than tradition or training. Truth is the revelation of His person. Is this not what He has been doing from the beginning of time? He is revealing Himself to us. The only criteria needed for intimacy with His nature is being revealed in the proper attitude (spirit). Therefore, the embrace of His person is never our background, previous environment, or cultural training. It is always attitude. There is no way to miss the heart of God unless one determines in his own heart to do so.

What was the attitude of the Jews of the Dispersion? They express it clearly in their conversation *one to another*. They ask, **"Whatever could this mean?"** (Acts 2:12). A literal translation of this from the Greek language would be **"What does this wish to be?"** In the Greek text the question begins with the word translated *what*. It is an interrogative pronoun. It can be translated "who," "which," or "what." It simply introduces a direct question. The second Greek word in this question is **could mean**. This word carries the idea of "to will," "to have a mind," "purpose," or "intent." The Jews of the Dispersion hear the disciples in their home dialects. They are greatly amazed and ask about the purpose of it. Why is it happening? The third Greek word in the question is translated ***this*** which completes the English translation. However, in the Greek text there is one more word which is left out in the English translation. It is the Greek word which is translated "am," "to be," or "to exist." So the Greek text literally states "What is the purpose of this to be (exist)?"

This is an amazing question. It has at its heart much more than a simple inquiry about meaning or the desire of an explanation. The idea behind the question is one of purpose. The Jews of the Dispersion have a desire or wish for this event to affect their lives. However, it is not the event alone that they are experiencing. The event takes on the purpose and design of the one who causes it or is the source of it. The One who is determining the purpose is the Holy Spirit. He is the Source. The ones who are asking the question seem to recognize that the purpose is focused on being rather than doing. They do not ask about the mechanics of how these disciples might be able to speak in these fifteen different languages. They do not want to know the doing, but what is it meant to be? So the question becomes, "How do we become a part of the purpose and wish of this event?" The Jews of the Dispersion recognize that God is doing something at this moment which directly involves them. They have left their homelands and come to Jerusalem for this very purpose. They do not want to miss it. They are seeking and open to whatever the wish or purpose of this event might be for them.

This is the heart of a seeker. One who is open approaches every event in his life with the same question. **"What does this wish to be?"** Those who ask this question have considered the things that might be undesirable as well as the blessings of life. While God may not have caused the event, He has certainly allowed it for a purpose. What does this event wish to be in my life? What was God's designed purpose when He allowed this to come my way? This is not a pity party focused on "why me?" It is a seeking heart open to being shaped by the existence of the event itself. **"What does this wish to be?"**

Part Two: The Wonder of Dispersion

The Jews of Palestine respond to the exact same event. The contrast of their attitudes is very obvious. Luke records their response. ***Others mocking said, "They are full of new wine,"*** (Acts 2:13). Luke reveals their attitude by his interpretation of what they said. This is the only time in the New Testament this Greek word translated *mocking* is used. It comes from the root word meaning "a joke." As Luke uses the word, it means "to deride, to make fun of, to mock, or to sneer." This group is not seeking to discover what this event could mean in their lives. They are filled with ridicule and accusation. They feel superior not only to the disciples who are from Galilee but also to the Jews of the Dispersion who might think this event has value. After all, they are the ones who are stable, have arrived, have it all together, and are the need of nothing group.

In addition to this, they accuse them of being drunk. This becomes obvious as we view Peter's response to their criticism. He preaches a powerful sermon of explanation. He begins by saying, ***"Men of Judea and all who dwell in Jerusalem, let this be known to you, and heed my words. For these are not drunk, as you suppose, since it is only the third hour of the day,"*** (Acts 2:14-15). The Greek word which is translated *new wine* it literally sweet wine. It was intoxicating. Drunkenness was common among the Greeks, but it was a grievous accusation in Jewish Palestine. It was considered obnoxious and sinful to be drunk. This again highlights the attitude of superiority over the disciples and what God is doing through them. The Jews of Palestine have an attitude of criticism and accusation which is the opposite of the Jews of the Dispersion, who are seeking and open.

It is of interest to me that this is not simply an attitude of indifference. The Jews of Palestine were responsible for the crucifixion of Christ. From their viewpoint, they had won. It was all over. Why don't they just go about their own activities of life and ignore this? They cannot! They are driven to respond to this great event. When God acts, we must respond either positively or negatively. There is no way to ignore Him or be indifferent to His actions. Truth demands response. When God moves war breaks out and people choose sides in the battle.

The Jews of the Dispersion seek and are open; the Jews of Palestine are closed and stale. The Jews of the Dispersion want to know what God intends this event to be in their lives. The Jews of Palestine refuse to allow this event to affect them. One group allows themselves to be taken to another level. They experience something new from God. The other group refuses to change and they criticize those who are open.

One Answer

Luke brings us to the climax of the two assemblies. There are two attitudes, but there is only one answer. Again Peter is the instrument through which this answer is explained. The answer is Jesus! The opening words of his message is *"Jesus of Nazareth, a Man attested by God to you by miracles, wonders, and signs which God did through Him in your midst, as you yourselves also know"* (Acts 2:22). Peter focuses his sermon on Jesus. He speaks of what they did to Jesus; they crucified Him. He quickly adds what God did to Jesus; He raised Him from the dead. He highlights the promises concerning Jesus. He presents the great and high position of Christ. *"Therefore let all the house of Israel know assuredly that God has made this Jesus, whom you crucified, both Lord and Christ,"* (Acts 2:36).

In a spirit of seeking the Jews of the Dispersion ask what the Pentecost event will be in their lives. The answer returns loud and clear – Jesus! It is the same for me. Everything is to bring me back to Jesus. He is to be revealed ever increasingly in my life. God designs and allows every event to bring me to Jesus. There is nothing outside of Him. Every circumstance has a purpose. It is Jesus. Let everything drive you to Jesus. Seek Him.

Acts 2:5-13

THE REVERSAL

The story of man in the Old Testament is one of constant moral failure and disobedience. However, the story of God in the Old Testament is one of constant redemption and second chances. This story begins with the dream of God for mankind. He fulfills His dream in His creation (Genesis 1 & 2). Adam and Eve share in the image of God and fulfill His heart in intimacy. Then the tragic appearance of self-centeredness enters the scene. It always destroys the dreams of God. We call it "The Fall" (Genesis 3). What else could we call it? Man demanded his independence and attempted to become his own god. Things went downhill from there! Cain kills Able. Things progress to the point that something so unredeemable takes place within man that God plans the flood (Genesis 6). There is only one family among the human race who can be spared.

The end of the flood is a new beginning for man. But it immediately goes bad. Noah gets drunk and experiences an episode with his sons (Genesis 9). A span of time passes. The family of Noah expands and a baby boy named Nimrod is born (Genesis 10:8). He is the son of Cush. The Scriptures describe him as *a mighty hunter before the Lord; therefore it is said, "Like Nimrod the mighty hunter before the Lord." And the beginning of his kingdom was Babel, Erech, Accad, and Calneb in the land of Shinar* (Genesis 10:9-10). Nimrod was *the mighty hunter* not of animals but of men. His name means "rebel." He was a tyrant in the sight of God, the first dictator. History informs us that Nimrod and his wife devised a new religion built around "the mother and child."

Evidently as the descendents of Noah moved from the East under the leadership of Nimrod they came to the plain in the land of Shinar. It was a comfortable place that was filled with plenty of resources. Here Nimrod became the founder of the Babylonian empire and led a rebellion against God. The story of the Tower of Babel takes place in this context (Genesis 11:1-9). This story parallels the first sin of Adam and Eve. Self-centeredness and independence motivate and dominate the scene. Only one thing can result from such an attitude. It is destruction.

This story is only found in these few short verses (Genesis 11:1-9). There is no other reference to it in any other Scripture. There is a message for us in the structure of these verses. The author begins by giving us a description of the self-centeredness of man (Genesis 11:1-4). The middle verse describes the intervention of God (Genesis 11:5). The last four verses give us the consequences of His actions and judgments (Genesis 11:6-9).

The first four verses about the self-centeredness of man and the last four verses with the consequences of God's actions and judgments revolve around the middle verse of His intervention on man's behalf. The two halves revolve around the coming of the Lord. *But the Lord came down to see the city and the tower which the sons of men had built* (Genesis 11:5). The author does not attempt to tell us God is absent or ignorant of what mankind is doing. He highlights the sovereignty of God and presents a contrast of man who in his arrogance builds a tower to reach up to God (Genesis 11:4). But the best man can do is so small and low that God still has to come down in order to touch him. It is a powerful lesson. The best man can achieve is so far beneath God that He must come down in order to be involved. This is the picture of the Old and New Testament. God always comes down to the man who is destroying himself. The incarnation is

Part Two: The Wonder of Dispersion

a picture of it! But our passage (Acts 2:1-13) concerning God's outpouring of the Spirit of Christ to indwell the believer is the most revealing. He has not abandoned us!

The first four verses of the story (Genesis 11:1-4) give details of the self-centered expression of the will of man. It begins with COMBINED. *Now the whole earth had one language and one speech* (Genesis 11:1). There was a great unity among the people of the whole earth. We do not know the population of the earth at this time. Some estimate there may have been around five hundred people. However, the basis of their unity was their linkage with each other through language. This immediately informs us that something is missing. God would be their king in a theocracy. He would be their provider, protector, and healer. The unity among His creation should be that they were His children. But their unity is based on themselves.

Immediately this self-centeredness focused on COMFORT. *And it came to pass, as they journeyed from the east, that they found a plain in the land of Shinar, and they dwelt there* (Genesis 11:2). Evidently all the people of the earth were traveling together as one body. They came to this beautiful plain which proved to have an abundance of resources. They decide to make this their home and live in the comfort of this valley. This was in direct violation of what God had commanded for them. *So God blessed Noah and his sons, and said to them: "Be fruitful and multiply, and fill the earth,"* (Genesis 9:1). They were seeking their security and comfort in themselves rather than in Him.

Their self-sufficiency is definitely highlighted in the next two verses. Verse three is about COME LET US. *Then they said to one another, "Come, let us make bricks and bake them thoroughly." They had brick for stone, and they had asphalt for mortar* (Genesis 11:3). In the next verse we are given the motivation behind this idea. It is also entitled COME LET US. *And they said," Come, let us build ourselves a city, and a tower whose top is in the heavens; let us make a name for ourselves, lest we be scattered abroad over the face of the whole earth,"* (Genesis 11:4). There is nothing hidden about what they feel or plan. It is said that every brick in the tower had a man's name written on it. This was an open rebellion against God, and independency from God.

In this middle verse (verse five) man begins to be aware of the presence of God and the consequences of this Presence. The passage is very clear that God decided to intervene in this situation. His intervention comes from the heart of love and not from anger. There is no attitude of revenge contained in the passage. There are four verses which proclaim the heart of God and the results of His presence. The first one begins with CONCERN (Genesis 11:6). *And the Lord said, "Indeed the people are one language, and this is what they begin to do; now nothing that they purpose to do will be withheld from them."*

The Hebrew word translated *proposed* is significant to the passage. It is used mainly of the Lord carrying out His purposes in judgment against wicked nations or of wicked men who devise schemes against God and the righteous. This word when used as a verb or a noun focuses on man's rebellion against God. It is not the deed itself which is evil, but how the deed relates to God. There is nothing wrong with building a city or a tower within a city, but it is what they proposed (purposed, designed) for the city and tower.

The Hebrew word translated *withheld* also portrays deep meaning for the passage. It has the basic meaning of "fortification" as in the great walls of a city. The deep concern of God is not just the building of the tower, but to what this will lead. They will continue to develop their security based on themselves. If one tower gives security (however false the security might be), they will feel the need for a second tower. It is a picture of the destructive power of sin. It is not just a simple deed which is a sin, but the escalating of the pattern of one's life. Rebellion goes from one degree to another. This is the concern of God for His people.

Verse seven is entitled COME LET US. This is a direct reference to the Trinity. God is going to give expression to His great concern for His people. *"Come let Us go down and there confuse their language, that they may not understand one another's speech,"* (Genesis 11:7). God strikes a blow at the very heart of their false security. He constantly allows the things we depend upon outside of Him to be removed. How else can He bring us to Himself?

The amazing result is CEASING. *So the Lord scattered them abroad from there over the face of the earth, and they ceased building the city* (Genesis 1:8). The building of the city was a result not a cause. It was a symptom of a false security. God never attacks the symptoms of my life, but He always deals with the heart's security. It is never about the actual activity but the source of it. God did not attack the act of building the tower and the city; rather He scattered them abroad over the face of all the earth, so the byproduct, the building of the city, ceased.

The natural result of this was CONFUSION. *Therefore its name is called Babel, because there the Lord confused the language of all the earth; and from there the Lord scattered them abroad over the face of the earth* (Genesis 11:9). There is an interesting word play taking place in this verse. The Hebrew word for *Babel*, also translated Babylon (Babili), means "gate of the god." It is a fitting name which expresses the selfish motive of the people. However, the Hebrew word for *confused* (balal) means confounded or confused. In the verse the author asks the reader to believe that the *Babel* means "confused."

There is another definite word play connected to this story. There is an inversion of the Hebrew phonetic sounds "lbn" (Hebrew word "nilbena" translated "let's make bricks" in verse three), and "nbl" (Hebrew word "nabela" translated "let Us go down" in verse seven). These plays on words tell us that the author is not really interested in giving us a nice story about

The Reversal | Acts 2:5-13

the origin of languages on the earth. This is not a mythological story where the author attempts to tell us how the various nationalities of man began. He sets the stage for the unfolding story of redemption. We leave this story filled with anxiety. At first there is no indication of redemption to give us hope. There is no protective mark for the fugitive (Genesis 4:15). There was no rainbow of promise in the clouds (Genesis 9:13) as there was after the flood. Will there be no second chance for these rebellious people?

The author gives a brief connecting genealogy (Genesis 11:10-26). He then thunders into the redemptive plan of God. Out of the scattered nations of the world He provides a plan of reversal. God is not done with the human race. God will form one nation (Israel) who will become His channel of blessing. His dream for Israel will be the re-establishing of a theocracy. Their unity will be Him! Israel did not cooperate with the plan. There is a re-occurrence of self-centeredness. The same disastrous course of the people of Babel is followed repeatedly by Israel. But God does not abandon His plan. He moves toward the final event which will reverse the Tower of Babel. It is Pentecost (Acts 2:1-4).

Most Bible scholars believe that there is an intimate connection between the story of the Tower of Babel (Genesis 11:1-9) and the Day of Pentecost (Acts 2:1-4). The action taken in the story of the Tower of Babel is reversed on the Day of Pentecost. This is the connection. The focus of most scholars seems to be on language. I propose to you several problems with this thought! One would expect that in a great reversal, God would strike a blow at the very heart of the issue. This assumes the heart of the story is language, but this is not true in both stories. God is not going to reverse symptoms such as language. He will go to the source of the issue.

In addition to this fact, one must notice that the language issue is not really reversed. In the story of the Tower of Babel, all the people who spoke one language are changed to speak in many languages. On the Day of Pentecost those who speak many languages are not changed to speak one language. Rather, Galileans who spoke one language ended up speaking many languages. Where is the reversal in this? There is a deeper issue confronting us!

As the story unfolds, the Tower of Babel is a symbol of human inventiveness and ingenuity. The people of the earth calculate their needs and consider the means of meeting those needs. This is a triumph of reason. Also the people create a brand new vision of how things might be. This is a triumph of imagination. The city is a picture of human ability to control and master the world. The author of Genesis says, **Then they said to one another, "Come let us make bricks and bake** (burn) **them thoroughly." They had brick for stone, and they had asphalt for mortar** (Genesis 11:3). This is a picture of technology. The people did not mine stone, but made bricks. This is the story of material power. The tower is a symbol of monumental architectural ability. Culture and civilization, forethought and planning all point to man's self-sufficiency. Mankind has turned to himself for his present and future security.

Do you recognize the details of this story in our day? It is a total picture of the present day human race. Our focus is on technology, material power, forethought, and planning. It is all about us! But let us not be too hard on mankind. Mankind is made up of individuals like you and me. Is this not our story as well? Is not our society founded on what we know? Are we not a people who are driven to figure it out, adjust it for personal benefit, and use it for self-comfort? Is this not our condition?

God has done something in Christ to reverse the condition. He has come down to where we are in the incarnate Christ and now the Spirit of Christ. His attempt is not to make better people. He is not working on improvement. He brings about a reversal of source which will change all of the symptoms. The answer is a Person, the Person of Christ. The self-sourcing which has destroyed us from generation to generation is now reversed. The outside God has now come to be inside. He has become our single source. He is our total security. There is nothing outside of Him. Peter will stand and proclaim it in the first sermon of the early church after Pentecost. It will be the single message of the Book of Acts.

I may not be able to make decisions for my society which bases their security on technology, material power, education, and planning. Yet, I can decide for myself. I may not even be able to adequately shift the source of my personal life from self-sufficiency which has been reinforced by my culture, but I can come to Jesus. He never intended for me to investigate the problem and solve it. The reversal which needs to happen in the heart source of my life must come from Him as well. He has revealed it to me; He has initiated the change; He will bring the change to pass. It is a simple question: Will I let Him?

PART THREE
ACTS 2:14-28

IN MY EYE

Acts 2:14

LISTEN TO ME

The Pentecost event (Acts 2:1-4) shakes the known and the unknown world. Things will never be the same again. Data and organized facts make little difference. But truth changes things forever! Once truth is realized, there is no turning back. Man lost what God intended for him in creation, and now God is restoring His original plan. Man is again filled with the Spirit of God. We have a copy of the very first message designed to explain the new level. Can you imagine the tone of such a sermon? Think of the expression on Peter's face as he preached this message to those gathered. Hear the boldness in his delivery.

Peter is preaching to the great crowd gathered at the Pentecost event. The atmosphere is filled with the strength of the Spirit. Make no mistake, everyone present is aware of something great. It is so unmistakable that all are jarred at the outset of the message. Luke goes overboard in his language to make us aware that this is not a normal preaching engagement. A brand new thing is happening. Man is being moved to a different level. It is the new level of Pentecost.

Luke uses three verses to introduce Peter's sermon (Acts 2:14-16). In the first of these verses (verse 14) he gives us the TONE of the address. In the second verse (verse 15) he reveals the correction or TRUTH as delivered by Peter. The third verse (verse 16) is an introduction to the TEXT from Joel which forms the base of Peter's message.

The actual delivery of the sermon is an important element in the communication of the message. Preaching the Gospel and lecturing on other subjects are distinctly different. Lectures have to do with the sharing of information and data, and they focus on the academic process. But the Gospel message is not on that level. Preaching has to do with the flow of the Spirit of Christ. However, it is the flow of the Spirit through the preacher which creates the force of the message. In a real sense the preacher is to become the message! It must be a fire in his very bones and spill from his heart.

Luke highlights this element repeatedly in these verses. To state the tone of the message, he writes, **But Peter, standing up with the eleven, raised his voice and said to them, "Men of Judea and all who dwell in Jerusalem, let this be known to you, and heed my words,"** (Acts 2:14). "I want to share with you" is a phrase which does not even begin to describe this preaching event. "Let us pause to briefly consider the Word," is not a proper description of this message. Peter stands before this crowd with a great proclamation. It can never be described as a devotional.

Let's begin with this, **But Peter, standing up with the eleven.** The Greek word translated *standing* is used in a variety of ways, one hundred and fifty-four times in the New Testament. It refers to a position of the body (Matthew 6:5), the ceasing or stopping of something that is moving (Matthew 2:9), and to stand firm or resist (Matthew 12:25). In our passage, this verb is in the form of a participle. It acts as an adverb giving content to the two main verbs which follow. What is really startling is that it is in the passive voice. This means that the subject is not responsible for the action but is receiving the action of the verb. At first view this seems a bit strange. One would certainly think that Peter is responsible for standing up before the crowd, but something is acting upon Peter. Luke tells us that this happening is not the average sharing of information. Peter is not standing as he has

Listen To Me | **Acts 2:14**

done so many other times to enter into another argument. He is not defending or protecting his position. One cannot look at this scene and say, "There Peter goes again. No one needs to pay attention to him." In light of the context we know that the Holy Spirit has placed Peter on his feet. This pronouncement is on a very high level.

The same thing takes place as Peter is placed before the council (Acts 4:7). After spending the night in jail, Peter is brought before the leadership of Israel. They ask for an explanation of the miracle which took place yesterday (Acts 3:7). Peter is filled with the Holy Spirit (Acts 4:8) and begins to preach to them. Again Luke tells us this happening is very significant. This is not just the ranting and raving of a man who is under pressure. Peter is not spilling out his carnal self-centeredness. This message is from another source!

There are two main verbs presented to us in our verse. The first one is *raised*. The meaning of this word is far beyond the idea of shouting. It literally means "to lift up." It is used to describe the ascension of Jesus Christ to the right hand of the Father (Acts 1:9). It contains the action of a sail being hoisted up (Acts 27:40). The truth which is to be proclaimed must be lifted up above all other ideas and concepts. Above all earthly explanations (Acts 2:13) or personal expression, the truth of this new level must be seen and heard. What is happening is not on the level of just another gathering. God takes charge of Peter and his voice becomes the instrument which lifts up the message above all others.

We now come to the third statement. It is the second verb in our text, and it is so strong that it elevates this scene above all others. ***But Peter, standing up with the eleven, raised His voice and said to them,*** (Acts 2:14). The Greek word translated *said* is only used three times in the New Testament. All three times are found in the Book of Acts (2:4; 2:14; 29:25). This is the same word Luke used to describe the speaking of the Holy Spirit through

129

the disciples in languages they did not know (Acts 2:4). It was a Divine utterance! Paul was confronted by Festus as he was defending his **heavenly vision** before King Agrippa (Acts 26:19). Festus accused him of being out of his mind (crazy). Paul replied, *"I am not mad, most noble Festus, but speak the words of truth and reason,"* (Acts 26:25). This Greek word means "to speak out loudly and clearly, or with emphasis." It is used in connection with philosophers and prophets. In the Old Testament it is used for the speech of the wise man, the fortune-teller.

It is easy to see what Luke's intentions are! He sets the tone and atmosphere for this first public explanation of the new level to which God has brought Christianity! He does it by the use of three words which form the context of the delivery of this message. The first is *standing*, the second is *raised*, and the third is *said*. Do you realize this combination is not used any other place in the New Testament to emphasize any other message? The disciples are experiencing a new level and it is like nothing anyone has ever witnessed. What is happening to and in the disciples cannot be contained in the average, normal, casual conversation. The indwelt Christ demands a completely new style of communication.

In Peter's next statement to the crowd we see that he recognizes what is taking place and the high importance or status of his message. He said, *"Men of Judea and all who dwell in Jerusalem, let this be known to you, and heed my words,"* (Acts 2:14). There are two parallel statements: **let this be known to you** and **heed my words**. These two verbal expressions are really only emphatic supplements, one of the other. They do not actually introduce any new information.

In the first phrase, the verb is **be**. It is an imperative which sets the tone for the entire statement. It expresses the intensity which is found within Peter as he is an instrument for the explanation, the truth. It is imperative they understand what he is going to explain. This is not optional; it is absolutely necessary.

What Peter has experienced and is going to invite others to participate in cannot be casually presented. This is not on the level of a salesman who is trying to make a living. This is the desperation of a heart that has seen truth. How can the message come forth without being a command?

The second phrase immediately follows: **heed my words.** The Greek word translated *heed* is a compound word. It combines the Greek words translated "in" and "ear." We might translate it, "listen." This is the only place it is found in the entire New Testament which makes it very significant. It highlights the seriousness compelled by the Spirit to place the truth in the ears of those around Peter. They must understand and respond. Peter must pressure them with the truth of the indwelling Christ.

Let's review what has been discovered. In our text Luke states the tone and intensity of the situation (Acts 2:14). Peter is about to preach an explanation of what has taken place in the Pentecost event. What is the tone of his delivery? He is *standing* which is a verb in the passive voice. Peter is being acted upon by the Spirit through what has taken place in his life. He is drawn to his feet by the passion of the indwelling Christ. Also Peter *raised his* voice. This is deeper in meaning than simply shouting or becoming loud. It is the idea of "lifting up." God has elevated every thing in Christian experience to a new level. Peter's preaching must reflect this new elevation. Luke also reports that Peter *said* to them. This is a translation of a Greek word which is only used three times in the entire New Testament. All of them are in the Book of Acts. In the Old Testament (Septuagint) this is used only for wise and significant statements given by prophets or wise men. This is a message which is elevated beyond normal communication.

As Peter begins to speak he uses two phrases which set the tone for his message. He says, **"Let this be known to you."** The verb *be* is in the imperative mood. There is urgency for openness and understanding. He commands them to stretch to

Part Three: In My Eye

a new level of understanding. He continues by saying, ***"Heed my words."*** This is equivalent to "listen." It is a double statement of emphasis. Peter expresses the extreme importance of what is happening. The atmosphere of the setting becomes very intense. This scene is elevated to a new level.

If that is not enough, Peter injects this same tone into the message as he preaches. The body of his message can be divided into three separate sections. Each section begins with a particular address or admonition (Acts 2:22, 29, 36). He begins his sermon with these words, ***"Men of Israel, hear these words:"*** (Acts 2:22). He urges them to recognize the sound waves coming from his lips. It is not the noise he wants them to hear. The Greek word has the idea of obedience. Jesus used this word at the close of several parables when He said, ***"He who has ears to hear, let him hear!"*** (Matthew 13:43). The emphasis of the Greek word is "come to know." There is urgency in his voice! He is desperate to communicate!

Peter introduces the second section of his message with another address. It is like calling out their personal names. He cries, ***"Men and brethren, let me speak freely to you"*** (Acts 2:29). This is a strange grammar construction in the Greek text. The actual main verb of the statement is ***let me.*** It is a translation of a Greek word which is composed of two very small words. The Greek words "ek" (from) and "eimi" (to be) are combined. Peter does not ask permission of the crowd. He says that the truth I am preaching to you is so great that it permits me to speak to you in this manner. The manner of my speaking is going to be ***freely.*** This is translated from two separate Greek words. The first means "among or amid." I am not going to do this behind your back but right in your face. The second word means "to express all that I am thinking." Something has captured me which I must reveal to you. I cannot hold back or soft pedal my words. I must forcibly tell you the truth. The truth I have experienced demands a complete exposure. Christ in His fullness has come to indwell us. It is a new level which compels a complete openness on my part.

The third section of Peter's message begins, *"Therefore let all the house of Israel know assuredly that God has made this Jesus, whom you crucified, both Lord and Christ,"* (Acts 2:36). The main verb in his opening statement is *let... know.* It is translated from the Greek word "ginosko." It is in the imperative mood. Again we see the strong, commanding, urging emphasis. In the verse, he does not speak of grasping data. If he speaks of information he would use the Greek word "gnostos." If he is only interested in them understanding the concept he would use the Greek word "oida" for perceiving. What he desires is for them to enter into intimate relationship with Jesus who has become Lord and Christ. "Ginosko" is the Greek word for the most intimate relationship in marriage.

He also adds a very interesting word to this emphasis. It is translated *assuredly.* It comes from a word group which can be translated "certainty," "sure," or "to safeguard." The actual Greek word he uses in our text can be translated "securely." This actual Greek word is only used three times in the New Testament. Judas instructed the leaders of Israel in the capture of Jesus by saying, *"Whomever I kiss, He is the One; seize Him and lead Him away SAFELY,"* (Mark 14:44). Paul and Silas were in Philippi. There was a slave girl who was possessed with a spirit of divination. When Paul and Silas were used as instruments for her deliverance, the magistrates threw them in jail. They commanded *the jailer to keep them SECURELY* (Acts 16:23). As Peter is preaching after Pentecost, he says, *Therefore let all the house of Israel know ASSUREDLY that God has made this Jesus, whom you crucified, both Lord and Christ,"* (Acts 2:36). In this passage, Peter urges the people of Israel to be intimate with Jesus who is Lord and Christ for certain, securely, and absolutely. This has to be! They must enter into the embrace. The reality of who Jesus is must become their personal reality.

Part Three: In My Eye

You cannot hear the tone clearly stated in the opening verse (Acts 2:14) without sensing a new intensity regarding the message. This is not a performance; there is no hidden agenda. The tone of the message is produced by the truth experienced. We have now experienced three different times within the message where Peter explodes with this same urgency. He is driven by the very reality of Christ who indwells him. He is captured by the resurrected Lord, the vision of the Kingdom, and now the indwelling Spirit. He burns with the truth! Everything has moved to a new level. The entrance level of the Old Testament has been replaced. The Spirit of Jesus within has superseded all they have experienced in commitment and relationship with Jesus in the flesh. Christ in you has become the new reality. This comes with a new level of intensity. Christ now consumes their lives.

How do you adequately express this? What should be the tone of your voice? Are you surprised I yell quite often? In our generation, one individual expressed it by crying out, "Take my life like a ten dollar bill and spend it all over town." He went on to express, "Let my life be like a candle which is lit on both ends until I am consumed for you." There is no room for a casual lukewarm attitude. Where does nominal Christianity fit into this picture? Christ has literally come to indwell the believer. The outside God has gotten inside. The dream and purpose of man has been filled. There is no room for yawning in this experience.

Whatever has duped us into the carefulness of man-invented strategies must be set aside. The author of the Book of Hebrews must have been yelling as he thundered into chapter twelve. ***Therefore we also, since we are surrounded by so great a cloud of witnesses, let us lay aside every weight, and the sin which so easily ensnares us, and let us run with endurance the race that is set before us*** (Hebrews 12:1). Every hindrance must be eliminated. We must not tolerate any element which might cause us to stumble. We must aggressively pour the reality of this message into our world. There is no time for strategy meetings. We must not soft pedal this message. We must compel every individual to embrace our Christ. We must fully enlist. We cannot delegate this to another. Senior adults cannot pass it to you. Teens must not think they can do it later. God calls us now!

Acts 2:15

GOD OR THE DEVIL?

The Pentecost event has amazed the great crowd. The Jews of the Dispersion are astonished by the things they have seen. They have sought and longed for a new and fresh movement of God. Could this be the end of their search? They raise this issue (Acts 2:12), *"What ever could this mean?"* Then we see the Jews of Jerusalem. They see nothing to astonish them. They are stale and narrow, and they are quite satisfied with the way things are. Their opinion of the Pentecost event is *"They are full of new wine,"* (Acts 2:13).

Luke addresses the issue through the preaching of Peter. Before he actually presents the sermon, he sets the stage for us. He presents the TONE of the message first (Acts 2:14). The TRUTH of the message follows (Acts 2:15). It is a bold statement of correction before the proper explanation is given. Thirdly, he shares the TEXT of the message (Acts 2:16-21).

In this study we shall examine the TRUTH of the message (Acts 2:15). Peter addresses both the Jews of the Dispersion and the Jews of Jerusalem in his overall message. The complete explanation of the Pentecost event (Acts 2:22-39) is focused on the Jews of the Dispersion. Their question is *"Whatever could this mean?* (Acts 2:12). Peter goes to great lengths to satisfy their seeking. It is a detailed explanation of the movement of God on our behalf.

In our text (Acts 2:15), Peter directly answers the statement of the Jews of Jerusalem. They do not seek to embrace any new movement of God. They are rigid and set in concrete. They explain the event away by saying, *"They are full of new wine,"* (Acts 2:13). It is a statement of mockery. Peter addresses their explanation. Their accusation is not worth more than one verse. Even if he gave more they would not listen. He simply says, *"For these are not drunk, as you suppose, since it is only the third hour of the day,"* (Acts 2:15). He gives them no deep spiritual insight. He does not reveal the unfolding plan of God. It is a simple statement of logic. He appeals to their intellect by saying how absurd their comment is. The third hour which is determined by sunrise is 9:00AM. Even those who are drunkards are not drunk this early in the day. This is especially true on a feast day such as Pentecost.

The key to understanding Peter's statement may be found in the Greek word translated *suppose.* This Greek word is only used five times in the entire New Testament and it is used in a variety of ways. It is used by Luke to describe the ascension of Christ (Acts 1:9). It is the word describing Jesus' response to a self-justifying lawyer who asks, *"And who is my neighbor?"* (Luke 10:29). It is a compound word meaning "under" and "to take." Its basic meaning is "to take from below." In our passage, there is a basic focus on the group that proposed this idea of drunkenness. The mockers have reached inside of themselves and proposed this idea. They do not seek beyond their own minds and hearts. They certainly are not open to a revelation from God regarding this matter. They explain everything from their own personal perspective. They do not seek an answer for what has happened. They already know the answer. If one is stuck in the mode of understanding everything within the framework of his own thinking, he is extremely limited.

When we limit ourselves to our own thinking, we most likely decide on a conclusion which is opposite of the real truth. That is the situation in our passage. The Jews of Jerusalem decide that the Pentecost event is a result of the devil. Drunkenness is considered by all Jews as obnoxious and sinful. Although drunkenness is common among the Greeks, it is a grievous accusation in Jewish Palestine. The Jews of Jerusalem view what God is doing as the work of the devil.

This is not the first time this has happened! They made this accusation enough times that they established a pattern. Consider the event recorded in Matthew 12:22-30. The fame of Jesus' miracles has spread over Palestine. On the occasion of a blind and mute man's healing **the multitudes were amazed** (Matthew 12:23). The man was actually demon possessed. A question spread through the members of the crowd. **"Could this be the Son of David?"** they asked (Matthew 12:23). The very suggestion that Jesus might be the Messiah is a threat to the authority of the Pharisees. They immediately attempt to make their conclusion that of the multitude. They say, **"This fellow does not cast out demons except by Beelzebub, the ruler of the demons,"** (Matthew 12:24). Again they attribute God's actions to the devil.

An amazing discourse results from their accusation. The initial response parallels our passage in the Book of Acts (2:15). Jesus approaches them on the level of logic (Matthew 12:25-30). What they say does not make any sense! How can they possibly come to this conclusion? They are educated and intelligent individuals. Their conclusion is a result of limiting their thinking to their own understanding. Self-centeredness dominates and determines all of their conclusions. To step outside of their self-centered thinking would be to risk being influenced by something beyond them.

They have not realized how destructive it is to approach everything in one's life from a self-centered view. It is simply the devil casting out his own demons which means he is **divided against himself** (Matthew 12:26). But this is the way self-centeredness acts. It will do anything to make itself look good. Self-centeredness is so focused on self that it cannot see the destruction brought about by its own actions.

This is what happens when a man thinks only of himself in his marriage and family. He gets married because he sincerely wants love and companionship. He desires a home, family and intimacy. But his self-centeredness demands its own way. He takes advantage of his wife. His lack of patience causes him to abuse his children in the discipline process. He spills a spirit of rebellion and death into his home. He builds barriers in his relationships. He destroys everything good in the home he sincerely wanted.

The same is true in the local body of Christ. All church members want the movement of God. There is a desire for revival and evangelism. Many individuals began attending because of their desire for love and fellowship. However, an attachment to tradition caused by self-centeredness brings division. Disagreements flourish and kill the Spirit of revival and evangelism. Love and fellowship give way to hatred and war. Self-centeredness destroys everything originally desired. It is the devil casting out his own demons.

This kind of situation is so serious that Jesus says it cannot be forgiven (Matthew 12:31-37). It is called "the blasphemy against the Holy Spirit." Jesus is very clear about the content of the unforgivable sin. It is not a deed or action, but it is spirit and attitude. Jesus is very forgiving to sinners, but He cannot and will not tolerate people with unholy attitudes. These people are not open and seeking. They are hypocrites focused on themselves, and they destroy everything around them in an attempt to save themselves. In reality, they attribute to the devil the very works of God.

The group gathered at the crucifixion of Christ expressed this same attitude. Jesus and the leaders of Israel were at extreme odds over the cross style. The "pour your life out" concept is foreign to the "grab for yourself" style. They did not just misunderstand the cross style but it greatly irritated them. They could not leave Jesus alone. His style was a threat to all they stood for! In their typical self-centered style they worked diligently to eliminate Him. Cross style deserves to be nailed to a cross. The deed is done (Matthew 27:35).

Even then they cannot help but express their bewilderment. They are again mocking Him as He pours out His life for others. The leadership of Israel (chief priests, scribes and elders) are yelling, *"He saved others; Himself He cannot save. If He is the King of Israel, let Him now come down from the cross, and we will believe Him. He trusted in God; let Him deliver Him now if He will have Him; for He said, 'I am the Son of God,'"* (Matthew 27:42-43). What a concept! They give expression to their very self-centered nature. They cannot conceive how anyone in intimacy with God can possibly be subjected to such a death as crucifixion. If Jesus really is the King of Israel, God will surely protect Him from such shame. If Jesus is truly the Son of God and doing the very works of God, will not God intervene on His behalf now? Therefore, if He has not been doing the work of God, indeed, He must be doing the work of the devil. So the cross is simply the climax or result of the work of the devil in the life of Christ.

Do you see the clear expression of their self-centeredness? If the leaders of Israel are intimate with God and are placed in such a circumstance, their self-centeredness will immediately use the power of God for their personal deliverance. They cannot possibly understand why Jesus does not do the same. God's activity in pouring out your life for others is totally foreign to their thinking. Thus, they ultimately attribute the crucifixion to demonic activity in the life of Christ when all the time God has planned it. They are again attributing the works of God to the devil.

But the pattern continues! The soldiers who are the elite of the Roman forces are guarding the dead body of Jesus. A Roman seal has been placed on the tomb. No one can possibly steal the body of Christ and propose the ridiculous conclusion of resurrection. However, God acts again. An angel of the Lord descends bringing a revelation of the resurrection. The fiercest of the Roman soldiers faint from fright. Upon reviving, they immediately run into Jerusalem to report the event to the leaders of Israel. It is one more of God's attempts to offer an opportunity of grace to these Jews. The soldiers *reported to the chief priests all the things that had happened* (Matthew 28:11).

The response of the chief priests is predictable for they follow the same pattern. *When they had assembled with the elders and consulted together, they gave a large sum of money to the soldiers, saying, "Tell them, 'His disciples came at night and stole Him away while we slept,'"* (Matthew 28:12). The key to their response is the Greek word translated *consulted together.* In the noun form it is translated "council." It paints the picture of a group of men sitting around the table discussing what they know. They turn into themselves for the answer to their dilemma. Out of their self-centeredness the decision is made.

They decide the disciples have stolen the body or at least that is their proposal. Stealing is of the devil. Therefore, the resurrection of Christ which is definitely the act of God is now being attributed to the devil. The source of this conclusion is their self-centered consulting. They constantly manipulate the people involved with their conclusions. *So they took the money and did as they were instructed; and this saying is commonly reported among the Jews until this day* (Matthew 26:15).

We need to ask and answer a series of questions for our personal lives! "How do we do this in our lives?" I want you to think carefully about those things against which you have taken issue. Do you have strong Biblical basis for your resistance or is it simply personal preference? My mind immediately rushes to many circumstances which have caused divisions in churches. I have experienced arguments and conflict over furnaces, communion tables, music and where the pulpit is placed. In one church great division arose over five gallon buckets of sand. Some caring people of the church were ministering to several homeless people from downtown. The homeless always needed to go outside between Sunday school and church to smoke. Those caring for these people had provided several buckets of sand at the front door of the building for the deposit of the remains of the cigarettes. The following Sunday morning the buckets were gone. They were found behind the building. Each time they were moved to the front of the building they would later turn up missing. Some folks did not want buckets of sand filled with cigarette butts in front of the church doors. Is this not attributing to the devil the works of God? Self-centeredness will not allow the individual to recognize that God is doing a new thing in the lives of people. It is easy to become so attached to tradition and self-centered patterns we find ourselves fighting against God. We attribute any deviation from our tradition to the work of the devil. What if God attempts to do a new thing as He did at Pentecost?

    A second question needs to be answered. "How serious is this issue?" Surely the impact of the truth discovered answers this question for us. When the Pharisees criticize Jesus for linking with the devil (Matthew 12:24), they shut the door to any activity of God in their lives. If we attribute what God is doing to the devil, there will never be any positive response to God's action in our lives. How will we ever receive any new instruction from God? Time and again Christ desperately attempts to communicate the truth to the leaders of Israel, even through the pagan soldiers at the resurrection, but they will not listen. They will not recognize the moving hand of God in the events which are shattering their traditions. Thus, they attribute to the devil the works of God.

    There is a third question of importance. "How can I tell if it is God's action or that of the devil?" Did you notice in each of the

Biblical illustrations above, it is self-centeredness which sources the confusion? You can never distinguish between God's action and the devil's without a complete death to self-centeredness. Those who seek and respond do not seem to have a problem. It is in openness we hear His voice and recognize His actions. The heart which seeks sincerely cannot miss His will. He will not allow that individual to be confused. This is a startling and comforting truth to one as ignorant as me.

Now we are confronted by a fourth question. "Can God use an event for His purpose which He did not cause?" Perhaps the devil causes an event and yet God utilizes this circumstance for His own will. Therefore, to fight against the circumstance caused by the devil would be to hinder the purpose of God. A powerful example of this is stated in the preaching of Peter in response to Pentecost. Peter says, *"**Him** (Christ), **being delivered by the determined purpose and foreknowledge of God, you have taken by lawless hands, have crucified, and put to death,"* (Acts 2:23). We must understand the depth of this truth. There seems to be two views of the crucifixion. There is the perspective of the men who think they are in charge. They plot in secret meetings to bring about the crucifixion. Their lawless hands do the work of the devil. Therefore the crucifixion is the result of the devil's action. But there is a second view. Christ is delivered by the determined purpose and foreknowledge of God. God is so sovereign and omniscient that He calculated into His plan the lawless deeds of men. He is so redemptive He changed what was intended to be bad into good. Jesus surrendered to what looked like the acts of the devil, because He knew it was the plan of God. Redemption was the result!

Can I be open and intimate with Christ? Can I know His heart and grasp His intent? Can I receive His mind until I know His thoughts? Can I live in every circumstance finding His will? Can His purpose be accomplished through me in all the confused circumstances of my day? Is this not His plan???

Acts 2:16-39

PETER'S EXPLANATION

The Pentecost event has taken place (Acts 2:1-4). The earth shaking reality of this happening is equal to everything God has accomplished up to this point. Everything is changed! No one can ever be the same again. The Jews of the Dispersion are completely awestruck. Luke highlights it five different times (Acts 2:6, 7, and 12). The Jews of Jerusalem react in their normal stale manner. They even slip into mockery (Acts 2:13). The entire movement of God is dismissed as they proclaim, *"They are full of new wine."* A proper explanation is desperately needed. The Jews of the Dispersion seek while the Jews of Jerusalem seclude themselves. The record must be set straight. Peter is on his feet. The Holy Spirit gives an amazing explanation with startling results.

Luke presents this explanation by making a contrast between man's view and God's view. The mockers have just had their say. It is puny, meager, and mechanical. Even a casual glance reveals how illogical it is. However, it is the best the reasoning of man can produce. God acts and men interpret it through the filter of their own minds. They are incredibly far from the truth. The huge dreams of God are reduced down to the understanding of man. But isn't this what God has faced year after year throughout the Old Testament? People with such limited capacities refuse to rely on the wisdom of God. Man, who was built to be an instrument of the movement of God, requires God to become a tool of his own designs. The best we can calculate is illogical. We even label the works of God as the actions of the devil.

BUT there is much more to it than this! God is acting. The dream of God for mankind is restored. What God intended in the creation of man was lost in sin but is now corrected. God has come to indwell man again. Everything which kept that from happening is made right. This is the crowning segment of man's redemption. God's step by step plan is accomplished. The devil views this Pentecost movement as deserving of only one simple statement; BUT God sees it as worthy of over one half of the chapter. The devil responds only by mocking; BUT God proposes the glory of mankind's restoration. The devil easily dismisses the event; BUT God must focus us on the reality of being filled with the Spirit of Jesus.

While the mockers dismiss the Pentecost event with a few words of mockery (Acts 2:13), Peter is on his feet (Acts 2:14). He spends only one sentence correcting the mockers (Acts 2:15) and then quickly moves into a full-blown explanation of the greatness of what God has just accomplished. He preaches a powerful sermon which greatly convicts the Jews of the Dispersion. Three thousand of them become Christians (Acts 2:41).

It is important that we view the sermon as a whole. The entire discourse is thoroughly saturated with Scripture. He simply refers to the Old Testament. These Jews are committed to the Scriptures. Peter thunders the news that the Old Testament Scriptures verify what God is doing. He begins with a Scriptural basis which was spoken by the prophet Joel (Acts 2:17-21). He then gives a three-verse explanation (Acts 2:22-24) which is based on a quotation from King David (Acts 2:25-28). Peter continues with more insight (Acts 2:29-33) based on a second quotation from King David (Acts 2:34-35). A definite progression dominates his message.

Peter begins with a strong quotation from the prophet Joel (Acts 2:17-21). In this passage from Joel, he captures the very heart of the Pentecost event. It is a quotation from Joel 2:28-32. We will deal with the details of this prophecy and its fulfillment in a later study. In our overall view, the important thing is to grasp the central theme of the prophecy. The resounding theme is given to us twice:

"That I will pour out My Spirit on all flesh:" (Acts 2:17).
"I will pour out My Spirit in those days;" (Acts 2:18).

Everything else in the passage has to do with the result of this great outpouring. Therefore, Peter's message boldly states that this prophecy has just been fulfilled in their presence. They have just experienced the action of God. He takes His very nature and plants it in the human life of mankind. Obviously the results of this action will take man to a new level of living. This was to take place in *the last days* (Acts 2:17). Peter boldly says, "The *last days* have arrived!" The emphasis of these *last days* is not judgment (although that may be present). It is not about church growth. The Spirit of Jesus is being poured out on the believers. Everything God has been working towards throughout the Old Testament has come to pass in this moment.

As Peter begins this message (Acts 2:22), he proclaims, "Let me share with you how we finally got here! It all happened through one man. He was not just a man. He was a man who made Himself totally available to God so God could do something through Him." Let us look at his sermon.

Doctrine of the Incarnation
The actions of God are taking place in Christ.
Acts 2:24

The first three verses of his sermon (Acts 2:22-24) are the explanation of the Scripture he quotes from King David (Acts 2:25-28). Notice this very important fact! He never says that Jesus is Divine. This is not a result of disbelief in Christ.

Certainly his belief is well established in his confession. ***Simon Peter answered and said, "You are the Christ, the Son of the living God,"*** (Matthew 16:16). But this is not his emphasis. Is this not a surprise? Would it not have been proper to cry out that the Divine Son of God has accomplished this? The very One they crucified was God!

However, Peter's emphasis is on what God is doing through this Man called Christ. Look at the strong statements in his sermon:

"Men of Israel, hear these words: Jesus of Nazareth, a Man attested by God to you by miracles, wonders, and signs which God did through Him in your midst, as you yourselves also know" (Acts 2:22).

"Him, being delivered by the determined purpose and foreknowledge of God…" (Acts 2:23).

"Whom God raised up, having loosed the pains of death…" (Acts 2:24).

This is a strong proclamation of the Doctrine of Incarnation. "Incarnation" means "to assume flesh." "The Doctrine of the Incarnation" means that the second member of the Trinity leaped from His throne to assume the body and nature of mankind. In one person, there was the total nature of God and the total nature of man in an indissoluble union. "Indissoluble" means you cannot split Him into parts. He is not half-God and half-man. He does not sometimes act as God and other times as man. In order for Him to become man, He was required to set aside those things He had as God. Everything which distinguished Him from man was set aside. Here was a man who totally responded to God for His moment by moment life.

The life of Christ is not explained in the fact that He is God, although we all believe that is true. His life is explained in the fact that He was a man filled with God. Jesus lived like He could not live through the power of the Holy Spirit. The miracles, wonders, and signs which He accomplished were only because God did them ***through Him*** (Acts 2:22). Even the tragic evil which appeared to be the result of **lawless hands, have crucified, and put to death** were really the **determined purpose and foreknowledge of God** (Acts 2:23). God simply would not allow Jesus to remain in death, but **God raised up** (Acts 2:24). If you desire to know how an individual lives when he is filled with God and constantly responds to God, Jesus is the answer.

The **last days** have now arrived! The prophecy of Joel is now fulfilled. How did we get here? It is through this Man called Christ, who though He is God, submitted to the incarnation. God became man and set aside everything which distinguished Him from man. He lived in total response to God. This is what enabled His crucifixion and resurrection to bring us to this moment. Without this we would still be under the Old Covenant with nothing but our performance and law. It is a new hour because of this Man called Christ! Peter bases this truth on the statement of King David (Acts 2:25-28).

Direction of the Incarnation
The unfolding plans of God are taking place in Christ.
Acts 2:29-33

The second point in Peter's sermon highlights the long range plans of God which are based on promises God made to King David (Acts 2:29-33). It was during a time of victory for King David and Israel. The Ark of the Covenant had just been returned to Jerusalem. David and the people were rejoicing with such delight. The Scripture says, **Then David danced before the Lord with all his might;** (2 Samuel 6:14). Through the prophet Nathan a message was given to King David. A key element in that message was this promise: *"Also the Lord tells you that He will make you a house. When your days are fulfilled and you rest with your fathers, I will set up your seed after you, who will come from your body, and I will establish his kingdom. He* *shall build a house for My name, and I will establish the throne of his kingdom forever ... And your house and your kingdom shall be established forever before you. Your throne shall be established forever,"* (2 Samuel 7:11-13 and 16).

It is indeed true that King David is **both dead and buried, and his tomb is with us to this day** (Acts 2:29). But **God had sworn with an oath to him** (Acts 2:30). This promise was centered in the coming Messiah. The throne of King David was to be protected by God. It would never disappear, but God would raise up from the seed of King David One who would reign on that throne forever and ever. King David, as a prophet, foresaw this (Acts 2:31). In Psalms sixteen he spoke concerning the resurrection of Christ from the dead. God would not allow **His soul ... left in Hades, nor did His flesh see corruption** (Acts 2:31). God simply intervened in the life and death of this Man called Jesus. **This Jesus God has raised up** (Acts 2:32). He was exalted to the right hand of God for the purpose of receiving the promise of the Holy Spirit. Due to these facts, we are now experiencing the very event which is being questioned! He has **poured out this which you now see and hear** (Acts 2:33).

Has this not been the plan of God from the very first disobedience of man? Did God not begin a restoration plan from the very beginning of sin? Is this not the fulfillment of the dreams of God for mankind? Is it not all found in the Christ who has provided the indwelling Spirit? King David was not the fulfillment of this. He is dead, buried, and certainly did not ascend into the heavens (Acts 2:34). But Christ, from the seed of David, has ascended. David saw it as a prophet and rejoiced in its truth. All of this has happened through the Man called Christ.

What is happening in the great Pentecost event has been the long range dream of God for us. To actually see the event and label it as a result of drunkenness is to reject God's long range plan. We must open ourselves to the indwelling of the Spirit as Christ did. As God moved through the Christ, He now wants to move through us. As Christ experienced the fulfillment of the dreams of God within His own person, so we must embrace the same fulfillment within us.

Dream of the Incarnation
What is taking place in Jesus is for you.
Acts 2:36-39

Peter thunders to the close of his explanation to the Jews. It is a conclusion which includes them. God has plans and dreams for His world. Instead of allowing these to be fulfilled, the Jews attempt to destroy them (Acts 2:36). They fought against all that God is accomplishing. But God is greater than their feeble attempts. *"God has made this Jesus, whom you crucified, both Lord and Christ"* (Acts 2:36). They join forces with the enemy. They, who were chosen to be an avenue of mercy, become a blockade of defiance. When this truth dawns on them they are shocked. *Now when they heard this, they were cut to the heart* (Acts 2:37). They cry out from the depths of their hearts for instruction in how to respond. They groan, *"Men and brethren, what shall we do?"* (Acts 2:37). How can we make this right? How can we undo what we have done? What can we do now that will make up for what we have done? We have crucified Christ!

The answer is clear! There is nothing you can do. No act or actions can set this right! The fact is there is a *"promise... to you and to your children, and to all who are afar off, as many as the Lord our God will call,"* (Acts 2:39). Will you respond to God at this moment? He is calling you now. It is a call to **Repent** (Acts 2:38). Give up a former thought and embrace a second thought. Please change your mind. You have lived in the attitude of crucifying Christ, but now you see a new truth. Will you abandon the former thought for the sake of the new which God has so graciously provided you? It is the baptism that John the

Baptist called you to a few years ago (Matthew 3). This very act of responding ushers in the forgiveness which God has already provided. You cannot make what you have done right. There are not enough religious deeds, regardless of how sacrificial, which can atone for your rejection of Christ who is the fulfilled dream of God. Will you in humility simply respond to what God is showing you now? If so, you will be forgiven and you will receive the ***gift of the Holy Spirit*** (Acts 2:38), the event which attracted your attention.

What God has done through the Man called Christ, He wants to do through you. All the fullness of God contained in Christ can now be in you. The God who acted through Christ now wants to act through you. That which attracted you to Jesus is a result of the Spirit of God. He is now yours as well! This is God's plan, embrace it!

Acts 2:16-21

THE TEXT OF PENTECOST

The ten tribes of Israel have been taken into exile never to return. The southern kingdom of Judah remains. However, Judah has not continued faithful to God. A sudden disaster falls without warning. An awe-striking black cloud descends upon the land. It is the dreaded locusts. In a matter of hours, every living green thing has been stripped bare. Did not God allow this to happen because of their sin? The prophet Joel, God's spokesman for that hour, rises to the occasion. His book, while only a brief three chapters is powerful in its impact. He contends that the judgments of God during the Day of the Lord will be far worse than the plague of the locusts. This disaster is a mere call to awaken and respond in repentance.

While there is a strong emphasis on God's inability to tolerate sin, the blessings which are to come are unparalleled. Peter highlights this section of Joel's prophecy as fulfilled (Acts 2:16-21). It becomes the text for his message which explains the event of the filling of the Holy Spirit which they just experienced. The focus of his quote from the Book of Joel is:

That I will pour out my Spirit upon all flesh; (Acts 2:17).

I will pour out My Spirit in those days; (Acts 2:18).

Everything in prophecy described by Joel is a result of this generous outpouring of the Spirit of God. There will be *prophesy, visions,* and *dreams* which all point to the sourcing of the Spirit of Christ. Even the *wonders in heaven above and the signs in the earth beneath* are a product of this new movement of God within the life of mankind.

The focus is not on God's final judgment of the world, although that may be mentioned. It is not on the final damnation of those who have rebelled against God, although that is certainly true. The entire prophecy is about the indwelling of God within the life of man. Joel is speaking about Pentecost! This results in salvation. In the prophecy there is a sense of completeness, of arrival. Pentecost is the final piece of the puzzle. It is the last nail driven into the board. The dream of God is fulfilled!

At first glance, one might think we have moved from a focus on Christ to a focus on the Holy Spirit. Peter completely corrects this in his message. We have arrived at this moment of the outpouring of the Spirit of God because of Christ. Christ became man and dwelt among us. Christ became an avenue for the great miracles of God (Acts 2:22). Christ, in submission to the Father, experienced the cross (Acts 2:23). Christ was raised from the dead by God (Acts 2:24). Christ was *exalted to the right hand of God* (Acts 2:33). He *received from the Father the promise of the Holy Spirit* (Acts 2:33). It is Christ who *poured out this which you now see and hear* (Acts 2:33). The only way any individual can enter into oneness with God is through Christ (Acts 2:38). We know the very Spirit an individual receives is the Spirit of Christ!

As we view the structure of the prophecy of Joel quoted by Peter, there are some definite aspects to this focus on the filling of the Holy Spirit. Let me list them for you.

Part Three: In My Eye

Period of Time

Peter begins his quotation from Joel by saying,

*And it shall come to pass in the last days, says God,
That I will pour out my Spirit on all flesh; (Acts 2:17).*

If this is compared carefully with the actual Book of Joel, you will find Peter does not quote it correctly. The Prophet Joel said:

*And it shall come to pass afterward
that I will pour out My Spirit on all flesh; (Joel 2:28).*

Peter changed the words to emphasize when this prophecy will take place. Joel says it is **afterward;** Peter says it is **in the last days.** This is not accidental or from a lack of memory. Peter interprets Joel's statement and applies it to his (and our) hour. Joel states this event will take place in the future, while Peter describes the present time period in which the Spirit of God comes in His fullness.

This phrase (**the last days**) is not unusual even in the Old Testament. The prophet Isaiah used it (Isaiah 2:2). The prophet Micah also used it (Micah 4:1). In both cases they refer to the time of the Messiah. The author of the Book of Hebrews introduces "God's Superior Revelation" to us by contrasting God's message, which came through the prophets, with the fact that God **has in these last days spoken to us by His Son, whom He has appointed heir of all things, through whom also He made the worlds;** (Hebrews 1:2).

In the coming of Christ the ancient economy was closed and a new, superior economy appeared. The **last days** signified the terminating of all the preparatory arrangements. We are no longer getting ready for anything since Christ has come! This was the emphasis John the Baptist preached. *"Repent, for the kingdom of heaven is at hand!"* (Matthew 3:2). The King of the Kingdom has arrived. The waiting period is over; Christ is here!

We are living in those days. All God wants to do within us is now available. Everything He has planned for you is at your finger tips. We do not need to wait for God to do anything else. It is all in place. These are the **last days.** We are living in the fullness of the Spirit. The prophets of old longed to experience and only saw by faith these **last days.** What a privileged people we are! There is no reason for us to live in defeat, confusion, or discouragement. Do not tolerate compromise! I am deeply concerned about an evangelical Christianity which wants to abide in an anemic, subnormal existence. The excuse is given that the final judgment has not come. We are still in the flesh. Therefore, we do not experience all God wants to do in us. This is not the emphasis of the New Testament. These are the **last days.** God has completed the work through Christ. Everything we need to be in intimacy with Him is now ours. There is nothing to stop us from experiencing the nature of God. We can be His! The thrust of this truth is that this is for you. You qualify! You are in the **last days.**

Presentation

Another strong emphasis in the prophecy of Joel is the picture of **pour out.** It is interesting that Joel would use these words to express the coming of the Holy Spirit. This phrase is not new to us in the New Testament. Jesus spoke to His disciples concerning fasting. He used the illustration of the new wine in old wineskins. New wine will cause old wineskins to break and **the wine is spilled** (Matthew 9:17). The Greek word translated

Part Three: In My Eye

spilled is the same as *pour out.* The picture is one of being completely emptied, spilling, or gushing.

Paul gives testimony to his past actions regarding the persecution of Christians. He admits to Christ, *"And when the blood of Your martyr Stephen was shed, I also was standing by consenting to his death, and guarding the clothes of those who were killing him,"* (Acts 22:20). The Greek word translated *was shed* is the same as *pour out.*

Luke gives us some additional information about the end of Judas' life (Acts 1:18). He tried to hang himself by tying a rope around a tree which was near a precipice. Evidently the rope broke *and falling headlong, he burst open in the middle and all of his entrails gushed out* (Acts 1:18). The Greek word translated *gushed out* is the same as *pour out.*

The definition of the word goes beyond the idea of simply "coming out." It carries with it the concept of abundance or lavished. It is the picture of a full bucket turned upside down. There is no holding back. There are no restrictions. Peter not only quotes this word in the prophecy of Joel, but also adopts it as his own description of the coming of the Holy Spirit. In the climax of his sermon, he says, *"Therefore being exalted to the right hand of God, and having received from the Father the promise of the Holy Spirit, He poured out this which you now see and hear,"* (Acts 2:33).

Christ has received the promise of the Father. He has not given His Spirit to us in meager portions. He has not restricted the gift of His Spirit. He is not bargaining with us about His presence. You CANNOT have as much of God as you want. You cannot choose a little or a lot. He will not give Himself in portions. He is extravagantly, lavishly, abundantly, without hesitation or restrictions giving Himself to us. The intent is that He will fill our entire being or not at all. All areas of our lives will be filled with His presence or we will not know Him. What a promise we have received! The thrust of this truth is that this is for you. You qualify! There is the fullness of God for you in the abundance of the outpouring of the Spirit of Christ. This truth is also demonstrated in the next great aspect of our text.

People Involved

When Joel used the Greek word translated *pour out,* he was contrasting the present coming of the Spirit of Christ with the few appearances of the Holy Spirit in the Old Testament. He continues with a similar contrast by saying, *"I will pour out my Spirit upon all flesh;"* (Acts 2:17). This presents a contrast with the restriction of the Spirit of Christ to certain privileged people throughout the Old Testament. He goes on to interpret his own prophecy in great detail. He gives us a list of those who are included in *all flesh.*

In the New Testament the Greek word translated *all* is used well over one thousand times. It is very important to know if an article is placed before the word. When an article is used it limits the word to a focused meaning. It focuses on a group and everyone within that group. However, when there is no article it emphasizes the broadest sense of the word. In our passage there is no article before the word! Joel is saying and Peter emphasizes the greatest view of the outpouring of the Holy Spirit. Also, this Greek word includes the idea of oneness, a totality or the whole.

As God speaks through the prophet Joel, He interprets His own prophecy with a list. The significance of the list seems to be found in the removal of all distinctions. There is no sexual distinction. *Your sons and your daughters shall prophecy.* The age distinction is quickly discarded. *Your young men shall see vision, Your old men shall dream dreams.* Even the status distinction is removed. *And on My menservants and on My maidservants.*

While these are the distinctions specifically mentioned in the prophecy, there are other divisions which are implied.

There are no racial distinctions. Think of the strong division between Jew and Gentile in the cultural environment of the New Testament. However, Paul cries out, *For you are all sons of God through faith in Christ Jesus. For as many of you as were baptized into Christ have put on Christ. There is neither Jew nor Greek, there is neither slave nor free, there is neither male nor female; for you are all one in Christ Jesus* (Galatians 3:26:28).

There are no educational distinctions. This is highlighted by the leaders of Israel gathered together to confront the apostles. Peter's reasoning and clarity is so powerful, they are amazed. *Now when they saw the boldness of Peter and John, and perceived that they were uneducated and untrained men, they marveled* (Acts 4:13).

The list goes on and on. There are no distinctions between personality types. Isn't it significant that this distinction is never highlighted? There is no past distinction. People who have committed sins in the past are not excluded; all are included. Even those who had been their enemies and responsible for the deaths of their companions (Saul of Tarsus) were included! There is no talent distinction. One cannot discover in the Book of Acts a prayer for God to foster certain talents in the church. Even when the apostles were searching for those who could "serve tables," they desired *seven men of good reputation, full of the Holy Spirit and wisdom...* (Acts 6:3). It was spiritual qualities they desired, not talent.

There was no prosperity distinction. Regardless of their personal economy status, they were included. It is simply never mentioned as an issue. There was no tenured distinction. From the very first recorded business meeting of the early church they were all included (Acts 1:15). The brothers of Christ who were converted during the cross event were included in the decisions as were the apostles who had been with Jesus the entire time of His earthly ministry.

Why are we so prone to distinctions? We seem to pride

ourselves in our differences. In our attitudes we foster the "haves" and the "have nots." We applaud the performance, the accomplishments of those with talent. Is it not an expression of our self-centered carnality? Something wonderful has taken place among the disciples. Jesus has become so dominant that nothing else matters. Christianity became totally about Jesus, not about the disciples and their distinctions.

The wonder of this truth is that you qualify. Everything God wants you to have is now here. There is nothing to hold you back. We are in *the last days*. The final piece of the puzzle has been put in place. Christ has accomplished all! He is everything God has dreamed for us. Concerning the distinction between Jews and Gentiles, Paul says, *For He Himself is our peace, who has made both one, and has broken down the middle wall of separation, having abolished in His flesh the enmity, that is, the law of commandments contained in ordinances, so as to create in Himself one new man from the two, thus making peace* (Ephesians 2:14-15). Outside of Christ, there are distinctions. Outside of Christ, we battle for position and make ourselves superior to others. But these are *the last days*. We are now in Christ and Christ is now in us! Regardless of all man-made distinctions, we are included.

Purpose

But there is one last aspect in our text. We have mentioned the idea of "arrival." We are in *the last days*. This is where God has been going throughout the entire Old Testament. Everything is now done. We have arrived! However, this is not in the sense "over." It is not that we now know it all. It is arrival in the sense of all that God wants us to have is now available to us. We have come to a new level in Christ. There is now going to be an accelerated revelation. Joel prophesied this; Peter proposed it.

Part Three: In My Eye

In the outpouring of the Spirit of Christ came **prophecy, visions, dreams, wonders,** and **signs.** Is it not interesting that he did not mention prosperity, health, and happiness? His list is focused on the expanded revelation of Christ. But this should not surprise us for John told us this in his Gospel account. John records the statement of Jesus, ***"However, when He, the Spirit of truth, has come, He will guide you into all truth; for He will not speak on His own authority, but whatever He hears He will speak; and He will tell you things to come,"*** (John 16:13). There is going to be an accelerated revelation of the truth. Jesus said, ***"I am the way, the truth, and the life,"*** (John 14:6). This is not an academic pursuit, but a spiritual revelation. This will not be given to a few as in the Old Testament, but all distinctions are broken down in the New Covenant.

You qualify! We are in ***the last days.*** Everything is yours because Christ is yours. Would you embrace His Spirit? Would you be embraced by His Spirit?

Acts 2:22

THE PROOF

On the Feast Day of Pentecost God restored to mankind the intimacy of His presence. It was the climax of His dreams for mankind and His purpose throughout the Old and New Testaments. The beginning was small. Only one hundred and twenty experienced His fullness at the start. What happened was so powerful it demanded explanation. Peter, moved by the Holy Spirit, stands to preach the revelation of God. He presents his text from the prophecy of Joel and then moves into his sermon.

Peter proclaims three verses of revelation and then supports it with a quotation from David (Psalms 16:8-11). The grammar structure of these three verses is significant (Acts 2:22-24). The opening statement of the verses presents to us a simple statement. ***"Men of Israel, hear these words;"*** (Acts 2:22). Then the rest of the three verses is one long sentence. It is somewhat complicated by its length; thus it can be confusing. The main subject of the sentence is a reflective pronoun which can be translated "self." It is "self" in all persons such as myself, yourself, or himself. It is used for emphasis. It sets the individual apart from everything else. It is therefore translated in our passage as ***you yourselves*** (Acts 2:22). This is not a general statement about the people of the world. Peter addresses the Jews who are in the temple area. They have surrounded the hundred and twenty who have just experienced Pentecost. What Peter says applies directly to them.

The main verb of the sentence is ***know*** (Acts 2:22). The English word ***know*** is a translation of the Greek word "oida." It means "to see, perceive, or apprehend." It can have the idea of physically seeing, but goes much deeper than sight. It is an inward grasping and understanding of the happening being perceived. This concept becomes the major thrust of Peter's message. He is not proposing new information to them or uncovering a hidden doctrine. It is not impossible for the Jews to see the truth though they are possessed by their tradition. They still have a chance. Peter literally says to them, "I am only telling you what you already know and understand! The only way this truth can confuse you is for you to choose confusion. You refuse to know!"

The same is true for us. What I do not know is not a problem for me. Herein lays my difficulty. I do know and refuse to obey. The thundering message of "prevenient grace" is light. This has come to all of us. He reveals Himself to everyone. Have we responded to His revelation? Are we walking in all of the light we have received? The message of Peter is only a presentation of what we already know and understand.

What is this revelation already revealed? It is the revelation of the person of ***Jesus of Nazareth.*** Peter opens with a short sentence, and the very first words of his lengthy sentence is ***Jesus of Nazareth.*** It is in the accusative case. This means it acts like a direct object which receives the action of the verb. Since the main verb is ***know***, Jesus becomes the focus of that action. The revelation of God is focused in this Person. If anything is clearly understood and seen of God, it is through this Person. The only possible avenue of insight into God is through Jesus. I am not speaking of a vision or dream which came to a special prophet. This is not what someone has told us they think they may have seen. This is not the opinion of a small group of people attempting to lure others. This is about ***Jesus of Nazareth.***

Peter does not present Jesus as "Jesus, the Son of God,"

though He certainly is that Person. He is not portrayed as the second member of the Triune Godhead, although this too is true. He is ***Jesus of Nazareth.*** He is literally "Jesus, the Nazarene." He is one of us. He has a birth certificate and a grandfather. A city of vile reputation is His hometown. Upon hearing Jesus was from Nazareth, Nathanael said, *"Can anything good come out of Nazareth?"* (John 1:46). He does not come to us as One from the highest, but One from the lowest. We do not see Him as One well connected, but One who is alone.

The very next words in the Greek text follow the English translation. They are ***a Man.*** This is translated from one Greek word which is also in the accusative case. This means it is a direct object also. These Jews not only know ***Jesus of Nazareth***, but they also know He was ***a Man.*** They experienced the miracles of Jesus. They heard His teachings. They were a part of the group responsible for the crucifixion of Christ (Acts 2:36-37). Jesus was not an historical figure about whom they read. He certainly was not an angel who appeared and disappeared from among them at various times. He was not the resurrected form of an Old Testament prophet, and He was not a ghost. Jesus was a literal, actual man! This crowd of Jews embraced Him as such. All of their conversations spoke of Him as ***a Man.*** Even the leadership of Israel dealt with Him as ***a Man.***

While there were certainly a variety of aspects concerning the presence of ***Jesus of Nazareth, a Man,*** there is only one thing which we must consider according to the text (Acts 2:22)! He is ***a Man attested by God to you*** (Acts 2:22). This statement forms an accusative phrase which receives the action of the main verb, ***know.*** The Greek word translated ***attested*** is actually a participle. In this case, it acts like an adjective giving content to ***a Man.*** It becomes clear that whatever is going on in this ***Man*** called Jesus, it is coming from God. The Greek word translated ***by*** is "apo." Its primary translation is "from." It basically means the going forth or proceeding of one object from another. In this case, the attesting is coming from God, the Father.

The Greek word translated *to* is "eis." It has the primary idea of motion into any place or thing. It is normally translated "in" or "into." First of all there is the action of what you already know and have experienced. This action is acting upon this **Man** called Jesus. He is an individual who is *attested*. This actually comes through or from the person of God. It is so personal that God has brought this to you as an individual. There is no way to say, "I did not know." This is not over your head. God has revealed it personally to you. You know!

The entire thrust of this idea seems to depend upon the word *attested*. It is for that reason we must thoroughly grasp its meaning and significance. The basic Greek word means "to show or display." The Greek word in our text has "apo" as a prefix. This gives it the idea of coming from someone or something. This Greek verb only occurs four times in the New Testament. These four times give us the various usages of the word. Paul said, **"For I think that God has displayed us, the apostles, last, as men condemned to death;** (1 Corinthians 4:9). Our Greek word is here translated **has displayed.** Here it has the idea of shown or displayed in terms of appointed or caused to be. The idea of appointment usually has to do with a high office such as a king or overseer. But the Divine action is strangely varied with a different set of values. God has appointed or made Paul and the apostles as objects of death. They are participating in the very fate of Jesus in suffering and death. This is the reversal of rank found only in the Kingdom of God.

Paul describes a coming day when the **man of sin** or **the son of perdition** will exalt himself. There will come a time when he will exalt himself as God, **so that he sits as God in the temple of God, showing himself that he is God** (2 Thessalonians 2:3-4). Our Greek word here gives the idea of displayed or showing, but it has the undercurrent of proving. He is displayed as God so he is authenticated as God because of where he is sitting.

The Proof | **Acts 2:22**

The final two times our word is used in the New Testament are in the Book of Acts. In the latter part of Acts, Paul is again in trouble with the Jews. He is brought before King Festus. The Jews **laid many serious complaints against Paul, which they could not prove** (Acts 25:7). You can see the usage of the Greek word translated **prove**. There is no evidence to convict Paul of the charges. The idea of show or display is certainly present, but it goes beyond that concept. There is a purpose involved which is to authenticate or validate.

Now the fourth place for the use of this Greek word is found in our passage. *"Men of Israel, hear these words: Jesus of Nazareth, a Man attested by God to you,"* (Acts 2;22). We can plainly see that Jesus was displayed or shown before them. He is **the express image of His person** (Hebrews 1:3). **He is the image of the invisible God** (Colossians 1:15). But this showing was for a distinct purpose. There was a goal or end result in mind. God was **attesting**, authenticating, verifying, and proving **Jesus of Nazareth, a Man.** Consider the translation from the Amplified New Testament: *You men of Israel, listen to what I have to say: Jesus of Nazareth, a Man accredited and pointed out and shown forth and commended and attested to you by God* (Acts 2:22).

The impact of the statement is that God, the Father, is accrediting, pointing out, proving, authenticating, validating, showing forth, and commending something which evidently was very important to Him. Perhaps it was the great power of God. Through Jesus, God the Father attempts to prove to the world His great power. Or maybe it is love. Perhaps through Jesus God wants to prove that He really does love mankind. The list could go on and on. However, according to our passage God is only proving one single thing. It is **Jesus of Nazareth, a Man!** God is accrediting, pointing out, proving, authenticating, validating, showing forth, and commending **Jesus of Nazareth, a Man.**

The focus of God is upon Jesus. Everything He does through Jesus is to promote, lift up, and proclaim Jesus. He is proving

Jesus! In order to grasp the full meaning of this, we will divide our study into two sections.

He Is The Messiah

In proving or attesting, ***Jesus of Nazareth, a Man,*** God the Father is authenticating who Jesus is. He is the Messiah. Do you realize how long the Father has been waiting to bring this one Man into this moment? In Genesis the record is given us of the sin of man. Adam and Eve violated the very desire and heart God had for them. But God would not let them go their own way. The dominant theme is that He promised redemption to them. He promised that the covenant relationship He had with them would be restored. This redemption would not come from an outside source, not even angelic beings. Even God could not set on His throne and manufacture this redemption. Man had gotten us into this mess and man would have to get us out. God promised that redemption would come from the victory the seed of woman would have over Satan. God assured Adam and Eve that redemption and restoration would be a reality in their lives and the history of their seed (Genesis 3:14-20). The Seed of the woman would restore, continue, and bring to full fruition God's Kingdom plans and goals. Jesus is this Seed!

Jesus is the **Man.** He is the One about whom the prophets have spoken. He is the One the universe has been groaning to embrace. Throughout the Old Testament, God kept the seed line open. God guarded and protected the coming of this One **Man.** He is the One God promised to sit on the throne of King David (Acts 2:30). He is the One God exalted to the right hand of the Father (Acts 2:33). He is the One God made Lord and Christ (Acts 2:36). The activity of God the Father is focused on this one **Man.** John the Baptist was made aware of this fact. He cried out, ***"Behold! The Lamb of God who takes away the sin of the*** *world! This is He of whom I said, 'After me comes a Man who is preferred before me, for He was before me,'"* (John 1:29-30).

In our passage, God the Father is approving, authenticating, and proving Jesus as this **Man.** He has done it through His life *by miracles, wonders and signs which God did through Him in your midst* (Acts 2:22). He has also done it through His death. This *Man* was *delivered by the determined purpose and foreknowledge of God* (Acts 2:23). This proof was also found in His resurrection. This *Man* is One *whom God raised up, having loosed the pains of death, because it was not possible that He should be held by it* (Acts 2:24).

Everything God has dreamed for mankind is found in this one **Man.** The phrase "in Christ" is used around two hundred times in the New Testament. This phrase is found eight times in Galatians, thirty-four times in Ephesians, and eighteen times in Colossians. A number of these references are not in the sense of incorporation but in the sense of instrumental. God has taken everything He wants us to have and placed it "in Christ." Christ is what He wants us to have! He *has blessed us with every spiritual blessing in the heavenly places in Christ* (Ephesians 1:3). The first chapter of the Book of Colossians is a list of those things found in the person of Christ, this **Man.** In Him we have *redemption through His blood, the forgiveness of sins* (Colossians 1:14). *He is the image of the invisible God, the firstborn over all creation* (Colossians 1:15). He is the great Creator. In fact, *all things were created through Him and for Him* (Colossians 1:16). *He is before all things, and in Him all things consist* (Colossians 1:17). *And He is the head of the body, the church* (Colossians 1:18). The list goes on and on.

This is not about what Jesus has done or will do! This is about the Person of Christ! He is the One who is being proven, *attested*, accredited, pointed out, authenticated, validated, shown forth, and commended. God wants to convince us of Jesus. The message God gave the prophets in the Old Testament was Jesus.

Part Three: In My Eye

The message of the New Testament is Jesus. There are no activities of God or possibilities of touching God outside of Jesus. Jesus said, *"I am the way, the truth, and the life. No one comes to the Father except through Me,"* (John 14:6). Do you grasp the all inclusiveness of Jesus? He is everything! No wonder Paul cried, *For in Him dwells all the fullness of the Godhead bodily; and you are complete in Him, who is the head of all principality and power* (Colossians 2:9-10).

He Is The Prototype

God, the Father, is authenticating the actual Person of Christ. He is the fulfillment of the plans of God as revealed in the Old Testament. This is summarized in the term, Messiah. However, the key aspect of the position of Messiah is the concept of prototype. Peter definitely proclaims this in his message. It is an explanation of what has just happened to them on this Day of Pentecost. God has come to indwell them. The Holy Spirit has been poured out upon them. What does this mean exactly? Jesus is the explanation. Peter, throughout his message, consistently proclaims Jesus as *a Man*. But He is *a Man* through whom God is acting! This is plainly seen in His life (Acts 2:22), His death (Acts 2:23), and in His resurrection (Acts 2:24). Everything which happens in the life of Christ occurs because God the Father acts through Him. This is what a man filled with the Spirit of God looks like!

Adam was created to be this, but he yielded to self-centeredness. He became the source of his own living. God needed another man to restore and rebirth His dream. He decided not to create another man as He did Adam. God decided to become that *Man!* He emptied Himself of all He had as God and became *a Man*. He was *a Man* totally submitted and surrendered to the sourcing of God. Nothing would happen through Him but what God produced. He would be filled with the Holy Spirit, a product of God indwelling *a Man.*

Could such a dream be possible? It did not work the first time; would it work the second time? What would be different about the second Adam? The second Adam would need to correct, make up, pay for, and redeem all the first Adam produced by his sin. He would need to live in total response to the Spirit of God and thus produce an entirely new breed of people. He would be the prototype of a new kind of man. God desired to redeem all of mankind, but He must do it through *a Man.* Jesus is that *Man.* God proved in Christ that the fullness of the Holy Spirit works. Man can be filled with God and be what he ought to be. Peter proclaims to the crowd, "What just happened to us, the one hundred and twenty, is what was taking place in Christ. It can now happen in you!" God has proven it!

The great crowd was *cut to the heart* (Acts 2:37). They wanted to know what they should do in response to this truth. Peter immediately points them to Jesus. They are to repent which means to give up the former thought and embrace the second thought (Acts 2:38). Jesus is the second thought! They are to be baptized into Jesus (Acts 2:38). They are to seek Jesus! I am joining them in seeking Him now.

Acts 2:22

THE PROOF - HIS LIFE

It is a new experience for the Jews of the Dispersion. They have just witnessed the outside God coming to live inside mankind in the lives of the one hundred and twenty disciples. Many manifestations of the occasion have raised a question in their minds. It is not a casual question. The question springs from the burning desire within them to experience the new thing God is doing. They are intense. They are seeking! Peter gives clear explanation under the strong inspiration of the Holy Spirit. This message will *cut* them *to the heart* (Acts 2:37).

The opening statement in Peter's message is focused on Jesus. He strongly emphasizes their present knowledge of Jesus, so he does not give them new information. After all, Christ lived His life in their midst. Peter clearly says that Jesus was *a Man.* He was born during their lifetime. He lived His life among them. They considered Him a man as they crucified Him. But Peter's statement to them is about *Jesus of Nazareth, a Man attested by God to you* (Acts 2:22). Through the life of Christ (Acts 2:22), through His death (Acts 2:23), and through His resurrection (Acts 2:24) God was proving the Person of Jesus. God was not attempting to prove His great power; He had already accomplished this in creation (Romans 1:20). He was not declaring His great wisdom; for all He made is manifesting it (Psalms 104:24). He is accrediting, pointing out, proving, authenticating, validating, showing forth, and commending

Jesus of Nazareth, a Man. This is His single focus!

This is such a key truth. God has placed all of His plans and purposes in the Person of Jesus. There is nothing or no one else! Jesus is the total focus of God. Everything God promotes is Jesus, and Jesus fulfills God's plan. There is no crisis where He will refer you to someone else. If you come to God with any question or issue, He is going to give you Jesus. It is very plain in the Scriptures that Christ is His eternal focus (Revelation 22:13).

What exactly is God's proof? The life of Christ is the beginning of the validation.

Miracles, Wonders, and Signs

Peter begins with the miracles, wonders and signs of Jesus. He opens His message with these words. *"**Jesus of Nazareth, a Man attested by God to you by miracles, wonders, and signs which God did through Him in your midst, as you yourselves also know"*** (Acts 2:22). This identical statement is made by the author of the Book of Hebrews. He spends an entire chapter presenting Jesus as superior to angels (Hebrews 1). He quotes scripture after scripture to validate it. He begins his second chapter with a severe warning. It is an appeal to focus on Jesus ***lest we drift away*** (Hebrews 2:1). In his warning he establishes a contrast. A word came from the angels which was so sure that everyone who disobeyed it was punished (Hebrews 2:2). If this was true for them, there is one possibility we shall escape. We have received greater revelation. The revelation which came to us was ***first ... spoken by the Lord*** (Hebrews 2:3). It was then ***confirmed to us by those who heard Him*** (Hebrews 2:3). This fact is added above all of this, ***God also bearing witness both with signs and wonders, with various miracles*** (Hebrews 2:4).

The phrase, ***wonders and signs,*** is found some thirty times in the New Testament. These two words are normally used together.

In the Book of Acts, the phrase, **wonders and signs**, appears four times, while **signs and wonders** is mentioned five times. These two words refer not to different classes of miracles, but to different aspects of the same miracle. The idea of **wonders** is the aspect of the miracle which is startling, imposing, or amazing. It is translated from the root Greek word which means "to keep, watch, connoting that which, due to its extraordinary character, is apt to be observed and kept in the memory." It is the overwhelming or shocking character of an event. The idea of **signs** is the spiritual end and purpose of the event. It is to lead to something out of and beyond itself. Thus a miracle is valuable not so much for what it is but for what it indicates of the grace and power of the Doer.

This is all verified by the word **miracles** in our text. This Greek word is where we get our word dynamite. It is used one hundred and nineteen times in the New Testament. However, in the New King James Version it is only translated "miracles" seven times. In the Gospels it is most often translated "mighty works." The majority of times throughout the remaining New Testament it is translated "power." In our modern day understanding the translation of **miracles** in our passage is a bit misleading. No doubt Peter includes the great miracle feats of Christ, but he emphasizes the flow of the resource of God which accomplished these and other activities.

What Peter is saying becomes clear when you understand the heart content of each of these three words. There is a captivating amazement about the life of Christ (**wonders**). It is certainly seen in the deeds of His life which point to a spiritual end and purpose, the very Person of God (**signs**). Escaping through Christ is the very flow of the resource of God (**miracles**). Although His ministry activities and His deeds of special miracles are included, the life of Christ is the captivating amazement which points to a spiritual end and is the very flow of the Person of God. Everything about Jesus, His miracles, His relationships, His attitude, His mannerisms, and His every day living, all shock you and cause you to see the wonder of the Father.

This truth is further highlighted by the fact that all three of the words are in the dative case. There are several usages for the dative case. The most frequent corresponds to our use of the direct object. The direct object is what receives the action of the verb, but Peter has already given this to us in the Person of Jesus. ***Jesus of Nazareth, a Man attested by God to you*** is an accusative phrase which acts as the direct object. Now Peter gives us this additional phrase which begins with ***miracles, wonders, and signs.*** In our text the dative case of this phrase is an instrumental dative. It is used to indicate the means by which a verb's action takes place. It generally corresponds to the English prepositions "with" and "by." Thus in our text Peter's statement is translated ***by miracles, wonders, and signs.*** God authenticates, proves, attests, points out, and commends Jesus by the very flow of His resource through the life of Christ. This flow astounds and amazes the world and points to the spiritual end of the Father.

Another startling fact is that the Greek word translated ***miracles*** in our text is the same Greek word translated ***power*** in Jesus' description of the coming of the Holy Spirit within the believer. Jesus said, ***"But you shall receive power when the Holy Spirit has come upon you: and you shall be witnesses to Me in Jerusalem, and in all Judea and Samaria, and to the end of the earth,"*** (Acts 1:8). Whatever the Father was doing in Christ is now happening in the believer. Whatever the Father was doing in and through the believer was started in Christ. The Father proved this life in Christ as He authenticated, pointed out, attested, and commended this reality. Jesus Christ is God's proof of man's possibility.

The Greek word translated ***miracles*** (Acts 2:22) and ***power*** (Acts 1:8) is "dunamis." All Greek words which come from the same Greek root word "duna" have the meaning "of being able or capable." It even has the idea of "to will." There is a contrasting Greek word which will help us grasp the concept. It is "ischus."

This Greek word stresses the fact of the ability while "dunamis" stresses the accomplishment. "Ischus" emph-asizes the actual inherent power, while "dunamis" implies ability or capacity to perform.

If you picture "ischus" as having substance or being a thing, then you can picture the use of that substance of power to accomplish something (dunamis). Jesus promised we will have the use of this substance. It is not that we will possess the power as if it is ours. The activity, demonstration, and accomplishment of this power happens through us as it did in Christ. God, the Father, is the substance of the power and Jesus is the stage upon which it is performed. The life of Christ is the proof that sons of God can exist in the flesh. Peter cries out to those who are hungry. The life of God flowing and sourcing a man is proven in Christ and is now promised to you. You can experience it as well. He cries, *"For the promise is to you and to your children, and to all who are afar off, as many as the Lord our God will call"* (Acts 2:39).

God Did

Peter continues to highlight this proof through the life of Christ. *"Jesus of Nazareth, a Man attested by God to you by miracles, wonders, and signs which God did through Him in your midst, as you yourselves also know"* (Acts 2:22). Notice the repetitive statement. The focus is on the activity and sourcing of God, the Father. Jesus is *a Man attested by God to you.* It happened through the instrument of *miracles, wonders, and signs which God did through Him.*

It intrigued me to discover the Greek word translated *did* is "poieo." We have highlighted this word repeatedly in previous studies. It is always used for the activities of Jesus. It accentuates not just the product of the deed, but the internal nature and sourcing of the deed itself. It is often used to speak of trees bearing fruit (Matthew 3:10). It is contrasted with duty, routine, and obligation which is something of an outside pressure and sourcing.

This same Greek word is used to describe God creating the heavens and the earth (Acts 4:24; 7:50; 14:15; 17:24). The physical creation came from the very internal nature of God. It is a reflection of the character and nature of who God is! No wonder Paul argues, *For since the creation of the world His invisible attributes are clearly seen, being understood by the things that are made, even His eternal power and Godhead,* (Romans 1:20).

Peter reveals that the attraction, amazement, and spiritual end of the sourcing which produced the life of Jesus is God, the Father. No wonder Jesus said to His disciples, *"If you had known Me, you would have known My Father also; and from now on you know Him and have seen Him,"* (John 14:7). Jesus is not the Father, but His life is the product of the Father's sourcing. Jesus went on to say, *"He who has seen Me has seen the Father,"* (John 14:9). No wonder Paul describes Jesus as **the image of the invisible God** (Colossians 1:15). The writer of the Book of Hebrews wrote that Jesus was the **brightness of His glory and the express image of His person** (Hebrews 1:3).

Peter cries out that the flowing resource which amazes us and points us to a spiritual end is God, the Father, demonstrating in and through Christ? This is his explanation of Pentecost. The one hundred and twenty believers experienced the very same thing in their lives. What they saw take place in Christ is now happening within them. As Jesus is sourced by the Father, so now the hundred and twenty disciples are being sourced by the Spirit of the Father. This is the beginning of the new level! Everything God has been doing up to this time is for this purpose. This same relationship is now promised to us (Acts 2:39).

Through Him

Peter is not done highlighting this truth. He restates it again. He proclaims, *"Men of Israel, hear these words: Jesus of Nazareth, a Man attested by God to you by miracles, wonders, and signs which God did through Him,"* (Acts 2:22). This Greek word translated *through* is very specific. It is a primary preposition which denotes the channel of an act. It is used for the instrument or intermediate cause. It highlights that which intervenes between the act of the will and the effect, and through which the effect comes. Thus it means "through, by, by means of."

Peter is very clear in what he proposes. Within the very nature of God, the Father, there is a creative power which is flowing through *a Man*. It produces an amazement and wonder in everyone who experiences this *Man*. The flow from the Father through this *Man* is for the purpose of proving, attesting, authenticating, pointing out, validating, and commending this *Man*. This *Man* is the channel or instrument through which God proves His supreme purpose for man. God wants to indwell man. Man was not built by God to source himself; but he was created for the sole purpose of being sourced by God. The realization of this has been lost for so long, it is questioned. Perhaps it is just a religious dream. Who will dare propose its possibility? Jesus is the answer. The reality of God living His life through mankind is proven in the Person of Jesus!

It started with Christ, but now has spread to the one hundred and twenty disciples. However, this is not intended for a few. The Jews of the Dispersion are included. It is to their children as well. But it is *to all who are afar off, as many as the Lord our God will call* (Acts 2:39). This is a promise!

In Your Midst

There is one more phrase which Peter adds to the life of Christ. *"Men of Israel, hear these words: Jesus of Nazareth, a Man attested by God to you by miracles, wonders, and signs which God did through Him in your midst, as you yourselves also know"* (Acts 2:22). Let me remind you of the subject and the verb of this long sentence. The Greek reflective pronoun translated *you yourselves* is the subject. The verb is the Greek word translated, *know.* Peter is only reminding them of what they have already grasped and understood. This is not a new revelation. As he closes this section of the life of Christ, he reminds them again of this reality. The life of Christ was lived *in your midst.*

The frequent use of this phrase in the Gospel of Luke and the Book of Acts cannot be overlooked. It underscores something remarkable and has strong theological implications. At the age of twelve, Jesus sits *in the midst* of the teachers in the temple (Luke 2:46). Jesus, the Master, assumes the role of a servant *in the midst* of His disciples (Acts 2:27). The disciples were terrified because Jesus Himself stood *in the midst* of them in His resurrected form (Luke 24:36). These are only examples of this emphasis.

This phrase is used immediately in the beginning of the Book of Acts. On the fortieth day of Christ's resurrection appearance, He is present among them (Acts 1:4). At the first recorded business meeting of the early church, Peter stood up *in the midst of the disciples* (Acts 1:15). This same emphasis is given in Peter *standing up with the eleven* as he preaches this great explanation to the Jews of the Dispersion (Acts 2:14).

Not surprisingly, Luke emphasizes this in Peter's sermon. The flowing resource of God, the Father, produces amazement and points to a spiritual end through *a Man* and was done *in*

the midst. This was not accomplished in a vacuum. It is not ancient mythology. This is not drug induced. What God dreams of accomplishing in our lives is "a daily living kind of thing." There is no way to side step the truth. God has proven, attested, authenticated, pointed out, validated, and commended this ***Man*** called Jesus. God is seen in His life. He proved once and for all that God can actually indwell us and live His life through us. We can be filled with the very nature of God. The results can be awesome to our world. Our families can be amazed and experience again the very flow of the Person of God. This is a promise which is to us (Acts 2:39).

Acts 2:23

THE PROOF - HIS DEATH: A DIVINE PLAN

How do you explain Pentecost? When you see someone filled with the Spirit of God, how do you explain what is happening within that person? The Spirit of Jesus has moved upon Peter to bring clarity to the Jews of the Dispersion and to us! This is not a matter of Peter's opinion. It is not about cultural environment. In reality, God gives us His explanation of this great event.

Pentecost must not be understood as simply an event. But this is true with all of the major events in the life of Christ. We see this forcibly in the cross. The crucifixion of Christ was not just a day in the life of Christ. The cross was not an experience for which Christ prepared and then from which He had to recuperate. This was the style of His life. He always lived the cross. It was fundamental in His thinking. It was His attitude and the expression of all his mannerisms. The cross style was the constant expression of the life of God living through Christ. That was Peter's explanation of Pentecost.

This same truth is found in the resurrection event. It was not just a great experience for Christ. The life of God flowing through a man could not be contained in death regardless of when or where it was confronted. The death of demonic possession could not survive the presence of the living God flowing through Christ (Matthew 8:29). *A Man* filled with the Spirit of God could go to the very heart of hell, but hell could not possess Him. He must be released *because it was not possible that He should be held by it* (Acts 2:24). The resurrection took place moment by moment in the life of Christ as He lived in a world filled with death.

This is true for the ascension or exaltation of Christ to the right hand of the Father. It was not just a great celebration to remember. The King who has been reigning from before time establishes a whole new Kingdom. In living through the fullness of the Spirit, Jesus actually opens a door to an entirely new breed, species of humanity. Pentecost is not simply an event for a moment. It is revelation of the heart of God. He establishes His Kingdom. It is not an event; it is a style!

How can we comprehend what is happening in one hundred and twenty men and women on this Pentecost Day? The explanation is based upon all that God had done in previous history. Peter begins with the text for his sermon as found in the prophecy of Joel. Pentecost is a product or fulfillment of the plan God has been working throughout the Old Testament. Everything has brought us to this point. Pentecost is the fulfillment of the dreams of God. He brings man back to the state in which He originally created Him. This is the restoration of mankind back to the full image of God.

The opening sentence of Peter's message is very simple. He says, *"Men of Israel, hear these words,"* (Acts 2:22). The second sentence, however, seems to be very complicated. It is a lengthy sentence which covers three verses. It appears the main verb is *know*, while the subject is *you yourselves*. Peter reminds them of what they already understand and have experienced. He forces them to verify the reality of what he proposes.

The focus of Peter's presentation is *Jesus of Nazareth*. But it is not *Jesus of Nazareth,* the Son of God (although this is true). He is *Jesus of Nazareth, a Man.* Certainly the audience being addressed understood this. They embraced Jesus as *a Man*. They crucified Him as *a Man*. They did not consider Him an angel or a ghost. However, there is one factor Peter desperately wants this crowd to understand. It is *Jesus of Nazareth, a Man attested by God to you*. The action of God was to prove Jesus. All the plans of God are fulfilled in Jesus. There is nothing outside of Christ. Jesus was not one of several plans; He was the plan. If you ask God for any solution to any problem, He is going to give you Jesus! He has no other answer.

How does this explain Pentecost? *Jesus of Nazareth, a Man* is God's explanation of Pentecost. Jesus was *a Man* filled with God. He was totally sourced by God. There was nothing happening in or through Jesus which was not the result of the Father. Jesus was the visible expression of the invisible Father. The sourcing of the Father through Jesus created amazement in His world which pointed everyone to the Father. All that is happening in Pentecost must be understood in the light of Christ. Peter explains Pentecost through Jesus' life (Acts 2:22), in Jesus' death (Acts 2:23), and by His resurrection (Acts 2:24). He begins with Pentecost being seen through the lens of the life of Christ. Jesus did not live as He lived because He was God (although He is most certainly God). Jesus' life was a product of what the Father did through Him. The amazing quality of Jesus' life (*wonders*) which pointed to the Father (*signs*) was the very flow of the Father through Christ (*miracles*). God has promised this same relationship to us (Acts 2:39).

Pentecost explained through the life of Christ is simple to understand. As God, the Father, moved through Jesus, *a Man*, He is now moving through us. Jesus was the prototype of what God intended for all of us. But His death presents something of a problem. Should not the power of God moving through Jesus deliver Him from such a cruel death as crucifixion? This particular death is one reserved for criminals, not individuals filled with God. The cross, in essence, is a sign of defeat. If the life of Christ is the wonder of God working through Him, His death is proof it does not win. Why did not the power of God contained within the life of Christ deliver Him from the cross? It would appear that God working and living through an individual would keep that person from the results of evil plans, sickness, and all things from the evil one. One can certainly understand the accusations at the foot of the cross. *"If you are the Son of God come down from the cross,"* they cried (Matthew 27:40). Others continued yelling, *"If He is the King of Israel, let Him now come down from the cross, and we will believe Him,"* (Matthew 27:42).

It is very important to consider that the writers of the Gospel accounts did not attempt to hide or belittle the cross. Matthew wrote His Gospel account as proof that Jesus was the Kingly Messiah. His main argument is one of authority. Over one half of his chapters are dedicated to the subject of the cross. He believed that the cross did not diminish the Divine authority, but increased it! How could this possibly be logical? Because it was planned! Jesus was not a victim; He was a victor!

Join me now in carefully investigating this study's verse (Acts 2:23).

Him

The Greek word translated *Him* is in the accusative case, a direct object (Acts 2:23). This relates directly to **Jesus of Nazareth, a Man,** which is in the same case. It can be translated "this person" or "the same." There is no question to whom Peter refers. The ones Peter addresses definitely know Christ as *a Man*, and they know He was crucified by their hands. The dominant subject is **Him.** Everything in this verse points to **Him.**

Being Delivered

The Greek word translated *being delivered* is also in the accusative case which makes it a part of this same direct object. However, this Greek word is not a verb. I realize that the way it is translated in our English text, it may appear as a verb. It is an adjective which gives content to *Him*. Therefore, this verse might read: "Him, the Delivered One."

The Greek word translated *being delivered* is only found in this passage in the New Testament. It is a compound word. It begins with the Greek word translated "from," and the Greek word meaning "given out or over, surrendered." This concept is given to us in abundance throughout the New Testament by the use of other words. Paul wrote, *"He who did not spare His own Son, but delivered Him up for us all, how shall He not with Him also freely give us all things?"* (Romans 8:32). The Greek word translated *delivered up* is an intensified form of "give." It designates the act whereby something or someone is transferred into the possession of another. This word is used one hundred and nineteen times in the New Testament.

By the Determined Purpose and Foreknowledge of God

What was the means of Christ's crucifixion? According to Peter it was *by the determined purpose and foreknowledge of God.* This statement is a dative clause, an instrumental dative. In the Greek language the word *by* is not there. It is used in the English translation because of the dative case. Peter explains the means of delivery. However, the article "the" is definitely present in the Greek writing and gives this phrase great strength.

The Greek word translated *determined* is a verb in the

participle mood. In this case it acts as an adjective giving content to the ***purpose and foreknowledge of God.*** It occurs mostly in the writings of Luke. It is only found twice in the rest of the New Testament (Romans 1:4 and Hebrews 4:7). God is always the subject of this verb with only one exception (Acts 11:29). Luke consistently uses this word to refer to God's great plan of salvation. It comes from the word meaning "boundary, limit." It means to mark out definitely, determine, appoint, constitute. It is the ***purpose and foreknowledge of God*** which marked out or appointed the death of Christ on the cross.

The Greek word (boule) translated ***purpose*** is dominantly used in the writings of Luke. It appears only three other times (1 Corinthians, Ephesians, and Hebrews). This word is used for the will, purpose, or intention as the result of reflection. This is distinguished from another Greek word (thelema) as seen in the executing of that counsel. Is it possible to imagine the Trinity in council? The conclusion was the cross event.

The Greek word translated ***foreknowledge*** is an important and often misunderstood New Testament word. Most often we consider it simply knowing something before it happens. This would mean the great omniscience of God knew about the crucifixion of Christ before it happened. This gave God the opportunity to respond to this action with a counter action. However, the concept of this Greek word is beyond this simple "fore" knowledge. In this verse ***foreknowledge*** is in the instrumental dative case. This shows that it was the means by which Christ was delivered to His enemies. It is not that God simply knew of the crucifixion; He actually caused it. This verse is not about God seeing ahead of time what will take place; He is actively involved in bringing about His plan.

Let us examine ***purpose*** and ***foreknowledge*** together. God, through His omniscience, saw the crucifixion. In His sovereignty He had already designed a redemptive plan which focused on Christ. This plan came from the reflective counsel of the Trinity.

He did not bend His plan to fit the activities of men; He encompassed the activities of men and bent them to fit His plan. This means the cross was the plan of God; it was the fulfillment of prophecy. This means God is actively responsible for the crucifixion of Christ.

How does this explain Pentecost? God, the Father, is proving Christ. Christ is the proof of the fullness of the God's Spirit. Here is how the Spirit-filled life appears. God proved Jesus by the amazing aspect of His daily living (**wonders**). He also proved Jesus by pointing us to a purpose beyond the activities He did (**signs**). It was caused by the consistent flow of His presence through this **Man** (**miracles**). But God also proved this same **Man** through His death. God flowed and lived His presence through the very essence of tragedy. Crucifixion was not in the best interest of Jesus' comfort. From the view of a world, things were not working out for Christ. It looked as if all of the events in the last week of His life have gone in reverse. Yet in the midst of the pain, suffering, and tragedy God was producing His supreme counsel through Christ.

If we are to understand the fullness of the Spirit of Christ in this setting, we must shift our focus. The Christian movement has focused on the comfort, happiness, and health of the individual. It is as if the outside God getting inside is for the purpose of fulfilling the individual. God lives within me to protect me, inspire me, fulfill me, and make me a wonderful person. All of these things may happen as a by-product of His presence. But the focus of the indwelling of God within the individual is the fulfillment of **the determined purpose and foreknowledge of God**. God has a plan which does not always focus on my immediate happiness and comfort. The fullness of the Spirit is not for the purpose of utilizing the power of God for my benefit; but for the dreams of God's eternal designs to be accomplished through my flesh. That may produce immediate discomfort, death, and denouncement.

Part Three: In My Eye

Will I allow Christ to flow His life through me for the fulfillment of His dreams? Will I abandon my personal agenda for the accomplishment of His sovereign plan? Will I set aside my personal comfort to embrace the necessary suffering of His desires? Is this what Paul meant when he cried, *"that I may know Him and the power of His resurrection, and the fellowship of His sufferings, being conformed to His death,"* (Philippians 3:10)? Listen to his call, *"We are hard pressed on every side, yet not crushed; we are perplexed, but not in despair; persecuted, but not forsaken; struck down, but not destroyed – always carrying about in the body the dying of the Lord Jesus, that the life of Jesus also may be manifested in our body. For we who live are always delivered to death for Jesus' sake, that the life of Jesus also may be manifested in our mortal flesh,"* (2 Corinthians 4:8-11).

The fullness of the Spirit is not a seeking of pleasure, comfort, and happiness. It is a seeking of His life manifested in and through us as it was in Jesus. Would the life of Christ not be manifested in our flesh in much the same pattern as it was in His own flesh? Christ in you is not for the purpose of self-satisfaction. This is not about solving all my problems and making everything for my benefit. God has always had bigger plans than this. Will I allow Him to fulfill His dreams through me regardless of the cost? God proved Jesus as *a Man* through whom He could fulfill His dream in the world. Will I be such a man?

Acts 2:23

THE PROOF - HIS DEATH: MAN'S ACTION

Academically understanding the crucifixion of Christ is no simple task. However, a spiritual understanding of this event drowns one in the depth of its reality. One can stay on the surface of the physical suffering or plunge into the heavenly realm where life is being changed. It is here we intend to journey. I am not sure how capable I personally am to make this journey; therefore, we must depend as always on Christ who has already walked this path.

Under the inspiration of the Holy Spirit, Peter is leading us. His message (Acts 2:17-39) must be understood as an explanation of the Pentecost event. One hundred and twenty men and women have just experienced the outpouring of the Spirit of Christ. The Jews of the Dispersion, numbering over three thousand, have been witnesses. In their amazement, they ask, *"Whatever could this mean?"* (Acts 2:13). Here in the context of this perplexity and questioning, Peter gives us insight into the heart of Pentecost.

The second sentence of his sermon is long and complex (Acts 2:22-24). The heart of the matter focuses on **Jesus of Nazareth, a Man attested by God to you** (Acts 2:22). The Greek word translated **attested** means "to display, show, validate, commend, and authenticate." What has just taken place in the lives of the believers has already been displayed, validated, or authenticated. This was done by God in the Man called Christ. He is the explanation of Pentecost. What took place in Him is now happening in the believers.

Peter continues in this great sentence to explain how God has proceeded with this proof. It took place in the life of Jesus (Acts 2:22). Jesus' life was a direct result of the flowing resource of the Spirit of God (***miracles***). The sourcing of the Spirit produced an amazement among all who came in contact with the life of Christ (***wonders***), and it always points them back to the Father from whence it came (***signs***). This is Peter's explanation of Pentecost. The believers are experiencing this same flow of the Spirit of God through their lives as Jesus did through His.

It is somewhat more difficult to embrace Peter's next thought (Acts 2:23). As the sourcing of the Holy Spirit produced the life of Christ, He also produces the death of Christ which is equally a demonstration of the resource of God. The activities of Jesus' life validated the reality of Pentecost; His death equally authenticated this filling of the Holy Spirit.

Immediately, this gives us the proper view of the crucifixion of Christ. Jesus was not a victim; He was a victor. As His miraculous life was a fulfillment of the sourcing and plans of God, so His death is the plan of God. God did not see in the future what wicked men were going to do and quickly adjust His plan to accommodate the actions of men. The Trinity actually counseled together and devised the crucifixion plan (***determined purpose***). God did not perceive what man was going to do and adjust His plans to include it; He planned His actions and included man in those plans (***purpose and foreknowledge of God***).

Purpose

There are several major conclusions to be understood from this truth. The first is the purpose of Pentecost. The indwelling of the Spirit of Christ is not for the benefit, aid, pleasure, or comfort of man. God did not create man only to discover he had major flaws. Upon discovering these weaknesses and inabilities God corrected them with the addition of Pentecost. Man was made in the image of God, which of necessity demanded the very indwelling of God's nature and life within man. The original purpose of man was all we see happening in the life and death of Jesus. The focus was never the comfort and pleasure of man's personal life, but the fulfillment of the dream of God. Mankind was to be the display of the very heart and nature of God. Jesus displayed the Father through His life. The visible image of the invisible God was revealed in Christ (Colossians 1:15). Jesus could truthfully say to His disciples, **"He who has seen Me has seen the Father,"** (John 14:9).

This is our destiny. We have the staggering privilege of being the body of God in our day. The issue is not our personal comfort and desires, but the fulfillment of God's dreams and plans. The eternal plan of God contained within the mind of God has come to indwell us. God did not create us and then come up with a plan. God first had a plan and we were created out of that dream. Our destiny is to fulfill the dream of God. Our life is completed in that fulfillment.

An example of this is John the Baptist. He was filled with the Holy Spirit from his birth (Luke 1:15). He was not shaped by his culture; his life was not dictated by traditions. His goal was never comfort or ease. Even in the early, tragic end of a successful ministry, he was being used by this indwelt Spirit. He was the forerunner; he was created by God for this purpose. Of necessity this involved the cross style. There was a call on His life beyond his personal desires. He was filled with God.

God has an eternal plan. If Pentecost is experienced in our lives it will mean the fulfillment of that plan even to the expense of our personal pleasure. We must remember this is not "an add on" for an exclusive few. This is the basic style of

Christianity. This is not "an advanced level" for those who are especially skilled. This is the normal. This is the fulfillment of the destiny of man!

Providence

What Peter is proposing in this one great sentence (Acts 2:22-24) is based upon the Scripture taken from the Book of Psalms (16:8-11). He is constantly saturating his message with the Scriptures. As we read this passage (Acts 2:25-28), the tone of this Scriptural basis becomes very clear. It is one of extreme confidence in the goodness of God. Listen to his words. ***I foresaw the Lord always before my face*** (Acts 2:25). The idea of *foresaw* is literally "to see before us," that is, "as present with us, to regard as being near." It conveys the idea of putting your confidence in someone, relying on him, or expecting assistance from him. The phrase ***always before my face*** expresses the Lord is always present to help me and to deliver me out of all my troubles.

This confidence produces great rejoicing and gladness (Acts 2:26). This was certainly expressed in the life of Christ. The author of the Book of Hebrews instructs us, *"looking unto Jesus, the author and finisher of our faith, who for the joy that was set before Him endured the cross, despising the shame, and has sat down at the right hand of the throne of God,"* (Hebrews 12:2). The wonder of the Spirit-filled life is the ability to look beyond the immediate circumstances to the fulfillment of the will of God, which is always good. The absolute certainty of this goodness is solidly located in the character and heart of God. It has to be good because He is good. This is His dream; it has rushed forth from the very heart of His inner drive. This dream is totally motivated by love, which is His character. Any discomfort for the moment is only for the fulfillment of the great plan of His love. You and I get to be included in this great plan which is really who He is. No wonder there is joy. He is directing and sourcing our living and our dying.

This confidence in the goodness and love of God produces singing in the midnight hours when one is in jail with a beaten back (Acts 16:25). When one is gripped with the fulfillment of the dreams of God, there is joy in the suffering of the cross. Pentecost is the flow of the Spirit of Christ through the life of the believer (***miracles***). It produces amazement (***wonders***) and always points back to Christ (***signs***). However, this same flow of the Spirit may lead us into discomfort and pain. Both can be produced by the flowing life of God through the believer.

Protection

There is one other important factor concerning the sourcing of God that brings us to death. There is great safety here! This is a vital part of the explanation of ***taken by lawless hands, have crucified, and put to death,"*** (Acts 2:23). There is absolutely no attempt on the part of Peter to eliminate the responsibility and guilt of those he addresses. Indeed, the crucifixion of Christ was because of ***the determined purpose and foreknowledge of God.*** It is by the hand of a sovereign God that Jesus was crucified. However, this does not dismiss the willing participation of evil men. They crucified Christ by an act of their free will. With their lips they quoted the law, but with their hands they willingly broke the law. Time after time the Spirit flowed through Jesus to call them to embrace God's Messiah. Time and again they rejected. There is no reduction of guilt (Acts 2:37).

It is amazing to realize that God used ***the lawless hands*** of men to accomplish His Divine purpose, yet never violated their will. The total sovereignty of God is presented alongside the complete responsibility of man. This great paradox is presented repeatedly throughout the Scriptures. It is boldly illustrated in the betrayal of Christ by Judas. Jesus said this about Judas. *"**And truly the Son of Man goes as it has been determined, but woe to that man by whom He is betrayed!**"* (Luke 22:22). Men are responsible not for God's plans but for their own sins.

The order of the Greek words as given in our text becomes very important at this point. Notice the phrase **have taken** is not present in the Greek text. It has been added in order to aid the flow of the English translation. Luke begins the verse with the Greek pronoun translated **Him**. He definitely wants you to understand he is still referring to ***Jesus of Nazareth, a Man***. This is immediately followed by the Greek phrase translated ***by the determined purpose and fore-knowledge of God***. It is then that the Greek adjective, **being delivered**, appears. Remember this adjective modifies the opening pronoun of the verse which refers to Christ as the Delivered One. Immediately following this is the Greek phrase translated ***by lawless hands***. This is the second instrumental dative phrase which expresses the means by which the action of this verse takes place. The next Greek word is translated **have crucified**. This is a Greek verb in the participle form. It is acting as an adjective. However, it is in the nominative case which means it modifies the main subject of the sentence. Peter is literally calling this great crowd the crucifiers. Finally the last Greek word in the text is translated ***put to death***. It is a verb in the indicative mood which means it is a simple statement of fact. This Greek word means simply to kill or murder.

So the structure of this verse is as follows: **Him** (Christ), the **delivered** One, was ***put to death by the determined purpose and foreknowledge of God*** and by ***lawless hands*** of you who ***crucified***. One easily sees that the action of this part of Peter's long sentence is the Greek word translated ***put to death***. Then Peter lists two equally instrumental datives which tell the means by which this was done. One is ***by the determined purpose and foreknowledge of God***; the second is ***by lawless hands***. If our lives are affected or influenced *by lawless hands* of men, are we not constantly experiencing in our lives evil things over which no one has control? The dreams and plans of God are constantly being thwarted because of the interference of wickedness. No one would deny there is a sense in which this is true. Theology teaches us the will of God abides in two categories. There is the primary will of God which was and is His supreme desire. However, there is also the secondary will of God which He accepts. It is the primary will of God that everyone should be saved. However, there is the will of God which accepts the free will of man. This presents the certainty that not all will accept His primary will.

How does this explain Pentecost? Pentecost is about the ***determined purpose and foreknowledge*** of God being accomplished through ***a Man***. It is not about the personal pleasure or comfort of that individual. God's dream and design must be accomplished through man. We have the privilege of linking with and being used by a sovereign God to fulfill the destiny of His creative desire. Nothing can stop this! In the fullness of the Spirit our lives are not determined by the whim of mystical fate. We are not at the mercy of the forces of evil. While our fellow man has free will and is responsible for his response, he will not be allowed to determine or affect the fulfillment of the dreams of God through our lives! The Spirit-filled believer is safe in the dreams of God regardless of how things appear in his circumstances. No wonder the author of the Book of Hebrews calls this "rest," (Hebrews 4). Now we understand why Paul and Silas sang at midnight in the midst of the pain of their beaten backs (Acts 16:25). We can now view the heroes of faith in a new way (Hebrews 11). Those looking forward to and those who actually received were all given vision through the eyes of the Spirit. Nothing could stop them! They were used by God to conquer their world. They became the instruments for the fulfillment of the dreams of God.

Part Three: In My Eye

The staggering reality is that this is not true for the individual outside of Pentecost. If the outside God has not come inside, there is no safety. When I am in charge of my own life and destiny, there is no control. I am not capable of warding off the forces of evil and the **lawless hands** of men. My best intentions and attempts will not be enough to protect. There is no purpose found in the crucifixions of my life. I am being moved from situation to situation by the mystical hand of fate with no reason or destiny. Does this not cause us to go to our knees for our children? There is only one safe place for my family. My children and my spouse must know the fullness of the Spirit.

God has proven this in Christ. What we see in Jesus' life and in His death is now ours. He is the beginning of the new relationship with God. Man can be filled with God. The outside God has come to be inside. We can be like Jesus!

Acts 2:24

THE PROOF - HIS RESURRECTION

The staggering truth of Peter's explanation of Pentecost is before us (Acts 2:22-39). Verses twenty-two through twenty-four are one long sentence. Verse twenty-four is a clause which presents the conclusion. Peter addresses the Jews of the Dispersion, the number of which is several thousand. The main subject is ***you yourselves*** (Acts 2:22). The main verb is ***know*** (Acts 2:22). He simply relates to them what they already ***know.*** They have the knowledge and understanding of ***Jesus of Nazareth, a Man attested by God to you*** (Acts 2:22). The focus of the statement is on the reality of God proving, attesting, validating, and authenticating the person of Christ. Peter then begins to list three distinct ways in which God has proven Jesus. We must interpret these facts in light of Pentecost. Peter gives an explanation of what has just happened (Acts 1:1-4).

As he begins, Peter highlights the life of Christ (Acts 2:22). Jesus, ***a Man,*** is the channel through which God manifested Himself. God revealed His person through Christ (***miracles***) which amazed and astonished His world (***wonders***). This revelation always points back to the Father (***signs***). However, this same life of God brings Jesus to death (Acts 2:23). Intimacy with God is not about our comfort, ease, and convenience. Intimacy is about the dreams and plans of God. Many times this brings us

Part Three: In My Eye

to a cross. Be assured God will never leave us there. Our passage is Peter's emphasis on the resurrection (Acts 2:24). The purpose of all of this is to explain Pentecost. God wants to accomplish this same thing in each personal life. It is a promise!

The subject of the clause in our text is **God.** He is the Prime Mover in the process, through the life of Christ. The main verb is *raised up.* This Greek word is the most common verb used for the resurrection of Christ. It is also used in its noun form (Acts 2:31), but Peter stresses the verb form of this word in his message (Acts 2:24-32). The Greek word used in our text is an action word, a verb. It is the same Greek word used for what happened to Peter as the Spirit of God moved upon him to preach at Pentecost (Acts 2:14). The focus of the resurrection of Christ is not on the event but on the action of God within the event. Our culture focuses on the event; the New Testament focused on the moving of God which is the heart of the event. We claim our salvation as an event; however, the heart of our salvation is the movement of God which was present then and now! Our salvation is not a noun; it is a verb.

Another surprising detail about this Greek word for *raised up* is its tense. Each time this word is used as a verb in connection with the resurrection of Christ, it is in the aorist tense. The only exception is when Jesus is quoted as speaking about His coming death and resurrection (Mark 9:31; 10:34). In these passages, the future tense is used. The New Testament writers apparently viewed the resurrection as only in the aorist tense. There is nothing like this tense in the English language. In its beginning stages, the Greek language only had the aorist tense. It was the "non-tense." Past, present, and future were developed later. The view of the aorist tense is external. It takes one outside the event or action, and it is seen from the beginning and the end. There is no concern with when it will happen; it is as if it has always been. Past, present and future are internal views. One stands in the middle of the event and views it as it happens (present), or as it is going to take place (future), or as it has already occurred (past). The aorist is the nearest tense we have to describe the view of God. He is outside the time zone and He views the resurrection as eternal.

In our passage Peter is not just reminding his listeners of an event which took place in the past, but he focuses them on the movement of God in Christ. It was not just in the past, nor is it in the future. It is not just in the now, which is the present tense. What God is doing in Christ has an eternal flavor to it. The time restraints do not apply. Peter develops this idea as his message progresses. This must be the reason John, in his Gospel account, consistently refers to the believer as already having eternal life. Within the framework of our time zone, the believer lives in the aorist tense.

One other factor concerning the verb of our passage is the active voice. This means the subject is responsible for the action of the verb. There is no question God is the source of all that is happening in Christ. Peter says so several times, leaving no room for argument or adjustment (Acts 2:24, 32). This is true in Jesus' exaltation as well as in the receiving of the promise of the Father (Acts 2:33). It even applies to His Lordship (Acts 2:36).

The next statement in our passage is *having loosed the pains of death.* The verb *having loosed* is in the participle form which makes it an adverb in this passage. It means to "untie, release, or untangle." It gives content to the verb translated *raised up.* This is a word which corresponds to the Greek word translated *should be held.* Peter paints the same picture twice for emphasis. This relates to the *pains of death.* The Greek word translated *pains* is in the feminine gender. It seems to relate to the idea of the birth pains of child bearing. Death could not keep Jesus any more than a pregnant woman can keep a child in her womb.

Then Peter explodes into the rest of the statement to explain *because* or why! He adds this last clause to his large sentence. God proved Jesus in His life (Acts 2:22) and in His death (Acts 2:23). He now gives us information to deepen our understanding in relation to the reaction of death to the life of the Spirit within *a Man*. He takes us beyond an activity God does for Jesus in raising Him from the dead. He explains Pentecost to the Jews of the Dispersion. He reveals to us how death responds when an individual filled with the Holy Spirit enters its realm.

He begins with *it was*. It is a translation from the Greek word "een." This Greek word means "to be" and is a focus on existence. This Greek word is contrasted with the Greek word "ginomai" which means "to become." These two Greek words are contrasted in John's Gospel account in the first chapter. Jesus is the "een" One (John 1:1). John the Baptist is the "ginomai" one (John 1:16). "Een" has an eternal value to it. This same Greek word (een) is used for the name of God at the burning bush. It is used in the great "I AM's" of Jesus. In addition to this, it is in the imperfect tense which means something happens in the past and continues into the present." God proved this man called Jesus. God moved His life through Jesus as He lived; He produced His death. But God continued to source Him even into the realm of death.

In this great sentence, Peter's concluding statement is *because it was not possible that He should be held by it* (Acts 2:24). A slight change was made in the translation which makes a tremendous difference in the interpretation of the statement. The justification for the change has to do with the Greek word which is translated *possible*. It is the Greek word "dunamis." We contrasted this word with the Greek word "ischus" in a previous study. "Ischus" is ability or resource. "Dunamis" is the flow of that resource in action. "Dunamis" is the Greek word translated *miracles* (Acts 2:22) and *power* (Acts 1:8). In light of this, the negative *not* should be connected to the Greek word translated *should be held*. The verse might read; *it was* (een, the state of being) *because* (why) *possible* (the flowing life of God) *should not be held by it.*

The "een" of the life of God was so powerful within this Man that it was *not possible* for Jesus to remain captured. This Greek word "dunamis" is an adjective translated "possible" which gives content to *it was*. Whatever is contained within **death** does not have the power or ability to contain the life of God sourcing *a Man*. Death exerts all the power it has and still cannot contain *a Man* filled with God.

The Greek word translated *should be held* is a verb in the infinitive mood. In the English grammar it is usually introduced with the word "to." This verb does not stand on its own but requires the main verb, *was* or "een." The negative ability to hold Jesus in death is tied into the existence of the life of God contained within *a Man*. This Greek word actually means "to forcibly seize, take hold of, arrest, or take into custody." It is absolutely impossible for death, in exerting this authority or power, to hold Jesus! It is because of the "een" (eternal) of God.

It is very significant that this verb is in the present tense. In the Greek language this means "now with a continual action." The present tense is moving from moment to moment and remains present. The resource of the nature of God, which is flowing through Jesus, is continually defeating the grasping ability of death. It is in the passive voice which means the subject is receiving the action. Since a verb in the infinitive tense does not stand alone, but relies on the main verb, its subject is also the subject of the main verb. The subject of the main verb in our clause is *it,* referring to the state of being, which is the flowing life of God. It was not death's fault that it could not hold Jesus. Death was acted upon by something greater than itself. Death could never hold the living nature of God. Peter is not saying that death could at one time hold the nature of God, but has lost its ability. Nor is he saying that Jesus earned the right to be liberated from the grip of death. His statement is that death has never had the ability to contain a man filled with the Spirit of God.

Part Three: In My Eye

Peter attempts to explain Pentecost to the Jews of the Dispersion. The Spirit of God has filled one hundred and twenty believers. What does this mean for these Jews of the Dispersion? It means to them exactly what it meant to Jesus. Death could not hold Him; death cannot hold them. He is not saying that they are liberated from the grasp of death because Jesus paid the penalty; rather He is saying they are liberated from the holding power of death because of the fullness of the nature of God indwelling them. It is the indwelling nature of God which makes man free from the binding power of death. If we are sourced by God we will not die; if we are sourced by death we are bound already and are dead.

To help clarify this, I would like for you to journey with me through the Gospel according to John. "Eternal life" becomes a common phrase in this writing. He starts with a strong emphasis on life. He gives us a proper picture of Jesus both from the eternal view as well as the human view. ***In Him was life, and the life was the light of men,*** (John 1:4). Again we must consider the Greek word "een" which is translated *was*. It has an eternal flavor to it, the state of existence, or to be. If we are not in relationship with Him who is life, we have no life in us. John highlights this truth from the outset of his Gospel account. Now let's go to the close of his account (John 20:31). ***But these are written that you may believe that Jesus is the Christ, the Son of God, and that believing you may have life in His name.*** Here he has captured his entire purpose for writing this account. In doing so he relates the necessity of having an intimate relationship with Christ (***believing***) which gives life. Is there any doubt that the theme of his writing is "life found in Christ?"

In between these two statements numerous references to life will be highlighted. All of these references will come from the lips of Christ as He speaks. There is one exception when Peter confesses directly to Jesus, ***"Lord, to whom shall we go? You have the words of eternal life,"*** (John 6:68). It is in the early chapters

Nicodemus, a ruler of the Jews appears. Within this discussion we discover our own limited knowledge as Nicodemus views life from a physical perspective. The very imagery of *born again* bespeaks ushering us into a new level of living greater than the present physical. The epitome of Jesus' message is given in a verse you have memorized. He says, *"For God so loved the world that He gave His only begotten Son, that whoever believes in Him should not perish but have everlasting life,"* (John 3:16). The Greek word translated *have* is in the present tense. This implies continual possession. The Greek word translated *everlasting* is also translated *eternal* in the previous verse. He says, *"That whoever believes in Him should not perish but have eternal life."* The Greek grammar and the Greek words of the last phrase in both statements is the same. The Greek word translated *eternal* has the idea of perpetual. When it is applied to life, it means the life which is God's and hence is not affected by the limitations of time. All of this is directly connected to the life of the Spirit within the believer (John 3:8). Jesus also connects this same life with the judgment in this passage. He says, *"He who believes in Him is not condemned; but he who does not believe is condemned already, because he has not believed in the name of the only begotten Son of God,"* (John 3:18).

It did not take long for the pressure to increase to the point the Jews wanted to kill Jesus. In the midst of these feelings, Jesus said, *"Most assuredly, I say to you, he who hears My words and believes in Him who sent Me has everlasting life, and shall not come into the judgment, but has passed from death into life,"* (John 5:24). What an encouraging statement! Jesus uses the same present tense grammar here. It is a bold statement to proclaim that anyone who is filled with the Spirit of Christ has eternal life now and will have eternal life continually. The Spirit of Christ contained within an individual cannot be held by death and death cannot inflict the judgment.

In the context of the feeding of the five thousand, Jesus

addresses the issue of bread. Since the Jews were complaining about Him, Jesus saw it necessary to give additional information. He said, *"I am the living bread which came down from heaven. If anyone eats of this bread, he will live forever; and the bread that I shall give is My flesh, which I shall give for the life of the world,"* (John 6:51). Now the Jews quarreled among themselves about how this could possibly be. Jesus went on to say, *"Whoever eats My flesh and drinks My blood has eternal life, and I will raise him up at the last day,"* (John 6:54).

The Jews became so frustrated they fell into name calling. They said to Jesus, *"You are a Samaritan and have a demon* (John 8:48). He denied that He possessed a demon but identified with the Father who indwelt Him. He could not simply think about Himself, but hurriedly said, *"Most assuredly, I say to you, if anyone keeps My word he shall never see death,"* (John 8:51). They could not comprehend His words and immediately took up rocks to stone Him (John 8:59).

As Jesus attempts to illustrate the truth, He speaks of being the Good Shepherd. He applies the various aspects of a shepherd's life to His own. He says, *"The thief does not come except to steal, and to kill, and to destroy. I have come that they may have life, and that they may have it more abundantly,"* (John 10:10). In the context of all Jesus says about life, this abundant life must certainly have at its heart eternal life produced by His presence within the sheep. He goes on to proclaim, *"And I give them eternal life, and they shall never perish; neither shall anyone snatch them out of My hand,"* (John 10:28).

Lazarus' death gave rise to a great teaching opportunity about eternal life. All the feelings and emotions we are prone to experience in the midst of death were present with Mary and Martha. With a tone of accusation, Martha told Jesus that Lazarus would not have died if He had been there. Jesus assured her that Lazarus would rise again, but Martha interpreted it to mean in the future resurrection. It was then that Jesus said, *"I am the resurrection and the life. He who believes in Me, though he may die, he shall live. And whoever lives and believes in Me shall never die. Do you believe this?"* (John 11:25-26). Is this reality? The resurrection has already taken place in those who believe in Jesus.

There are three major chapters in the Gospel according to John which are focused exclusively on the coming Pentecost event (John 14, 15 and 16). Verse after verse is dedicated to the coming of the Holy Spirit. These powerful words are spoken to the disciples in a private setting in the upper room before the Garden of Gethsemane event and His crucifixion. He tries to get them focused on what He is going to experience and where it will take them. They are going to know intimacy with God. He said, **"At that day you will know that I am in My Father, and you in Me, and I in you,"** (John 14:20). How could there be a tighter or more intimate relationship than that? He even told the parable of The True Vine (John 15:1-8) to illustrate this oneness. Just before going to the Garden of Gethsemane, He broke into His great high priestly prayer (John 17). In the third verse of that prayer He cried, **"And this is eternal life, that they may know You, the only true God, and Jesus Christ whom You have sent,"** (John 17:3). In previous studies we have discovered the Greek word for ***know*** is "ginosko." It is not simply about knowledge or information. It is a relational term. It is the Biblical word for the most intimate relationship in the marriage union (Matthew 1:25). Intimacy and relationship with God is eternal life.

Now we view this great Gospel truth through the eyes of Pentecost. Intimacy, knowing, believing have all come together in the fullness of the Holy Spirit. God has come to indwell man. God, who is life, cannot be contained in death. The flowing resource of God living through Jesus may have brought Him to death, but death could not hold Him. It was child's play; there was no contest. The flowing resource of death does not match the flowing resource of Life! This is promised to us!

Part Three: In My Eye

Think of the staggering ramifications of this for your life. We live in a world where death is constantly confronting and surrounding us. Spiritual death constantly attempts to swallow the church. Where are the people of life? Who will be filled with the Spirit and march into their world?

Acts 2:24

THE PROOF - DEATH IS CONQUERED

What is Peter saying about the resurrection of Christ in relation of Pentecost? That is what we desire to discover. In our last study we attempted a detailed analysis of verse twenty-four. Everything in Peter's message must be interpreted in light of what has just happened to one hundred and twenty believers. The Jews of the Dispersion witnessed the event and they wanted to know, **"Whatever could this mean?"** (Acts 2:13).

Peter's explanation focuses on **Jesus of Nazareth, a Man attested by God to you** (Acts 2:22). God proved, authenticated, and validated the fullness of the Spirit in Christ. What the life of God in Christ did for Him, it will do for all men! It is now happening in the one hundred and twenty believers and is promised to us. One of the startling factors is the issue of death and resurrection (Acts 2:23-24). The fullness of Christ in the believer is not just for the sake of this present living experience. Christ is to live His life through the believer, not just on concrete streets, but on streets of gold as well. The indwelling of the Spirit is an eternal experience. It defines our essence as Christians. To remove this is to cease to be Christian either here on earth or in heaven.

The life of God flowing through Jesus not only produced His living, but also produced His death (Acts 2:23). It has become important to me for the Spirit of God to produce my death. It is then it will have significance. The death of Christ counted in the redemptive plan of God. Should not my death count in the same plan? John the Baptist's death played a key role in preparing for the death of Christ. Could not my death be used in such a manner? Am I at the whim of accidents or freak events? Does happen-chance dictate my existence? Should I not be filled with God as Jesus was and in this oneness find direction even for my death?

This also applies to the resurrection from the dead. Everything Peter explains about the experience of Christ becomes mine when the same Spirit flows through me. The flowing life of God in Jesus produced His life, death and resurrection. The picture is vivid concerning the *resurrection* (Acts 2:24). Jesus did not enter into death and hell only to be trapped there. God, the Father, did not need to rush to His rescue and raise Him from the dead. Rather the picture painted is that of a man filled with the Spirit of God. When the flowing life of God in a man confronts death and hell, hell and death are powerless.

Obviously, the significance of the resurrection is seen in light of the greatness of death. Death is a strong enemy. We know that it takes the great movement of God to bring victory from it. In our passage, death is referenced three times. Verse twenty-three concludes with it: ***Him, being delivered by the determined purpose and foreknowledge of God, you have taken by lawless hands, have crucified, and put to death.*** It appears twice in our present text: ***whom God raised up, having loosed the pains of death, because it was not possible that He should be held by it*** (Acts 2:24).

Peter uses three completely different words to make this reference. The Greek word translated ***put to death*** (Acts 2:23) is "anaireoe." It is from two words: an emphatic or up (ana) and to take (haireoe). This is translated "to slay, murder, or take off." This corresponds with the idea of death as that which imprisons an individual or holds them. This Greek word is used as a verb in the clause of our long sentence. The emphasis is on the movement or the action of death. The Greek word in our text (Acts 2:24) translated *death* is "thanatos" which is a noun. Then at the end of the verse, death is referred to by a pronoun. However, in each case they are related to the illustrated action which is happening. In the first case, it is the entangling pains likened unto child birth, which is being untied or *loosed.* The pronoun which refers to death relates to "take hold of" or "forcibly seize."

Peter highlights the greatness of the resurrection by placing it firmly in the context of the severity of death. He points out the strangle hold of death upon a man so strongly, the resurrection is almost lost in the tragedy. This again reminds us, we must know the strength of our enemy in order to understand the greatness of our Conqueror. For this reason, let me remind you of the exposition of this verse (our previous study on Acts 2:24). In this long sentence, **God** is definitely the subject of this climatic clause. The resurrection is presented to us in the verb form (***raised up***). This emphasizes the fact that it is not an event but a movement of God within the event. This resurrection verb is in the aorist tense. This places us outside the event which gives us an eternal view of what God is doing. It is not about what God is doing, has done, or will do, but simply about what happens when a man filled with the Spirit comes in contact with death. Death can no more hold that man than a pregnant woman can keep her child in her womb. Death in all of its fury cannot contain the life of God filling a man!

Cause of Death

In light of this expositional study, it might be wise for us to understand the Biblical background concerning death. Let's begin with a deep awareness that death is simply the opposite of life and was never intended. As seen in our study (Acts 2:22-24), death is all that is experienced outside of the fullness of the Spirit of Christ. It was intended by God that man should live sourced by God. The moment man is not sourced by God, he is dead. This reveals to us the reality of life and death. Life is Christ; death is the absence of Christ. Anything outside of Christ is death. No wonder John cries, *"In Him was life, and the life was the light of men,"* (John 1:4). This places life completely beyond the simple definition of breathing, eating, or functioning. Death is not the absence of these things. This leads us to the conclusion that death is not a natural process. It may be the way man is now, but it was not the way man was created by God. Man was created by God to be sourced by God, thus to live. Death is foreign, something to be greatly feared. It is no more regarded as a natural process than the resurrection. It is caused!

What is the cause of death or separation from the sourcing of God? It is contained within the very pride and self-will of man. Consistently this cause is called "sin!" Therefore, when one seeks to discover the cause of death he is really seeking the cause of sin. Death shapes our concept of sin. Paul said, *"For the wages of sin is death, but the gift of God is eternal life in Christ Jesus our Lord,"* (Romans 6:23). If life is found only "in" Christ, then death is found "outside of Christ." Our text (Acts 2:22-24) teaches us that a man sourced by the Spirit of Christ is alive, but when he is sourced out of himself he is dead. Therefore, death is caused by self-sourcing. This must become the definition for all sin – self-sourcing. Sin has always been man wanting to live out of himself and not living out of Christ. It is a sourcing issue. To identify sin by deeds is to miss the heart of the matter. Sin is never about right and wrong. Even the best deed sourced by man remains a sin and produces death.

Perhaps this helps us understand the fallacy of the law. Understanding this principle, it is easy to see the law never brings life, but always produces death. Even if man keeps the entire law, he lives in death. For some reason, chapter seven in the Book of Romans has become controversial. Paul simply presents mankind from the viewpoint of the law. He strongly declares that sin is produced by the law (Romans 7:7-12). He says, *"And the commandment, which was to bring life, I found to bring death,"* (Romans 7:10). He further says, *"The law is holy, and the commandment holy and just and good,"* (Romans 7:12). So the problem is not the law. The problem is man relying on himself to keep the law. Paul calls this "sin!"

He then breaks into a powerful discourse of the struggle contained within the heart of man (Romans 7:13-25). Listen to his plea. *"Has then what is good become death to me? Certainly not! But sin, that it might appear sin, was producing death in me through what is good, so that sin through the commandment might become exceedingly sinful"* (Romans 7:13). It is after this deep awareness, he concludes, *"I am carnal,"* (Romans 7:14). Here is the core of all sin. It is the *carnal* which is an attitude of self-will and self-sourcing. Even the good deeds that I want to do end up being bad. This so dominates that what I hate is what I produce. No wonder he cries, *"Now if I do what I will not to do, it is no longer I who do it, but sin that dwells in me,"* (Romans 7:20). He summarizes this state in which he exists the *body of death* (Romans 7:24). When I am sourced by Christ, I live; when I source myself, I die. Every attempt I make to affect my own escape from death and to merit life by my achievements is simply another effort to live from myself. This only entangles me the more in sin and therefore death. The law which set out to lead me to life ends up leading me to death.

What a tragic dilemma in which to dwell. How will I ever escape? The best I can do is still filthy rags in His sight and only produces more death. At the close of the chapter Paul breaks into praise for all is not lost! He cries, *"I thank God – through Jesus Christ our Lord!"* (Romans 7:25). He begins the next chapter by saying, *"There is therefore now no condemnation to those who are in Christ Jesus, who do not walk according to the flesh, but according to the Spirit,"* (Romans 8:1). He continues by explaining what he means by **walking according to the flesh**. It is a sourcing issue. The flesh in this passage is the carnal self-centered mind. It is man living out of himself. Whenever this takes place, man is dead. But life is produced by the Spirit of Christ sourcing the individual. He says, *"For to be carnally minded is death, but to be spiritually minded is life and peace,"* (Romans 8:6).

Continuing Death

Death (self-sourcing) is never viewed as simply extinction. Death is not something which takes place when your lungs quit breathing and your heart stops beating. An individual is dead even when eating and breathing. Death is the immediate condition of an individual who is self-sourced. Therefore, death is never viewed as something which happens to an individual and he ceases to exist. Everyone exists forever either in life or in death.

Our culture compartmentalizes everything; it is the way we think. This was not so in the Biblical culture. They thought in terms of the whole; it is what they emphasized. In salvation, we break it into sections such as "saved," "sanctified," "discipleship," and "heaven." The Biblical culture simply thought of "salvation." It was all contained in this one word. This is true of death. We speak of "physical death," "spiritual death," "judgment," and "eternal death (hell). This is not a proper Biblical view. All of these aspects of death exist in the New Testament, but all within the category of death. Paul explained, *"For the wages of sin is death, but the gift of God is eternal life in Christ Jesus our Lord,"* (Romans 6:23). Obviously Paul was not simply referring to physical death. He viewed the whole of what happens in an individual who is sourcing himself.

The Scripture is filled with the progressive revelation of God. Therefore, one sees this concept developing through the Old Testament and into the New. Sheol is a Hebrew word which is normally translated "grave" (Psalms 88:3, 5). There seems to be two main compartments to this "abode of the dead." The upper compartment is referred to as "Paradise" (Luke 23:43). The lower compartment is called "Hades" (Acts 2:27, 31). It was believed that all went into this one place, Sheol (Ecc. 9:2-3). It was a place where love, hate, envy, work, thought, knowledge, and wisdom were absent (Ecc. 9:6, 10). The atmosphere of such a place is bleak. There is no light; it is a place of shadows (Job 10:21-22). It would be a place of soul sleeping.

It is strongly presented to us in the New Testament that something happened to Sheol. There was a drastic change which altered the construction of the abode of the dead. The end result was the establishment of heaven and hell. What was, is no more! When an individual physically dies, he does not go to Sheol for sleeping, but is transported directly to heaven or hell. Paul assured us, **"We are confident, yes, well pleased rather to be absent from the body and to be present with the Lord,"** (2 Corinthians 5:8). The Bible does not give us a complete explanation of what actually took place in the great transition. We cannot, nor do we want to, be dogmatic. Rather we are searching and open for truth.

Christ - Solution To Death

This we know for certain! Jesus is the answer! A man got us into this mess; it will take a man to get us out of this mess. But where is the man who is not in the mess? The only man who could bring us to life would be one who is not under the domination of death. Obviously God could not find a man who was not controlled by death. Paul said, **"For all have sinned and** *fall short of the glory of God,"* (Romans 3:23). Of course, **the wages of sin is death** (Romans 6:23). So God decided to become the Man. Christ is the Man who is not controlled by death!

Peter explains Pentecost to the Jews of the Dispersion and to us. He presents the explanation of Jesus. He is the example of what a man filled with the Spirit of God is like. His life was not self-sourced. This would have been sin and therefore death. He was a man who was sourced by God. What was taking place in one hundred and twenty disciples was going on in the person of Christ. The Spirit of life produced life within and through Him. He did not do or live because He was God (although He was and is God). He did what He did because He was a man filled with God.

Since Jesus was not controlled by death, but by the Spirit of life, His death was not the death of a normal man who was already controlled by death. God had to bring Him to death (Acts 2:23). Since sin pays the wages of sin, He had no wages to collect. God made Him to be sin for us. Paul explained, **"For He made Him who knew no sin to be sin for us, that we might become the righteousness of God in Him,"** (2 Corinthians 5:21). God brought Jesus to death for our sakes. But the same God who brought Jesus to death has brought Him to life (Acts 2:24). A Man filled with the Spirit of God went into Sheol, the place of death and judgment. We have so little information about the activities which took place there (Ephesians 4:7-10). What happens when a Man who is being produced and sourced by the Spirit of God marches into Sheol? It could not contain Him. Things could not remain the same. A New Covenant is established. Judgment takes place. Eternal life is given. No wonder Jesus told us we will never die (John 11:26).

Death is no longer death for the believer. Paul quotes Hosea the prophet.

The Proof - Death is Conquered | **Acts 2:24**

> *"O Death, where is your sting?*
> *O Hades, where is your victory?"*
> *(1 Corinthians 15:55)*

He explains that the sting of death is sin (1 Corinthians 15:56). Sin is found in self-sourcing; self-sourcing has been eliminated by the sourcing of the Spirit. Therefore, death no longer has teeth to devour us. It is the picture presented of Jesus in our passage. He is a Man filled with the Spirit who has marched into the middle of death, but death had no way to hold Him. The life of God sourcing Him was constantly untangling Him. This happens in all the death entanglements of this life and in the next. The grasping hold of everything outside of Christ in this life could not get a grip on Him. The judgment of death and hell could not contain Him. This is not because He was God but because He was filled with God. What happened in Him has also happened in one hundred and twenty believers and is now promised to us. We are free in Christ.

Acts 2:25

A MAN'S CONCENTRATION

A great crowd of Jews *from every nation under heaven* are listening intently to Peter's explanation of Pentecost. They earnestly seek an answer to the question, *"Whatever could this mean?"* (Acts 2:12). The Holy Spirit moves on Peter! Cultural environment and tradition have nothing to do with the explanation. This message comes from the heart of God. Peter uses quotes from the Old Testament in a very impressive manner. As he explains the life of Jesus, Peter matches his personal statements with quotes from the Scriptures. There are as many verses dedicated to the statements of Scripture in his message as are dedicated to his personal insights.

Peter begins with the prophecy of Joel (Acts 2:16-21). The one hundred and twenty believers are experiencing an event that God planned and promised for many years. This is the fulfillment of *I will pour out of My Spirit on all flesh* (Acts 2:17). Peter then gives a practical life explanation in the next three verses (Acts 2:22-24). God authenticated the out-pouring of the Holy Spirit in *Jesus of Nazareth, a Man.* He did it through the life of Christ, His death, and His resurrection. All that was true of Jesus is now true for us. We have just entered into a new intimacy with God.

Peter bases this thought on a Psalm of David (Psalm 16:8-11). He begins his statement with a Greek word translated *for* (Acts 2:25). It is the Greek word "gar" which is a causative particle. It expresses the reason for what has been. But often this Greek word assumes a reaction on the part of the hearer to what has gone before and gives, in its clause, the reasons for this reaction. No doubt Peter anticipated astonishment from the Jews of the Dispersion. After all, they had been responsible for the crucifixion of Christ. How could they have missed the wonder of what God was doing in this Man? What was taking place in Christ is the highest spiritual reality God has planned for mankind. It is almost to startling to grasp!

What is the basis of this? How could God fill a man, even *Jesus of Nazareth?* They have been carefully looking for the "new thing" which God is going to accomplish. They recognize it in the experience of the one hundred and twenty disciples. How could they have missed it in Christ? How can they now enter into this experience after what they did to Christ?

Peter anticipates their reaction and takes them back to their Scriptures. It is here we clearly see the fundamental truth which opens the possibility of all God wants to do within us. It is found in this Psalm (16:8-11). Above all other Psalms this one is especially considered a "Messianic Psalm." At the original writing of the Psalm, David writes concerning himself. This is the wonder of the Scriptures! God says something through David which goes far beyond the scope of his life. As Peter points out in his sermon, there is absolutely no way this Psalm could apply or be fulfilled in David. Peter says, **"Men and brethren, let me speak freely to you of the patriarch David, that he is both dead and buried, and his tomb is with us to this day,"** (Acts 2:29). Since David is both **dead and buried** among them, this Messianic Psalm could not be about him. It is **Jesus of Nazareth, a Man** in whom this Psalm is fulfilled. The flow of God's life through Christ, which produced His life, His death, and now His resurrection, fulfills the details of this Psalm in every way.

However, there is additional information and details given

to us within this quotation of the Psalm. Up to this time the entire focus has been on God who initiated and sourced all that took place in Jesus. But what was the inward spiritual condition which allowed this to happen? How could Jesus maintain this flow of the Holy Spirit in every activity? This seems to be the personal question which we consistently ask. Sometime, at my best moments, I can experience God sourcing me, but how do I maintain this moment by moment? How can I maintain the consistent sourcing of the Spirit of God in my life? This is the most practical aspect of this spiritual reality. We all agree about the power of God, and we certainly embrace the fact that God loves us all. But how do I live in this every day in all situations? What is the key factor which releases this reality within me?

Peter's sermon is an explanation of Pentecost to the Jews of the Dispersion. What is presently in the one hundred and twenty disciples is exactly what was and is within Jesus. What God is doing in and through Jesus is made plain. Now through the statements of David, Peter highlights the attitude present within Jesus which releases this resource. This must be the same attitude or spiritual condition within us, if we are to experience the same sourcing. What is this condition?

Look anew at the quotation of King David,

> *I foresaw the Lord always before my face,*
> *For He is at my right hand, that I may not be shaken*
> *(Acts 2:25).*

Remember this is a Messianic Psalm. David is writing these words about himself, but God intended it concerning Christ. With this in mind, it is as if Jesus is speaking these words about Himself.

The Greek word translated *foresaw* must be understood in light of the completed phrase, *always before my face*. This is a strong statement. The strength of the focus cannot be overstated. It is all consuming, all encompassing, and God the Father is appearing in the presence of Jesus. The absolute focus and concentration of *Jesus of Nazareth, a Man* upon His **Lord** (Father) is overpowering; it is as if there is nothing else.

The Greek word translated *before...face* is actually two words combined. The first Greek word would be translated "in." It has the idea of "in, on, at, and by any place or thing, with the major idea of resting." The object is neither moving nor going any place. It is compared with the Greek word "eis" which is translated "into" and implies motion. Another Greek word of comparison is "ek" which is translated "from" which indicates motion out of. Therefore, the Greek word translated *before* actually means "remaining in place." The second Greek word translated *face* can also be translated "eye" or "countenance." The meaning of the statement is that something has come to rest in the very eye, face, or presence of the individual. All of this indicates a strong focus.

This is further emphasized by the Greek word translated *my* which is a part of this same phrase, **before my face.** This Greek word is an emphatic form of me or mine. It is a statement of ownership. Since this is a Messianic Psalm, Jesus states this about Himself. Obviously He refers to His Father. The Father is the object which is in the very eye of Christ without any motion of coming or going. He is the permanent fixture or the remaining vision of Christ. Jesus takes ownership of this focus.

This is further emphasized with the word *always.* It is an interesting translation. This is one of those few places where one English word is the translation for two Greek words. Most often it is the reverse. It is not a compound word, but two different and separate Greek words. The first word is often translated "through," "during," or "with." It implies motion through a place. In our passage, time is the issue. This gives us the meaning of continued time or indefinite time. It can be used in the sense of throughout or during as in "during the whole night," (Luke 5:5), "during forty days," (Acts 1:3). The second word contains the idea of oneness, totality, or the whole. When these two Greek words are used together, the idea of "through the entire time" is conveyed. Thus, we have the translation *always.*

We have a double emphasis on the consistency of what is happening. Something has come to rest in the very eye, face, and presence of Christ. It is consistently there throughout time. Nothing is more valuable to Him. Not even the most startling of events distracts Him. Whenever we come close to Him, this one factor is present. This gives content to the opening statement from our text, *"I foresaw the Lord."*

Do not lose sight of the fact that this is a Messianic Psalm, a statement concerning Christ. The Greek word translated *foresaw* is a compound word. The two words are "before" and "see." It can have the meaning of seeing something before or previously. However, in our passage this verb is in the middle voice. This means that it has to do with personal preference. It means to see before oneself, having before one's eyes, or figuratively, of what one has vividly in mind. This verb is in the indicative mood which means it is a simple statement of fact. There is no argument involved. It is in the imperfect tense. It is an action which took place in the past but continues into the present. This also verifies the continuing action of *always.* The focus of *Jesus of Nazareth, a Man* cannot be questioned. He lives with a constant focus on His Father. His mind is constantly aware (practicing His presence) of the presence of the Father. There is no variation. This is the one fundamental, unchanging, and never-ceasing factor of His life.

In order to be certain we understand the importance of this focus, he adds another key phrase: *For He is at my right hand, that I may not be shaken.* He begins this statement with a conjunction, *for.* It is a different Greek word than found at the beginning of this section (Acts 2:25, see discussion above). This Greek word is most often translated "that" or "because." He gives the basis or reason for his above statement. ***Jesus of Nazareth, a Man*** is sourced by the very Spirit of God. The spiritual condition which enables this filling is His constant (***always***) focus upon the Father. How is this focus maintained? He is now going to state the reason!

The key to this statement is found in the subject and the verb, ***He is***. In the Greek language this is one word. It is the third person singular of the Greek verb translated "to be." He highlights the state of being, not the doing of the Father. The "I am's" of Jesus come from this verb. The focus of Jesus is upon the Father's Person. The Father does not visit Jesus to give Him instruction. It is not during times of great distress that Jesus calls upon the Father and the Father comes to Him. No, Jesus is in intimate relationship with the Father. The presence of the Father (state of being) comes into His very eye, face, and presence. He is not using the Father for His personal advantage. Jesus is not forced to focus on the Father for without Him He will fail. This is not a means to an end. Circumstances cannot affect this focus because it is not about Christ's personal gain. Jesus is captured by the Father, because the Father is actually there. It is a state of being.

Jesus describes it as ***at my right hand.*** In the ancient world, a bodyguard always stood on the right side of the one he was protecting. In this position he could cover him with his shield and still have his right arm free to fight. The right hand is also mentioned because that was the place of dignity and honor. In our passage, the right hand is used in reference to the entire person. The Father is in the dominant position in relationship to Christ. It is another way of saying what He has already said. The Father has captured the very eye of Christ. The Father is in the very face of Christ until He can see nothing else. No circumstances can get between Christ and the Father. His concentration is stronger than any interference!

There is another important emphasis made in the Greek

word translated *at*. The actual Greek word is "ek." The statement is **He is ek my right hand.** This Greek word is contrasted with "apo." Both of these Greek words imply motion away from an object. However, "apo" refers distinctly to this motion coming from nearby or around the object, while "ek" always relates to the motion coming from within the object.

This presents two outstanding insights into the concentration of Christ upon His Father. The presence of the Father, while it is a state of being, is also in motion. We should not be surprised concerning this truth. We discover it repeatedly in the Scriptures. Jesus is focused on the Father not because of what the Father is doing, but because of what He is being. However, the state of being is one of great action and accomplishment. The Father's state of being is so powerful it can be described as motion. The energy of the Father's state of being always affects and changes everything around it. The Father defeats every enemy of Christ. It is not a defense of doing, but His very presence defeats the enemy.

This tremendous truth is coupled with the fact that the motion is from within. The action of the state of being is from the very heart or nature of God Himself. The focus of Christ is not upon a facsimile of the Father. Christ is not captured by a portrait or statue of the Father or even ideas about Him. Christ is not focused on an organization or career; this is not theological or conceptual. The Father Himself, state of being, who is in motion within Jesus has absolutely mastered His vision.

Jesus was twelve years of age (Luke 2:42). During the Feast of the Passover His family took Him to Jerusalem. As they left Jerusalem, they assumed Jesus was in the company with which they were traveling. They had gone an entire day's journey when they realized He was not with them. It took an entire day to return to Jerusalem. They searched another three days for Him throughout the city. In desperation, they went to the temple to seek Divine aid. There He was! They must have been very stern with Him (Luke 2:48). His patient answer was, **"Why did you** *seek Me? Did you not know that I must be about My Father's business?"* (Luke 2:49). In the Greek text, the word **business** is not there, but is added for clarification in the English. Jesus' statement was, *"Did you not know I must be about My Father?"* Even at age twelve Jesus recognized His dominant focus! It is the Father; His state of existence (*I must be*) was the Father. Nothing else is going on in His life.

This is intimately connected to Peter's explanation of Pentecost. Jesus is the clear and precise explanation of the fullness of the Holy Spirit. He is sourced by the Spirit of the Father. This is maintained consistently because Jesus is totally focused on the Father. The very nature of the Father fills Jesus and sources Him, and it is this same nature which consumes His vision. His very eye becomes filled with the state of being of the Father's presence.

The consistency of the focus of Christ upon the Father allows the constant sourcing of the Holy Spirit. This is highlighted again in the final phrase of our passage. He says, *"that I may not be shaken."* This clause must be seen in the context of Christ's focus on the Father which allows the sourcing. The Messiah must not be shaken from this focus. This must be constant in His life if He is to know the constant resourcing of the Spirit of the Father. What will enable Jesus to maintain this focus? It will not be the power of His mind or discipline. This will not come about because He wills it to be so. The phrase begins with two Greek words translated *that*. It is a phrase consisting of "in order that" or "not." When these are combined it means "in order not," "so that not," or "rest." Why has the Father come in His moving state of being? Why has the Father come to remain in a constant position in the eye of Christ? He does so to keep the focus constant. The One who is responsible for the constant focus is the Father! The Father enables the focus; the Father is the focus; the Father fills and sources the focus. There is no way to be distracted if Jesus responds to the Father.

He climaxes this last clause with *shaken.* In the context of our passage, it expresses the idea of wavering, to move back and forth. It is in the subjunctive mood which suggests a possibility. It is not a certainty, but is desired. The consistent flow of the Holy Spirit sourcing the life of the Messiah is one of focus. It is hopeful that His focus will remain constant, but it is not guaranteed. The Messiah must respond to the Father's presence (state of being), Who has come to be in His eye.

All of this is to explain Pentecost to the Jews of the Dispersion. What has happened in the lives of one hundred and twenty disciples is exactly what was and is taking place in Jesus. He was sourced by the Spirit of God. He lived in total dependence and surrender to the flowing resource of God. How could He maintain this on such a consistent basis? It was because of His focus! His gaze was fixed on the Father. He never wavered from this view. But even this was not produced by His will or determination. The Father came and captured Him. The Father was constantly on His right hand. The Father surrounded, encompassed, and enveloped Him. There was no struggle to remain focused. He relaxed in the presence of the Father and responded to His love.

This is now promised to us! Jesus said, *"As the Father loved Me, I also have loved you; abide in My love,"* (John 15:9). He also said, *"As the living Father sent Me, and I live because of the Father, so he who feeds on Me will live because of Me,"* (John 6:57). Is there anything else needed? Could I respond and rest in Him?

Acts 2:26

A MAN'S CELEBRATION

Peter is preaching an amazing sermon. It is the explanation of the Pentecost event. The words are coming from his mouth, but the Spirit of God is moving through him, sourcing those words. The Jews of the Dispersion, having just witnessed the Pentecost event, are open and responding to the new thing God is doing through Pentecost. They are eager to know how they too may experience Pentecost just as the one hundred and twenty believers. How can this apply to their lives?

Jesus is the explanation! This is Peter's opening sentence. God proved Pentecost in **Jesus of Nazareth, a Man.** He did it through the life of Jesus, His death, and His resurrection. The focus of the explanation is on sourcing. The essence of the Spirit of God sourced everything which flowed from the being of Christ. The central issue of Pentecost or Christianity is sourcing. It is not about theological correctness, proper behavior, or right versus wrong. It is about sourcing. Who is responsible for what is coming through and from you? Is it coming from you or through and from the Spirit of God?

Peter is very much aware that this kind of statement will produce a reaction. Certain questions will be raised. How can this happen in my life? If I experience Pentecost, how will I maintain a consistent sourcing of the Spirit? He forcibly says the answer is still found in Jesus. He quotes to us a Messianic Psalm (Psalm 16:8-11). This passage can easily be broken into three sections. These three sections combined give us the secret of how ***Jesus of Nazareth, a Man*** maintained on a consistent basis the sourcing of the Spirit of God even in and through death. The three sections are **CONCENTRATION** (Acts 2:25), **CELEBRATION** (Acts 2:26), and **COMMUNION** (Acts 2:27-28).

Jesus' concentration was completely on the Father. This is a Messianic Psalm. This means we must take these words as those of Christ. He boldly says that the Father is in His eye. His entire vision is the Father. The Father is so large in His eyesight that Jesus can see nothing else. This vision is not a picture of the Father, ideas about the Father, or a statue of the Father. The actual Father, in the essence of His Spirit is present. His very presence acts like a body guard which defeats every enemy. Jesus is able to maintain this vision of His Father because of the Father. He does not have special discipline, techniques, or meditation methods. It is the Father Himself who sources the consistency. As Jesus sees the Father, He is captured by Him. Because He is captured by the Father, He consistently sees the Father. The very presence of the Father sources the consistency. Jesus is simply responding to the Father. Remember this is an explanation of Pentecost. What is happening in Jesus is now transferred to the disciples. This is also promised to us. This is the key to our lives as well.

The overflow of this is **CELEBRATION** (Acts 2:26). This seems to describe the tone of the response which is constantly going on in the life of ***Jesus of Nazareth, a Man.***

Therefore my heart rejoiced and my tongue was glad; Moreover my flesh also will rest in hope (Acts 2:26).

He begins with the Greek word translated ***therefore.*** There are two Greek words which are translated into this one English word. The first Greek word is the same as in the above study for the Greek word translated ***always.*** It is a primary preposition denoting the channel of an act, through, or during. It implies motion, through a place. The second Greek word can be translated "that thing." So a proper translation beginning this great statement would be "through that thing." What was the constant attitude present through the concentration (Acts 2:25)? If Jesus lived in a total focus on the Father, He was in His eye, what was happening in the inner life of Christ through it all?

The Messiah seems to realize that His life is filled with "rejoicing." **Rejoiced** is a translation of a compound Greek word. The first word is "well" and the second one is "mind." This is an entirely different Greek word than what Paul uses in Philippians as he instructs us to **Rejoice in the Lord always. Again I will say, rejoice!** (Philippians 4:4). Paul uses the same Greek word Jesus used in the Sermon on the Mount concerning persecution. **"Rejoice and be exceedingly glad, for great is your reward in heaven,"** (Matthew 5:12). However, the Greek word Peter is using here in quoting David is only used fourteen times in the New Testament. Six of those times it is translated "merry." It is an interesting word because it is a verb used in the context of relationship. It is used strongly in the Parable of the Prodigal Son. Upon the return of the son, the fatted calf was killed and a party was given. Jesus said, **"And they began to be merry,"** (Luke 15:24). The elder brother accused the Father by saying, **"You never gave me a young goat, that I might make merry with my friends,"** (Luke 15:29). It has the connotation of having a party with one's friends. Paul makes the use of this word plain in asking a question, **"For if I make you sorrowful, then who is he who makes me glad** (merry) **but the one who is made sorrowful by me?"** (2 Corinthians 2:2). Since this Greek word has to do with relationship, it becomes very important in regard to intimacy with God. The chief sin in one's relationship to God is denial of God as the cause of joy. When I depend upon circumstances, materialism, or power to determine my merriment, I have sinned. In Stephen's great message to the Jews he related the story of the golden calf. He said, **"And they made a** *calf in those days, offered sacrifices to the idol, and rejoiced in the works of their own hands"* (Acts 7:41). The golden calf was not their only sin, but they had shifted the cause of their joy to something other than God.

This becomes significant in the context of our passage concerning **Jesus of Nazareth, a Man.** It was through those things such as His life and His death that the focus on His Father strengthened. In the context of His relationship with the Father, there was a "well mind." He lived in dependence on the flow of the indwelling Spirit. This brought the spirit of merriment. It took place in His **heart.** It is exciting to see that the usage of this word in the New Testament does not depend upon the Greek concept or usage of the word but is influenced by the Old Testament. It refers to the inner person. It is the seat of understanding, knowledge, and will. It takes on the meaning of conscience. It is described most effectively by Peter in his challenge to wives. He calls them to something beyond *merely outward* adornment – *arranging the hair, wearing gold, or putting on fine apparel – rather let it be the hidden person of the heart, with the incorruptible beauty of a gentle and quiet spirit, which is very precious in the sight of God* (1 Peter 3:3-4). *The hidden person of the heart* describes well the New Testament concept of *heart.*

In our passage, *therefore my heart rejoiced,* **heart** is the subject and **rejoiced** is the verb. It is interesting this verb is in the passive voice. This means the **heart** is not responsible for the merriment. This is not a matter of getting oneself into a positive mental state. We are not being challenged to discipline our thought process to blot out all negative thoughts. The **hidden person of the heart** of the Messiah is being acted upon by the very relationship of intimacy with the Father. He is living in a party, making merriment. But He is being brought to death! Yes, it is a death *delivered by the determined purpose and foreknowledge of God.* Even in death, the relationship is intimate and flowing in merriment.

The next clause in our passage is most exulting. ***Jesus of Nazareth, a Man*** exclaims, ***"and my tongue was glad;"*** (Acts 2:26). The Greek word translated ***tongue*** can mean the organ of the body or often it stands for speech or language. The Greek word translated ***was glad*** is a compound word. The first Greek word means "much;" the second Greek word means "to leap." Therefore, this Greek word means "to leap for joy, to show one's joy by leaping and skipping." This kind of activity denotes excessive or ecstatic joy and delight. Often in the Old Testament Septuagint this Greek word is used to speak of rejoicing with song and dance (Psalms 2:11; 20:5; 40:16; 68:3). This verb is normally found in the middle voice which has to do with personal preference. He is not expressing a quiet spirit of contentment. This is not resting as in napping. This is a party where things are getting out of hand. Merriment is taking place with my best friend, the God who is sourcing me. It is an occasion to dance on the table, blow party whistles, and play loud music! I just cannot help myself!

Both verbs, ***rejoiced*** and ***was glad***, are in the aorist tense. It adds a timeless element to His condition. This corresponds to the Hebrew perfect tense as found in the original writing in the Psalms. As focus upon the Father is ***always*** present in His life, so also is the jubilant merriment. Do you see the interworking of these two concepts?

Peter is describing and explaining the Pentecost event. The explanation is Jesus! That which flowed in and through Jesus is now happening in the disciples. This is promised to you. Here is what you can expect when you are filled with the Spirit. When God sources you, look for these things. Jesus will be your total vision. Not because you refuse to see anything else, but because you cannot see anything else. You are captured by Him. You see Him, therefore He captures you. Since you are captured by Him, you see Him. This produces in your inner person a merriment which is not affected by circumstances, pressures, or even death!

The next major phrase in the Messiah's statement is just as startling. He says, *"Moreover my flesh also will rest in hope,"* (Acts 2:26). ***Moreover*** literally means "the continuation of a condition or action." It can also mean "in addition, further, or besides." How could there be anything more? To experience all we have just proposed would be more than one could expect in a multitude of lifetimes. It only points us to the abundance of His presence when flowing through ***a Man***. There seems to be no end to the extravagant benefits.

It is very valuable for us to grasp the full significance of the reference to ***my flesh***. The actual Greek word does refer to the physical body as distinguished from the spirit or soul. Many scholars believe this statement in our verse is in regard to the hope of the resurrection. Peter has just preached about the Spirit of God producing the death of Christ. Now he quotes the Messianic Psalm in which the Messiah is expressing His hope and trust in God who will raise Him from the dead. However, there is room for a larger and deeper interpretation than this.

In the preceding statement the Messiah has revealed the joy and merriment within His ***heart*** and ***tongue***. We discovered the ***heart*** is the ***hidden person of the heart***. This joy is a condition of the inner most person which certainly affects the flesh but is not dependent upon it. The Greek word translated ***tongue*** can most definitely refer to the organ in the body. As stated above, it can also refer to speech or language. However, David originally wrote this in the Hebrew language. In the original Psalm the Hebrew word is actually translated ***glory***. It expresses the idea of abundance, honor, and dignity. This Hebrew word expresses the glory of God filling the temple. This would not be a focus on the physical presence of God, but the Spirit and essence of His presence. Peter, in quoting this Psalm, followed the translation of the Septuagint rather than the Hebrew text. In this change the translators shifted from the glory (Hebrew) to the tongue (Greek). In light of the total statement, the Messiah is expressing the condition of the inner person (**heart**). What is being expressed is not just from the physical tongue but from the very soul, being, or essence of His existence.

With this in clear focus, we must view the statement of ***my flesh*** as an expression of something beyond the physical body. This is not a statement of the confidence the Messiah has in the physical resurrection from the dead. As we have understood from Peter's sermon, the resurrection is more than an event. It is not just a physical resurrection of the body, although that is included. The resurrection is a state of being which flows from the indwelling and sourcing of the Spirit of God within the individual. So the idea of ***flesh*** in this verse must be seen as greater than just the physical. It represents the entire person.

This is further seen in a proper understanding of the concept of ***will rest in hope***. The Greek word translated ***will rest*** literally means to dwell in a tent or tabernacle, to camp. This Greek word is used by Jesus in the Parable of the Mustard Seed. He tells us of the smallest seed the Jews possessed which grows into the largest tree in their land. It ***becomes a tree, so that the birds of the air come and nest in its branches*** (Matthew 13:32). This portrays the idea of lodging or remaining. The birds do not simply alight temporarily in the tree but nest and permanently dwell.

Jesus of Nazareth, a Man says, "***Moreover my flesh also will rest in hope.***" Some scholars have interpreted this to be an expression of the Messiah's faith. He could yield His flesh to death in confidence of the physical resurrection. So ***hope*** is the resting place, the camping site, or the permanent dwelling of His flesh in death. However, in understanding ***flesh*** as more than the physical body we begin to perceive a deeper meaning of this statement. ***Hope*** is not the place of dwelling, but literally means "as may be hoped." The place of dwelling is His focus on the Father.

The Messiah said in the beginning of Peter's quotation (Acts 2:26) that the Father was in His eye. This vision is so dominant, He cannot see anything else. No circumstances or difficulties are able to distract Him. This focus on the Father is absolutely consistent. This is not a picture of the Father, and it is not an idea or doctrine of the Father. The actual essence of the life of the Father has come to be His body guard. This means because He is seeing the Father He is consistently focused on the Father. Therefore, the Father is producing or sourcing the focus. Jesus is simply responding to the stimuli of the Father's presence. This produces merriment in the depths of His inner being. It is so strong it permeates His entire life even to the physical body. Since His entire being, both spiritually and physically dwells, permanently lodges, rests, or nests in this focus, He may continue to hope in the Father. The Messiah will continue to live in the fullness of the Father. What the Father has been doing within Him, the Father will continue to do through Him. The unseen future holds no fear because of the dwelling place of the focus on the Father.

Peter is explaining Pentecost. Pentecost is Christianity. The Old Covenant is now gone and the New Covenant is present. **Christ in you** is now ours (Colossians 1:27). As the Father sourced Jesus, so Jesus now wants to source us. How can this be maintained on a moment by moment basis? The key is in the focus. We must focus on Jesus as Jesus focused on the Father (Acts 2:25). You and I can experience this same focus which takes place in the same sourcing of the Spirit. This will produce the same jubilant merriment which Jesus experienced in relationship with the Father. This sourcing can permeate our lives until He is our lodging place. We can live in the eternal hope of this focus and sourcing continues forever. Even in crucifixion there is no fear. The life both physically and spiritually is consumed by the focus of His presence. Christ is ours; we are His!

Acts 2:27

A MAN'S COMMUNION

Peter, filled with the Holy Spirit, is being used by God to explain to the Jews of the Dispersion the outpouring of the Spirit of Christ. His explanation is for us as well. He focuses his explanation on Jesus. In order to understand Pentecost, we must understand Jesus. ***Jesus of Nazareth, a Man*** was the proof of Pentecost. God sourced this **Man** so all could see and understand the full potential God intends for mankind. God sourced the life of Christ (Acts 2:22), the death of Christ (Acts 2:23), and the resurrection of Christ (Acts 2:24).

What was the spiritual condition of Jesus which allowed this sourcing? Furthermore, how did Jesus maintain this sourcing moment by moment? To answer these questions, Peter reverts back to the Old Testament Scriptures. There must not be any chance of misunderstanding. This is not Peter's opinion, cultural perspective, or memorized answer. The explanation comes from King David who speaks concerning the Messiah (Acts 2:25). It is a quotation from a Messianic Psalm (Psalms 16:8-11).

The Father sourced Jesus because of His spiritual condition. The key element was Christ's focus. The **CONCENTRATION** of Christ was on the Father (Acts 2:25). The Father appeared in the eye of Christ until He could see nothing else. The Father is the source of the concentration as Christ responds to His appearance. As the Son sees the Father, He loves Him. As Jesus loves the Father, He is driven to see Him. As Jesus sees the Father,

He loves Him. This drives Jesus to see Him. The very presence of the Father perpetuates the concentration.

This produces a condition of **CELEBRATION** within the inner most person of Christ (Acts 2:26). There is a merriment which resembles a party flowing between the Father and Son. It affects the entire being of Christ which enables Him to have hope. The very dwelling place of the Spirit filled Man is the presence of the Father. This fullness enables Him to hope in all situations, even His death and resurrection.

Then the Messiah breaks into an outburst of this celebration (Acts 2:27). It is an expression of worship as the Son actually speaks to the Father. The Messiah is giving details of the depth of the **COMMUNION** which takes place between them in the fullness of the Holy Spirit. Remember this is an explanation of Pentecost. Everything true of *Jesus of Nazareth, a Man* is taking place in the one hundred and twenty disciples. It is also promised to you.

The beginning statement of this worship is *"For You will not leave my soul in Hades,"* (Acts 2:27). This statement is so important and powerful that Peter restates it as he continues preaching. He interprets this statement in light of the promise of the Father to King David (Acts 2:30). It is a validation of the resurrection of the Messiah according to Peter: *"he, foreseeing this, spoke concerning the resurrection of the Christ, that His soul was not left in Hades, nor did His flesh see corruption,"* (Acts 2:31). This is an Old Testament statement of the New Testament reality proposed in verse twenty-four. God was proving Pentecost in *Jesus of Nazareth, a Man.* One of the proofs was found in the resurrection. *A Man* filled with the Spirit could not be contained in death. Death is pictured as long, gigantic fingers reaching to seize, capture, and imprison the individual. He gives the picture of a baby trapped in his mother's womb. Death can no more hold the person filled with the Spirit than a pregnant woman can keep her baby in her womb. When one is filled with the Spirit, he can move into the midst of death with complete freedom from fear. Death is anything which is not sourced by the Spirit. All the aspects of death connected to daily living fall by the wayside. They try to entangle us, but it is not allowed because of the Spirit of Christ. The seizing fingers of death slide from the believer. This is also true for death as contained in physical and eternal death. Jesus told us, *"And whoever lives and believes in Me shall never die. Do you believe this?"* (John 11:26). The reason for the truth of this statement is the intimacy of the fullness of the Spirit. Death is no longer death. The sting has been removed. Evidently there is something so powerful and explosive within the relationship of the Spirit of Christ and the believer that death is no longer a threat!

The depth of the relationship producing this reality is expressed in the verb of the opening sentence of our passage. It is *will (not) leave*. *Leave* is a combination of two Greek words. These two words can be translated "in" and "forsake, abandon, or desert." It means to "leave behind in any state or place." Jesus is obviously speaking of His Father who is in His eye.

The Messiah's proclamation is strong; the Father will not abandon or leave Him. The intertwining of the Father and the Son is so tight that there is no possibility of separation. There is a complete unity between them. They cannot be divided even by death. It is the picture of the vine and the branch relationship (John 15). The two are distinct yet not the same; but they are so united you cannot see where one leaves off and the other begins. This is the man filled with the Spirit of Christ. Peter is explaining Pentecost. The fullness of the Holy Spirit is a state of intimacy with Christ. It is so tight and complete He cannot go off and leave you.

We must carefully investigate this key word. The Greek word translated *leave* (engkataleipo) is actually a compound word. The first Greek word is "en" which is used numerous times in the New Testament. The second Greek word is "kataleipo." This word is used twenty-four times in the New Testament. It means "to forsake, abandon, or leave behind." One would think this word (kataleipo) would have been adequate to express the cry of the Messiah's heart in our passage. But when Peter quoted this Psalm, he used the Greek word "engkataleipo." This states the basic idea of forsaking or leaving behind, but strengthens the relational aspect of the statement.

Let us review the use of the Greek word "en." You may remember from previous studies the role this word plays in comparison with "into" (eis) and "from" (ek). Both of these words indicate motion either away from or towards. But the word "in" has no motion. It bespeaks the fact of resting, remaining, or abiding. In the New Testament this word is used in regard to a person being filled with something. Sin is not a simple deed, but actually lives in a person (Romans 7:17-20). The opposite of this is God's Spirit living within the believer (Romans 8:9-11; 1 Corinthians 3:16). Life, joy, faith, and the Word are said to be in people because of the presence of the Spirit of Christ (John 6:53, 15:11; 2 Timothy 1:5; John 5:38). ***All the treasures of wisdom and knowledge*** are found in Christ (Colossians 2:3). The mystery and the life are both hidden in God (Ephesians 3:9; Colossians 3:3).

Most important for us is the use of this word for the inner relationship between God and a person. There are frequent statements that God actually works in a person (1 Corinthians 12:6; Philippians 1:6, 2:13; Colossians 1:29). Paul seems to present a formula which he emphatically states as **Christ in you** (Romans 8:10; 2 Corinthians 13:5; Colossians 1:27). This description was highlighted by Jesus in the upper room discourse on the promise of the Father (John 14, 15, and 16). In describing His own relationship with the Father He said, *"Believe Me that I am in the Father and the Father in Me,"* (John 14:11). He continued, *"I am in My Father, and you in Me, and I in you,"* (John 14:20). In describing the coming experience of the fullness of the Spirit,

Jesus said, *"He dwells with you and will be in you,"* (John 14:17).

This gives us a good understanding of the use of "in" (en). Remember this is the first of two words combined together in the Greek word translated *leave* (engkataleipo) in our text (Acts 2:27). The second word (kataleipo) is really interesting for it is also a compound word. It is the Greek word which can be translated "down," and the Greek word which can be translated "forsake" or "leave." The first Greek word translated "down" can mean "down from," "down upon," or "down in." It has the connotation of "deep throughout." This second Greek word translated "forsake" or "leave" can mean "fail," "wanting," or "deficient."

If this has become clear in your thinking, you are automatically asking a question. Why would they place the word "in" (en) at the beginning of the word "leave" (kataleipo) and form a whole new word (engkataleipo)? Clearly something distinctive is being stated by the use of this word. This is not about simply leaving something behind as in leaving a message, but has to do with relationship. This Greek word (engkataleipo) is used ten times in the New Testament. Each time it is used there is relationship involved. It is the word used in the statement of Christ on the cross when He cried out, *"My God, My God, why have You forsaken Me?"* (Matthew 27:46; Mark 15:34). Paul also used this same term in referring to Demas. He said, **"Be diligent to come to me quickly; for Demas has forsaken me, having loved this present world, and has departed for Thessalonica"** (2 Timothy 4:9-10).

In this Messianic Psalm, the Messiah is giving us deep insight into the intimacy and oneness found in the fullness of the Spirit. The Father is in the eye of the Son. This is not an acquaintance relationship. This is not a mutually beneficial relationship. This is not even a need based relationship. The unity is deep in the fullness of the Spirit; there is no possibility of separation. The security of the relationship is found in unity and oneness. There is no deficiency even in the realm of the dead. This relationship supersedes every circumstance of life and death.

This concept is even further expanded by the direct object of the verb. Jesus says, **"For you will not leave my soul in Hades."** The focus of the action of the verb is on the direct object, *my soul*. This was startling to me. Perhaps I have had the wrong interpretation of *soul*. When *soul* is suggested, I immediately think of the part of my being which is in the image of God. It is the spiritual aspect of my life where God intends to indwell. This interpretation is not what Jesus is saying in our verse. The Greek word translated *soul* has to do with "the principle of life." It is contrasted with physical death. This Greek word can be used for both man and animals.

An example can be found in the story of a man who fell asleep in church. Let this be a warning to all who might be tempted to do this. Paul is preaching. A man falls asleep while sitting in a window. He falls three stories to the ground and dies. **But Paul went down, fell on him, and embracing him said, "Do not trouble yourselves, for his life** (soul) **is in him"** (Acts 20:10). So this Greek word translated *soul* is used in the New Testament to refer to the natural life existence of men. It becomes a word which encompasses the essence of my existence. Thus, it is used in our passage. The Messiah is saying that the intimacy He has with the Father is so strong that who He is cannot be separated from the Father. The Father has become the heart of His DNA. The Father is not a warm jacket Jesus wears. The Father is the center ingredient of every cell of Christ's being. There is no way to separate the Father from who He is. Any attempt of separation would destroy Him. It would be easier to remove the mother's or father's genetic makeup from their child than to separate the Father from the life principle of Jesus.

We must see this in the context of Peter's explanation of Pentecost. The Father is sourcing Jesus. The spiritual condition of Jesus which allows this is the consistent concentration on the Father. The Father has gotten into the eye of the Messiah, and Jesus has responded to this vision. This has produced merriment (party) between these two with the undercurrent of the absolute confidence of hope. The communion is so strong between them; there is no possibility of separation. Not even **Hades** (the realm of the dead) can disturb this party of unity. If one can experience a party with the Spirit of the Father in **Hades**, what could be the circumstances which could separate us from Him? The Messiah is describing the depth of the communion found in the fullness of the Spirit!

The second phrase in our passage is just as intriguing. It says, **"Nor will You allow Your Holy One to see corruption,"** (Acts 2:27). Here is a bold statement of confidence in relationship. The verb **will allow** is a Greek word which focuses on source. It comes from the Greek word "didomi" and means "to give or bestow upon." This word is the most common expression for the procedure whereby a subject deliberately transfers something to someone or something so that it becomes available to the recipient. In our sentence, it is in the negative. The Father who is in the eye of the Messiah and with whom there is a depth of communion and unity WILL NOT GIVE corruption to the One who is filled with the Spirit.

Let us examine the logic of the total picture found here. Peter is explaining Pentecost to the Jews of the Dispersion. Jesus is the explanation. He is a man who is sourced by the Father. Everything He has is given to Him by the Father. His life with all of its aspects is sourced by the Father. Even Jesus' death is given to Him by the Father. His resurrection is certainly a gift of the Father. Jesus is totally dependent upon the Father for every function. The spiritual condition within Jesus which allows this sourcing is His absolute concentration on the Father. The Father is in His eye. Jesus simply responds to the Father which strengthens the focus. This produces merriment (party) within the relationship. Hope and confidence flow from this intimacy. This relationship is so intimate separation is impossible without the destruction of who Jesus is. The Father has become the DNA of the essence of Christ. It is so strong it can exist even in the realm of death. The absolute certainty of this is found in the sourcing of the Father. The Father would never source the Son with corruption. The Father is life and light. The Father will never give the Son destruction, damnation, or corruption. If this is true in Jesus, it is true in us through the fullness of the same Spirit. Obviously the key is found in the total sourcing of the Spirit of God.

This is further highlighted by the Greek word translated *to see*. It is not simply to physically see. It means to perceive, grasp, understand, or know. It has an inward focus. This is especially important when we attempt to comprehend the meaning of *corruption*. Many Bible scholars interpret this word to refer to the physical body of Jesus. They specifically relate this to the decaying of the body of Christ during His three days in the grave. They are very strong in declaring that Jesus' body did not experience any form of returning to dust. When the blood stops circulating to the cells of the body, the decaying process begins in the body. Some believe this did not happen to Christ. I have not been able to embrace this concept! It violates the focus of Peter's sermon. Peter is explaining Pentecost. Jesus is the complete explanation or example of the content of Pentecost. What happened to Jesus is taking place in the one hundred and twenty disciples, and is promised to you. This would mean I would not need to be embalmed when I die for my body will never experience decay. But that is not true. Peter expresses that it was not even true for King David (Acts 2:29).

However, the main difficulty is basing this truth on this passage and especially the Greek word translated *corruption*. This same word is used by Luke in his Gospel account. Jesus is instructing His disciples not to worry. He said, **"Sell what you** *have and give alms; provide yourselves money bags which do not grow old, a treasure in the heavens that does not fail, where no thief approaches nor moth destroys* (Luke 12:33). In the revelation of the second trumpet in the Book of the Revelation, we see the same word. ***And a third of the living creatures in the sea died, and a third of the ships were destroyed*** (Revelation 8:9). In our text in the Book of Acts, one must see this word in this same way. The focus is not on the body not decaying, but upon the entire destructive power of death (**Hades**). The focus is on the liberation from the destruction that is brought about by death. This is further verified in Paul's sermon when he said, **"And that He raised Him from the dead, no more to return to corruption,"** (Acts 13:34).

The Messiah is once again declaring the depth of intimacy found in the communion of the fullness of the Holy Spirit. There is no chance of destruction for the one who is filled with the Spirit of Christ. The core of every cell of his being is throbbing with the life of God. The intimacy is so deep He will not abandon the believer, nor give him destruction. Our total confidence and hope is found here. As this was experienced by Jesus, so this is now promised to us. The oneness Jesus had with the Father, we are now to experience with Him. Every circumstance of life must be faced with the awareness of His presence. He will not abandon us nor give us destruction!

Acts 2:28

A MAN'S COMMUNICATION

Jesus' inner heart is full of worship. He is giving wonderful expression to that worship in a Messianic Psalm. He moves from CONCENTRATION (Acts 2:25) to CELEBRATION (Acts 2:26). This produces a change in language from speaking about His Father to actually addressing Him in worship. There is a COMMUNION (Acts 2:27) expressed in His worship. The Father and Son have become one. They cannot be separated. There is a COMMUNICATION established. The Son cries, **"You have made known to me the ways of life;"** (Acts 2:28).

The communication level between the Messiah and the Father who has filled Him is very strong. This does not surprise you. It matches the level of the intimacy between them. There is correspondence between intimacy and communication. One must not think there can be barriers and communication will still take place. If I am not hearing clearly, I may not be embracing properly. The intimacy level must be the beginning place of correction.

This is highlighted in His opening statement in verse twenty-eight. **You have made known** is a translation of one Greek word. It is used twenty-five times in the New Testament. It is completely beyond the idea of "to say." It is not on the level of a simple conversation. It is not the equivalent of writing someone a note. In the New Testament this has to do with announcing. It is blaring, even bold. It means "to make known publicly or explicitly." If one investigates the appearance of this Greek word in the New Testament (twenty-five times), they all relate to God or the salvation event in Christ.

In our passage, the level of communication must be understood far beyond yelling or shouting the information. He is not necessarily saying that God, the Father, forcefully informed Him. It has to do with communication derived from intimacy. For instance, there is a communication level unique to husband and wife. It comes from years of intimacy. It is beyond verbal statements. Some men call it "the look." One just knows how the other feels or thinks. This depth of communication is present between Jesus and His Father. The Father is able to share the depth of His heart and passion. But not only is the Father able to share it, the Son is able to grasp it. It comes from the intimacy they have together. In our relationships with each other, there are very few people with whom you can share everything. You say to that person, "I can't tell this to anyone else. They just would not understand." This person understands because you have shared many experiences together, some of overwhelming joy and some of incredible sorrow. You share on a very intimate level. The Father is revealing the depth of life to the Son. This happens because they have become one.

You must constantly remember this entire discussion concerns the explanation of Pentecost. Jesus is the explanation for the fullness of the Spirit. He is sourced by the Father. What takes place within Him is now happening in one hundred and twenty disciples, and it is promised to you and me. This sourcing of the Father comes because of the spiritual condition of Jesus. He is totally concentrated on the Father. The Father is in His eye (Acts 2:25). This produces an amazing celebration (Acts 2:26). It is on the level of high-spirited fun which takes place between the Father and the Son. Out of this comes worship which is an expression of the depth of the communion they experience together (Acts 2:27). It is impossible to separate them. Even death cannot untangle who the Father is from who Jesus is. Now we see the wonder of the communication happening between them (Acts 2:28). This is all taking place within the experience of Pentecost. This is no longer unique to Jesus, but was given to the disciples and now to you and me.

Jesus must have spent hours with the disciples in the upper room explaining this (John 14, 15 and 16). He attempted to get them ready for His death, resurrection, and ascension. They were deeply troubled because He kept speaking of His departure. They could not imagine life without Him. How could He describe this to them? He said, **"No longer do I call you servants, for a servant does not know what his master is doing; but I have called you friends, for all things that I heard from My Father I have made known to you"** (John 15:15). Jesus used the same Greek word as found in our text. To move from a servant to a friend is a shift in intimacy. In the context of this intimacy Jesus is now communicating to us. It is Pentecost.

Paul was deeply aware of this reality. He had experienced both the old and new covenants. Of all his contemporaries he has been the most zealous for the traditions of the fathers (Galatians 1:14). He had lived in the mystery of the Old Testament. It was a shadow in which the revelation had **been hidden from ages and from generations, but now has been revealed to His saints** (Colossians 1:26). The revelation of the hidden mystery is very simple, yet it is immersed in riches and glory. Here is what has been revealed to the saints. **To them God willed to make known what are the riches of the glory of this mystery among the Gentiles: which is Christ in you, the hope of glory** (Colossians 1:27). Paul uses the same Greek word found in our text. Think of the intimacy found in **the riches of the glory of this mystery!** Christ is in you. This is the hope of glory. This is the intimacy level which enables Christ to make Himself known to us.

The Book of Ephesians is such a powerful treatment of what

is happening in the unseen world. Paul begins by declaring that God has spoken into being every good thing He wants us to have (Ephesians 1:3). He has placed them all in Christ. He then begins to list these great blessings. It is only a partial list, but it is completely overwhelming. He has chosen us. He has adopted us. Holiness is ours. We have become accepted. Redemption is ours through His blood. He has given the *riches of His grace which He made to abound toward us in all wisdom and prudence, having made known to us the mystery of His will, according to His good pleasure which He purposed in Himself,* (Ephesians 1:7-9). The Greek word in our text appears again. The intimacy level of being in Christ, accepted in the Beloved, enables a communication beyond knowledge. It is what is *purposed in Himself.* We know the mind of Christ.

Let us return to our passage in Acts. *You have made known to me the ways of life;* (Acts 2:28). It appears the most effective way to grasp the meaning of *life* is to see it in the context of the ministry of Jesus. In ministering to Nicodemus, Jesus spoke of being lifted up like a serpent in the wilderness. The purpose of which was *"whoever believes in Him should not perish but have eternal LIFE"* (John 3:15). *"For God so loved the world that He gave His only begotten Son, that whoever believes in Him should not perish but have everlasting LIFE"* (John 3:16). The conclusion is simply stated by John the Baptist. *"He who believes in the Son has everlasting LIFE, and he who does not believe the Son shall not see LIFE; but the wrath of God abides on him"* (John 3:36). Jesus continued in ministry by speaking to a Samaritan woman. He offered her water and said, *"But the water that I shall give him will become in him a fountain of water springing up into everlasting LIFE"* (John 4:14). Jesus pleaded with the people of His day, *"Do not labor for the food which perishes, but for the food which endures to everlasting LIFE, which the Son of Man will give you,"* (John 6:27). In speaking about Himself, Jesus said, *"For the bread of God is He who comes down from heaven and gives LIFE to the world"* (John 6:33). The crowd responded with a desire for this bread. Jesus continued, *"I am the bread of LIFE"* (John 6:35). In the same discourse Jesus declared, *"And this is the will of Him who sent Me, that everyone who sees the Son and believes in Him may have everlasting LIFE;"* (John 6:40). The crowd began to complain about His statements. Jesus continued to clarify, *"Most assuredly, I say to you, he who believes in Me has everlasting LIFE. I am the bread of LIFE,"* (John 6:47-48). In further explanation Jesus said, *"I am the LIVING bread which came down from heaven. If anyone eats of this bread, he will LIVE forever; and the bread that I shall give is My flesh, which I shall give for the LIFE of the world"* (John 6:51). You can do further research yourself to see how Jesus used this Greek word.

Life was used in early Christianity to characterize salvation. The Old Testament shows a strong contrast between the dead gods of the world and the Living God. The actions of our God prove He is alive. The dead gods were manufactured by the hands of men. Men had to take care of these gods. \They were served, protected, and given provisions. Our Living God is one who acts in our behalf. He delivers us. The Old Testament contains the abundant stories of the great deliverances of our Living God in our behalf. This is the Living God who is sourcing **Jesus of Nazareth, a Man.** His sourcing is one of LIFE. Whatever is contained in this word is flowing through Jesus to His world. This is what has now possessed the hundred and twenty disciples. This is what is promised to you and me!

There is a significant connection between the LIFE and the "way." It seems to be at the very heart of the communication between the Father and the Son. This communication is far beyond the sharing of data or information. It is completely outside the realm of drawing Him a map or showing Him a path. This seems to be the danger in referring to Christianity as a journey. We immediately think of the Bible as a road map.

We study carefully to make the right turns and stay on the correct way. While this symbolism is valid we must constantly be aware of the danger it suggests.

Perhaps the author of the Book of Hebrews clarifies it. Here is his declaration: *"Therefore, brethren, having boldness to enter the Holiest by the blood of Jesus, by a new and LIVING WAY which He consecrated for us, through the veil, that is, His flesh, and having a High Priest over the house of God,"* (Hebrews 10:19-21). I was really intrigued by the use of the word *boldness*. This is translated from a compound Greek word. It is the words "all" and "the act of speaking." It is used to express freedom or frankness in speaking all that one thinks or pleases. This describes Jesus as He was relating the first prediction of His death and resurrection. *He spoke this word openly* (Mark 8:32). Especially in Hebrews and First John the word denotes confidence which is connected with communion with God through Christ. This new communication enables us *to enter into the Holiest*. The Greek word translated *to enter* is a compound word. It is the combination of "into" (eis) and "way" (same Greek word in Acts 2:28). An astonishing embrace has happened in Christ. We have been given the ability to communicate on a whole new level to the extent it has placed us into a new way.

What has made this possible? The Hebrew author cries out, "It is *by a new and living way,*" (Hebrews 10:20). The Greek word translated *new* as used in this verse is significant. This is the only time it is used in the entire New Testament. It is like God saved this word for a special emphasis as related to Christ. Its original meaning was "freshly slaughtered." Jesus is the new way, the freshly slaughtered sacrifice. He opens the new communication level to God. What seems odd is for the Hebrew author to continue to call this death sacrifice the *living way.* The *living way* is the cross way. He continues to clarify that the *way* was *consecrated for us* by Christ. The Greek word translated *consecrated* is a compound word. "In" and "to make new" are the meaning of the two words. He is pictured as the High Priest who has been freshly slaughtered for the purpose of taking us through the veil right into communication with the heart and mind of God. He is the *living way.* Through intimacy (communication) with Him, we have intimacy (communication) with the Father.

Let us return to our passage in Acts. ***You have made known to me the ways of life*** (Acts 2:28). This is a good time to review. ***You have made known to me*** is not in the realm of data or information. It is in the embrace of personal intimacy. Between the Father and the Son is a level of oneness that allows the Son to grasp the inner heart of the Father. The depth of the communication is directly tied to the depth of the intimacy. This same depth is promised to us. It is not academic achievement but the intimacy of Pentecost. The outside God has come inside. In the oneness of the fullness of the Spirit a new level of communication has taken place. In this embrace ***the ways of life*** are shared. We might have expressed this as "revealed," "comprehended," or "made plain." However, these words miss the intent. They indicate separation or mastering the material. This intimacy is the sharing of the minds until we know, not because we have learned, although there is a maturing process. It is not because we have spiritual disciplines, although He has been disciplining our lives. It is because we have been embraced by Him in oneness.

This is expressed in the word *ways.* It is important to note in the original Psalm (Psalm 16:11) this appears as singular. We must not approach this as if there are several possibilities; rather there is only one way of life! The Greek word translated *ways* is found one hundred and one times in the New Testament. However, nearly one-third of all occurrences are found in Luke's writings. Since the statement in our passage is coming from the lips of Christ (a Messianic Psalm), it might help us to consider two other major occurrences where He used this imagery.

In the Sermon on the Mount Jesus declared, *"Enter by the narrow gate; for wide is the gate and broad is the way that leads to destruction, and there are many who go in by it. Because narrow is the gate and difficult is the way which leads to life, and there are few who find it"* (Matthew 7:13-14). The danger of these two verses is to interpret them out of their context. One could conclude that there are two possibilities with two destinations. It is my responsibility to "find" the path which leads to life. It is like trying to find a path in difficult terrain, or coming across a narrow entry after a lengthy search. This would reduce the Scriptures to a road map which I must follow explicitly without detours.

However, we must view these two verses (Matthew 7:13-14) in light of their context, the Sermon on the Mount. Jesus establishes the "seeking-finding" concept. Even at the end of these two verses, He says, *"and there are few who find it,"* (Matthew 7:14). In the verses just prior to this statement (Matthew 7:7-12), Jesus focuses on the "seeking-finding" con-cept. He indicates that "finding" is guaranteed in the "seeking." "Opening" is certain in the "knocking!" "Receiving" is to be expected in the "asking!" He stated this same concept earlier (Matthew 6:33). The focus of the Sermon on the Mount is not the road map, performance list, or self-searching routine. It is the mystery of the Divine action whereby if we seek (respond) He will find us!

There are those Bible scholars who believe the great theme or proposition of the Sermon on the Mount is the opening Beatitude:

Blessed are the poor in spirit,
For theirs is the Kingdom of heaven (Matthew 5:3).

Those who have nothing with which to buy, no status by which to claim, and no merit by which to demand have the Kingdom of God as their own!

Narrow is the gate and difficult is the way is because it runs cross grain to our very self-sourcing nature. Pride demands that we must find; brokenness requires we must be found. Self-accomplishment requires the claim of achievement; seeking (responding) implies accepting. Self-reliance promotes the "I must do it" attitude; inability demands "I must be enabled." This is "relational" language. The imagery of the *way* is not about the discovery of a road and carefully walking in this safe path. It is about Christ who is ***the way, the truth, and the life*** (John 14:6).

This brings us to another strong declaration of Jesus concerning the *way* (John 14:6). Your understanding of the context is essential in light of its statement. In John's account of the Gospel these chapters (14, 15 and 16) are a long discourse given by Jesus in the upper room. He is at the moment of betrayal and crucifixion. The focus of the discourse is the purpose for all that will take place in the next few days. His death, resurrection and ascension will be to accomplish the fullness of the Spirit. Jesus said, ***"I will pray the Father, and He will give you another Helper, that He may abide with you forever – the Spirit of truth, whom the world cannot receive, because it neither sees Him nor knows Him; but you know Him, for He dwells with you and will be in you. I will not leave you orphans; I will come to you,"*** (John 14:16-18). This statement is not about His second coming. It is about the outside God getting inside. This is Pentecost.

Jesus begins His discourse by encouraging His disciples. He understands their dismay over His immanent departure, but it is only because they do not fully comprehend all He has tried to teach them (John 14:1). In the Father's household (family) there are many dwelling places, not mansions (John 14:2). Up to this time, the disciples have only seen one dwelling place; that is Jesus. He is filled with the Spirit. Jesus is going to go away (crucifixion, resurrection and ascension) in order to prepare more dwelling places. He is going to prepare them to become dwelling places. If Jesus participates in the difficulty of going away and prepares them as dwelling places, He will come again (not second coming) and receive (a Greek word always used regarding people, a term of intimacy) them to Himself (John 14:3). The result will be that where He is (state of being) they will also be (state of being). Where He goes, they know. They also know the *way* (John 14:4).

Thomas totally misses the point (John 14:5). Road maps, destinations, and traveling dominate His thoughts. From this view He does not know where Jesus is going or how he could get here. Jesus explains, ***"I am the way, the truth, and the life. No one comes to the Father except through Me"*** (John 14:6). In the rest of the three chapters (John 14, 15 and 16) Jesus speaks of the indwelling of the Spirit of Christ. What Jesus accomplished for us is found in who He is. The *way* is not about road maps and traveling, but about intimacy and relationship.

One hundred and twenty disciples have received the fullness of the Holy Spirit. A large crowd of Jews witness this outpouring. Peter is moved upon by the Holy Spirit to give an explanation. His entire sermon focuses on Jesus as the clarification. ***Jesus of Nazareth, a Man*** is filled with the Father who sources His life, His death, and His resurrection (Acts 2:22-24). It was the absolute CONCENTRATION (Acts 2:25) of the Father that enabled this spiritual condition in the Son. The result of this was CELEBRATION (Acts 2:26), which was high-spirited fun permeating Jesus' entire being. As Jesus breaks into worship, He addresses the Father. His worship reveals the depth of His COMMUNION (Acts 2:27) with the Father. They are so welded together, they cannot be separated. In the depth of their relationship there is found a paralleled depth of COMMUNICATION (Acts 2:28). As the Father and Son embrace they explicitly reveal life. It is life in abundance, in the eternal, and in every aspect of Jesus' being. It is ***the way of life***. He did not find this in performance or the mapping of travel. He found it in the intimacy of the embrace and the Father in His eye. This is present in Jesus. It was given to the disciples. It is promised to you!

Acts 2:28

THE ULTIMATE GOAL

In my younger days of ministry, I was somewhat repelled by those who had a futuristic view of Christianity. During revivals in those days, the closing night would always be focused on heaven. The song evangelist would feature our future in glory land and the old saints would get blessed. None of this seemed to resonate with me. I thought probably it was just my age and this would change as I got older. Now I am "old" but find my feelings the same.

It is very dangerous to speak like this due to misunderstanding. Not everyone is in the same place. We are certainly not against the blessings and plans of God for the future in eternity. However, the focus for the future has often been streets of gold in front of great mansions. This is not unlike many of the world religions which have proposed the future life will abundantly provide those things we sacrificed or do not have in the present. Often our expectations of the future have been an expansion of the present focus. Could the focus on life without pain, suffering, and death in the future be a product of the circumstances we are struggling with in the present? Could the physical comfort of big mansions in the future life be a result of the focus on a materialistic struggle in the present? While this may not be evil, it should not be the determining factor of our perspective.

There is a Biblical principle which remains true in all of the writers of the New Testament. Eternal life is not that which is to come, but is that which is started now. John highlights this repeatedly in his Gospel account. Our life in eternity is an expansion of this life. We must not view them as separate or different lives. Eighty years on this earth is really brief compared to the infinite eternal life. Yet, it is very significant. It is so valuable we must embrace it as much as we look forward to eternal life. This life is not one thing and eternal life another. They are stages to the same living experience. One is the expansion of the same substance experienced in the other.

We do not consider our childhood as one life and our adulthood as a separate or different life. Our childhood is very brief in comparison to the time span of adulthood. However, it is in this childhood that the very roots of adulthood are found. Our responses, concepts, and attitudes of life are all shaped in our childhood. The patterns we establish in this period become a determining factor in the quality of our adult living. While childhood may be vague in our memory, it is very influential and is not considered a separate life. So it is with the linkage between our life in this time zone and our eternal life. One does not live one way in this time zone and then have a different life in eternity. The patterns, direction, and style of life are determined in our present life and will be expanded in eternity. Eternity is an expansion of what we are already experiencing in this life!

This is the concept expressed by the Messiah in our passage. Peter explains to the Jews of the Dispersion the essence of Pentecost. ***Jesus of Nazareth, a Man*** is his explanation. Jesus is sourced by the Father in the same exact manner we are to be sourced by Jesus. Everything expressed in Jesus is promised to us. However, we must have the same spiritual condition which allows this sourcing. It is the same spiritual condition found in Jesus. This is described for us by Jesus in a Messianic Psalm (Psalm 16:8-11) which is quoted by Peter (Acts 2:25-28).

Jesus was totally focused on the Father (CONCENTRATION, Acts 2:25). The Father was the pivotal point of influence and resource. Jesus was captured, mastered, and obsessed by the Father. During this focus there was a CELEBRATION taking place (Acts 2:26). It was high-spirited fun as they made merry. This happened within Jesus and the Father. It spread from His heart, to His emotion, to His countenance, and to the very tone of His life. Even His physical body found resource in this merriment. The strength of this condition spilled forth into worship. It was an expression of the depth of the COMMUNION between them (Acts 2:27). The Father and Son are inseparable. The depth of this relationship is expressed in COMMUNICATION (Acts 2:28). The Father was in Jesus' eye (Acts 2:25), then in His heart (Acts 2:26). The Father was in His cell structure (Acts 2:27) and even in His ear (Acts 2:28).

Communication is not accomplished until the recipient has understood. The communication is determined by the depth of the intimacy between them. Jesus spoke of this to His disciples in the upper room before His crucifixion. He said, **"However, when He, the Spirit of truth, has come, He will guide you into all truth;"** (John 16:13). It is a causative statement. The Holy Spirit is going to wrap His arm around you and cause you to be brought into the full knowledge and understanding of the Person of Jesus. In the depth of the union with our heart, He knows how to reveal Himself to us! Obviously the *way of life* is Jesus. So the opening statement in our passage gives expression to this revelation. *You have made known to me the ways of life;* (Acts 2:28).

There is one more clear statement in our passage. It is the climax of His expression of the intimacy between the Father and the Son. He cries, **"You will make me full of joy in Your presence"** (Acts 2:28). In many ways this statement becomes the great summary of everything Jesus has already spoken in the Messianic Psalm. He is expressing one more time the details of His spiritual condition.

The Greek verb of this great statement is translated, *You*

will make full. Notice it is in the future tense. In the Greek language the future tense has a very significant aspect about it. The future tense is the only tense which expresses only a level of time. It does not refer to the completion or duration of an action. If this statement (Acts 2:28) is really a summary of the entire Psalm, the verb tense used in the various explanations up to this point are all going to take place in the future as well. The past tense refers to what has taken place in my history and has end. The present tense gives a picture of now which also is quickly completed. The future announces the continuation in the days ahead with no prospect of ending.

In this last statement, Jesus grasps all He has experienced with the Father and proclaims it will continue in the future. Whatever happens in the resurrection, ascension, and exaltation will be a continuation of what He has already been experiencing. He may have new circumstances with new surroundings, but what has been His life up to this point will continue to be His life in the future. What sources Him in these days of earthly ministry will continue to source Him in the eternal dwelling.

In the future, the Father ***will make full***. The Greek word comes from the idea "to complete" or "to finish." It means to fill, supply abundantly with something, impart richly, or to permeate and invade. This same Greek word is used in connection with the devil. He has the ability to activate this in our lives. But Peter said, ***"Ananias, why has Satan filled your heart to lie to the Holy Spirit and keep back part of the price of the land for yourself?"*** (Acts 5:3). Satan desires to fill, permeate, and complete his work in us. Will this not also be true of eternity? If Satan is allowed to accomplish this in my present life, why would he not continue it in the future? Eternity is an expansion of what I now experience!

This same Greek word is used by Luke as a description of the Pentecost event. ***And suddenly there came a sound from heaven, as of a rushing mighty wind, and it filled the whole house where they were sitting*** (Acts 2:2). He uses the imagery of an echo (Greek word for *sound*). The fullness of the Holy Spirit has come from the Father and is rebounding and reflecting from the believer. The believer is *filled*. You will remember from previous studies this word is contrasted with the Greek word translated "filled" in verse four. This Greek word is used in verse two as well as in our study verse and it paints the picture of a container being filled with content. The outside content is coming inside the container. It is *filled*!

It cannot be an accident that Jesus uses this same word to describe what will take place in His future life. Peter's explanation of Pentecost is about Jesus. What happened in the life of Jesus is now happening in one hundred and twenty disciples. It is now promised to us. Jesus is sourced by the Father. This sourcing is now ours to claim. Evidently it is not just a time zone sourcing. The Father did not give this to *Jesus of Nazareth, a Man* because He needed it to make it through this life. When Jesus ascended to the right hand of the Father as *a Man*, did He no longer need this sourcing of God's life? No, He needs this same sourcing in the heavenly realms. The fullness of the Spirit defines human beings! We will not cease to be human beings in the eternal realms; we will not become angels. We will be people filled and sourced by God. Jesus is the prototype.

Peter continues in his sermon to highlight the sourcing of the Father through Jesus even after death. Jesus did not raise Himself from the dead, but was raised by the Father (Acts 2:24; 2:32). In eternity Jesus is to occupy a position at the right hand of the Father. In this position He is going to be sourced by the Father. Peter preached, **"Therefore being exalted to the right hand of God, and having received from the Father the promise of the Holy Spirit, He poured out this which you now see and hear,"** (Acts 2:33). The redemptive work to mankind continues in Pentecost, being sourced by the Father through Jesus. The Father is the source of the outpouring of the Holy Spirit!

This is promised to us in eternity as well. As we experience the fullness of the Holy Spirit here, we will experience it there. The spiritual experience we have now will be our spiritual experience in eternity. It is an expansion of His Divine presence. If you and I do not have the sourcing of the Spirit in this present life, we will not experience it in the life to come! Death is not a cure. It is certainly not a magic wand which miraculously transforms me. It is a transition from this stage of my life to another.

As Jesus highlights this continuation into the future, He focuses on two important issues which simply verify this truth. First, there is *"You will make me full of joy,"* (Acts 2:28). This is very significant. The Greek word translated *joy* is the same Greek word translated *rejoiced* (Acts 2:26). Jesus describes His spiritual condition which allows the Father to source Him in His earthly ministry. The Father is in His eye (CONCENTRATION – Acts 2:25). The more Jesus sees the Father the more Jesus loves the Father. The Father draws Jesus into His very presence. The intimacy and oneness is on the highest level. He is one with the Father. The oneness has a natural result. It is CELEBRATION. *"Therefore my heart rejoiced, and my tongue was glad;"* (Acts 2:26). The Greek word translated *rejoiced* comes from a root word meaning "well minded." It is not the same "rejoice" to which Paul refers in his writings. It is often translated "merry." In the English dictionary it means "high-spirited fun." Jesus describes His life on this earth as one of intimacy with the Father that results in high-spirited fun at the heart of His being.

Now He restates this same thought (Acts 2:28). In the future, the same spiritual condition will exist. He will no longer be in this time zone, but He will continue to be sourced by the Father. Eternity for Him will be an expansion of what He is already experiencing in this present world. Intimacy with the Father will continue to result in a "well mind" and a heart that is filled with "high-spirited fun." The same relationship Jesus has had with the Father will continue into eternity. As the Father has sourced Jesus in earthly living, so He will source Him in eternal living!

Part Three: In My Eye

This is promised to you and to me. Peter explains the Pentecost event. What is taking place in the lives of one hundred and twenty believers is what Jesus experienced. This is the Promise of the Father, and it is now ours. It is ours forever. Our bodies cannot tolerate the stress or the anxiety of sourcing our own lives. Our minds collapse under the pressure of responsibility when we are alone. We were designed for the indwelling of the Father. Jesus is the pattern. His life was not the removal of conflict, battle, or strife. It was His dependency on the sourcing of the Father in the midst of all circumstances. In the middle of upheaval, there is high-spirited fun at the core of His living. If this is not true now, it will not be accomplished in death. Death is a transition of what we are now into we will be forever. Eternity is a continuation of our present spiritual patterns and directions.

There is a second thought which verifies this same truth. Jesus is saying, **"You will make me full of joy in Your presence,"** (Acts 2:28). His choice of words is very significant. He has restated the CELEBRATION of merriment which has come as a result of the intimacy He has with His Father. Now He is going to restate His CONCENTRATION on the Father. The same Greek word translated *presence* in our verse (Acts 2:28) is used by Jesus in His beginning statement. He said, **"I foresaw the Lord always before my face,"** (Acts 2:25). *Presence* and *before face* are translated from the same Greek word.

This Messianic Psalm was originally written in Hebrew and then translated into Greek. In the Hebrew language there was no word for *presence*. They used the idea of "being in your face." As it was translated into the Greek language, a compound word was used. The first word indicates motion toward and the second word means the area around the eye. It expresses the idea of coming into or toward your eye (face). Jesus is expressing His CONCENTRATION on the Father at the beginning of this Messianic Psalm. The Father has gotten in His eye. He could not see anything else. Everything else is overshadowed by the

Father's presence. The Father is the center point of everything that happens in His life. The entire life of Jesus revolves around the Father. He simply cannot see anything else.

This concept is highlighted with the use of the Greek word translated "in" as found in our passage (Acts 2:28). It is an unfortunate translation because it confuses us with the first statement of Christ (Acts 2:26). As Jesus spoke of His CONCENTRATION on the Father He used the Greek word which is translated "in." In our translation it is stated as *before*. This gives us the picture of remaining or no movement. The Father has come to the very eye of Christ and is dwelling there! Now in this concluding statement Jesus uses the Greek word which is normally translated "with" (Acts 2:28). It is a word which expresses a form of relationship. The relationship is usually personal. It designates the person in whose fellowship or accompaniment something takes place.

Jesus, in his final hours before the crucifixion, opens His heart to the disciples. In relating the fullness of the Spirit who will come to be with them, He says, **"And I will pray the Father, and He will give you another Helper, that He may abide with you forever"** (John 14:16). He is not speaking of the Holy Spirit simply accompanying the believer. It is not in the sense of a guardian angel that protects us from unseen dangers. He will be "with" us in the sense of relationship. Listen to the final statement of the Apostle Paul in his second letter to the Corinthians. He wrote, **The grace of the Lord Jesus Christ, and the love of God, and the communion of the Holy Spirit be with you all. Amen.** (2 Corinthians 13:14). This is not a desire that our experience with God would be as one carrying a rabbit's foot or four leaf clover. This is relational. To experience the Trinity in intimacy is the heart of Christianity. It is then that grace is known, love is experienced, and oneness of communication is embraced.

The Messiah is expressing His present experience of this depth of relationship in His opening statement (Acts 2:25). The

Part Three: In My Eye

Father is in His eye. The Father remains the single focus of Jesus' life. This is the spiritual condition which allows the sourcing of the Spirit. Now as He closes this great statement He boldly proclaims this will continue in the future. As He ascends to the right hand of the Father and assumes His rightful place as King of the Kingdom, this will continue. This intimacy between them is not only a time zone embrace, but an eternal oneness. What has been experienced in the present will follow into eternity.

Peter explains Pentecost to us. Jesus is the explanation. As the Father sourced Jesus, He will also source us. We must have the same spiritual condition Jesus had. As this is established in the present time zone and flows into the eternal realms for Jesus, so what is established in our present will expand in our eternity. What is your intimacy level with Jesus now? Will you be satisfied with this level when He comes again?

PART FOUR
ACTS 2:29-35

DAVID'S MESSAGE

Acts 2:29-30

GOING BEYOND

Peter is preaching. The Jews are listening. He comes to the most crucial portion of his message. ***Jesus of Nazareth, a Man*** is the explanation of Pentecost. It is radical to them. How can this be? They actively engaged in crucifying Jesus. He is dead! Peter boldly announces ***this Jesus God has raised up.*** He is not dead; He is alive! Then Peter gives the most earthshaking news of all: God has established a Kingdom through Jesus on an entirely different plain than they can conceive. It is far beyond their expectations.

The Jews had a certain expectation of the coming Messiah. We can only understand our passage (Acts 2:29-30) in light of what they believed in that hour. After the return of Judah from the Babylonian captivity at the end of the Old Testament, there was four hundred years of constant turmoil. They remained in their own land but were dominated by foreign powers. Their way of life, their culture and their religious practices were under constant threat. The latest interference came from the Roman Empire. These Jews made many attempts to solve this problem. Groups of zealots formed military bands to attack the Roman soldiers in their land. Barabbas was part of this force (John 18:39-40). However, these resistance fighters were only minor irritations to Rome.

The Sadducees were a wealthy group of men who formed one half of the ruling body of Israel, the Sanhedrin. They took a very liberal approach to government. Every possible connection

Part Four: David's Message

with Rome was utilized for financial benefit. Instead of fighting or resisting, they tolerated and compromised. The zealots were an irritation to these Sadducees as well. Anything or anyone who upset the present relationship with Rome was a threat to their financial arrangements.

There was another group made up of the general population of Israel. They were the common folks. They realized the forces against them were unmovable. However, Jehovah God had promised the Messiah, and they believed He was their only chance. They had a growing awareness that God was about to do something startling in their world. The circumstances of their lives demanded a movement of God, a fulfillment of His promise. Their hope was focused on a Messiah. Everyone understood the Messiah would be the Son of David. Matthew begins his Gospel account by highlighting the lineage of Jesus through King David (Matthew 1:1-17). Jesus was the Son of David.

At the peak of the miracles of Christ, He fed the five thousand men besides women and children. The crowds were convinced Jesus was the One God had promised. He would change their economy, establish their nation, and liberate them from oppression. He is the Son of David. They decided to make Him King *by force* (John 6:15). The Son of David would rule on the throne from Jerusalem! This same desire was even more forceful at the Triumphal Entry of Jesus into Jerusalem! They cried, *"Hosanna to the Son of David!"* (Matthew 21:9). This was so widespread that the Pharisees proclaimed, *"Look, the world has gone after Him!"* (John 12:19). These common folk wanted to make Jesus King!

The crucifixion of Christ destroyed any hope of such an earthly rule. The disciples were obviously caught in this expectation as well and were totally dismayed by His death. But His resurrection was a restoration of their hope. He attempted to focus them on the Promise of the Father when He appeared to them for forty days. As He instructed them, they interrupted

Him with this same earthly rule focus. They asked, *"Lord, will You at this time restore the kingdom to Israel?"* (Acts 1:6). After forty days of teaching on the Kingdom of God, they still could not get beyond their earthly view of a throne in Jerusalem with Israel ruling the world.

If this was true of the disciples, who had on the job training with Jesus, what about the Jews of the Dispersion? These Jews come to Jerusalem for only two or three months a year during the feast days. They heard a lot about Jesus but they did not have much experience with Him. The leadership of Israel swayed them to participate in the crucifixion. They had a picture of the Son of David ruling on the throne in Jerusalem, and Jesus did not complete this picture for them. In their minds, Jesus was causing more problems than He was solving. King David would be raised through his son or perhaps resurrect himself to come and restore the Kingdom of Israel. Their view was a temporal Kingdom of God ruled by King David.

Peter does not viciously attack this group of Jews. In the Spirit of Christ, he simply highlights what God has been doing through Jesus. These Jews of the Dispersion missed it. They were so engrossed in their own ideas of the Messiah they missed the Divine action of God. They placed the actions of God in their box of requirements which caused them not to recognize God when He moved. Please do not fall into this trap! Do not box Him into your theology or traditions! You must see with the eyes of Christ!

Go Beyond Your Traditions
Acts 2:29-31

Peter is forceful in his approach. He does not treat them with disrespect, but confronts them with truth. What is the truth about their **patriarch David? He is both dead and buried,**

and his tomb is with us to this day. Does this sound like a great deliverer to you? We have looked at King David as the **patriarch**. This is a translation of the Greek word which means "founder of a nation." This is an important reference to David since Peter is going to explain the establishment of a new Kingdom. In Israel's history, there was never a king equal to King David. The prosperity, world respect, and power of the Kingdom of Israel were never greater. When the Jews considered what Israel should be, they thought of the rule of King David. The restoration of Israel in those days was their hope and longing. They thought it would be wonderful if King David would be raised from the dead and they could duplicate what he established in ancient days, the whole earth was afraid of Israel. The disciples had no problem seeing Jesus overtake Rome; no one could hurt Him since He had been raised from the dead. He could march on Rome, overthrow Caesar's throne, and bring it to Jerusalem. Each disciple would have a throne and they would all rule together.

Peter now gives an explanation of Pentecost to the Jews of the Dispersion. What is promised to you is far beyond your wildest thoughts. You are trapped among the dead. Your thinking is from the realm of the dead, and your traditions have the smell of death about them. Why? Is it because you base it on one who is dead? The **patriarch David ... is both dead and buried, and his tomb is with us to this day** (Acts 2:29). Pentecost is about the alive Jesus. ***This Jesus God has raised up, of which we are all witnesses*** (Acts 2:32). Even David in his prophetic role understood this. He received a promise from God which he embraced by faith. God promised that an individual of the lineage of King David would be raised up to sit on his throne. But He did not mean there would be one who was simply born of the lineage of King David. He would overthrow the Roman Empire and establish the Kingdom of Israel on earth. NO! God raised up Christ from the dead. He has ascended to the right hand of the Father for the purpose of establishing an eternal

Going Beyond | **Acts 2:29-30**

Kingdom. In fact, His Spirit has descended to sit on you as if you were His throne of dominion. He has established the Kingdom within you. Please do not limit the Kingdom of God to your traditions based on a man who is dead.

What about us? Think about the things which have become so important to us. We put great value on our belief system. We are divided over the theologies of John Calvin and John Wesley. We debate the opinions of these two men on a daily basis. We argue back and forth quoting them as the authority, and the truth is that both of these men are dead. But Jesus is alive! His established Kingdom is reigning not only at the right hand of the Father, but also in the inner lives of men. Will we embrace Him and the fullness of His ruling in our lives in this moment?

The tradition of Sunday school is another thing about which we argue. Many of us were raised in Sunday school, and it was a sacred time of training in our lives. We experienced Sunday school teachers who won us to Christ by their dedication and love. Should we not continue to have Sunday school as we always have? How can we abandon such a sacred tradition? Wilberforce, the founder of Sunday school, is dead. We must go beyond our sacred traditions to the One who is alive. His name is Jesus. Will we allow Him to indwell us in His fullness and do a new thing in our world for this day?

Another avenue of spiritual training throughout the years is the ancient hymns. We have worshipped through them and their theology has been burned in our brains. We can sing them from memory. How can we abandon the sacred tradition of the hymns in our time of worship? But the authors of the hymns are dead. We must go beyond our traditions based on the dead. We must move to the One who is alive. Could Jesus give us new expression because He lives within us?

When we think of the dead who have influenced our traditions, we must not fall into the trap of thinking about the Bible being written by the dead. Those who penned the words of the

Part Four: David's Message

Scriptures are dead, the Author is not! God is alive and wants to speak His Word to us in this hour. Peter gives an explanation of Pentecost. God raises Jesus from the dead. The Father establishes an eternal Kingdom through Jesus. He came to indwell us. We must move beyond our traditions to embrace the King who lives within us.

Go Beyond the Temporal
Acts 2:32-33

There is one thing which causes me fear: could it be we have viewed the reality of Pentecost (the outside God coming inside) only in light of the temporal? I went to an English dictionary to gain a proper understanding of this word, temporal. It is something which is related to or limited by time. It is that which is related to a material world and only lasts for awhile. It is not eternal and it passes away. Christianity is not temporal! In fact, *you* are not temporal!

The Old Covenant was temporal. It was founded in time; it would be fulfilled in time; it would cease in time. The Old Covenant was waiting for its fulfillment in the New Covenant. Pentecost is the event where we stepped from the best of the Old Covenant into the wonder of the New. The transition is dramatic. Peter attempts to describe it to the Jews who are engrossed in the temporal Old Covenant. Their sacrifices are limited to this world. They take the life of a lamb according to a schedule which is established in this time zone. They offer prayers at the appointed time period. They are very strict about the observance of the Sabbath day which is one day set aside out of a week. It is so temporal. Everything they cherish which gives them value is temporal! The patriarchs of old are a heritage which places them on a different physical plain than other people; but is it temporal. The Jews' hope is in **we have Abraham as our** *father* (Matthew 3:9). During the Triumphal Entry of Jesus into Jerusalem, these Jews cry out, *"Hosanna! Blessed is He who comes in the name of the Lord! Blessed is the kingdom of our father David that comes in the name of the Lord! Hosanna in the highest!"* (Mark 11:9-10).

They see their relationship with God as significant only in the temporal realm. Their security is based on temporal men who are used by God to establish their heritage in the temporal. They understand the promise of God to bring deliverance in the temporal circumstances by establishing another temporal kingdom. The Sadducees do not believe in the resurrection of the dead, therefore, there is nothing beyond the temporal! While the Pharisees do embrace the resurrection of the dead, it is very vague and undefined. It is basically a belief that does not affect their lives.

If this group of Jews is going to grasp what has happened in the lives of one hundred and twenty disciples, they must go beyond their temporal box. *This Jesus God has raised up, of which we are all witnesses* (Acts 2:32). He is *exalted to the right hand of God, and has received from the Father the promise of the Holy Spirit*, and *He poured out this which you now see and hear* (Acts 2:33). The new King is establishing a Kingdom which bridges the gap between the temporal and the eternal. Jesus is not King on David's throne in Jerusalem, but as David's Lord, He is ruler of an eternal and heavenly Kingdom.

We must carefully apply this truth to our lives! Our eyesight is so limited to this time zone; *Christ in you* is not a bandage to get you through this life. The Kingdom within you is the Kingdom of the ascended Lord who is resurrected from the dead. He has infused you with His eternal life. The fullness of His Spirit enables you to live in the eternal Kingdom is injected into your now. As Jesus approached the last week of His life, it was natural that He would spend time in prayer. In John 17, right before heading to Gethsemane, Jesus prays the high priestly prayer.

You need to read it carefully and understand His perspective as found in the concept of *the world*. The Greek word (kosmos) means "order, regular disposition, and arrangement." In other words, the world is a system, a way of thinking, or a kingdom. Jesus prayed, *"I have given them Your word; and the world has hated them because they are not of the world, just as I am not of the world,"* (John 17:14). We are *in this world*, but not *of this world*. Pentecost was not given to aid you in your pursuit of this world. Do not prostitute the Spirit of Christ by trying to manipulate His benefits for advancement in this Kingdom of the world. Radically break with any focus on this world for the purpose of one focus: Christ. The Spirit of Christ takes you beyond the temporal.

Go Beyond the Temporary
Acts 2:34-35

We want to now add one other thought for the sake of clarity. This world system is temporary. Everything connected to it, valuable in it, and esteemed by it is passing away. The world system is boxed into time. The present leaps quickly into the past, and it is gone. In a snap of a finger, the future disappears into my past; it is gone. We look back and remember. David's throne was temporary. Many bowed before him and called him, "King," or "Lord." But *he is both dead and buried, and his tomb is with us to this day* (Acts 2:29).

David, by faith, went beyond the temporary. He saw through the eyes of faith One who would ascend and *sit at My right hand* (Acts 2:34). He did not experience the indwelling King, but understood the eternal ruling of this King. Christ was raised from the dead; He ascended to the right hand of the Father. The eternal Kingdom is established by Him. This Kingdom is not boxed into the temporal or temporary. God placed the Kingdom

Going Beyond | Acts 2:29-30

(Jesus) within you. You are now in this eternal Kingdom and He is in you! You must go beyond the temporary.

Peter explains Pentecost to us. We must not focus the power of the eternal Lord dwelling within us in the temporary. Our lives must not be spent in constant concern for the temporary time zone. Our focus must be on what matters forever. Tears must not be spilt for the temporary; we must weep for that which is eternal. Let us not exhaust ourselves for what has no eternal significance; let us wear ourselves out for the forever. Do not attempt to utilize the eternal power of God for the temporary when God wants to acclimate you to the eternal.

Healing is temporary. Everyone in the New Testament who was healed is now dead. Christ can and does heal! But the healings of the New Testament were always for the bigger purpose of the eternal. Every miracle of Christ was a sign. The miracle was not pointing to itself but to something beyond itself. The purpose of the miracle was not just to solve the immediate problem, but to highlight the intervention of the eternal into the temporary world. Christ was not interested in a temporary fix. He quickly deserted the multitudes because they were only interested in the temporary. They came wanting free bread (John 6), but Jesus gave them such strong teaching that the crowd quickly went away. He pointed them beyond their temporary need, and they quickly lost interest.

Someone will always ask the question, "Why don't we see as many miracles in our time as during the time of the Bible?" The reason is the same as in the Scripture when Jesus' miracles became less frequent: the crowds were only interested in the temporary.

This would be a great opportunity to examine our personal perspective. The Holy Spirit calls us to go beyond our traditions and certainly the temporary. Let us become people who share the eternal perspective of Christ.

Acts 2:29

A PATRIARCH

Peter begins this section with a very specific introductory statement. Evidently he felt it was essential to the content of his presentation. The subject matter was especially close to the heart of his audience, the Jews. He must properly prepare them before he attempts to disturb and expand their grasp of the truth. Thus he says, ***"Men and brethren, let me speak freely to you"*** (Acts 2:29).

Peter addresses the multitude by calling them "brothers." He used the same term for the one hundred and twenty believers in the upper room (Acts 1:16). It was the beginning of the first recorded business meeting of the early church. He expressed the same desire in our passage to unite with the Jews of the Dispersion to discover the truth for life. It is a way of identifying himself with his listeners. He is not speaking as a critical outsider who does not properly understand. Rather he has the same Jewish heritage and maintains the same Jewish traditions and beliefs.

He begins with ***"Let me speak."*** He does not ask permission from them; rather the truth he proclaims is so great it gives him the right to speak. The permission for speaking to them comes from the content of the truth itself. If in preaching, Sunday school teaching, or witnessing, we rely on our audience to inspire our message, we will quit in discouragement. Our inspiration must not come from the audience but from the greatness of the truth.

He adds the word *freely* to his statement. It is literally, "with freedom." It is an expression of two Greek words. The first (meta) is "with." It expresses the idea of "together or in your midst." Peter is not speaking so softly they cannot hear and he is not speaking behind their backs. They have asked for an explanation of Pentecost; therefore, Peter declares the truth to their faces. The second Greek word (parreesias) means to speak everything without reserve. Peter is not going to hold anything back. Fear of offending his audience is set aside. He is going to express everything he has on his mind as the Spirit guides him.

In this passage Peter establishes a contrast between Christ the risen Lord and David the patriarch. His contrast is not difficult to understand. He just quoted four verses of King David's writings from an Old Testament Psalm (Psalm 16:8-11). This was in response to the reaction of the great crowd to Peter's initial explanation of Pentecost. This is a great Messianic Psalm. David wrote about the circumstances of his own life, however, God inspired him to write beyond what he knew. Jesus, the Messiah, is speaking these words. This could be difficult for the Jews of the Dispersion to understand, complicating Peter's explanation. They crucified Jesus and held Him in contempt. King David was a great hero of the Jewish faith. They initially may have considered King David as the fulfillment of this Psalm. Peter wants to be very clear: King David cannot be their focus in this Psalm. He calls them to go beyond one of the greatest kings their Jewish tradition produced and embrace the new King who now rules.

Peter immediately presents a contrast between the ***patriarch David*** and "Jesus, the King of the Kingdom." It is unusual that he refers to David as ***the patriarch*** (Acts 2:29). This word is only used in three statements in the New Testament (Acts 2:29; 7:8-9; Hebrews 7:4). Only once is the word connected to King David. It is reserved for Abraham, Isaac and Jacob. It is used for the father and founder of a family or tribe. David was the greatest King of Israel, but certainly not the father or founder of Israel.

Part Four: David's Message

We might assume Peter is being generous in his reference to David for the sake of gaining the attention of the Jews. It is more likely he is making a statement which calls their attention to a greater truth. David could easily be considered *the patriarch* of the kingly lineage of Israel or the father of the royal family.

The first King of Israel was Saul, who took the throne under the circumstances of the Philistine aggression. David was his successor, and Solomon, David's son, was the third king. The extension of power for the kingdom of Israel was greatest during the latter two reigns. However, after the death of Solomon the northern ten tribes broke away. They refused to give allegiance to the dynasty of David, and thereafter had their own kings. No one dynasty long held the throne in the northern kingdom called "Israel." In the meantime, the tribes of Judah and Benjamin maintained their own kingdom called "Judah." The kings were entirely of the Davidic dynasty. The last Davidic king was Zedekiah who was captured by Nebuchadnezzar. Judah entered into the Babylonian captivity for seventy years. This ended the Kings of Judah ruled by the Davidic dynasty, or did it?

Peter reminds these Jews that God made a promise to David. His throne would not pass away; it would be an eternal throne. God was going to bring forth from the lineage of King David one who would establish the throne of Judah forever (Psalms 132:11; 2 Samuel 7:11-17). Peter points this out in his sermon (Acts 2:30). ***Jesus of Nazareth, a Man*** is the fulfillment of prophecy. He is the new king of a different kind of Kingdom.

It is very important to understand the undercurrent of Peter's message. There is a tremendous movement of God taking place in the person of Jesus. He is reestablishing everything back to the way God intended it in the beginning. We are being restored in every aspect of our lives from what happened as a result of the fall. The climax of this great change is Pentecost; the outside God coming inside. We experience the full measure of what happened in Jesus! This places the Kingship of Christ on a completely different level than the Kingship of David. The contrast is startling!

Wrong - Right

One aspect of the contrast is wrong and right. The kingship of David was never right. It is true God chose David as king. He said, *"I have found David the son of Jesse, a man after My own heart, who will do all My will"* (Acts 13:22). While David was God's choice as the King of Israel, God never intended Israel to have an earthly king. Israel was established as a theocracy not a monarchy. The people of Israel were to be a unique nation within the world. All the other nations of the world had men as their kings; but Israel was to be ruled by God. The people of Israel came to Samuel, the prophet, demanding a man king. They said, *"Now make us a king to judge us like all the nations,"* (1 Samuel 8:5). Samuel was very upset by this demand. However, *the Lord said to Samuel, "Heed the voice of the people in all that they say to you; for they have not rejected you, but they have rejected Me, that I should not reign over them"* (1 Samuel 8:7). At the heart of Israel's request was the rejection of the kingship of God in their lives. They were not rejecting God as their deliverer, one who would rescue them. They simply wanted to rule over themselves.

God instructed Samuel to warn the people. He said, *"You shall solemnly forewarn them, and show them the behavior of the king who will reign over them,"* (1 Samuel 8:9). Samuel told them what an earthly king would do. He would take their strong sons and form a massive army. Some of them would be enlisted to farm his land and manufacture weapons for war. Their daughters would be taken to serve his household. A king would take the best of their fields, vineyards, and olive groves. He would take ten percent of their grain, sheep, and earnings

Part Four: David's Message

as taxes. The people will become his servants. ***Nevertheless the people refused to obey the voice of Samuel; and they said, "No, but we will have a king over us, that we also may be like all the nations, and that our king may judge us and go out before us and fight our battles"*** (1 Samuel 8:19).

God permitted the demand of the people, but it was not His will. It was wrong! Everything the prophet Samuel predicted for the nation of Israel took place. The taxes were high; the palaces were expensive and extravagant. They had a king who demanded their support. The people had to provide for their king; he had needs. They had to fight for him. One of King Solomon's first major feats was the construction of the temple in Jerusalem. A work force of thirty thousand was employed in cutting timber from the cedars of Lebanon. There were eighty thousand cutters of stone in the quarries of Jerusalem and seventy thousand ordinary workmen. Also Solomon erected a considerable complex of buildings north of the City of David. His own palace was probably even more magnificent than the temple, for it took almost twice as long to build (1 Kings 7:1). There was a separate palace for his chief wife, Pharaoh's daughter (1 Kings 7:8). All of these were elaborately furnished. The extravagance of these buildings endangered the economy, despite the flourishing commerce.

Peter is preaching a powerful message to the Jews. Through their ancestors they had made the wrong choice. While they held King David in high esteem as the founder of the royal line, they must recognize how God is bringing redemption to them. He is redeeming their royal line. What was wrong is now being made right! This is not about King David; this is about Christ! He is now setting upon the throne; it is an eternal throne, the Kingdom of God.

Your earthly kings took from you; King Jesus is giving to you. You furnished the man power by which your kings reigned; King Jesus is filling you with His power. You provided everything for your kings; King Jesus is providing everything for you. He is filling you with His Spirit, empowering you with His ability, and equipping you for your day. The eternal Kingdom has come to be within you. Your old kings became enamored with power and what they could get. King Jesus lives for what He can give. He delights in providing everything for you. Would you live in response to Him? Remember back in your history before your forefathers demanded a king. In those days, God was your King. He provided everything for you. He gave you manna from the sky, quail in the bush, water from the rock, a land for your inheritance, protection from your enemies, and even caused your shoes to last. He delighted in providing for you. Your forefathers demanded an earthly king; in so doing they rejected the provision of God for their lives. They moved from the place of safety and provision to a place of insecurity and lack. God is giving you another chance. This is the new covenant. God is redeeming your royal line. What is wrong has been made right! Jesus is King!!

Pentecost is far beyond receiving power to do some miracles. It is completely beyond an emotion or warm feeling. It is the very invasion of our lives by the One who is King. We recognize all other kings as selfish, dependent or weak. We will no longer acknowledge them as our rulers. Our King came to reign within! We become the very territory of His Kingdom. He is the Provider and the Provision of all that is needed within this territory. He will build the structure of our lives, provide the resources necessary for living, and defend the borders of our existence. He is our King.

In his explanation of Pentecost to the Jews, Peter quotes a Psalm written by King David. While David penned the words, we must clearly understand this is not about him. The depth of relationship between man and God as described in the Psalm does not begin to relate to David. He may be the founder of the royal line, **the patriarch**, but **he is both dead and buried, and his tomb is with us to this day** (Acts 2:29). God raised Jesus from

Part Four: David's Message

the dead; God the Father ascended Jesus to His right hand. Jesus is exalted. Jesus receives from the Father all that is promised. God makes Jesus both Lord and Christ.

We must not long for King David and "the good ole days." God is doing a new thing in Christ. Everything which is true about Jesus is now being offered to you. The same intimate relationship is now yours. Jesus is a prototype for all God wants to do in mankind. The Kingdom of God is now here in fullness and God reigns within. All that was wrong has now been made right.

How does this apply to us? We are not Jews; my forefathers did not demand an earthly king. We have always fought for freedom. The physical act of the Israelites wanting a man king is only a surface revelation of the desire for man to rule over man. We really want to be our own king. We invite God to be a part of our lives. We recognize the need to have Him involved in the great crisis moments. We are certainly open to miracles and His help in the time of need. We are willing to even acknowledge our need for salvation and heaven when we die. But in the meantime we really want to rule over our own lives. We want to provide for ourselves.

This may be why we continually attempt to reestablish an Old Testament in the New Testament hour. We want to live in the old covenant when King David's dynasty ruled. Self raises its head to provide for our lives, fight our battles, and do our own thing. We want the credit for the success of our own living. After all it is my life; I have worked hard. Even if God is involved, He is a helper rather than a ruler. Calling upon Him to help me only verifies the fact that I am really in charge. I don't mind His aid but I want to dictate when He aids me and in what way He aids me. I am willing to use all the resources available to me in order to look good. Self loves statements like "God helps those who help themselves." Self thrives on trying, attempting, doing my best, doing my part, or working at it.

Self loves to serve God; because it is all about "my" service.

How grateful He should be to have me. I have had an abundance of experience; I have much talent; He could certainly use my wisdom. Self loves to live its life for Christ; because it is all about what I am doing. It is the Pharisaical approach to life. Jesus told a parable *to some who trusted in themselves that they were righteous, and despised others* (Luke 18:9). There were two men who went to the temple to pray. One was a Pharisee and the other was a tax collector. Listen to the expression of king self: *The Pharisee stood and prayed thus with himself, "God, I thank You that I am not like other men – extortioners, unjust, adulterers, or even as this tax collector. I fast twice a week; I give tithes of all that I possess"* (Luke 18:11-12).

In Pentecost Christ restores everything back to what God intended in the beginning. Man no longer provides; he is filled with the Spirit of Christ. Man no longer does the best he can do for God; God does His best through mankind. We no longer live our lives for Christ; Christ lives His life through us. We no longer try and attempt in our own power; we surrender, relax and depend on God. We have a King who delights in providing for us. Pentecost is God's call for us to die to self provision. Let us renounce King David (self) and embrace our new King: Jesus.

Acts 2:29-30

THE PATRIARCH APPROACH

The great day of Pentecost has just taken place. One hundred and twenty disciples have just been filled with the Spirit of Jesus. God has moved Christianity to an entirely new level. God's dream for mankind has just reached its climax. God wants to live within man and source him. He has already accomplished it in Jesus and now God begins to fulfill it in all mankind. Three to five thousand Jews of the Dispersion recognize this event as the new thing God is doing in their day. They ask the question, **"Whatever could this mean?"** (Acts 2:12).

Peter, filled with the Holy Spirit, is moved by God to give an explanation. He begins with a text from the prophecy of Joel (Acts 2:17-21). The body of his sermon introduces the person of *Jesus of Nazareth, a Man* (Acts 2:22). God proved Pentecost in and through the person of Christ. He proved the fullness of the Spirit of God sourcing a man through the life of Christ (Acts 2:22), through His death (Acts 2:23) and through His resurrection (Acts 2:24).

This brings a resounding reaction from the crowd. They participated in crucifying Christ. How can they ever expect to experience Pentecost in their lives after what they have done? Peter quotes an Old Testament Psalm to them. This is a messianic Psalm (Psalm 16:8-11). Jesus, the Messiah, declares His spiritual relationship with the Father. Through this Psalm, we begin to understand the depth of the Pentecost experience.

Evidently Peter feels that further explanation is definitely needed. There may have been among the Jews a belief that this psalm was fulfilled in David. Although he wrote the Psalm, it needs to be understood without question **Jesus of Nazareth, a Man** fulfilled it. In kindness and clarity Peter highlights the truth of Pentecost as seen through the context of David's life.

Peter uses the contrast between man's provision and God's provision. He contrasts what God can do with what man can do. Man's plan is seen against the backdrop of God's plan. But isn't this always the contrast? The Jews learned this lesson in the Old Testament; now they are relearning it in the New Testament. It seems every generation has to be taught this lesson again. We can say it, teach it, preach it and even demonstrate it. With all of that we remain one generation away from the loss of God's movement through us.

It soon becomes apparent that not only does each generation have to learn this for themselves, but every individual must relearn the lesson a multitude of times. Why do we so easily forget? I think I have sufficiently learned the lesson only to realize in some particular situation I have once again depended on myself. God forgive me! In my heart I have learned the lesson and embraced it. However, I seem to have patterns which my heart has not corrected in many everyday life experiences. But God is progressing through my life, step by step, correcting and changing every aspect of my living. The lesson is so crucial; it is a matter of life and death. In fact, life and death is the contrast of the lesson. Man consistently produces death and God consistently produces life.

This is the resounding emphasis of Peter's explanation of Pentecost. He emphatically speaks of man's death and God's life. The opening statement of the body of his sermon focuses on this (Acts 2:22-24). He boldly says that God was delivering **Jesus of Nazareth, a Man** over to mankind. He knew full well that they would take Him **by lawless hands**. They would crucify and put

Part Four: David's Message

Him to death. But God's provision is life. Peter's description of the life of God moving within man as a result of Pentecost is startling (Acts 2:24). All that death proposes is nullified by the Spirit of God. A man filled with the Spirit of God is raised up. In fact, the Spirit of God is constantly generating life within him, so that death cannot possibly hold or imprison him.

God had this great plan for life from the beginning. *For David says* this *concerning Him* (Acts 2:25). Peter quotes an Old Testament Psalm written by David (Acts 2:25-28). The heart of this Psalm is the intimacy between the Spirit of God and the Messiah. He develops this close communion through the first two verses and then explodes into the declaration, *"You will not leave my soul in Hades,"* (Acts 2:27). Death has no part in the fullness of the Spirit. If God is the source, there is life.

Man's Provision - Death
Acts 2:29

Now Peter thunders into our verses (Acts 2:29-30). He uses a blaring contrast between death (man's provision) and life (God's provision). In our previous study Peter calls David, *"the patriarch."* This title is never used for King David except by Peter in this sermon. That title has always been reserved for Abraham, Isaac and Jacob. They were the founders of the new nation. King David does not qualify for consideration in that category. However, he was considered the founder of the royal line. All the kings of Judah were of the lineage of King David to the close of the Old Testament.

We also discovered that while David was chosen by God to be king, the concept of an earthly king was not's God's will. God certainly permitted it but He did not will or want it. The very desire for man to rule man was a direct rejection of the Lordship of God (1 Samuel 8:7). What did the ruling of man over man produce throughout the Old Testament? It constantly stimulated death. Over and over again there was defeat and captivity. Israel, who was to live in the provisions of God, lived in the provisions of man. Anything sourced by man produces death. The only moments of life in Israel were when God directly intervened in their behalf. The patriarch approach always produces death. It is man ruling over himself.

Peter reminds the Jews of this truth as illustrated by King David himself. He preaches, *"Men and brethren, let me speak freely to you of the patriarch David, that he is both dead and buried, and his tomb is with us to this day"* (Acts 2:29). This is not just a simple statement. You can see the strong emphasis on death in David's statement even in the English translation. Peter says that David is not just dead, but he is *dead and buried*. In fact, David is not just dead and buried, but *his tomb is with us to this day.* The Greek text from which this is translated is even more dramatic and emphatic. The phrase begins in the Greek text with the word *that* (hoti). It is a conjunction used to introduce the object, contents, or argument to which the preceding words refer. Peter has introduced the subject as *the patriarch David*; he is now going to state clearly the argument at hand. Here is what the patriarch approach produces. Immediately following this conjunction is a different conjunction *both* (kai). This is a simple continuative conjunction which marks the progress of a continued discourse. In other words, one idea is being added to the other idea. The next Greek word is translated *he is dead* which is followed by the conjunction *and* (kai). Immediately the Greek verb translated *buried* is used which is followed by the conjunction *and* (kai). Peter closes the sentence with *his tomb is with us to this day*. Notice carefully the consistent use of the conjunction *and* (kai). He is building a case by stacking one piece of evidence on top of another.

In addition to this, each verb is in the aorist tense. We do not have anything like this tense in the English language. It is the Greek tense which is a non-tense. In other words, it is not considering *when* David's death and burial took place. It is a total focus on the actual verb event. Peter is calling the Jews to consider the fact that David actually died and was buried. The proof is found in the tomb which they annually white wash. Visitors came during the feast days to Jerusalem and paid their respects to the remains of King David. There may have been some Jews who believed the Psalm Peter quoted in his sermon (Acts 2:25-28) was actually about King David. Peter is clarifying the fact that this was not even remotely possible. The entire royal line (man ruling over man) produced nothing but death. The patriarch approach is one of death!

At the time Peter delivered this sermon, the Davidic line was obscure. The wealth and glory that had once accompanied this lineage was gone. Joseph and Mary, both descendants of this line, were poor peasants living in Nazareth of Galilee. It was a small town with an awful reputation. There is no hope Judah will have a King from this royal line without the direct intervention of God. We can clearly see what man produces; it is death.

Does this directly apply to us? The spiritual principle is the same. How can we possibly be the exception to the spiritual dynamics of the ages? Would you be willing to trace this principle through the history of your personal life? Everything that is sourced by you has resulted in death. You and I have lived in the patriarch approach. How many times have we hung our hands by our sides and cried out, "I have tried my best!" All our planning, scheming, and manipulating have done nothing but bring destruction. The best we have been able to build is in rubble. Even the moments of so called success are fleeting. Everything which is lasting and valuable must be sourced by Jesus!

How can we identify with kings, the royal line, who rule in our lives? The chief characteristic is dependency. When we depend on our education instead of Jesus, has it not become our patriarch, the king? Education may be used by God, but it must not be the source of my life. Do I live out of the resource of my talent? God has given me talent. Should I use it? The answer is "yes," but when I depend on it instead of Him then it becomes the patriarch of my life. My personal traditions and experiences are of value, but they must not become the source for my actions. How easy it is for religion, theology, or ethical rules to become the source of my life instead of Jesus. The moment it happens we miss the heart of the Gospel. Death is always the result. It would be tragic to meet every Sunday morning in the church and spill death into our present generation. If we use the patriarch approach to teach or act we are producing certain death! Dependency on Jesus produces life. Would you join me in choosing life?

Acts 2:29-30

THE PROPHETIC APPROACH

Peter is preaching to a large group of Jews. He clearly uses language and illustrations they will understand. He is answering their request to explain Pentecost, the fullness of the Holy Spirit. He uses a very strong contrast between David, the patriarch, and David, the prophet. The patriarchal approach is man ruling over himself; it always ends in death (Acts 2:29). The prophetic approach is God ruling over man; it always brings life.

However, it is very important to understand the concept of kingship or ruling. It is not ruling as a king who resides in a palace or oversees a multitude of people. We all give respect to the king, pay our taxes, and follow his rules. This was the patriarchal approach. Some have tried to expand this approach by combining it with the prophetic approach. Christ, our King, doesn't rule from a throne in heaven, but has come to live within us. He is much more involved than before, but it is still limited. Christianity is a combination of my efforts and His efforts. He does His part and I do my part. He depends on me for some things and I depend on Him for some things. I am always open for Him to help me. This indicates I am doing it and He is simply an asset when needed. This mixture is a compromise of the prophetic approach. It is simply the patriarchal approach with a few cosmetic adjustments to make it appear prophetic. It still produces death. Let's go to our passage and carefully examine the prophetic approach.

God's Provision - Life
Acts 2:30

On his own, man can only produce death. The resource of David is exhausted (Acts 2:29). The patriarchal approach must be rejected by all. It *is both dead and buried, and his tomb is with us to this day.* If we have exhausted all of our personal resources to produce life and found nothing but death, we are in total dismay. Hope is gone; there is nothing left to do but white wash the tomb of our own activities of death. At this point, Peter's face must have taken on a glow. He must have raised his voice with thrilling excitement. Hope began to spill from his message. There is one way out!

With great passion, Peter cries, *"Therefore,"* (Acts 2:30). This Greek word is used to express either the mere external connection of two sentences, the one follows upon the other, or also the internal relation of cause and effect, that the one follows from the other. In this case it is certainly not cause and effect, or is it? Does not life display itself in the midst of death? Is this not the fundamental of the cross principle? In the midst of the emptiness of our self-effort, there appears the sufficiency of Christ's fullness. When dismay is all you can see, look carefully for hope. Christ will provide it. As destruction eliminates all possibilities, it cannot stop the movement of His life. Life is found in the middle of death.

This patriarchal approach of the royal line, man ruling over man, has ended in death. It is obviously going to produce nothing but more death. What if David could shift from being the patriarch to being the prophet? The prophetic role is vastly different than the patriarchal role of establishing a royal line of rule. The prophet spoke not his own thoughts, but what he received from God. He was not the source of the inspiration, but was a recipient of God's resource. He was not the provider,

Part Four: David's Message

but with open hands he received provision. He did not solve the problem, but was used by God as a part of the solution. Instead of an instrument of death, he becomes the instrument of life.

The central issue of the Biblical prophet was the phenomenon of sourcing. The Old Testament prophet does not parallel the sacral figures of the pagans; he is not a magician. He does not force or manipulate God. On the contrary, he is under Divine constraint. It is God who moves upon the prophet. God invites, summons, and impels him. God sources the prophets who must transmit exactly what he receives. Repeatedly the Old Testament Scriptures restate what God spoke to Moses, *"I will raise up for them a Prophet like you from among their brethren, and will put My words in His mouth, and He shall speak to them all that I command Him"* (Deuteronomy 18:18). Jeremiah, the prophet wrote, *"Then the Lord put forth His hand and touched my mouth, and the Lord said to me: 'Behold, I have put My words in your mouth"* (Jeremiah 1:9).

This is verified by the experience of the prophet, Balaam. Balak, a Moabite King, was frightened by the victories of Israel over their enemies. He hired Balaam to curse the Israelites. When Balaam began to pronounce the curse, it became a blessing upon Israel. Balak was tremendously upset and said to Balaam, *"What have you done to me? I took you to curse my enemies, and look, you have blessed them bountifully!"* So he answered and said, *"Must I not take heed to speak what the Lord has put in my mouth?"* (Numbers 23:11-12). After further attempts Balaam again says, *"Did I not tell you, saying, 'All that the Lord speaks, that I must do?'"* (Numbers 23:26).

If this is true for the Old Testament prophet, how much more this must be true for the individual who is filled with the Spirit of God. We moved to a new level at Pentecost. Peter describes the depth of this experience. The new level is not a patriarchal approach where the royal line of self-sourcing dominates. It is the prophetic approach where the indwelt Spirit of God sources the believer. "Self" is not living its life for Jesus; Jesus is living His life through "self." We no longer are serving Jesus, but Jesus is serving through us. I do not speak for Him: He is speaking through me. A dramatic shift has taken place. Self-sourcing produces death. Jesus-sourcing produces life.

Present

Peter gives us a basic understanding of how to experience the prophetic approach. He says, *"Therefore, being a prophet, and knowing that God had sworn with an oath to him that of the fruit of his body, according to the flesh, He would raise up the Christ to sit on his throne,"* (Acts 2:30). He begins with the idea of PRESENT. He refers to David as *being a prophet.* The Greek word (huparcho) translated being is two Greek words combined into one. The first (hupo) means "under" with the connotation of "from which things come forth." The second (archo) means "to begin." Thus it has the idea of "be present, to be, or to exist."

This is an entirely different approach than the "patriarch approach." David was the founder of a royal line which came from the desire of man. Man wanted to rule over man. This was not God's will nor was it sourced by God. Man created this; God permitted it; it produced death. The prophetic role was totally opposite of this. There was no prophetic line. It was not about ruling. God selected the individual and he came into existence as a prophet. They did not come from the same tribe or have the same characteristics. There were no educational requirements; it was not purchased by certain financial qualifications. God sourced the prophetic role. It was a state of existence for God.

The call (sourcing) of God is the common thread permeating the prophetic role throughout the Old Testament. There are such vast differences in the personalities and ministries of the various prophets. Elijah is wild and somewhat isolated (1 Kings 17-19). On the other hand, Elisha plays more of a pastoral role (2 Kings 4). Amos thunders a message which has a strong social conscience. Deborah is the wise governor (Judges 4-5). Isaiah is the distinguished courtier; Jeremiah is the sad visionary; Ezekiel is the exiled priest. There are many more male prophets than female. But gender is never raised as an issue. The female prophets are never seen as unacceptable or inferior. Regardless of gender, personality types, or backgrounds, they all are sourced by God.

Not only was the existence of the prophets sourced by God, but He also sourced all of their activities. Often the prophet foretold the future which is the case in our verse. How could this be done truthfully and accurately without Divine sourcing? What man knows the future? The omniscient God who is sourcing man knows the future. The question for the prophet is not "what should I do?" God was calling the prophet to "be!"

I fear we have participated in the patriarchal approach rather than the prophetic approach. Our focus has been on what God wants me to "do." We have seen our role as ruling while God aided and blessed our activities for Him. What God wants me to "be" is the issue of the New Testament. All of my energy must be spent on seeking Him; I must have no other concentration. His call (sourcing) has come to my life. In Him I discover life.

Perceives

Peter presents a second aspect to the prophetic role. He says, *"Therefore, being a prophet, and knowing that God had sworn with an oath to him that of the fruit of his body, according to the flesh, He would raise up Christ to sit on his throne,"* (Acts 2:30). It is PERCEIVES. The prophet seemed to know information others did not. It was not about data or simply information. Although there were schools of the prophets, it was not about education. The entire prophetic role was about knowing the mind and heart of God. They were pastors or ministerial monitors of the people of God. They admonished and reproved. They seemed to know what God thought about the situation at hand. The prophet saw the spiritual principles of the ruling of God in the nation and applied it in clarity.

The Greek word (eido) translated **knowing** means "to see." It is seeing far beyond the physical, but grasping, understanding, and perceiving. In our passage David is fulfilling the prophetic role. He foresees the spiritual principle of God's redemptive plan. By faith, he sees the facts of the coming Messiah, His reign, and fulfillment of the royal line. God's future plan is unlocked for David. He lived in the hope of the enterprise of God's activities. He knew he was in the flow of this movement. How could David live in such a perspective? God was sourcing this prophetic view. If David only knew the royal line (patriarch approach), the end would **be both dead and buried, and his tomb is with us to this day.** But David moved into the prophetic approach. As he was sourced by God he saw life and knew the dreams of God fulfilled in Christ.

You and I are confronted with the same issue. We can live in our own sourcing. We can do the best we can with the knowledge we have available to us. We can "figure it out" to the best of our education and training. Or we can move to a new level. Christ can source our thinking. We can "know." We can see with the eyes of Jesus. We have the possibility of knowing what we cannot know. Sourcing from our own minds leads to death, sourcing from His mind leads to life. Let's choose life!

Acts 2:30

THE PROPHETIC PROMISE

Peter laid the ground work for the explosion of great truth. Our passage spills forth from the center of his message. The context is Pentecost. But it is not just the Pentecost event. It is Pentecost, the climax of what God wants to do in mankind. It is Pentecost, the restoration of fallen man. It is Pentecost, the intimacy of God and man in union. In light of this, Peter's entire explanation is about the sourcing of the Holy Spirit in and through *Jesus of Nazareth, a Man.* Every section of his sermon focuses on "sourcing."

The heart of his message is his contrast between "the patriarchal approach" (Acts 2:29) and "the prophetic approach" (Acts 2:30). The patriarchal approach features David as the founder of the royal line. It was wrong and produced nothing but death. God never intended man to rule over man. Man was looking to man as the source of His needs. Self-sourcing only produces death. Even when we do the best we can, there is death. Our resource will never lift us to the level of life.

The prophetic approach always produces life. The prophet was sourced by God. He was not a product of education, heritage, cultural surroundings, or talent. He was selected and sourced by God. The only common denominator among the prophets was the calling of God. God moved to redeem the patriarchal approach, the royal line. He did not want to leave us in death. The key issue in Pentecost is "sourcing." Thus, the key issue in

The Prophetic Promise | **Acts 2:30**

Christianity is "sourcing." It is not about a right deed over against a wrong deed. It is about what sources the deed. Even the best deed sourced by self is wrong.

Jesus' preaching ministry was filled with parables. The consistent thread throughout all of the various categories of parables is "sourcing." The Parable of the Vine and the Branches (John 15:1-8) is definitely focused on the sourcing of the life of the Spirit. Jesus tells this parable in the center of His discourse on the coming of the Holy Spirit (John 14, 15, 16). It is a physical illustration of the indwelling of the life of God which is to come. As the vine flows its life source into and produces the branch, so the Spirit of Jesus will flow into us. The only obligation of the branch is to "abide." Nine different times Jesus stresses this word. If the branch "abides," it will be sourced by the vine. It spontaneously produces fruit if it "abides."

The Parable of the Sower (Matthew 13:1-8) is about how the soil responds to the sourcing of the Sower. The production of the soil is not about works, talent, or ability. It is about responding to the seed of life which the sower has implanted into the soil. Bearing fruit is about the generating life of God being turned loose within our lives to manifest itself. Paul called it the fruit of the Spirit.

The Parable of the Wheat and the Tares (Matthew 13:24-30) is about "sourcing." The wheat and the tares are in the same field; they are allowed to grow together. However, the wheat is sown by the owner of the field; the tares are sown by an enemy. They may appear much alike for a time. But at the harvest, it is easy to distinguish between the poisonous tares and the valuable wheat. It is not about the "doing" of the tares or the wheat, but it is about their source.

The Parable of the Mustard Seed (Matthew 13:31), the Parable of the Leaven (Matthew 13:33), and the Parable of the Pearl of Great Price are much the same. Each one tells the heart of the Kingdom of Heaven. The mustard seed is the smallest of all seeds. But it sources the greatest of trees. The Kingdom of God (fullness of the Spirit) is like this mustard seed. The leaven in the meal will permeate the entire loaf of bread. It will determine its size and shape. It sources the loaf of bread. There is a merchant who is seeking the pearl of great price. He forsakes everything for this one pearl. This one great pearl is the focus of his entire life; he is sourced by it.

Even the Parable of the Prodigal Son (Luke 15:11-32) is a story about sourcing. The great sin of the prodigal was separation from the Father. Redemption is pictured as coming back home. The Father restores him to intimacy. The ring is placed on his finger; a robe is placed upon his back. He is again sourced as a son!

Now Peter declares the same issue as the explanation of Pentecost. God has filled man again. We are now sourced by the Spirit of Christ. Peter explains this in the language and setting of the Jewish community. Therefore, he gives the contrast of the patriarchal approach and the prophetic approach. The patriarchal approach brings nothing but death (Acts 2:29), but the prophetic approach focuses on life. He says, **"Therefore, being a prophet, and knowing that God has sworn with an oath to him that of the fruit of his body, according to the flesh, He would raise up the Christ to sit on his throne,"** (Acts 2:30).

The word **therefore** has the content of cause and effect. It presents to us the principle of the Kingdom of God. Life is found only in the midst of death. When man has exhausted his best, God is there to produce life. As long as you are working, manipulating, and calculating, He will let you. When you have collapsed, He can bring life. The royal line has produced nothing but death, God is now going to bring life in the midst of death.

He begins with the idea of PRESENT. He refers to David as **being a prophet**. The Greek word (huparcho) translated **being** is two Greeks words combined into one. The first (hupo) means "under" with the connation of "from which things come forth."

The Prophetic Promise | **Acts 2:30**

The second (archo) means "to begin." Thus, it has the idea of "be present, to be, or to exist." This is a different approach than the "patriarchal approach." David was the founder of a royal line which came from the desires of men. Man wanted to rule over man. This was not God's will nor was it sourced by Him. Man created this; God permitted it; it produced death. The prophetic role was the total opposite. There was no prophetic line. It was not about ruling. God selected the individual and he came into existence as a prophet. They did not come from the same tribe or have the same characteristics. There were no educational requirements; it was not purchased by certain financial qualifications. God sourced the prophetic role. It was a state of existence produced by God. This is the call for our lives.

Peter presents a second aspect to the prophetic role. He says, **"Therefore, being a prophet, and knowing that God had sworn with an oath to him that of the fruit of his body, according to the flesh, He would raise up the Christ to sit on his throne,"** (Acts 2:30). It is PERCEIVES. The prophet seemed to know information others did not. It was not about data or simple information. Although there were schools of the prophets, it was not about education. The entire prophetic role was about knowing the mind and heart of God. They were pastors and ministerial monitors of the people of God. They admonished and reproved. They seemed to know what God thought about the situation at hand. The prophet saw the spiritual principles of the ruling of God in the nation and applied it in clarity.

The Greek word (eido) translated ***knowing*** means "to see." It is seeing far beyond the physical, but grasping, understanding, and perceiving. In our passage, David is fulfilling the prophetic role. He foresees the spiritual principle of God's redemptive plan. By faith, he sees the facts of the coming Messiah, His reign, and fulfillment of the royal line. God's future plan is unlocked for him. He lived in the hope of the enterprise of God's activities. He knew he was in the flow of his movement. How could David

Part Four: David's Message

live in such a perspective? God was sourcing this prophetic view. If David only knew the royal line (patriarch approach), the end would be both **dead and buried, and his tomb is with us to this day.** But David moved into the prophetic approach. As he was sourced by God he saw life. He knew the dreams of God fulfilled in Christ. Jesus wants to source us with His mind.

Promise

The PROMISE of God is the basis for this sourcing. Peter says, *"Therefore, being a prophet, and knowing that God had sworn with an oath to him that of the fruit of his body, according to the flesh, He would raise up the Christ to sit on his throne,"* (Acts 2:30). The sure foundation of the promise given to David is an oath. In fact, in Peter's statement he gives this idea a double emphasis. Not only did David receive assurance of the promise by an oath from God, but God also swore. In reality the "swearing process" and the "oath process" are the same, which gives this emphasis a double thrust. In other words, it is very hard to miss that the basis of the prophetic role (sourcing of God) is the very integrity of God!

The Greek word (horkoo) translated **oath** originally designated the staff held when swearing an oath. This was not to be treated lightly or superficially. There was a ceremony involved which placed the oath in a formal setting. This took great thought and purposeful planning by the person in charge. This was a very serious event. The sacredness and binding character of the oath was strengthened in the swearing. Both ideas are presented in our passage which highlights its importance. The pattern for the swearing of an oath is found in the Book of Hebrews. *For men indeed swear by the greater, and an oath for confirmation is for them an end of all dispute* (Hebrews 6:16). This was common practice for the Jews to whom Peter is preaching. The settling of a dispute was accomplished when an individual swore by God. So every oath has these two elements. The first element is the promise being made, and the second is the appeal to the omniscient God, the One who does not let us get by with falsehoods.

But in our passage Peter elevates the situation to another level. God is the one who is swearing the oath. The Hebrew author addresses this issue as well. ***Thus God, determining to show more abundantly to the heirs of promise the immutability of His counsel, confirmed it by an oath, that by two immutable things, in which it is impossible for God to lie, we might have strong consolation, who have fled for refuge to lay hold of the hope set before us*** (Hebrews 6:17-18). When God decided to swear an oath, He searched for a higher power. God found no higher power than Himself! Therefore, He based His oath on Himself. It is *impossible for God to lie.*

The prophetic role (God sourcing us) is based on the very strength of the character of God. It is unquestionable. This is the foundation of Peter's explanation of Pentecost. Man sourcing himself (patriarchal approach) always ended in death. God sourcing us (prophetic approach) is based upon the promise of God fulfilled in Christ being raised from the dead and sitting on the throne of the Kingdom. If God is not trustworthy and sure, we must continue to do the best we can with our self-sourcing. If God is true, we dare not hesitate in surrendering our lives to Him. We must die to all of our self-sourcing which always leads to death. We must allow Him to be the source of our lives which is life!

Participation

Here is the most radical aspect in Peter's message. God makes promises and He keeps them. Accepting the sovereignty and majesty of God is fairly easy for most of us. However, listen to Peter's sermon. *"Therefore, being a prophet, and knowing that God had sworn with an oath to him that of the fruit of his body, according to the flesh, He would raise up the Christ to sit on his throne,"* (Acts 2:30). God is including us! He is not just doing something for us. He wants to do something through us. He is not sourcing something outside of us, but He is sourcing us. This sourcing is not apart from Him; it is sourced by Him.

By faith, David knew that God would source his flesh in making him King of the Kingdom. The order of words in the Greek text as translated into the English would read, "of fruit the body." The Greek word translated *of* is "ek." It is the idea of "from" with a specific focus on it originating from within another object. The Greek word translated *body* is also proceeding from the loins of their father. Obviously in our passage (Acts 2:30) it is used for offspring. God promised to David that one of his offspring would sit on the throne in the eternal Kingdom of God.

Evidently Peter considers this emphasis to be significant. Repeatedly he highlights it in his message. As he begins the body of his sermon explaining Pentecost, he says, *"Men of Israel, hear these words: Jesus of Nazareth, a Man attested by God to you"* (Acts 2:22). Peter underscores the reality of God's restoration of mankind coming through mankind. Man got us into this mess; man must get us out of this mess. God cannot redeem us from afar. But where is the man who is not in the mess? God cannot find such a man. God decides to become that needed man. God joins us in our humanity. He becomes one of us. The incarnation takes place; Jesus is the Man. God sources redemption, but He sources it through mankind. This is the greatness of Pentecost. God does not want to do something to us; He wants to do something in us.

The danger in this great truth is the tendency to divide the activity between God and man. We speak often about "my part" and "God's part." We readily admit God has the bigger part. My part may only be a meager five percent and God's part is ninety-five percent. This is dangerous and exceedingly wrong! The truth of the matter is I have no part in the performance or activity. It is wrong to speak of "my part" and "His part." It is *all* God's part. Surely I am to be involved! Do I not participate in the Christian life? The answer is a bold "YES!" This is the message of Peter. God did something through David. David's responsibility was simply to respond to the activities of God. This is the role of the prophet.

Performance oriented people find it very difficult to grasp this concept. Simple illustrations become very necessary. What part does a glove have in the accomplishment of a task? It provides no energy. It certainly does not supervise. It can claim no glory. The glove is energized, directed, and controlled by the hand within it. The dreams, goals, and desires of the hand are the passion of the glove. The glove is sourced by the hand.

The glove has no choice in the matter. Therefore, it has no other option. We find ourselves both with choice and with options. We can decide to attempt life on our own. We can source ourselves and accomplish nothing but death. But God calls us to participate with Him on a new level. It is the level of response. We can live in constant response to the movement of God in our lives. This produces life.

Primary

This brings us to the primary focus of the message. It is Jesus. Peter says, *"Therefore, being a prophet, and knowing that God had sworn with an oath to him that of the fruit of his body, according to the flesh, He would raise up the Christ to sit on his throne,"* (Acts 2:30). The intent and focus of this verse is Jesus. David shifts from being **the patriarch** to being ***a prophet***.

As a prophet, he is sourced by God. In this state of being, he grasps and perceives the authority of the person of God. Based upon this authority a promise is made. God promises to do something through David which will mean life on a new level. This new level is Jesus. The same life which is sourcing **Jesus of Nazareth, a Man** is now sourcing me. There is a new Kingdom with a new King.

In the translation quoted above, the phrase, ***according to the flesh, He would raise up the Christ***, is included. In most other translations it is removed since it is not in the earliest Biblical manuscripts we now have available. This means in this verse the name of Christ is not mentioned. Some people may be very disturbed by this fact. However, Peter clarifies the issue in the following verse: *"he, foreseeing this, spoke concerning the resurrection of the Christ, that His soul was not left in Hades, nor did His flesh see corruption,"* (Acts 2:31). There is absolutely no doubt that Peter believed David was referring to Christ in this statement. In fact, it was not just Christ, but the resurrected life of Christ. How can a dead man rule on the throne of David in an eternal Kingdom? God will have to source that life!

God took the patriarch approach (man ruling over man) and redeemed it. The prophetic approach is God sourcing the very life of man. What could only produce death has been transformed by the power of God through Christ. David descended into the realm of Hades and his body knew corruption (Acts 2:29, 34). But Christ was sourced by God and ascended from Hades without knowing corruption. He was exalted by the power of God ***to the right hand of God, and having received from the Father the promise of the Holy Spirit, He poured out this which you now see and hear*** (Acts 2:33). He is exalted; He is empowered by the Father for ministry; He is protected from His very enemies. This is all being sourced by the Father. During this time, ***the patriarch David… is both dead and buried, and his tomb is with us to this day.***

You and I are confronted with a choice. It is the same choice confronting the Jews of the Dispersion. They were ***cut to the heart*** and responded to the sourcing of God. They painfully admitted they participated in all that brought death, the patriarchal approach (man ruling over man). What will we choose?

Acts 2:31-32

RESURRECTED LIFE

Peter's explanation of the Pentecostal event continues. He focuses his discussion on the infilling of the Holy Spirit. He gives only one version and he never strays from the subject. In his clarification of Pentecost he speaks of ***Jesus of Nazareth, a Man***. Jesus is the Man who is an adequate illustration of Pentecost. In our humanness, we might give various interpretations of Pentecost. We might attempt to explain Pentecost by means of theology. But theology would limit the indwelling of the Spirit to our own thinking and understanding. We might package the event in an historical context, but this would place the fullness of the Spirit in our past. We would then study it only as an historical event. A philosophical approach places it in the realm of opinion which we could debate. NO! Peter forcibly states that Pentecost must be explained only in terms of Jesus.

In Jesus, we experience one who is totally sourced by God. We see through every day events of life how the fullness of the Spirit works. We understand not only empowering for great ministry, but intimacy. Oneness with the Father and the Son demonstrated in the life of Christ creates within us a passion for the same. It is seen as possible for our lives. Once discovered we cannot live without it. This intimacy is displayed in Christ as the ultimate for mankind. It is our purpose and destiny. It is the fulfillment of the dream of God for us all.

If you survey the message of Peter, it appears Pentecost,

Resurrected Life | **Acts 2:31-32**

as demonstrated in Jesus, is about life! Every section of Peter's explanation highlights this idea. The opening sentence of the body of his sermon (Acts 2:22-24) points us to the resurrected life of Christ. The Spirit of God is so powerful in His fullness even the depth of Hades cannot contain it. As Peter quotes a Messianic Psalm (Acts 2:25-28) life is promoted. Once again we see that the worst death can produce does not affect life in the Spirit. The ways of life are revealed (Acts 2:28).

Peter restates the same emphasis in the new section we are studying (Acts 2:29-33). The Spirit of God within Jesus produces life. Peter suggests there is a great contrast between life and death. The patriarchal approach was total death. Man ruling over himself left him to no resource but his own. This was death in every aspect. But Christ brought us a new approach. It produces nothing but life. The Spirit of God ruling and sourcing man brings life. How can we know this for sure? Where is the proof? It is found in *Jesus of Nazareth, a Man*!

Peter proclaims David as a prophet (Acts 2:30). His prophetic role is focused entirely on the insight God gave him in the form of a promise. He actually foresaw (had knowledge of it before it happened) the coming of Christ. More specifically, he grasped the wonder of life produced by the Spirit of Christ, the resurrection (Acts 2:31).

Peter cries, *"This Jesus God has raised up, of which we are all witnesses"* (Acts 2:32). The wonder of this statement is not only in the words he uses but in the order of those words as it is found in the Greek text. In the Greek language the speaker or writer would move the most important items of his statements to the front of the sentence. Allow me to share the order of the Greek words in this sentence.

The first word is the Greek word "touton" translated *this*. It highlights this person as the object of a verb or preposition. It can be translated "this one," "Him," "the same," "that," or "this." There is no doubt to whom Peter refers. He points directly to *Jesus of Nazareth, a Man.* The second Greek word in the sentence is not translated into English. It is the Greek word "ton." It was originally a demonstrative pronoun meaning "this," or "that." However, it eventually evolved into an article such as "the." It is used in the Greek language as an emphasis. It is emphatic. The third Greek word is translated Jesus. A literal translation would read as follows: "This one the Jesus." Peter is absolute in his statement and his entire focus is on the person of Christ. There can be no adjustment to the statement.

The fourth word in the Greek text is a compound Greek word (anesteesen) translated **resurrection**. It comes from "again" and "to stand." Thus it means "standing again." It is used in a variety of ways but most significantly for the resurrection from the dead. The fifth word is the Greek word "ho." It is a definite article and is most generally "the." In this verse it is used to emphasize the sixth Greek word, **God**. If we were to read our verse in the order of the Greek words it would read, "This one the Jesus stood up the God of whom all we are testifiers." As we proceed we will analyze this great statement.

Person of Jesus

Even the casual reader of this verse (Acts 2:32) would agree the focus is on Jesus, the Person. Peter begins this sentence in the Greek with Jesus. Remember this helps determine the emphasis of the statement. He places the definite article "the" before the name of Jesus. This makes Him emphatic and particular in the sentence. The first word of Peter's statement in this verse is a Greek word translated "this one," "Him," "the same," "that," or "this." These facts present to us a threefold foundation for Jesus being the major focus of this statement. If you carefully examine Peter's sermon you will discover he does this two additional times. A total of three times he emphatically points to Jesus as

Resurrected Life | **Acts 2:31-32**

this same Jesus (Acts 2:23, 32, 36). He recalls for his audience their knowledge of and acquaintance with ***Jesus of Nazareth, a Man*** (Acts 2:22).

The strength of the statement seems to focus on Jesus being the same. In other words, the Jesus of whom Peter speaks now is the same as the Jesus he referred to earlier. Let's view afresh the opening statement of the body of his sermon which is an explanation of Pentecost. He says, **"Men of Israel, hear these words: Jesus of Nazareth, a Man attested by God to you by miracles, wonders, and signs which God did through Him in your midst, as you yourselves also know…"** (Acts 2:22). In our previous study we discovered the main subject of this sentence is ***you yourselves***. It is a reflective pronoun which is the pronoun of the self (himself). It is a stronger focus on the individual than the normal pronoun. Peter addresses this group concerning Jesus with no one else in mind. This becomes important as we discover the main verb of the sentence. It is the word, ***know***. The direct object which receives the action of the knowing is ***Jesus of Nazareth, a Man***. This links the person of Jesus, to whom he refers, to their knowledge. Their knowledge of Jesus was totally limited to His manhood. They knew Him only as a Man they could crucify. They did not view Him as an angel, the Messiah, or as God.

Now Peter in the middle of his sermon says, "This same Jesus to whom I referred at the beginning is the same One to whom I am referring now." He is ***Jesus of Nazareth, a Man***. This is not a different person from the One you knew. He has not evolved into something else. He has not ceased to be a Man, One like you. He is the same. However, I want to add a factor to your knowledge of Him. **"This Jesus God has raised up,"** (Acts 2:32). I have found this same emphasis repeatedly in the Book of Acts. This seems to be a real concern in the minds of the apostles. They do not want anyone to think that after His resurrection Jesus was someone different than before His

Part Four: David's Message

resurrection. Certainly the resurrection of Jesus changed Him. Peter cries out, "Absolutely not!"

This has to do with the heart of Peter's explanation of Pentecost. The Spirit of God was sourcing ***Jesus of Nazareth, a Man.*** In fact, it was the Spirit of God within Him causing His life which was demonstrated in ***miracles, wonders, and signs*** (Acts 2:22). This same Spirit of God sourced the very death of Christ (Acts 2:23). But this same Spirit of God caused life to continue within Him (Acts 2:24). Therefore, the life of Jesus before His resurrection which was sourced by the Spirit of God is the same life being sourced by the Spirit after His death. He is the same Person sourced by the same Spirit. The only thing that has changed is the circumstances surrounding Him.

Jesus was dependent on the Spirit of God for His life before His death, but after the resurrection He now sources Himself? No! The same dependency He experienced before the resurrection is the same dependency He has now. The references Peter makes to this fact are very impressive. It is the Spirit of God which sourced Jesus resurrection (Acts 2:32). Jesus ***poured out this which you now see and hear*** because He received it from the Father. It is the Spirit of God that sourced Jesus as the Messiah and as Lord (Acts 2:36). It was the sourcing of the Spirit of God which ascended Jesus and placed Him at the right hand of the Father (Acts 2:34). Jesus continues to be an explanation of Pentecost. The sourcing of the Spirit of God is to be an eternal sourcing. This is the defining factor of the people of the Kingdom of God. This is what makes us who we are.

This really means the attitude of Christ before His crucifixion is the same after His resurrection. Do not think He was loving and kind before His death, but He is judgmental and mean after His resurrection. His mission before His death was redemption; His mission after His resurrection is redemption. He prayed for you before He was crucified (John 17:20). He is interceding for you after His resurrection (Hebrews 7:25). He did not peel off His Calvary love gloves after His death and wipe His hands of you! He loves you the same. He is sourced by the Spirit. God became man, a real man. As a man He limited Himself to the only resource man needs, the Spirit of God. This was an eternal sacrifice. He never gave up His attachment to us. One like us, with the flesh of humanity, made it to the right hand of God. He is like us!

Remember Jesus is a prototype of who we are. Jesus is painting a picture of the life of a Christian. In Jesus we see what God dreamed for us. The life which is sourced by the Spirit of God is the life we will have forever. The individual who is sourced by the life of the Spirit is presently living the resurrected life. What we are through the sourcing of the Spirit in this present time zone will be expanded in the eternal realm forever. We must be sourced by Him!

Position of Jesus

As we continue to view our verse (Acts 2:32) there is another obvious fact. The entire focus of the verse is on the PERSON OF JESUS. What is so important about Jesus? The one single factor Peter highlights about Jesus is the resurrection. ***"This Jesus God has raised up, of which we are all witnesses,"*** (Acts 2:32). While this is true of this verse, it is also true of the Peter's sermon in its entirety. As we begin to follow Peter's explanation of Pentecost as found in Jesus, it becomes very clear that the resurrection of Christ from the dead is a fundamental issue. The sourcing of the Spirit of God within Christ did produce miracles and even His death. While this is definitely mentioned (Acts2:22-23) the thrust of his argument and proof rests upon the emphasis of the Spirit of God producing the resurrection from the dead. There is the negative approach as he says that death could not possibly hold the Man filled with the Spirit (Acts 2:24, 31). There is the prophetic approach, David received this promise generations ago (Acts 2:30-31). Then there is the positive approach as the eye witnesses validate its reality (Acts 2:32).

The only real proof of the entire matter is Jesus' resurrection from the dead. Everything else is subjective and mystical. Peter can preach that one hundred and twenty disciples are filled with the indwelt Spirit of Christ, but how can he prove it? There is another group that said, *"They are full of new wine,"* (Acts 2:13). How can it be proven that Jesus ascended and is sitting at the right hand of the Father? Only a few actually saw Him ascend. How do they know where He went? The only validated, historical evidence is the resurrection. All the rest of the truth hangs on the reality of the resurrection of Christ. This was the promise made by God with an oath to King David (Acts 2:30-31). If this promise is true, we must embrace all Peter is preaching. If this promise is not true, then do not believe any of it!

It becomes very evident that the entire outpouring of the Holy Spirit, the Promise of the Father, is dependent upon the resurrection of Christ from the dead. If death had conquered Him, there is no ascension, and He would never have **exalted to the right hand of God** (Acts 2:33). If He was imprisoned in Hades, He would never have **received from the Father the promise of the Holy Spirit** (Acts 2:33). If the resurrection is not true then Jesus did not pour **out this which you now see and hear** (Acts 2:33). If we are convinced of His death and His resurrection, then we must embrace the ascension and the outpouring of His Spirit.

The culture of Peter's day viewed all the activities of Jesus as "redemption." His death was not separated from His resurrection. His death, resurrection, and ascension were all connected as one event. His death, resurrection, ascension, and outpouring of the Spirit were "salvation." If we embrace one aspect we must embrace all. The resurrection of Christ was not more essential or important than any other aspects of redemption. However, it was the key to their witness. As Peter says, *"Of which we are all witnesses,"* (Acts 2:32). The disciples could validate this aspect of the redemption event.

In a previous study from Acts chapter one, we discovered this same amazing truth. Luke highlights this truth in the first recorded business meeting of the early church. The one hundred and twenty needed to replace Judas who was now dead. There was a single qualification for the replacement of the apostle. He must **have accompanied us all the time that the Lord Jesus went in and out among us, beginning from the baptism of John to that day when He was taken up from us,** (Acts 1:21-22). Why would this requirement be so important? **One of these must become a witness with us of His resurrection** (Acts 1:22). This gives us key insight into the purpose and role of the twelve apostles. Their purpose was not to provide adequate leadership for overseeing the various regions in which evangelism would take place. It was not so new programs would be established and promoted for the new church plants. The entire purpose was to be *a witness with us of His resurrection.* Luke describes the ministry of the apostles after Pentecost as evangelism began to take place. *And with great power the apostles gave witness to the resurrection of the Lord Jesus. And great grace was upon them all* (Acts 4:33).

The entire focus of the message of the early Church throughout the Book of Acts is the resurrection of Christ. It is in every message and conversation. We already viewed it in this first message preached by Peter explaining Pentecost. Immediately after Pentecost, Peter and John were involved in a miracle at the Gate Beautiful. The surrounding crowds were greatly moved giving Peter the opportunity to preach to them. The results were, **Now as they spoke to the people, the priests, the captain of the temple, and the Sadducees came upon them, being greatly disturbed that they taught the people and preached in Jesus the resurrection from the dead** (Acts 4:1-2).

Part Four: David's Message

As the Book of Acts unfolds into the evangelism of the Apostle Paul, we see the message of the resurrection being strongly delivered to the Gentiles. *Then certain Epicurean and Stoic philosophers encountered him. And some said, "What does this babbler want to say?" Others said, "He seems to be a proclaimer of foreign gods," because he preached to them Jesus and the resurrection"* (Acts 17:18; see 17:32). Paul's message before the council was the resurrection. *But when Paul perceived that one part were Sadducees and the other Pharisees, he cried out in the council, "Men and brethren, I am a Pharisee, the son of a Pharisee; concerning the hope and resurrection of the dead I am being judged!"* (Acts 23:6). As Paul was before Felix, the governor, giving his defense against the accusations of the leaders of Israel, he said, *"I have hope in God, which they themselves also accept"* (Acts 24:15). At the close of his defense he boldly proclaimed, *"They ought to have been here before you to object if they had anything against me. Or else let them who are here themselves say if they found any wrongdoing in me while I stood before the council, unless it is for this one statement which I cried out, standing among them, 'Concerning the resurrection of the dead I am being judged by you this day' "* (Acts 24:19-21). Paul was then presented before King Agrippa who wanted to hear his defense. Paul told him of his heavenly vision and that *"the Christ would suffer, that He would be the first to rise from the dead, and would proclaim light to the Jewish people and to the Gentiles"* (Acts 26:23).

Provision of Jesus

However, there is one other factor in our verse (Acts 2:32) which must not be ignored. Peter is very definite in his message that Jesus did not raise Himself from the grave. Jesus was not the source of His own resurrection. He is emphatic concerning his focus on Jesus. Peter is equally definite about the resurrection of Christ from the dead. But above all he must convince you that **God has raised up** Jesus. The most important issue in interpreting Peter's sermon is to remember it is an explanation of the Pentecost event. Every phrase, every sentence must be seen in light of the outside God coming to be inside.

As we have highlighted previously in Peter's sermon, the resurrection is a result of the outside God living inside. ***Jesus of Nazareth, a Man*** was filled with the Spirit of God; therefore life was generated within Him. The resurrection was not just an event He experienced but a life which He lived because of the indwelt Spirit. No one who knew Christ should be shocked at the physical crucifixion. He lived the crucified life in a consistent life style. The cross for Jesus was not an event only; it was a life style. He was always giving Himself away; He never thought about Himself. He lived in the fullness of the Spirit as He continually surrendered Himself to the Spirit. It is equally true that no one who knew Jesus should be surprised at His resurrection. He was constantly living a life generated by the Holy Spirit. As the world of death and darkness continually attempted to engulf Him, life was quickened within Him. The Spirit of God so penetrated Him, death could not prevail. He was sourced by God.

This is promised to us in the fullness of the Spirit. We are to be sourced by God. Life is the undefeated proof of our testimony. We can say that God lives within us; but how is this mystical aspect proven? We can speak of knowing Christ, but how is this validated to a world who does not know Him? Here is the factor the world can see; here is the proof. We live in the midst of death; we are sourced by the Spirit.

Acts 2:33-35

ASCENSION - DESCENSION

Peter is explaining Pentecost in a powerful sermon. His focus is on Jesus. Everything God has accomplished in ***Jesus of Nazareth, a Man*** He now wants to do in and through us. Jesus is the beginning of an entirely new species of humanity. The significant difference between Jesus of Nazareth, a Man and all those who have gone before Him is Pentecost. This marks the beginning of a new source for man. While the prophets of old have prophesied concerning this radical change, it was not understood. Who could grasp what mankind could be if sourced by the nature of God?

Therefore, when the outside God came to actually be inside it was shocking to the Jews of the Dispersion. They recognized Pentecost as the new thing God was doing. They were anticipating this great event. Immediately they broke into seeking and responded with a question, *"Whatever could this mean?"* (Acts 2:12). Peter was moved upon by the Holy Spirit to give clear understanding of what God was doing in mankind. Every word of his sermon must be interpreted as an explanation of Pentecost (Acts 2:14-39).

As we come to our passage, Peter comes full circle in his sermon. He explains, *"Therefore being exalted to the right hand of God, and having received from the Father the promise of the Holy Spirit, He poured out this which you now see and hear"* (Acts 2:14-39). This event started with the sound which

Ascension - Descension | Acts 2:33-35

amazed the multitude (whether it was the sound of the rushing mighty wind or the sound of the fifteen different languages being spoken by Galileans). Peter explains it as the fulfillment of the prophecy of Joel. Then he introduces Jesus as the explanation of Pentecost. He was sourced by God in His life, death, and resurrection (Acts 2:22-24). Peter continues by expounding David's connection with Messianic Psalms (Acts 2:25-26). However, David is dead while Jesus is alive in the resurrection of the sourcing of the Spirit. He is now exalted to the right hand of the Father and is fulfilling the promise of the outpouring of the Spirit. This is what the crowds had heard and seen which brings us back to the sound.

This can be reasoned in reverse as well. The sound which they heard was the result of the outside God coming inside. It was contingent on Jesus receiving from the Father the promise. This was contingent on Jesus ascending to the Father's right hand. This was contingent on His resurrection which was contingent on His death. This was all based on the promise of God made to David.

The passage (Acts 2:29-35) establishes a series of contrasts. There is actually a series of subordinate contrasts which give content to one major contrast. The overall contrast is very easy to identify. It is simply "The Patriarch Approach – Man's Provision" contrasted with "The Prophetic Approach – God's Provision." The very nature of sin from the beginning is man's desire to provide for himself. All deeds of sin have at their heart an independent attitude rejecting a dependency on God. This independent attitude was distinctly expressed by Israel when they desired a man king. During the first third of Jewish history God was King of Israel. It was a theocracy. After all the benefits and blessings experienced by Israel from this relationship, Israel decided they wanted to rule over themselves creating a monarchy. It wasn't that they did not believe in God. They did not want to totally eliminate His involvement in their lives. They just did not want

Part Four: David's Message

Him as their King, their Provider. They wanted to provide for themselves. Unless, of course, circumstances got out of hand and required that God rescue them. God became their backup plan.

The patriarch David was a symbol of this. He was the founder of the royal line. The royal line was focused on man ruling over himself. It was man providing for himself. The first discussion we had of a contrasted subordinate was WRONG – RIGHT. The patriarchal approach was WRONG. God did not intend it; it was not His plan. When Israel demanded a man king, they rejected God (1 Samuel 8:19). Israel was saying, "No." But God would not reject us! God was and is aggressively involved in redeeming us from ourselves. This is Peter's explanation of Pentecost. God will move upon man's provision and raise it to a new level. He promised a provision which is now fulfilled in Christ. God brought us back to what He intended in the beginning. The King is reigning within. He is our provision.

The second subordinate contrast is DEATH – LIFE. Man's provision always results in death. Regarding the patriarchal approach, David is **dead and buried, and his tomb is with us to this day** (Acts 2:29). Even his royal line has become obscure. Everything man provides, protects, and promotes ends in decay. Even man's best attempts are futile. But the prophetic approach (Acts 2:30) is a promise from God. He is going to act; He is going to provide. Peter describes all that God provides (Acts 2:31-35). It is the provision of Pentecost. Throughout this provision there is the emphasis of "life." It is found in Christ who could not be held by death because of the fullness of the Spirit. God raised Him from the dead. The fulfilled Kingdom is a Kingdom of life.

We now come to the third subordinate contrast. It is ASCENSION – DESCENSION. We are once again faced with the startling statement which is found twice in Peter's sermon (Acts 2:27, 31). It is also quoted a third time in chapter thirteen (Acts 13:35). For Peter to quote this statement so often must mean it has significance. Moreover, the essence of the truth of

Ascension - Descension | **Acts 2:33-35**

this statement is seen in the New Testament present tense reality (Acts 2:24). While the word "ascension" is not used, Peter's quote certainly highlights it. Peter reminds us for the second time in his sermon; *"He, foreseeing this, spoke concerning the resurrection of the Christ, that His soul was not left in Hades, nor did His flesh see corruption"* (Acts 2:31).

Let us be sure and remember there is no ascension without a descension. There is no resurrection without death. In fact, life is only found in the midst of death. In Peter's sermon, there is no mention of the ascension without the context of the resurrection. Also, there is no mention of the resurrection without the context of death. In Peter's presentation the resurrection is a distinct portion of the ascension. He refers to the resurrection three times. Two of those three times, he refers to the resurrection in the verb form (Acts 2:24, 32). The resurrection must be seen as the act of ascending. The Greek word translated resurrection (Acts 2:31) means to lift up.

While all we have said is true as seen in our passage, notice this is in a physical sense. Jesus physically dies and is physically raised from the dead. Then He physically ascends as witnessed by His disciples (Acts 1:9-11). However, it is just as important to notice the spiritual emphasis in our passage. The spirit of submission (death to self-centeredness, cross style) is maintained in the heart attitude of Christ at all times. He does not ascend from the sourcing of the Father to a self-sourcing. Is Jesus not **exalted to the right hand of God** (Acts 2:33)? Yes! However, the Greek verb translated "being exalted" is in the passive voice. This means the subject (Jesus) is being acted upon or receives the action of the verb. His position of honor and authority at God's right hand is received by Him in the spiritual attitude of death. Jesus cannot claim the outpouring of the Holy Spirit upon the believers as that which He sourced. He **received from the Father the promise of the Holy Spirit** (Acts 2:33). He was sourced by the Father as He lived in the spiritual attitude of the cross. The physical aspect of the resurrection, ascension, and outpouring of the Holy Spirit all took place in the context of the spiritual attitude of submission, death to self-centeredness.

Is this not the lesson we must learn? We can never physically experience the resurrection unless we physically die. Neither can we physically ascend to heaven unless we physically descend to death. But this is much bigger than just the physical accomplishment of going to heaven. Intimacy with Christ, the fullness of His Spirit, or being sourced by God will never spiritually take place unless we experience the spiritual death of the cross. It is in the brokenness of the cross style we can ascend to these spiritual realities. Life is only found in the midst of death. This spiritual submission is so necessary even the physical depends upon it.

Do you realize how hard it has been for Peter to grasp this reality? Let's go back to the ministry of Jesus to His disciples (Matthew 16). Jesus had tremendous results with great multitudes. But they did not grasp His heart. He decided to focus His efforts on His disciples. He had only six months before He would experience the cross. He took His disciples into Gentile territory in an attempt to escape the pressure of the multitudes. His teaching would focus on the crucifixion. He begins with the first prediction of His death and resurrection (Matthew 16:21). It was not a brief statement but a continual teaching according to the passage. Jesus was aware that the disciples believed He was the Messiah, but they did not comprehend the content. They thought of Him as a military Messiah who would deliver them from Rome. They wanted Him to restore Israel to her proper place among the nations of the world. They desired thrones and power in this earthly kingdom. They did not understand Jesus was establishing a Kingdom of the cross style. Everyone in this Kingdom would live the style of bleeding, suffering and dying. It would be in the midst of dying that life would come!

The disciples aggressively argued with Him about this cross style. In fact, Peter openly rebuked Jesus to His face. Jesus

Ascension - Descension | **Acts 2:33-35**

responded by recognizing that Peter's statement was of Satan (Matthew 16:22). Jesus gave the call to all Christians, **"If anyone desires to come after Me, let him deny himself, and take up his cross, and follow Me"** (Matthew 16:24). Where exactly is Jesus going? He is going to descend. But it will be in the midst of the descent that He will ascend. While this may be a physical descension followed by a physical ascension, don't miss the spiritual context. Jesus already embraced the cross. His life style, the cross style, is a direct result of His submission to the Father. He is being sourced by the Father in the midst of rejecting self-sourcing. The sourcing life of the Father is only found in the midst of death.

Now Peter is expressing the same truth in his explanation of Pentecost. If the heart of Pentecost is about the sourcing of the Spirit instead of self-sourcing, Peter must highlight the cross style. While there was a physical descending from which the physical resurrection and ascension took place, the heart of the matter is the spiritual reality. The physical resurrection took place because Jesus was sourced by the Spirit. The physical ascension occurred because Jesus was sourced by the Spirit. There was a spiritual death to all self-sourcing in the heart of Christ. In the midst of this spiritual death, life came! If we desire life in our families, churches, or our own lives, we must live in the death of self sourcing. All self-sourcing must be crucified with Christ that the life of Christ might source us.

The argument the disciples had with Jesus lasted for at least six days (Matthew 17:1). It must have been some kind of debate. How difficult this was for Jesus. Having said all He could say, He called for a prayer meeting. Jesus took three disciples with Him to the mountain to cry out to the Father for revelation of the cross style. His prayer was answered as Jesus was transfigured on the mount. The sourcing of the Spirit within Him began to be manifested through Him so the disciples could see it. Moses, representing the law, and Elijah, representing the prophets, came

Part Four: David's Message

to fellowship with Him. They spoke only of His crucifixion, thus verifying what Jesus had told His disciples (Luke 9:31). During this visitation the Father overshadowed the mountain. He continued to verify the cross style by placing His stamp of approval on Jesus. He told the disciples, ***"This is My beloved Son, in whom I am well pleased. Hear Him!"*** (Matthew 17:5). Jesus was a bleeding, suffering, dying Messiah. But it was not just physical; this was already taking place in the inner heart of Christ. He was not calling His disciples to another event, but to a heart condition in which they could live!

It is certain that Peter finally grasped the truth of the Mount of Transfiguration. He explains Pentecost in terms of this same dying. Jesus descended and from that descension came the ascension. But the ascension was not just in the physical. The very source of the resurrection and ascension was the sourcing of the Spirit of God within Christ. He was sourced by the Spirit because He refused to be self-sourced. He experienced the crucifixion of the heart, long before the physical crucifixion event. It was the condition of His nature. This allowed the sourcing of the Spirit.

This is the call of the Spirit to our lives. Everyone wants God to intervene in their lives. We want God to give us good luck, bless our finances, provide good health, and make our children beautiful. We want to go to heaven, but not too quickly. We become very disappointed with God when He does not grant us these things. Peter explains Pentecost as the establishment of a new Kingdom. It is the Kingdom of the cross style. Self-sourcing must die; in the midst of this death there will be life, the sourcing of the Spirit.

John the Baptist understood this. He became the bridge from the Old Covenant into this new indwelling of the Spirit, the New Covenant. When Peter, James, and John came down from the Mount of Transfiguration, they expressed confusion concerning the ministry of the forerunner. They did not recognize John the

Baptist as the promised Elijah (Matthew 17:10). They viewed their future through the eyes of self-sourcing. They saw the forerunner as a military general who would pave the way for the ruling of the earthly Messiah. John the Baptist did not fill this role. Jesus described John's role for them, *"But I say to you that Elijah has come already, and they did not know him but did to him whatever they wished. Likewise the Son of Man is also about to suffer at their hands"* (Matthew 17:12). John the Baptist, the Elijah, foreran the cross style. He was submissive. He was not self-sourced. He lived in the style of the cross. He foreran the pattern Christ would follow. Christ brought life in the midst of John the Baptist's death. Life is found in the midst of death.

This is clearly stated in the physical realm. John the Baptist lived in the wilderness not a fancy house. He wore simple cloths not fancy robes. He ate simple food not expensively prepared meals. He physically suffered for his message. He died declaring it. However, do not miss the spiritual realm. His attitude was never one of self-sourcing. At the height of his ministry and fame, he cried, *"It is He who, coming after me, is preferred before me, whose sandal strap I am not worthy to loose"* (John 1:27). He lived the dying.

This is the call of Christ upon our lives. This is the explanation of Pentecost. We must die to our self-sourcing that the Spirit of Christ might source our lives. ***Jesus of Nazareth, a Man*** is the prototype. There is no ascension without descension. Life is found in the midst of death. Who will join Jesus in descending?

PART FIVE
ACTS 2:36-39

I PROMISE YOU

Acts 2:36

THE WRONG CONCLUSION

The most important physical element in the understanding of the Scripture is "context." If you interpret a verse outside of the writer's intended flow, you are in violation of the Scriptures. The context of our passage is "Pentecost." The New Covenant is startling; three to five thousand Jews of the Dispersion stand in amazement. They cry out, *"Whatever could this mean* (to be)*?"* (Acts 2:12). God uses many shocking interventions to introduce this new spiritual level. Because these Jews are open and seeking, God abundantly reveals the truth to them.

The Holy Spirit moves upon Peter and he gives a clear explanation of the meaning of the event (Acts 2:14). He saturates his sermon with Scripture. He begins with his text (Acts 2:16-21). There he quotes from the prophet Joel (Joel 2:28-32). The body of his sermon is a clear statement (Acts 2:22-24). It is the basic proposition or theme of his message. Every word, phrase, and sentence of his message is an explanation of Pentecost. He will address no other subject. The theme of his explanation is ***Jesus of Nazareth, a Man*** (Acts 2:22). God proved Pentecost in this Man. The New Covenant is an outside God coming to live inside man. In the Old Testament God was always outside. There were requirements which man was to accomplish. He was to fulfill the law by his own personal discipline and resource. In the New Covenant, everything changes. God indwells mankind and we are sourced by Him. Jesus is the first Man since Adam and Eve to experience this indwelling. He is the beginning of the Kingdom of God among us.

In our passage (Acts 2:36) Peter begins the conclusion of his message to these Jews. It is a very strong statement. **"Therefore let all the house of Israel know assuredly that God has made this Jesus, whom you crucified, both Lord and Christ."** Carefully note the word *assuredly.* In the Greek text it is the first word in the sentence. This word is the emphasis or the highlight of the statement. It is a translation of the Greek word "asphaios." Its literal sense is "safe, safely, secure, or unshakable." It is used to highlight the certainty or stability of a thing, as in a "sure" anchor (Hebrews 6:19). It is used often for the guarding or safekeeping of a person or thing. Some examples would be the capture of Jesus in the Garden of Gethsemane (Mark 14:44), securing the grave of Jesus (Matthew 27:65-66), the careful locking of a prison (Acts 5:23), of guarding prisoners (Acts 16:23), and of fastening feet in the stocks (Acts 16:24).

Peter begins to conclude his message to the Jews of the Dispersion. They participated in the crucifixion of Jesus. They did not accept Jesus as the Messiah. They missed all the truth that God proclaimed through Jesus. This is far beyond theological differences. Do not view them as one denomination against another, but they are all spiritually one. They are lost! As those who are involved in deep sin are lost, so these Jews of the Dispersion are lost. As those who consistently crucify Christ afresh with their evil deeds are without eternal life, so these Jews, having crucified Jesus, are also dead. They are very religious, but they are without hope. What an awful state in which to dwell.

Peter begins his concluding remarks with a strong declaration. It is a statement which is absolutely secure; it is locked down. It is totally safe to rest your life upon it. Let this one sure truth shape your theology. There is no give and take, no compromise or adjustment in this reality. This declaration is the fundamental which establishes the foundation of everything God desires for your life. If you grasp this all is well; if you miss this you are damned. This is the big, huge issue! It is the fact *that God has made this Jesus, whom you crucified, both Lord and Christ.* This is the final statement in Peter's explanation of Pentecost.

Did you hear the certainty of this great statement? The security of this statement is made by the interaction of its elements. There is absolutely no compromise. To hedge on any aspect of this great truth is to be lost. There are no minor issues in the presentation. You cannot embrace some of the aspects without accepting them all. You cannot pick and choose.

Caused

God has caused this! That is why it is so certain. The sovereign hand of Almighty God moved and the result puts it beyond question or suspicion. There is no debate concerning the reality of this statement. However, a deeper issue concerning this fact is found in the Greek word (epoieesen) translated *has made.* This verb comes from the Greek root word "poieo." It is the Greek word used to bespeak the action of trees as they bring forth fruit (Matthew 3:10; 7:17; 13:23, 26). It is the same Greek word used to speak of the creative actions of God (Acts 4:24; 14:15). But the depth of the word contains a meaning far beyond "habitual doing," and is a concept expressed by the Greek word "prasso." Prasso is never used in connection with Jesus or God, the Father.

The Greek word (poieo) from our passage speaks of motive or creative flow. It is the picture of an artist whose creative, artistic nature is flowing through his brush to produce a masterpiece on the canvas. In other words, what God is doing in Jesus is a product of the very inner heart of His being. It is an expression of His nature. Paul calls himself *less than the least of all the saints* (Ephesians 3:8). He was selected to *preach among the Gentiles the unsearchable riches of Christ* (Ephesians 3:8). The content of this message was the revelation of *the fellowship of the mystery* (Ephesians 3:9). It was hidden in God from the beginning of the ages; but now it is *made known by the church to the principalities and powers in the heavenly places* (Ephesians 3:10). If you ask, "Why was it hidden and now made known?" The answer is clear! It was determined by the *eternal purpose which He accomplished* (epoieesen) *in Christ Jesus our Lord* (Ephesians 3:11). The Greek word (epoieesen) translated *accomplished* is the exact word in our passage (Acts 2:36). It is even the same grammar form. This revelation came from the deep, eternal purpose in the heart and mind of God. The revelation is that which is taking place in *Jesus of Nazareth, a Man*.

Paul also tells us that *God was in Christ reconciling the world to Himself, not imputing their trespasses to them, and has committed to us the word of reconciliation* (2 Corinthians 5:19). Therefore, *we are ambassadors for Christ, as though God were pleading through us* (2 Corinthians 5:20). He continues by revealing the very foundation for this! *For He made* (epoieesen) *Him who knew no sin to be sin for us, that we might become the righteousness of God in Him* (2 Corinthians 5:21). The Greek word (epoieesen) translated *He made* is the exact word in our passage (Acts 2:36). It is even the same grammar form. God has embraced our sin in Christ. It is a product of His deep internal heart love for us. His nature would not be satisfied until we *become the righteousness of God in Him*.

Peter is now standing before the Jews of the Dispersion. His explanation of Pentecost is clear and concise. The outside God coming to live inside must be seen in the context of Jesus. Pentecost is explained and understood in and through Jesus. The creative flow which caused Jesus is now available to us. It comes from the very center of God's heart. We can become a part of the heart of God. The creative, artistic heart of God

The Wrong Conclusion | Acts 2:36

painted a masterpiece in the life of Christ. This is what the heart of God wants us to be. He made it possible through Christ in Pentecost.

There is one other aspect to this great action of the heart of God which we must thoroughly understand. Jesus was willing to accept the causing of God. The creative "causing" came from the very center of God's heart; but there was also the consenting of Jesus heart! The Jews were persecuting Jesus; in fact, they *sought all the more to kill Him* (John 5:18). It began with Jesus breaking their Sabbath and was heightened by claiming that God was His Father. In their minds, they thought He was *making Himself equal with God* (John 5:18). Listen to the answer of Jesus, *"Most assuredly, I say to you, the Son can do* (poiein) *nothing of Himself, but what He sees the Father do* (poiounta); *for whatever He does* (poiee), *the Son also does* (poiei) *in like manner. For the Father loves the Son, and shows Him all things that He Himself does* (poiei); *and He will show Him greater works than these, that you may marvel,"* (John 5:19-20). All of these Greek words are from the same root Greek word "poieo."

All the Father is doing (poieo) comes forth from His creative, artistic heart; the entire "doing" (poieo) of the Son is a result of that same heart. The Son set aside His own agenda and resource for the throbbing heart of God. The Son refuses to source Himself in any way. In total submission to the Father, He becomes an expression of the heart of the Father. This is Peter's explanation of Pentecost. What is happening in Jesus is a direct result of the sourcing of the Father; it is also a result of the submissive response of Christ to the Father. He set aside all He had within His own right as God, allowing the Father to source Him. The secret to releasing all of the eternal purpose of the Father is a willing response. Jesus lived in this open response to the Father.

Part Five: I Promise You

Conclusion

Now we come to the second aspect of Peter's concluding statement. He says, "You have come to the wrong conclusion!" Listen to his exact words, ***"Therefore let all the house of Israel know assuredly that God has made this Jesus, whom you crucified, both Lord and Christ,"*** (Acts 2:36). He leaves absolutely no room for a wrongful identification of Jesus. Not one of those listening Jews could wonder to whom he was referring. The news of the crucifixion of Jesus was still the topic of conversation in Jerusalem. The local newspapers were full of the event's details. The circumstances of this crucifixion were so dramatic; the event was the news of the day. The individual that God caused is the exact One that they crucified. There can be no mistake in identity.

Peter strongly emphasizes this identity in his language. God caused **this Jesus**. The Greek word (touton) is often translated "this same." It is an adjective which modifies Jesus. It is a finger which points directly to Jesus whom Peter is describing. He does not want them to misunderstand his statement. Planted between **this** and **Jesus** is the Greek word (ton) which is not translated in the English sentence. It is the definite article which is normally translated "the." A literal translation of this Greek statement would be "***this*** same (touton)" "the (ton)" "***Jesus*** (leesoun)." This definite article highlights again the specific Jesus whom Peter presents to the Jews. All three of these Greek words are in the accusative case which serves as a direct object of the verb. Peter displays the particular and specific Jesus whom God, the Father, has "caused."

Peter's next statement gives content to Jesus. The Jesus God has caused is the One ***whom you crucified***. All through his sermon Peter highlights all that God has caused through and in this Jesus. He sourced ***miracles, wonders, and signs*** through

Him (Acts 2:22). He raised Jesus from the dead (Acts 2:24, 32). God the Father conquered Hades and corruption through Jesus (Acts 2:27). He fulfilled His promise to David (Acts 2:30). Jesus is seated at the right hand of the Father in exaltation (Acts 2:33). Jesus received from the Father the promise of the Holy Spirit; Pentecost was the day of the "pouring out." God sourced all of this in the same Jesus!

How did the Jews of the Dispersion respond to Jesus? ***You crucified*** Him! The very Jesus you crucified is the Jesus I am declaring to you. ***You crucified*** Him! You came to the wrong conclusion. You were so set in your own traditions you did not see what God was doing in and through Jesus. Your self-centered agendas manipulated your vision; you were blind to the sourcing of God. You were totally religious, but unmoved by the action of God in your midst. You came to the wrong conclusion. It was not a misunderstanding or a misjudgment. No one can say, "We did not know!" God was faithful to give revelation after revelation to you. You came to the wrong conclusion.

But wait!!! God has not set you aside. He has brought you to Jerusalem year after year seeking a new thing. He continued His "causing" without hesitation. What He did in and through Jesus He is doing again in one hundred and twenty believers. It is a new demonstration to you. He caused these humble, uneducated Galileans to speak in your dialects. You heard ***them speaking in*** your ***own tongues the wonderful works of God*** (Acts 2:11). The Holy Spirit moved upon Peter to give clear explanation of what is happening in Jesus and now in one hundred and twenty believers. You are given another chance! Will you come to a different conclusion?

God has not changed His mind or removed His opportunity. God has not shut down the redemptive operation in Christ. God has not ceased His activity and therefore you have missed your one chance. All the resource is still before you. All He presented to you in the person of Jesus, He is presenting to you

Part Five: I Promise You

now. Will you come to a different conclusion? God has done it all and it is still available. The whole issue rests upon your conclusion. Don't crucify Jesus; embrace Him. Don't resist in your stubbornness; walk in open responding. Will you come to a different conclusion?

Do you see the clear cut application of this scene in your life? You and I have come to a wrong conclusion! We have self-sourced our lives. God abundantly reveals Himself to each of us repeatedly. Each time we self-source our lives we crucify Jesus as certainly as the Jews of the Dispersion. We came to the wrong conclusion. But God has not abandoned us. The promise is still in place. All He wants for you He is still offering. Will you come to a different conclusion?

There is no question! This is the destiny of man! Here is a pure example and promise of who we were created to be. The only thing which can hinder this sourcing is our own self-sourcing. God promised it just as He proved it to Jesus. What the Father is doing in Jesus, He wants to do through us. As God "caused" Jesus, so He wants to "cause" us. Do not miss it! He is waiting for your conclusion.

Acts 2:36

LORD AND CHRIST

It is a universal fact that everyone is religious. The sociologists of our world boldly declare this. They have never found a tribe or group of people, however isolated, that did not have an established worship of a higher power. The issue for our generation is not the existence of God. Admittedly there are some atheists in our time. But they are the residue of several generations of good Christianity. The pagan world does not produce atheists. It takes several generations of Christianity to produce comfort and stability. In the midst of those blessings people become focused on themselves. Their self-sourcing becomes strong and they eliminate God.

The issue of our world is not the existence of God, but what kind of God is He? This really matters. The base of the world's religion is a search for this God. How can we find Him? When we find Him, how can we manipulate Him to get what we desperately need? It is the picture of the pagan who has a god of rain. He dances and offers sacrifices in order to entice this god to place the proper rain on his crops. This approach establishes a performance or doing base. If I do the right things, offer the right sacrifices, or make the right prayers, I will be rewarded with what I need. This promotes self-sourcing. While my god is the ultimate power, I am the one who earns or merits his favor.

Christianity has an entirely different focus! It has often been stated, "Religion is man's search for God; Christianity is God's search for man!" God broke in on us. He intercepted our lives. The theological term for this is "prevenient grace." Prevenient means "going before." This is the grace (love) of God that has gone before. In other words, God initiated His contact with us. We did not search for Him; He searched and found us. This is not based on our manipulation, performance, or merit. It is not based on us at all! This is about God and what He decided to do. His nature demands His involvement. Redemption is not a "pet project." He is not experimenting. God's nature drives Him to be redemptive. He is expressing Himself. If we do not thoroughly understand this great truth, all we have is confusion. The practical expression of Christianity is the expression of the nature of God. Anything which is not the expression of the nature of God is not a part of Christianity.

Peter boldly declares the heart of Pentecost! He roots the explanation of Pentecost in the nature of God. The outside God came to be inside man. The individual who is filled with God is filled with His nature. In practical life, how will this look? The answer is found in ***Jesus of Nazareth, a Man*** (Acts 2:22). Jesus is the demonstration of this indwelling. God, the Father, came to source Jesus. Jesus is the expression of the nature of God. Everything the Father is doing in Jesus He wants to do in us. However, Jesus is unique. He is the first One to experience the sourcing of the Father since Adam and Eve. As the first Adam was the means by which the whole human race fell into self-sourcing, so this second Adam will be the means of grace by which the whole human race can be restored to the sourcing of the Father. It will require His life, death, resurrection, and ascension. These will all be sourced by the Father. Having accomplished this, God exalted Jesus to the His right hand (Acts 2:33). The Father gave Him the Promise which is now poured out (Acts 2:33). Man can now be sourced by the Father. The same nature of God living in Jesus is now living in us!

What did this nature of God dwelling in Jesus cause in

Him? If Jesus was sourced by God, what were the results of this sourcing? The nature of God produced the very life of Jesus (Acts 2:22; it produced the death of Jesus (Acts 2:23); it also caused the resurrection of Jesus (Acts 2:24). This was all a part of the plan that God was sourcing in this Man! But, this same nature sourced the exaltation of Jesus (Acts 2:33). In fact, this nature caused and creatively produced, Jesus as Lord and Christ! Jesus is not Lord and Christ because He earned it. It is not because He is God that He is Lord. In fact, if Jesus was made to be Lord and Christ, then there must have been a time when He was not Lord and Christ. This drives us to define and discover the content of who Jesus has become.

Content

The focus of the content is **both Lord and Christ**. Peter presents the idea of Jesus being **Lord and Christ** as absolutely inseparable. In other words, Jesus cannot be **Lord** without being **Christ**. He cannot be **Christ** without being **Lord**. They cannot be separated in experience or theology. He is very strong on this issue. If you see the actual Greek text it looks like this: "kai kurion auton kai Christon." There is a double emphasis on the linkage of the two titles, **Lord and Christ**. This is done by the Greek word (kai) translated **both** beginning the phrase. The same Greek word (kai) is then inserted between the two titles. Notice also the Greek word "auton" which is not translated. It is a pronoun of the "self." It is used to intensify the statement or emphasis. Jesus Himself is **both Lord and Christ**. He is not sometimes one and then the other. He is always both.

We must not develop a theology that allows us to separate these two. Any theology that indicates Jesus can be my **Christ**, Savior, and Redeemer without being my **Lord**, Master, and Owner is false. Any assumption that Jesus will save me from my sins but allow me to maintain ownership of my own life must be dismissed. The proposal of salvation without being in the Kingdom in which the Lord reigns is ridiculous. We must not develop a theology which violates His nature.

Jesus ascended to the right hand of the Father. He received from the Father the ownership of the Kingdom of God. The Greek word (Kurion) translated *Lord* means owner, possessor, and master. Jesus is the agency through which God established the Kingdom. Jesus ascended to the heavens with the Kingdom in His hands. He gave it to the Father in humble submission. Now the Father announces that Jesus is King of this Kingdom. He received this position from the Father. The Spirit of Jesus comes to indwell me. He cannot deny Himself (2 Timothy 2:13). He cannot be other than who He is.

Some years back, at the close of a revival service, a teenage girl was kneeling at the altar of prayer. Her life was complicated with overwhelming problems. I knew her situation and I could speak frankly to her. At the close of the prayer time I asked her this question. "Have you ever totally surrendered your life to Christ?" She hesitantly admitted that she had not. Her statement was, "I have never totally surrendered my life to Christ. I am saved, but I am just not sanctified!" She was establishing two different realms of God's grace. She believed she could receive forgiveness from Christ and not embrace Him as Lord. That is impossible and it was the basis of her spiritual problem.

I fear this is an expression of our evangelical language. It creates such confusion. We speak of Jesus as Savior (Christ) and then Jesus as Lord. Sometimes we have even proposed the question, "If Jesus is our Savior (Christ) will you allow Him to be your Lord?" The difficulty with this question is that it suggests an individual could continue to have Jesus as Savior without Him ever being Lord. This is absolutely impossible. They are not two categories. He is **both Lord and Christ.**

The Lordship of Jesus is not a secondary or additional issue in Christianity. It is a salvation issue. The difficulty in our understanding seems to be in the area of surrender. I can surrender all to Jesus now, but it is always what I know at this point in time. Surrender is never stagnant, but always expanding. As I grow in Christ my surrender must grow as well. He reveals truth to me which expands my embrace of Him. This means I am totally surrendered today and I must be totally surrendered tomorrow. My surrender must expand to truth revealed tomorrow. There is never a time I can be less than totally surrendered to be Christian.

The writer of the Book of Hebrews illustrated this truth in Jesus. In describing Jesus, he said, *"though He was a Son, yet He learned obedience by the things which He suffered"* (Hebrews 5:8). Bible scholars relate this statement to Jesus' experience in the Garden of Gethsemane. There is no indication in the statement that Jesus had been disobedient. He was always totally surrendered to the Father. However, in the Garden of Gethsemane, He moved into a situation He had never before experienced. His "total surrender of yesterday" had to expand to embrace this new experience in order to be "totally surrendered today." This is the continuing experience of the believer. We never arrive. At the beginning of Christian experience, Jesus is Lord; at the end of the Christian experience, Jesus is Lord. If I am filled with the nature of God, I will experience who He is. He is **both Lord and Christ.**

To accept the indwelt presence of the Spirit of Jesus, I must embrace Him as Lord and Christ. What does it mean for Him to be **Lord**?

Controller

In a very practical view His Lordship will appear as controller or owner. The word "Lord" is used in such a variety of ways in our language and culture. It was so in the days of Peter as well. One of the strong usages of this word in Peter's culture was the connection of the term with royalty. Many of the emperors of that day adapted the term "Lord" as their title. It is applied to the possession of ownership of something or someone. Even in our passage there is an indication of a progression in the unfolding of His Lordship. He has become Lord! It is sovereign authority of the Owner of all things (God the Father) who has bestowed upon Jesus the ownership of the Kingdom of God. He has been made **both Lord and Christ.** Paul referred to himself as the slave (doulos) of Jesus (Romans 1:1). He sees himself as totally owned and under the authority of One who made it to the right hand of the Father.

This is so strongly proclaimed and believed in the New Testament that it became a creed. ***Therefore God also has highly exalted Him and given Him the name which is above every name, that at the name of Jesus every knee should bow, of those in heaven, and of those on earth, and of those under the earth, and that every tongue should confess that Jesus Christ is Lord to the glory of God the Father*** (Philippians 2:9-11). This confession will ring upon the lips of everyone. It will be so predominate there will be absolutely no question about its reality. Everyone will admit it; every tongue will confess it; every knee will bow to it.

Jesus is the owner. He is not the owner of all things because He is God (although He is). He is the owner of all things because He is a man who is filled with God. It was through the Spirit-sourced Man that death, life, and ascension took place. He is not coming against me as the God who can eliminate me. He is coming to me as a Man sourced by the very nature of God who has paid my price. He owns me. He does not own me to use me; He owns me to set me free. I am free to participate in His nature.

Bring this thought into the context of this passage! Peter is preaching to several thousand Jews. Can you make your way into this great crowd and hear the message as if it is to you? You made Jesus a criminal. You displayed Him naked before an entire world in shame and embarrassment. You degraded Him to the lowest level of your society. He is not worthy of burial. You would have left Him to rot on the cross and His bones to be picked bare by the vultures. This is your view of Jesus.

But God has a different view. He is Lord! Wait! While He owns you, He has not come to throw you to the wolves. He does not desire to punish and destroy you with the blows of His mighty hand. He comes with the nature of God; He flows with the heart of the Father. There is a promise to you. Everything that is going on in Him, He now wants to give to you. He can do this because He now owns you. You are no longer owned by the devil. The evil of your own nature no longer possesses you. You have been bought and paid for with a great price. You have a new Lord!

Christ

He is not only **Lord**, He is **Christ**. Do you understand how strong a statement this was to the Jews of the Dispersion? All their lives they had dreamed of the coming Messiah. The Hebrew word "Messiah" is the equivalent of the Greek word "Christ." It literally means "the anointed One." In this sense "the chosen One." Their hope rested in the coming of the Deliverer. Every morning, the first words spoken by them were, "Could this be the day?" Every lamb offered on the sacrifice altar pointed to this hope. He would be a man; but a Man offered and appointed by God to be King of the Kingdom. Peter cries out to them, **"God has made this Jesus, whom you crucified, both Lord and Christ,"** (Acts 2:36).

How did the Jews of the Dispersion view Jesus? They thought He was a fake and pretender. They did not see Him worthy of their time or attention. He was a bothersome human being who deserved to be eliminated. He was the object of their fun and mockery. They did not see anything worthwhile in Him.

Part Five: I Promise You

They crucified Him. How have you and I viewed Jesus? We made Him the object of our profanity. His name is connected with every evil and bad thing that happens to us. We stand before our crucifixion of Him and mock Him as surely as those of days gone by. "He saved others; He cannot save Himself or us," we cry. He is the great Savior of the world. The angels declared it at His birth; yet we continue on in our sin for we do not believe He can save us. He is love; yet we continue to hate and divide. He is the revelation of eternal things; yet we continue to give ourselves to that which rots and rusts. He is the wisdom of God, but we will not go beyond our stupidity. We view Him as worthless. In the ancient days He was at least worthy of crucifixion. We don't even have time to do that to Him now. We simply ignore Him as if He does not matter.

Wait! There is a promise. God, the Father, gave it to Him. God, the Father, took His entire nature and filled this Man. He is a Spirit-sourced Man. Through Him the Father brought redemption. The Father sourced Him to be the very owner of the Kingdom and the very redemptive source for your life. All that is within Him can now be given to you. The nature of the Father is yours through the One who is **both Lord and Christ**.

Acts 2:36

KNOW AND KNOWING?

Peter uses a variety of elements to explain Pentecost; yet all the elements are singular. In that explanation we find many aspects to apply to our lives; yet all the aspects are the same. We must consider the many perspectives of Pentecost; yet all these viewpoints must be seen through the same lens. It is ***Jesus of Nazareth, a Man***! Jesus is the core of the conclusion of every interpretation and application.

In securing my education I attended a strong Wesleyan holiness seminary. I went with the rigid purpose of establishing a Biblical theology of holiness. During my first year there my level of excitement was high. The school had an annual holiness convention, and they invited a well known preacher of holiness to come and speak during that week. He spoke in morning chapel and evening worship, and I never missed a service. I sat in the front row on the edge of my seat. I had a notebook and pen, along with my Bible, ready to take notes. This was my time to find clarity from the Scriptures about holiness. At the end of the week, my notebook was empty and my head was shaking in dismay. He filled the hours with explanation, but my heart was sad. This strong proponent of holiness had proposed holiness without Jesus. In all of those hours of speaking he had not mentioned Jesus even once.

Peter's sermon is twenty-six verses long (Acts 2:14-39). His entire sermon is focused on Jesus. We must understand every verse in the light of Jesus. There is no holiness outside of Him. Each time the Evangelical Church steps outside of Jesus to develop a doctrine, we divide and destroy ourselves. When we highlight miracles, wonders, and signs (Acts 2:22) apart from Jesus, we produce sensationalism and racketeering. When we see death (Acts 2:23) outside of Jesus there is nothing left except hopelessness. The gifts of the Spirit apart from Christ produce spiritual stars and are demonic.

In light of this, there is no surprise that Peter begins his explanation of Pentecost with Jesus and ends it with Jesus. He explains every aspect of life in terms of Jesus. The Pentecost event is the inauguration of a whole new existence which makes us like Jesus, sourced by the Father. What is our involvement with miracles? What should be our concept of death? How should we view the resurrection? How am I personally to relate to the history of Israel? What is the significance of the exaltation of Jesus to the right hand of the Father? All of these questions find their answer in **Jesus of Nazareth, a Man**. Everything the Father is doing in Jesus is related to us because of Jesus!

There is a contrast between Peter's presentation of Jesus at the beginning of the sermon and his statement concerning Jesus at the close. He begins on one level and ends on another level. He moves us from where we are to where Pentecost can take us! The body of his sermon begins with a sentence which is three verses long (Acts 2:22-24). In previous studies, we discovered the subject of this long sentence. It is **you yourselves** (Acts 2:22). This is a translation of a Greek word (autoi) which is a reflective pronoun. A reflective pronoun is a pronoun of the "selves." It is not just "him" but "himself." This is a stronger focus on the antecedent than a normal pronoun. Peter, at the beginning of his sermon, addresses the Jews of the Dispersion. He has some hard things to say to them. He wants them to clearly understand that he is speaking to them. Luke clearly defines who they are. This is a very select group. They are three to five

Know and Knowing? | Acts 2:36

thousand in number and they are from fifteen different countries (Acts 2:9-12). At the end of his sermon, Peter contrasts the Jews of the Dispersion with all Jews. He says, **"Therefore let all the house of Israel..."** (Acts 2:36). He is addressing all the Israelites of every generation. The Greek word (oikos) is used to refer to a whole people or nation as descended from one ancestor. In this instance this group is identified as Israel. This is a very strong statement. Peter addresses all the generations of Israel. He speaks to Abraham who must know the truth about Jesus. Every descendent of Abraham must know what God is doing in Jesus! This is verified by the far reaching extent of **the promise** (Acts 2:39). It extends to the future generations of Israelites and to those **who are afar off**. Those who **are afar off** are clarified **as many as the Lord our God will call** which includes us. Even the Gentiles are included in this address. We must know what God is doing in Jesus.

Peter's message, originally intended to explain Pentecost to a specific group of Jews, is expanded to include the whole world. What God is doing in Jesus is so big it demands the attention of everyone. This message must be broadcast over every sound wave in all generations of time. It must be understood by each individual because of its value to their lives. No one is to be left out. No one can exclaim, "This does not apply to me!" The world must know what the Father is dong in and through Jesus.

There is a second part to this contrast. Peter contrasts the verb of his opening sentence with the verb of his closing sentence. The subject of the long sentence which began his explanation is **you yourselves**. The verb of that sentence is **know** (Acts 2:22). In the climatic sentence of this sermon the subject is **all the house** while the verb is **let know** (Acts 2:36). While in the English translation they may appear the same, they are the translation of two different Greek words. This creates the contrast.

In the opening sentence the Greek word (oida) is translated **know**. It is in the indicative mood which means "a simple statement of fact." It is in the perfect tense. This means that something has occurred outside of the present moment which has continual results into this present moment. It is in the active voice which means the Jews of the Dispersion are responsible for knowing what they are experiencing. This Greek word (oida) specifically focuses on perceiving, understanding, or grasping. It is often translated "to see." In the context of this opening sentence, Peter tells the Jews of the Dispersion what they already have seen and understood. They have known **Jesus of Nazareth, a Man**. They knew, meaning they perceived Him as a man. They did not think He was a ghost, angel, or vision. They nailed Him to a cross because they perceived Him as a man.

Is this not true for all of us? No one can consider Jesus of Nazareth in the realm of fairy tales. He is not a myth or fable. Each one of us must deal with an historical Jesus who actually existed. Honesty with historical facts demands that you and I deal with this real person called Christ. The great question is one which came from Pilate during the secular trials of Jesus. He asked the Jewish crowds, **"What then shall I do with Jesus who is called Christ?"** (Matthew 27:22). You must do something with Him! You cannot ignore Him!

However, the final statement of Peter's sermon takes us to a new level of consideration. The subject expands from a group of Jews of the Dispersion to all the generations of Israel and to even all the Gentile world. Everyone must be brought into the knowledge of this new level. The verb of this final sentence is also **know**; but it is a translation of a different Greek word (ginosko). It is a relational term. It is not primarily about date or information. It takes a person from reading about an event in the newspaper to actually being on the scene and experiencing the event. "Ginosko" is embracing the event. This is the Greek word which is used for the most intimate relationship in marriage.

This particular Greek word, while it is used in a variety of ways throughout the New Testament, always has an atmosphere or tone in its usage. It relates to familiarity acquired through experience or association. It is not relationship from a remote position, but requires embrace or involvement. It also carries with it an ongoing, continuing aspect. There is a progression in the "knowing."

In the opening statement of Peter's sermon, he reveals the Jews as knowing Jesus on the level of perceiving and understanding that He was a man. They acted on this data. They did not question this information. Now at the close of his message, Peter calls them to a new level of "knowing." Their understanding must progress to an embrace of His person. Jesus must cease to be an object of their rejection; He must become the individual they embrace, get to know, and experience as **both Lord and Christ**. They must embrace Him in light of Pentecost. They must embrace Pentecost in light of Him. They must move from the level of seeing Him through the eyes of tradition and religious ceremony to what the Father is sourcing in Jesus.

Size of the Truth

There are two more categories in which we need to see the contrast. How big is the truth? I can master data. I can comprehend and figure out information. This kind of knowledge is all within my control. I can view *Jesus of Nazareth, a Man* through the eyes of my tradition and ceremonies. I can argue where He is wrong and how He should be stopped. I can set aside claims He might impose on my life as unrealistic and unreasonable. I can study the law, the oral traditions of the elders; I can calculate where He stepped over the boundaries of our sacred orders. I can justify the crucifixion. Crucifixion was not the best, but it was *expedient that one man should die for the people* (John 18:14). After all, there are significant ramifications if Rome gets word of this Radical. If we do not take care of Him, they may judge us all by Him. Isn't this all reasonable?

While this data may indirectly affect my life, it is more like the affect of a flat tire. It is a political issue on which we must vote. At the close of his message, Peter calls the Jews of the Dispersion to a different level of involvement in the truth. God was sourcing this Man. Jesus was caused by the Divine movement before our very presence. We must experience this! If the Father **has made Jesus both Lord and Christ**, we cannot vote on it and go home. This affects my life. My relationship with my wife is changed; how I raise my children is now different. This truth is so big it pulls me into His heart. Jesus, being sourced by God, and being given the primary position of a new realm (**both Lord and Christ**), cannot be treated lightly. It must go to the depths of my soul; it must burn in my bones.

There is such a strong parallel between the Jews of the Dispersion and us. They accepted the data that Jesus was a Man. They voted on this fact and crucified Him. Have we not done the same? Have we not simply learned the theological data and gone on sourcing ourselves? Now God has broken into their midst with one hundred and twenty demonstrations of the same thing He was doing in Jesus. Does this show His desperation to communicate the size of the truth He has displayed? Will you go to a new level with me?

Substance of the Truth

In the confines of their culture and social activities, these Jews simply heard the rumors of Jesus performing miracles. But you know rumors are only partially true. These Jews of the Dispersion were probably not a part of the great crowds which followed Jesus. If you read the description of those crowds, you will be amazed. It was a multitude of handicap people. Oh, the multitudes are so easily swayed with every magician who comes along. Even if it all happened exactly as they say, so what? We know Him on the level of another miracle worker claiming the right to be heard.

But Peter cries, "Wait!" We must embrace Him on another level. This Jesus you pushed aside as another magician has been sourced to a new level. He is now **both Lord and Christ**. This is a call to allow Him to reign in your life. You have the incredible opportunity to walk into the midst of a new Kingdom which God caused through Christ. You can know this Kingdom not as data (oida) but by experience (ginosko). The Kingdom *can* be within you.

Isn't this the need of our lives? This is not an attempt to convert you to a belief system. We are not interested in an adjustment in your life style. This is not someone's performance of a magic trick to stir your emotions and cause you to enlist. This is a call to step into "ginosko." Paul grasped this reality. He cried, "I want to *be found in Him, not having my own righteousness, which is from the law, but that which is through faith in Christ, that righteousness which is from God by faith; that I may know* (ginosko) *Him and the power of His resurrection, and the fellowship of His sufferings, being conformed to His death* (Philippians 3:9-10). Oh, the wonder of it all! Can I actually know about Him? Can I fully know Him in all the wonderful aspects of who He is? Can I know Him in His Lordship? Can I know Him in His position as Christ? Can I by experience be intimate with His person?

Sameness of the Truth

What is the bottom line? You knew and watched. You saw and perceived. You embraced Jesus as a man. There is no doubt in your mind about this information. In our case, we accepted Him as God out there. He is the creator of all things. I embrace

Part Five: I Promise You

the theology of Him being the Savior of the world. I am willing to embrace His church and its practices. I realize the practice of decency and purity is proper and best for me and my children. I embrace Him on the level of "oida."

Now will you embrace Him on a new level? Will you let God do in you what He has been doing in Christ all of this time? God sourced Jesus even in His Lordship and position as Christ. Will you allow Him to source you into this new Kingdom? Will you let Him flood your very being with experience, and intimacy, and bathe you in Himself? Will you enter into the realm of living which can only be experienced because God caused Him and now wants to cause you?

Acts 2:36

LORD AND CHRIST

Jesus is Lord! The early church believed this. It was the central Christian confession concerning Jesus. Paul wrote, *"That if you confess with your mouth the Lord Jesus and believe in your heart that God has raised Him from the dead, you will be saved"* (Romans 10:9). Is this not the creed proposed by the early church? In the midst of the confusion over the spiritual gifts, Paul clarified all issues by saying, *"Therefore I make known to you that no one speaking by the Spirit of God calls Jesus accursed, and no one can say that Jesus is Lord except by the Holy Spirit,"* (1 Corinthians 12:3). Is it any wonder that Paul declares this will be the confession at the end of the ages? The revelation of Christ will be so pronounced *every tongue should confess that Jesus Christ is Lord, to the glory of God the Father* (Philippians 2:11).

Peter could not explain Pentecost without focusing on Jesus. How could he focus on Jesus without declaring His Lordship? The closing, climatic statement of his explanation is, *"Therefore let all the house of Israel know assuredly that God has made this Jesus, whom you crucified both Lord and Christ,"* (Acts 2:36). In the Septuagint (the Greek translation of the Old Testament) the Greek word translated "Lord" appears over nine thousand times. In over six thousand of those passages the Greek word (kurios) translated "Lord" replaces YHVVH, which is Yahweh or Jehovah. This was the name revealed by God to the people of Israel through

Part Five: I Promise You

Moses (Exodus 3:14). It was a name held in such high esteem that by New Testament time it was rarely spoken aloud.

I have no problem declaring Jesus as Lord. I vigorously join in worship, singing the songs which pronounce His Lordship. I do so without thinking through this concept. I have always assumed that Jesus is Lord in the same sense that He is God. I have never struggled with the content of His Lordship. In other words, what exactly do I mean when I boldly confess Jesus as Lord? Is He Lord in the sense that He is sovereign, creator, or almighty? Do I do the very thing the Jews of the Old Testament days did? Am I simply substituting another name (Lord) for the title of God?

In our study, Peter boldly pronounces the Lordship of Jesus. He clearly defines this position in a different way than another name for God. In a previous study we discovered the contrast between Peter's opening statement in his sermon (Acts 2:22-24) and this climatic, closing statement (Acts 2:36). At the beginning of his sermon, Peter addresses the Jews of the Dispersion. He refers to them as *you yourselves*. However, at the close, Peter wants *all the house of Israel* to grasp the truth of his statement. As Peter begins his message, he speaks of that which the Jews of the Dispersion know (eido). At the close of his sermon, Peter calls for an expansion of their relationship. He wants them to move from facts and information to knowing through experience (ginosko). They must now embrace Christ in relationship.

There is one fact in both the beginning and closing of Peter's sermon which he does not contrast. It is a parallel. He refers to the action of the Spirit of God in Jesus as *did* (poieo) in the opening and *has made* (poieo) in the closing. This word highlights the creative nature such as a tree bearing fruit. Peter declares that God proved Pentecost in the life of Jesus. He did it *by miracles, wonders, and signs which God did through Him in your midst* (Acts 2:22). It was the creative flow of the Spirit of God in Jesus which brought these things to pass. Now at the climax of his message, Peter again refers to this creative flow. The same nature which sourced the miracles through Jesus is now sourcing His position as **both Lord and Christ** (Acts 2:36).

The miracles of Jesus were a result of the sourcing of the Spirit. Now the position of Lord is also sourced by the Spirit. This is a radical idea! It suggests that the position of **both Lord and Christ** is a new position as found in the New Covenant. From this we must make the assumption that there was a time when this position did not exist and Jesus did not have this title. God is eternal. This means He is not limited by the element of time. He transcends all things including the binding limitations of our time frame. I can make an attempt to describe this perspective; however, anything I might say would fall short of the reality of the case. I do not have this perspective. Perhaps, from the reality of God's perspective, Jesus has always been in the flesh. From the perspective of my time He was born in the flesh. An eternal God made entrance into my era. The Scripture speaks of His birth from the view of my time zone. There is undoubtedly eternal truth beyond this view, but how can I grasp it?

It appears that Peter is doing the same thing. In the opening statement of his sermon he proclaims that God proved Pentecost in **Jesus of Nazareth, a Man** (Act 2:22). This was done **by miracles, wonders, and signs which God did through Him.** The verb, **did** (poieo) is in the singular number, aorist tense, active voice, and indicative mood. Now in the closing statement he cries **that God has made this Jesus, whom you crucified, both Lord and Christ** (Acts 2:36). The verb, **has made** (poieo), is in the singular number, aorist tense, active voice and indicative mood. They both have the same grammar structure. Peter refers to Jesus becoming Lord and Christ in the same way He refers to the accomplishment of the miracles. There was a time before Jesus did miracles and then He did miracles that were sourced by the Father. There was a time before Jesus was Lord and Christ and then His position as Lord and Christ was sourced by the Father.

Part Five: I Promise You

It is fascinating that in both of the above situations the verb (poieo) is in the aorist tense. We have discussed this tense in other studies. It is the non-tense. The verb does not focus on when the event took place, but rather it directly points to the action of the event itself. In a sense, by using this tense Peter tells us not to struggle in trying to understand the time zone perspective versus the eternal zone perspective. He calls us to embrace the wonder of the establishment and cause of this position of **both Lord and Christ**.

We must understand that man was made in the image of God. After creating all things, God expressed *that it was good* (Genesis 1:25). **Then** (after that) God decided to move to a new level in the creation (Genesis 1:26). It had to do with making man *in Our image, according to Our likeness* (Genesis 1:26). This is described in terms of man having **dominion over the fish of the sea, over the birds of the air, and over the cattle, over all the earth and over every creeping thing that creeps on the earth** (Genesis 1:26). This is about ruling which is a lordship position. The Greek word translated *let Us make* (poieo) is the same word Peter uses to describe the sourcing of this new position, **both Lord and Christ**. Paul refers to Jesus as the *image of the invisible God* (Colossians 1:15). In other words, what God attempted to do in and through Adam, He has successfully done in and through Jesus.

In the Genesis account, it is written, **then God said, "Let Us make man,** (Genesis 1:26). This is the last stage in the progress of creation. These very words show the peculiar importance of the work to be done. In the next chapter of Genesis we are given more detail concerning this activity. **And the Lord God formed man of the dust of the ground, and breathed into his nostrils the breath of life; and man became a living being** (Genesis 2:7). The action of God in creating man is described differently from all the other creations. He formed man. The basic meaning of this Hebrew word is "to form" or "to fashion." Its primary emphasis is on the shaping or forming of the object involved.

It is used to describe a potter who forms the clay vessel. This special involvement was due to the peculiar distinction of man being *in Our image,* after ***Our likeness.*** Peter highlights the value of the idea by using the words twice.

Man was to be God's representative. He would not represent God in the sense that God was absent and man was sent to act in his behalf. In a real sense, God made a physical world, but He was invisible to this visible world. The image of God was an expression of a relationship God would have with man. There would be a uniting, saturating, indwelling, or permeating of God and man. Man would be sourced by God who indwelt him. Thus, everything man did would demonstrate what God is doing. By the sourcing of God, man would have ***dominion*** which is to rule, control, or have power over. This is a Lordship concept.

The tragedy of the fall (Genesis) was completely beyond the act or deed. Man was radically changed from being sourced by God to being self-sourced. He relinquished his sourced rule and authority over all things to Satan. One quickly discovers Satan claims everything as his kingdom. In the temptation of Christ (Matthew 4:1-11), the devil offered to give to Jesus ***all the kingdoms of the world and their glory.*** How did he get authority over all created things? We gave it to him!

In this context, view Jesus who is being sourced by God as ***both Lord and Christ.*** He reclaims first place, the position God gave man in the first place during creation. In all the Greek lexicons the descriptions of ***Lord*** always combined two major ideas; power and authority.

Power

God has newly established His Kingdom in Jesus. Jesus was the first One since Adam to be sourced by the Spirit of God. He echoed the message of John the Baptist, ***"Repent, for the*** *kingdom of heaven is at hand"* (Matthew 4:17). Jesus is the One who is again *crowned with glory and honor.* He has been set *over the works of Your hands.* All things have been put *in subjection under His feet* (Hebrews 2:7-8). Jesus is the beginning of the end of the age. Through His death, resurrection, and ascension, Jesus usurps the position of Satan as having power and authority and reclaims it. But let us not forget Peter's explanation of Pentecost. Jesus did none of this because He is God; He accomplished all of this because He is a Man sourced by God. Man is the one who gave Satan this power; now the Man sourced by God will be the One who will take it from him.

The Greek word translated "power" is "dunamis." It is the Greek word from which we get the English word "dynamite." It emphasizes not the actual resource itself, but the flowing action of that resource. In other words, the power of the Lordship of Christ is the flowing resource of the Spirit of God within and through Him. His Lordship results from and is caused by, the sourcing of the Spirit of God. By the resource of the Spirit, God re-established through Jesus that which failed in Adam. The Kingdom of God is now complete in Christ. It is a Kingdom constituted by humanity; but it is humanity sourced by God. Jesus was the first One and is responsible through the sourcing of the Father for its existence. He is not Lord because He is God. He is Lord because He is a Man sourced by God. God has brought it to pass!

How incredible is it that one of our humanity actually made it to the right hand of God? He has our skin, our body. No wonder the author of the Book of Hebrews cries out after seven chapters saying only one thing. *"We have such a High Priest, who is seated at the right hand of the throne of the Majesty in the heavens,"* (Hebrews 8:1). Jesus is able to plead our cause for He is one of us. He is Lord of the Kingdom. It is a new position which is sourced by God.

A summary at this point is needed. Jesus is **both Lord and**

Christ. This Lordship position needs to be understood from two aspects: power and authority. It must be clear that the power of this position is sourced. Jesus is not Lord because He is God, but because He is Man being sourced by His Father. This power does not put Him in charge to act as King out of His own will and desires. He is enabled by the Father. This power is not a resource Jesus experiences apart from the Father. In other words, the Father does not grant Jesus the power, then sit back to see what Jesus does with it. The Father, through the Spirit, is the power indwelling Jesus. Jesus knows the flow of the power through intimacy with the Father.

All of this gives clear understanding to our position in the Kingdom. Peter's explanation of Pentecost is Jesus. What is happening in Jesus is now taking place in us. He is the prototype and therefore is unique. However, we also have this same derived power from the indwelt presence of the Spirit of Jesus. We are destined to reign with Him. Paul gave this as a ***faithful saying:***

For if we died with Him,
We shall also live with Him,
If we endure,
We shall also reign with Him
(2 Timothy 2:11-12)

John, the Revelator, proposed this same tremendous idea. In the heavenly realms he heard a new song:

"You are worthy to take the scroll,
And to open its seals;
For You were slain,
And have redeemed us to God by Your blood
Out of every tribe and tongue and people and nation,
And have made us kings and priests to our God;
And we shall reign on the earth" (Revelation 5:9-10).

Part Five: I Promise You

Authority

Authority is the second aspect of this Lordship. This authority means "to rule because of ownership." At first glance, you might think this ownership is based on creation. God, the Creator, has the right to own everything. This is the foundation of Jesus' ownership. This brings us to the interaction of **both Lord and Christ**. These two elements cannot be separated. The Greek word (Christos) translated **Christ** is the same as the Hebrew word (Mashi'ach) translated "Messiah." It means to smear or anoint, thus, the Messiah is the "anointed One." He is set aside or anointed for the task of delivering Israel and establishing the Kingdom of God. Deliverance will involve the crucifixion, resurrection, and ascension. Peter describes all of this as sourced by God.

The Lordship of Jesus is intimately connected with His role as Christ. He delivers or redeems us. We are owned, not because He is creator, but because He is Savior. We are twice owned. We are owned, not because He made us, but because He bought us. Paul describes this by saying, *"He has delivered us from the power of darkness and conveyed us into the kingdom of the Son of His love,"* (Colossians 1:13). We relinquished authority to Satan, but Jesus has come! The Father picked us up, carried us, or transported us from the authority of Satan to the Kingdom of Jesus. He sourced all of this through *Jesus of Nazareth, a Man*. Ownership now belongs to Jesus who is a Man sourced by God.

The attitude of the ownership is very important. It is not an attempt of a tyrant. He is not a dictator. In Him we have a High Priest who sympathizes with our weakness. In fact, He *was in all points tempted as we are, yet without sin* (Hebrews 4:15). We are His beloved bride for He loves us and gave Himself for us (Ephesians 5:25). He is the One who washed our feet (John 13:1-7). We are the branch which is intimately connected to

His life source. We bear His fruit and participate in His purpose (John 15:1-7). He is **the good shepherd. The good shepherd gives His life for the sheep** (John 10:11). We are privileged to belong to His fold.

Should we not respond? Let nothing distract us from Him! Count it joy that He is both **Lord and Christ**!

Acts 2:36

POWER AND AUTHORITY

Jesus is Lord! What a statement. It is at the heart of all Christianity. Can the sovereign power of God be questioned? Is He now over all things and who can disagree with Him? Paul addresses the philosophers at Mars Hill in Athens. He chose to speak to them about their altar which had the inscription "To the Unknown God." He cried, "Let me make Him known to you! **God, who made the world and everything in it, since He is Lord of heaven and earth, does not dwell in temples made with hands"** (Acts 17:24). John, the Revelator, gives such forceful insight into the final victory we will experience as Christians. The scenes around the throne of God are filled with awesome worship. They set the tone for what we should be about in this present hour. There were four living creatures, **they do not rest day or night, saying:**

> *"Holy, holy, holy,*
> *Lord God Almighty,*
> *Who was and is and is to come!"* (Revelation 4:8).

There were twenty-four elders who sat before God on their thrones. They would fall on their faces and worship God saying:

> *"We give You thanks, O Lord God Almighty,*
> *The One who is and who was and who is to come,*

Because You have taken Your great power and reigned" (Revelation 11:17).

Who will stand in His presence and dispute His Lordship? Who would be bold enough to claim to be greater than Him? Do we not all bow at His feet and cry, "Holy, holy, holy, Lord God Almighty?" I have no problem with this emphasis and want to join my voice with the multitudes around the heavenly throne. BUT this is not what our passage proposes! In the closing statement of Peter's sermon explaining the Pentecost event, he boldly proclaims, **"Therefore let all the house of Israel know assuredly that God has made this Jesus, whom you crucified, both Lord and Christ,"** (Acts 2:36).

Sourcing of the Position

Let me remind you of some essential facts found in the context of this sermon. In the opening statement of his sermon, Peter says, **"Men of Israel, hear these words: Jesus of Nazareth, a Man attested by God to you by miracles, wonders, and signs which God did through Him in your midst,"** (Acts 2:22). The miracles, wonders, and signs were a result of what God did through Jesus. "Did," in verse 22, is a translation of the Greek word "poieo." It is singular number, aorist tense, active voice, and indicative mood. The Greek word translated "**has made**" in verse 36 is also "poieo." It is a singular number, aorist tense, active voice, and indicative mood. In other words, they are the exact same. The very same way the Father sourced **miracles, wonders, and signs** through Jesus is the same way He is now sourcing Him as **both Lord and Christ**. Jesus has not always been Lord because He is God; this is a different position. Peter gives new content to the position as He describes Pentecost.

Part Five: I Promise You

Sequence of the Position

As Peter describes the life of Jesus in his sermon, he does so in a progression. He begins with the Father sourcing ***miracles, wonders, and signs*** (Acts 2:22). He progresses to the amazing truth of the Father sourcing the death of Jesus (Acts 2:23). He quickly moves to the action of the Father which raised Him from the dead (Acts 2:24, 32). But it is this same sourcing which exalted Him ***to the right hand of God*** (Acts 2:33). While in this exalted position, God sourced Jesus with ***the promise of the Holy Spirit*** (Acts 2:33) which enabled Him to pour out blessing. Now Peter thunders to the climax of his explanation. While the Jews of the Dispersion participated in humiliating Jesus by placing Him on a cross, God sourced Him in a new position of ***both Lord and Christ*** (Acts 2:36).

Seat of the Position

God is establishing something brand new. What was is no longer; what is has just been established. We heard this from the announcement of John the Baptist. He proclaimed, ***"Repent, for the kingdom of heaven is at hand!"*** (Matthew 3:2). There has been no authentic prophet for four hundred years. It is not surprising the people came from all over Israel. He was announcing the presence of a new Kingdom, the Kingdom of God. The focus of the Kingdom is upon the King of the Kingdom, Jesus. How should we respond to His arrival? We should repent. We should give up a former thought to embrace a second thought. We set aside what has been to embrace what is to be.

Within the person of Jesus a new thing is taking place. He is the first One to be filled with the Spirit. What does this mean? He is sourced by God. He is the beginning of an entire new species. God is producing a new breed of people in and through Jesus. They are called sons of God. They are unlike anyone else in history. They are people who are intimate with God. They are sourced by God and they are Kingdom people.

The cross of Christ is an amazing event. It is here that Jesus shed His blood. There is a tremendous study on this subject in the context of the Jewish culture. The Jews believed that life was in the blood (Leviticus 17:11). One important aspect of the blood from their view was the presence of the seed of life. The sperm of life was found in the blood. On the cross God placed the seed of His life into the womb of the world. A new breed of humanity was born from the cross. This new breed would be sons of God, possessing the very nature of God, and being sourced by the very presence of God. Jesus is the beginning of this new humanity.

Since Jesus is the first human being since Adam to enter into this Kingdom, He is being honored by the Father. Because He is the first human being to be sourced by God to establish this new Kingdom, God gives Him the position of ruling in this Kingdom. The Apostle Paul captured this truth. He understood what God was doing in and through Christ. He told us that God was working **the exceeding greatness of His power toward us who believe** (Ephesians 1:19). What exactly does that mean? How does it affect us? He says that it is the same power **which He worked in Christ when He raised Him from the dead and seated Him at His right hand in the heavenly places** (Ephesians 1:20). Where exactly is this place of authority? It is **far above all principality and power and might and dominion, and every name that is named, not only in this age but also in that which is to come** (Ephesians 1:21). What is the position of Jesus in this place? **And He put all things under His feet, and gave Him to be head over all things to the church, which is His body, the fullness of Him who fills all in all** (Ephesians 1:22-23). Is Paul not speaking of the Kingdom of God, the body of Christ? Jesus is the new King of this new covenant Kingdom which is made up of people who are sourced by God.

Substance of the Position

In the previous study, we dealt with this subject, but we must clarify it so you thoroughly understand. There are two aspects contained in the content of this new position of Jesus in the Kingdom of God. Jesus is **both Lord and Christ** (Acts 2:36). Let me remind you that He is not one or the other; He is both. The language is very strong. These two ideas are absolutely inseparable. They cannot be separated in experience or in theology. If you were to see the actual Greek text, it would look like this: "kai kurion auton kai Christon." When translated directly into the English, it reads; "and Lord self and Christ." There is a double emphasis on the linkage of the two titles, **Lord and Christ**. This is done by the Greek word (kai) inserted between the two titles. Notice also the Greek word "auton" which is not translated. It is a pronoun of the "self." It is used to intensify the statement or emphasis. It other words, Jesus "Himself" is **both Lord and Christ**. He is not sometimes one and then the other. He does not have two hats but only wears one at a time. He is *always* both. There is no chance of embracing Jesus as **Christ** without embracing Him as **Lord**. Do not expect Him to be your **Christ** without Him being your **Lord**.

It appears the basis or content of His Lordship is the fact that He is Christ. The Greek word (Christos) translated Christ is the same as the Hebrew word (Mashiach) translated "Messiah." It means to smear or anoint; thus, the Messiah is the "anointed One." God set Jesus aside and anointed Him for the task of delivering Israel and establishing the Kingdom of God. Peter described this in his explanation of Pentecost. God, the Father, sourced the cross, resurrection, ascension, and now the outpouring of the Holy Spirit. This all has to do with the establishment of this new breed of human beings who are sourced by God and from the Kingdom of God. Obviously the Lordship of Jesus is intimately connected to His role as the Messiah, Christ. He delivered and redeemed us.

Jesus, sourced by the Father, ascended to the right hand of God. He finished the great task of establishing the Kingdom of God. He hands the Kingdom to His Father. Since He has been sourced by the Father He claims no right to it as if He brought it about on His own. He claims no ownership within Himself. He does not demand the right to be Lord which has to do with owning. Jesus relinquishes all rights and claims to the Kingdom since He is sourced by the Father. As He turns to depart, the Father calls Him back. The Father sources Him as King of Kings and Lord of Lords; He gives Him the Kingdom. It is not His in self-sourcing, but is His through the sourcing of the Father. He is head of the Kingdom through the sourcing of the Father. Therefore, the attitude or content of the Lordship is determined by the character of the Father who is sourcing the position.

This reality is contained within the Greek word (kurios) which is translated Lord. It is clearly seen in the contrast between two Greek words which can both be translated "lord" and "master." These two Greek words are "kurios" and "despotes." The difference between the usages of these two words is the attitude or practical expression of their function. A man was "despotes" in relation to his slaves, but he was "kurios" in relation to his wife and children. He was Lord and Master (despotes) over his slaves because he owned them. He could buy and sell them at his whim or desire. There was no thought of their welfare or what was good for them. It was a matter of business and personal benefit. After all, slaves were simply property. He was only linked to them through business and personal comfort. They did not have his DNA; his heritage was not theirs. They did not have the family name. They were not sons.

Let me say it again: a man was "despotes" in relation to his slaves, but he was "kurios" in relation to his wife and children. Both words can be translated Lord or Master, but the attitude is different. It is because the linkage is different. Contained within "kurios" is a limited moral authority where the individual who is Lord takes into consideration the good of those over whom he is Lord. Yes, Jesus is Lord, but we are family. He has been given and is sourced as Lord by the Father. He is our big brother who has paved the way and established the Kingdom. How often He told us this: *"No longer do I call you servants, for a servant does not know what his master is doing, but I have called you friends, for all things that I heard from My Father I have made known to you"* (John 15:15).

The Scriptures describe this relationship between us and our Lord. He is our great High Priest. *Seeing then that we have a great High Priest who has passed through the heavens, Jesus the Son of God, let us hold fast our confession* (Hebrews 4:14). Is He not Lord and Master? Yes, but He who serves as a big brother will serve in the position of priest. *For we do not have a High Priest who cannot sympathize with our weaknesses, but was in all points tempted as we are, yet without sin* (Hebrews 4:15). You must understand His Lordship! He has been where we have been and experienced what we have experienced. He is not one who has known nothing but wealth and prestige. We are not simply His slaves to be used as property for His personal benefit. We are His blood; we are kin to the Trinity. The life source that is sourcing Jesus is sourcing us. We are His brothers!

We are His bride! We are not His prostitute to be used and forgotten. Paul instructed us as husbands *love your wives, just as Christ also loved the church and gave Himself for her* (Ephesians 5:25). This is the attitude of His Lordship (kurios). He does not treat us as slaves but as His bride. He has great plans and purpose for us. He has dreams to be fulfilled in and through us. The reason He gave Himself for us, His bride, is *that He might sanctify and cleanse her with the washing of water by the word, that He might present her to Himself a glorious church, not having spot or wrinkle or any such thing, that she should be holy and without blemish* (Ephesians 5:26-27). Paul continued to encourage a husband to love his wife as he would love himself, because the husband and wife are one flesh. *For no one ever hated his own flesh, but nourishes and cherishes it, just as the Lord does the church. For we are members of His body, of His flesh and His bones* (Ephesians 5:29-30). He is Lord as "kurios" not as "despotes." We are not His property as a slave owner, but we are His lover. We are one flesh with Him!

We are the branch who is intimately attached to Him, the vine. As the branch bears much fruit so we are His disciples and the Father is glorified (John 15:8). Are we not essential to Him? Does He not value us? Are we not an extension of His very life? Does He not accomplish His will through our lives? Are we not an expression of His DNA? As Jesus finished the great parable of the True Vine, He cried, *"As the Father loved Me, I also have loved you; abide in My love"* (John 15:9). This is the attitude of His Lordship.

The disciples were standing stiffly against the wall. The table was spread with the meal, but no one was eating. Are they not hungry? Disciples are always hungry. The problem is that there was no servant at the door to wash their feet. How can they lounge at the table and eat together with dirty feet? No one dare suggest the idea of washing one another's feet. If I washed your feet, then I would be admitting you are bigger and better than I am. I will never do that; so they stand staring at the food. Jesus has been detained and arrives a bit late. As He comes through the door, He immediately sees the situation. He does not have to pray about the issue; He does not have to search the Scriptures for the will of God. Jesus simply knows what to do. It is His natural, spontaneous nature. The Father is sourcing Him. He grabs a bowl and a towel. He washes the feet of each of His disciples, including Judas. He is Master and Lord. This is the content of His Lordship. He said, ***"You call Me Teacher and Lord, and you say well, for so I am. If I then, your Lord and Teacher, have washed your feet, you also ought to wash one another's feet"*** (John 13:13-14). Has He not revealed the heart of His Lordship?

We have a Lord. We are His Kingdom. Everyone in the Kingdom has the same sourcing, including Jesus. We are a new breed of humanity. We have His mind and His heart. We are Christ like, for what sources Him also sources us.

Acts 2:37

HEARING

Chapter two of the Books of Acts is an amazing chapter. Pentecost, the outpouring of the Holy Spirit (Acts 2:1-4) is the main event. It is the context of the content of the chapter. Luke dedicates the content of the chapter to a contrast between two groups of Jews. The difference between these two groups is their response to Jesus' infilling by the Holy Spirit. This may be a statement of the only two responses possible regarding the coming of the Spirit. The majority of the verses Luke dedicates to the Jews of the Dispersion. Two verses he dedicates to the Jews of Jerusalem (the leaders of Israel).

The Jews of the Dispersion are described as those who **were dwelling in Jerusalem Jews, devout men, from every nation under heaven** (Acts 2:5). They represent fifteen different nationalities from all over the world (Acts 2:9-11). Many of them were a product of the exile of the Old Testament days. They lived in foreign lands but came to Jerusalem for several months each year. They were driven by a conviction that God was going to do a new thing. It would no doubt happen during the feast days and occur in the temple. They came year after year in anticipation and longing to experience the new blessing from God. Obviously when God did a "new" thing, it would be different from anything they had ever seen up to this time. How would it occur? What would it look like?

The chief characteristic Luke highlights in the contrast is

Part Five: I Promise You

the "openness" of the Jews of the Dispersion. Their anticipation reveals itself in their constant watchfulness. They are looking for God to move in a new way. They come to Jerusalem every year in expectation, and they spare no expense in doing so. Most of this chapter (Acts 2) Luke dedicates to an explanation of God's response to them. All of God's actions in the chapter (after Acts 2:1-4) happen in them. God allows them to hear the message in their own languages (Acts 2:5-12). He moves upon Peter to deliver a message explaining Pentecost (Acts 2:16-36). God convicts them in the depths of their hearts (Acts 2:37). Three thousand of this group are filled with the Holy Spirit and form the base of the early church in Jerusalem (Acts 2:41). This is all in response to their openness.

Luke contrasts the Jews of the Dispersion with the Jews of Jerusalem. While the Jews of the Dispersion are open and awaiting God's movement, the Jews of Jerusalem are closed, narrow and have rigid attitudes. The Jews of Jerusalem are introduced and described only in one verse (Acts 2:13). They are called "mockers." It is not difficult to pinpoint exactly to whom this phrase refers. At the crucifixion of Jesus, Matthew records, **"Likewise the chief priests also, mocking with the scribes and elders said,"** (Matthew 27:41). These are the leaders of Israel. The Greek word (empaizo) translated *mocking* used in Matthew's account means "to act like a child," "to jeer," or "make fun."

I would ask you to allow the seriousness of both of these groups to grip your heart. The greatest sacrifice of all times is taking place. God's own Son is giving His life to change the course of the history of mankind. He is the Lamb of God for which they have been waiting. The leaders of Israel are making fun of Him. Now the Word has been accomplished. God has exalted Jesus to the position of the King of the Kingdom. The promise of the Father was placed in the nail scarred hands of Jesus. God pours out His Spirit on mankind in fulfillment of prophecy. The fall of mankind in the Garden of Eden is now corrected. This is the day of the fullness of the Holy Spirit. What response do the leaders of Israel exhibit? They act like children, jeering and making fun (Acts 2:13).

In Peter's introduction to his sermon, there is only one verse which acknowledges the leaders of Israel's response. God simply dismisses them, and He gives them no revelation. Peter says, **"For these are not drunk, as you suppose, since it is only the third hour of the day,"** (Acts 2:15). The heart of this verse is found in the Greek word (hupolambano) translated *"suppose."* It comes from the idea of "taking up a thought." It is actually a compound word. The two combined words are "under" and "to take." In this setting, it gives us the picture of reaching down under or within for the answer. This group of Jews are not asking or seeking, but answering and judging. The leaders of Israel turned inward to their narrow traditions and patterns. What was happening in the one hundred and twenty disciples did not fit any of their thoughts; it was a new thing! They dismissed the new action of God in the fullness of the Spirit as drunkenness or a result of the devil. They are not open to new revelation but are limited to their own understanding.

God moves from the leaders of Israel to those who are open and responding. Luke highlights the open hearts of the Jews of the Dispersion throughout chapter two in the word "*hear*" or "*heard.*" It is the Greek word "akouo." This Greek word is the summary of their response to the message preached by Peter explaining Pentecost. This Greek word (akouo) means "to hear." However, in relation to a teacher it is used to describe a disciple's understanding or hearing with the ear of the mind (Matthew 11:15; John 8:43, 47; 1 Corinthians 14:2). This is the phrase, **"He who has ears to hear, let him hear!"** (Matthew 11:15). It is used in the sense of "to give heed" or "to obey." In the context of our chapter (Acts 2), it is used in the sense "to understand" or "to comprehend."

Luke writes, **Now when they heard** (akouo) **this, they were**

Part Five: I Promise You

cut to the heart, and said to Peter and the rest of the apostles, "Men and brethren, what shall we do?" (Acts 2:37). The grammar structure of this sentence highlights the "hearing." The Greek word (akouo) translated **when they heard** is a participle. This means it is a verb which can be used as an adjective. It is the nominative case which places the act of hearing as an adjective to the subject of the sentence. The subject is focused on those who were hearing, understanding, or comprehending which cut them to the heart. This participle is in the aorist tense; it is the non-tense. The focus is not on the past, future, or present tense. The focus is not on when they heard but on the act of their hearing. This is another way of highlighting the importance of "hearing." It is in the active voice meaning the Jews of the Dispersion are responsible for this action. They have responded. It is their openness which has allowed the truth to penetrate their lives.

There is great significance in comparing this response at the close of Peter's sermon with his opening sentence. Peter follows his Scriptural text with the body of his message. The opening phrase is *"Men of Israel, hear* (akouo) *these words:"* (Acts 2:22). Peter pleads with the Jews of the Dispersion to be open, responsive, and receptive to the revelation of his explanation of Pentecost. Everything will change in their lives if they will just **hear**. This will bring an extreme change in their understanding alone! They will move from being quite content in participating in the crucifixion of Christ to the extreme guilt of their actions. Viewing Jesus as a threat to Jerusalem will change to Jesus being the fulfillment of God's dream for them. Fighting against the new faith of Christianity will change to embracing and participating in the early church. They will be baptized in the name of Jesus and participate in Pentecost. This is the radical change which will be brought about by "hearing."

It is important to recognize that their "hearing" did not start at the close of Peter's sermon. It was not the wonder of his speaking ability that opened their minds and hearts. They were not captured by the emotion of the Pentecostal moment. They have had the chief characteristic of openness and seeking throughout this chapter. God caused the Galilean disciples to speak in the fifteen different languages of the Jews of the Dispersion in direct response to their seeking. *And when this sound occurred, the multitude came together, and were confused, because everyone heard* (akouo) *them speak in his own language* (Acts 2:6). They were absolutely amazed by what they saw and heard happening through the disciples. As they began to reflect on this event, they were amazed at the fact the disciples were all Galileans (Acts 2:7). They asked, *"And how is it that we hear* (akouo), *each in our own language in which we were born?"* (Acts 2:8). They began to rehearse among themselves the content of what they were hearing. They cried, *"We hear* (akouo) *them speaking in our own tongues the wonderful works of God,"* (Acts 2:11). It was so evident that Peter realized they comprehended and understood. In his sermon, he said, *"Therefore being exalted to the right hand of God, and having received from the Father the promise of the Holy Spirit, He poured out this which you now see and hear* (akouo)*"* (Acts 2:33). Hearing (akouo) is the fundamental aspect of response which allows the movement of God in their lives. Is this not the cry of what God wants for all of us? Could we just listen to Him?

Luke distinctly contrasts the hearing of the Jews of the Dispersion with the non-hearing of the Jews of Jerusalem. There was no way the Jews of Jerusalem could *hear*! God was moving in Pentecost and it did not penetrate their lives at all. There was no understanding of God's new thing among them. They made a joke of it by mocking. Did they not "hear" the *sound from heaven, as of a rushing mighty wind*? Did they not "hear" the Galilean disciples speaking in fifteen different dialects? Did they not "hear" Peter's explanation of Pentecost? It does not matter if they physically heard it or not, they simply did not "hear."

The lack of hearing did not occur because Peter was an uninteresting preacher or the singing was off key. This is characteristic of their lives. In a confrontation with these very same Jews in Jerusalem, Jesus explained the problem. He understood that they claimed Abraham as their father, yet they sought to kill Jesus, because His word had no place in them (they did not hear). If Abraham was really their father they would have been like Abraham, seeking and open. But they really have another father. Jesus asked them, **"Why do you not understand My speech? Because you are not able to listen** (akouo) **to My word"** (John 8:43). He boldly told them that their father was the devil. He concluded by saying, **"He who is of God hears** (akouo) **God's words: therefore you do not hear** (akouo)**, because you are not of God,"** (John 8:47).

How can a person know for sure they are listening (akouo) to God? The answer is clear in our passage: **Now when they heard this, they were cut to the heart, and said to Peter and the rest of the apostles, "Men and brethren, what shall we do?"** (Acts 2:37). We have discovered the subject of this sentence. It is the act of hearing. The verb is equally important. The verb is the Greek word (katanusso) which is translated **they were cut**. This is the only time the word is used in the New Testament.

"Kata" is a prefix on the root word "nusso." "Kata" means "from" and is placed as a prefix for the purpose of intensifying the root word. "Nusso" means "to prick or pierce." Luke states that the Jews of the Dispersion were pierced and pricked thoroughly or all the way through their hearts. This verb (katanusso) is in the passive voice which means the subject is receiving the action of the verb. The Jews of the Dispersion are not responsible for this piercing; they are being acted upon. It is in the indicative mood which means it is a simple statement of fact. It is in the aorist tense, which is a non-tense. The focus is not on when the action of the verb took place, but is on the act of the piercing.

"Piercing through" naturally takes place when one is "hearing" (akouo). If you want to remain as you are, do not be open and seeking before the Lord. If your comfort is high priority, do not be open and seeking before the Lord. If you want to live undisturbed and unchanged, do not seek or listen to Jesus. His very presence will pierce your heart. His light will confront your darkness. Expect to be shaken at the core of your existence when He speaks and you listen.

We must carefully examine the piercing of the truth in the lives of the Jews of the Dispersion. They came every year to Jerusalem in sincere worship on the feast days. They consider themselves respectable, law abiding, and above average in their Jewish faith. They observe the proper sacrifices and maintain the six hundred and thirteen oral traditions of the elders. They participate in the crucifixion of Jesus; this is completely justifiable in their present state. He was an extreme threat to the law of Israel. They are simply following the leadership of those members of the Sanhedrin who know the total situation. They have no guilt for their actions; in fact, they feel good that they are participating in the protection of their faith.

They are open and seeking for all God wants to do. They want to embrace the new thing which God is hopefully going to accomplish in Jerusalem. They came year after year looking for this new thing! They participate in the new thing without even knowing it. The crucifixion brings about the resurrection which moves to the ascension. The Father has given the Son His promise to be poured out upon all flesh. Pentecost explodes upon the world. God honors the seeking spirit of this group of Jews even though they participated in the crucifixion. He goes all out in extravagant ways to awaken and astound them. The ***sound from heaven*** (Acts 2:2) certainly gets their attention. They are confused (Acts 2:6), ***amazed and marveled*** (Acts 2:7), and ***amazed and perplexed*** (Acts 2:12). This is a direct result of the Galilean disciples speaking in fifteen different dialects they did not know. It absolutely shocks the Jews of the Dispersion. This is totally unnecessary in regard to the communication of truth. It was not necessary for them to hear the message in their home languages. Peter preaches in only one language. In fact, the Galilean disciples are simply shouting **the wonderful works of God** (Acts 2:12).

All of this only intensifies the hearing of the Jews of the Dispersion. Then God moved upon Peter with a clear explanation of Pentecost. The truth of what God is doing in the new thing is all found in Jesus! The very Jesus they crucified is the new thing God is doing in their midst. The awareness of this reality pierces them to the depths of their very beings.

The subject of the sentence is the act of hearing. The verb is the thorough piercing or pricking. The direct object that is receiving the action of this piercing is **the heart** (Acts 2:37). The Greek word (kardia) translated **heart** is one you will recognize. The Old Testament concept focuses on the heart as the seat of the desires, feelings, affections, passions, and impulses. **For the life of the flesh is in the blood** (Leviticus 17:11).

If you do not want to be affected here, you should not **hear**. Openness and hearing are dangerous in maintaining the rigid adherence to traditions. If you want to stay as you are do not open your ears or mind to the voice of God. If you grasp His truth it will affect the very core of your living. He will threaten all the established patterns, the very thoughts we have comfortably accepted will be disturbed. We are drawn into new truth which produces guilt. We will see all that we are in light of all that He is. It is startling!

But this is what we really want! Life is found here. Ultimately it is the only safe place for us. Let us rush to Him in openness and **hear**.

Acts 2:37

WHAT SHALL WE DO?

We do not talk enough about prevenient grace. Regardless of how many preachers focus their sermons on this great concept, it is never enough. There is something about the human condition which either forgets about it or begins to take it for granted. I can speak of it in every sermon and not be over emphasizing its truth. Prevenient grace needs to become the lens through which we see all things. Perhaps you respond by saying, "I thought Jesus was to be the lens of my life!" That is so true, because Jesus is prevenient grace. Another word for "grace" is "love." "Prevenient" means "going before." Prevenient grace is the love of God that goes before.

Long before you seek Jesus, He is seeking you. You only love Him because He first loved you. The only reason you desire Him is because He has wooed you to Himself. He came after you; you did not come after Him. You did not cry out to Him. He has been calling out to you. *For God so loved the world that He gave His only begotten Son, that whoever believes in Him should not perish but have everlasting life. For God did not send His Son into the world to condemn the world, but that the world through Him might be saved* (John 3:16-17). God *loved*; God *gave*; God *sent*. You are simply the recipient of the action of God. He is all over you. He is knocking on your forehead. He is pestering you with love. He will not let you go! He has taken the initiative. It is prevenient grace.

This reality is the basis for Christianity. Since God has come to you, He is seeking response. Therefore, Christianity is not "doing" but "responding." You must make this shift in your thinking. God is not waiting for you to do something before He will move on your life. He has moved on your life and is waiting for you to respond. "Doing" is an emphasis on accomplishment. I am the source of it. I must accomplish the task. Our lives have been trained in this thought. In school, we must master the material, learn the lessons, and pass the tests. Once we have done this we graduate. We are recognized for our achievement. "Responding" is a different thought process. It bespeaks the presence of someone else interacting in my life. I am not on my own. I am responding to someone beyond myself. This is Christianity. Jesus is not waiting for me to master the material or get it right. He has come to enable, source and empower me; will I respond?

This is the wonder of the passage in our study. *Now when they heard this, they were cut to the heart, and said to Peter and the rest of the apostles, "Men and brethren, what shall we do?"* (Acts 2:37). Do you hear their cry? Notice that it comes from the depths of their hearts. They verbalize it through their souls and emotions. We must analyze their question, *"What shall we do?"*

Context of the Question

I want you to embrace this group by placing yourself in their situation. They are not bad people; in fact, they are called **devout men** (Acts 2:5). The Greek word (eulabes) translated **devout** is a compound word. The first word (eu) means good, well, right, rightly. The second word (iambano) means to take. The **devout** individual is one who has the right attitude and reverence. He received things with discernment and has proper estimation of something.

The first occurrence of this word (eulabes) is concerning Simeon, the old man at the temple (Luke 2:25). He is ***devout*** waiting for the consolation of Israel, the promise of the coming Messiah. He was one who had well and rightly received the promises of God; he was one who has taken seriously God's promises in God's Word. The second occurrence is in connection with the Jews of the Dispersion and it is from our passage. They are called ***devout men*** or God-fearing. They are individuals who accept God's command that His feast should be kept with every male Israelite required to appear at the sanctuary (Leviticus 23). It was to occur fifty days from the offering of the barley sheaf at the beginning of Passover (Exodus 23:16; 34:22). They were people who rightly and seriously received God's commandments.

They were anticipating a new movement from God. They dedicated themselves to seeking this movement by leaving their homes and coming to Jerusalem especially during the feast days. They immediately recognize the outpouring of the Holy Spirit on the one hundred and twenty believers as the new movement of God. They are ***confused*** (Acts 2:6), ***amazed and marveled*** (Acts 2:7), and ***amazed and perplexed*** (Acts 2:12). In openness, they immediately begin to ask, ***"Whatever could this mean?"*** (Acts 2:12).

The Holy Spirit through Peter gives a powerful revelation of Jesus, the One they crucified. He describes how they took Jesus ***by lawless hands, have crucified, and put to death*** (Acts 2:23). After describing the mighty working of God in Jesus through the resurrection, exaltation, and outpouring of the Promise of the Father, he again reminds them they crucified Him (Acts 2:36). They are cut to the heart. They experience an overwhelming realization. They are in a desperate situation from which there is no deliverance. Think of what has just dawned on them. They have been guilty of crucifying Christ. Even if He was just an ordinary man, they have crucified an innocent man. But it is far beyond this. They have crucified the Son of God. He is God's answer to everything they have been expecting. They longed for God to intervene; He has in Jesus. They crucified the very answer for which they prayed. They dug a hole out of which they cannot crawl. They are helpless; they have no hope; there is no answer for them. In this statement, they are throwing up their hands in absolute desperation. What a revelation!

Have you ever been there? I am not talking about circumstances coming in on you, and you search for solutions. My reference is not to bills you cannot pay which are forcing you into bankruptcy. This is not about your awareness that your mistakes are the reason for your crumbling marriage. All of these situations may awaken you and become the means by which God brings you to this realization. But our discussion is about something much more serious. What God dreamed for your life you have treated as valueless. What God did in and through Christ, you pushed aside. God desperately wants intimacy with you, but you have straight armed Him out of your life. God provided everything you need in Jesus and you source yourself. In reality, you took Jesus out and crucified Him. The climactic statement of Peter's sermon is about you. Peter preached, *"Therefore let* (place your name here) *know assuredly that God has made this Jesus, whom you crucified, both Lord and Christ"* (Acts 2:36). It is much worse than that. When we source ourselves we continue to crucify Jesus.

"What shall we do?" is not a cry for a list of rules or activities which will undo the situation. Let's call a committee meeting; let's develop a plan. This is not "do" in the sense of an action, performance, or accomplishment. There is no way out of this. There is nothing we can do. What action could I "do" which would balance what I have already done? Do you see it? This is not about good deeds or bad deeds. If I do more good deeds, they cancel out the bad deeds. How much money would it take to repay Jesus? How much service would He demand? There is no amount of "community service" which will make it right.

My debt is huge; I am guilty. There is no way back for me. Is this not a cry of desperation? Is there not an answer contained within the question itself? Must I not assume there is absolutely nothing that can be done?

Center of the Question

I made an interesting discovery when I studied this question, *"What shall we do?"* You will find this question in similar words seven times in the New Testament. Three times it is in response to the preaching of John the Baptist (Luke 3:10-12). Twice it is used in connection with the conversion of Saul of Tarsus (Acts 9:6; 22:10). The Philippian jailer is shaken into giving this same response (Acts 16:30). Then we find it in our current passage of study. If you are not familiar with each of these situations, take time to investigate the details.

There is a distinct contrast between the two found in Luke's Gospel account and those found in the Book of Acts. The difference is the establishment of the New Covenant in the outpouring of the Holy Spirit. John the Baptist's preaching was a preparation for the Kingdom of God. When the people and the tax collectors asked this question, John the Baptist gave them specific activities to accomplish. He gave them rules and instructions which applied to their particular situation. After Pentecost the answer to this question is given in terms of prevenient grace and response.

In the case of Saul of Tarsus, the awakening is so severe he is shaken to the core of his very being. He was **advanced in Judaism beyond many of** his **contemporaries in** his **own nation, being more exceedingly zealous for the traditions of** his **fathers** (Galatians 1:14). What more could he do? He missed the thrust of what God is doing in Jesus. The scene is desperate; there is nothing to do. So obviously he is not asking for an instruction

Part Five: I Promise You

manual on how to rebuild his life or directions on how to correct his course.

An equal situation is happening in the life of the Philippian jailer. He awakes from his sleep and finds the prison doors open. The movement of the Holy Spirit brought about an earthquake which shook the prison. The jailer immediately supposes that the prisoners have escaped. The Scriptures say he ***drew his sword and was about to kill himself*** (Acts 16:27). Paul makes him aware that the prisoners are all there. Do you see the desperation of the scene? The jailer does not request instructions on how to make things right. There is nothing to do in this crisis hour.

The Greek word translated ***do*** in each of these situations is "poieo." This very word points you to something greater than just an activity or a duty to make things right. This Greek word appears so often in our studies. It is the word used for trees ***bearing*** fruit. Trees do not "do" fruit; it is the process of "poieo." Our understanding will be increased if we translate the word ***do*** as "respond." It is not about doing, but responding. In the English language there is a different emphasis for "doing" compared to "responding." The emphasis of "doing" is on "self." When someone speaks of what they have been doing, it is about their personal accomplishments. They are responsible; they achieved it. However, "responding" is an emphasis on interaction. When someone speaks of responding, they highlight something beyond them to which they are reacting. Christianity is never a "doing." It is always a "responding." We emphasized this at the beginning of this study and we are repeating it again on purpose. It is so vital!

Through the years I have used crazy illustrations in an attempt to describe this. For instance, in days gone by my wife would meet me at the airport as I returned from revival meetings. She would wrap her arms around me and give me a great big kiss. I did not turn to the people standing around me and exclaim, "Did you see me kiss my wife?" The reason is simple. I did not kiss my wife. Those around me might persist,

"But we stood right here and watched you. You had your arms around her; your lips were pressed to hers." This is all true; but I did not kiss my wife. She kissed me. What was my role in the kissing? I was simply responding! Those who were watching us could not tell, but I knew. We carefully watch an outstanding Christian. We congratulate him on all he is "doing" for Jesus. He quickly corrects us by saying, "I am not doing anything; I am simply responding."

This is surrender on a new level. The difficulty with the emphasis of surrender is we naturally slip into the "doing aspect." We think in terms of surrendering things. What thing should I surrender now? Do you see the self-sourcing involved in this activity? In fact, we often struggle with the difficulty of "taking it back." This idea comes from going to an altar of prayer and giving something to Jesus only to pick it back up and take it home with us again. But the focus of this activity is on "self." I am so bad I cannot even surrender completely or correctly. I must simply respond which allows Jesus to do in me what He desires.

Conclusion of the Question

I wish I could hold you right at this point. I would like to suspend you in this suspense. What will Jesus do to me? If I surrender in simple response to Him as described, how will He treat me? If my Christianity moves from self-accomplishment to responding, what will He accomplish in me? If I move from a "doing" religion to a "responding" Christianity, what will be the results?

The answer is clear as found in our passage in the Jews of the Dispersion. It will take several studies to see the details of what Peter is proposing in the concluding two verses of this paragraph (Acts 2:38-39). But we can easily grasp the overall concept. He will embrace you with the warmth of His Spirit;

Part Five: I Promise You

you will know intimacy with Him. What was displayed in ***Jesus of Nazareth, a Man*** now happened in one hundred and twenty disciples. This experience is also promised to you. The intimacy Jesus knows with His Father is the same intimacy you can know with Him.

This is summarized in the statement "***and you shall receive the gift of the Holy Spirit,***" (Acts 2:38). The outside God will come to be inside. The sourcing of the Spirit is yours. In this phrase there is a double statement or emphasis on the idea of "response." He definitely says, ***"You shall receive."*** He also says, "It is ***the gift of the Holy Spirit.***" "Receive" is the translation of the Greek word "lambano." In the New Testament sense it means to actively take; this verb is partially in the passive sense which means to receive. Peter uses this word in the middle voice. According to the context, Jesus is aggressively, extravagantly pouring out the Spirit of God upon us. We aggressively respond to this generous ***gift of the Holy Spirit*** from our own personal desire. This is highlighted again in the word ***gift***. The Greek word (dorea) means to give. It is a free gift with emphasis on its gratuitous character. It is given or granted without return or recompense; therefore, it is unearned. It is given or received without cost or obligation; therefore, it is free! It is unnecessary or unwarranted; therefore, it is unjustified.

Will you respond?

Acts 2:38

CONTEXT OF RESPONDING

"What shall we do?" When an employee begins the day asking his employer that question, we expect the employer to give a "to do" list. The day will be considered successful if all the tasks are accomplished. In athletic competitions, *"What shall we do?"* is very clear. We must aggressively execute the plays or skills we have practiced better than the opposing team. The final score of the game will verify if this was accomplished. In education, *"What shall we do?"* is plainly delineated in the lesson plans. The students must master the material; the scores on the final test will testify to how well they have done. Even in the church there is an answer to the question, *"What shall we do?"* We have a mission statement which we fulfill with our programs and activities on the calendar. The annual report measures how well we did with our attendance and paid budgets. Is there not a pattern established through all of these areas of life?

Peter has just finished his powerful explanation of the Pentecost event. The truth of Jesus was lodged in the hearts of the hearers. **Now when they heard this, they were cut to the heart** (Acts 2:37). They immediately follow the pattern in the above paragraph. They ask, *"What shall we do?"* You would expect the answer to be a list of items to accomplish or instructions for proper performance. Would you not expect a "check list" bringing corrections to the things that are wrong? A list of new rules would allow this group to measure how much they have changed. How can they correct their situation if they do not know what old activities to change and new activities to perform?

Peter gives a powerful answer to the question. ***Then Peter said to them, "Repent, and let every one of you be baptized in the name of Jesus Christ for the remission of sins: and you shall receive the gift of the Holy Spirit"*** (Acts 2:38). Is this not a list of beginning activities for them to accomplish? The very first activity they should do is *repent* and this should be followed by the second activity to *be baptized in the name of Jesus Christ*. Obviously this is only the beginning of the activities they will need to perform; but we do not want to give them so much as to overwhelm them.

While this approach certainly dominates every area of our self-sourced culture, it is not the approach of Peter or the Scriptures. This group was *cut to the heart*. The truth of Jesus was applied to their lives through the power of the Holy Spirit. This is prevenient grace. This is not a result of Peter's persuasive speaking or the emotion of the Pentecost event. There is a deep, internal movement of the Spirit of Christ bringing revelation of reality and truth. This group finds themselves in a pit from which they cannot escape. They are trapped with no way out. They are guilty with no possible way of undoing or correcting. What activities could they perform which would correct what they did to Jesus? No wonder they are *cut to the heart*.

Therefore, Peter's call to *repent* is not an activity they can accomplish. It is not a duty they can "do." It is a call to "respond." You do not *repent* and God comes in response to your activity. Rather God moves on your heart and you respond. This response is called "repentance." Repeatedly in our previous studies we have dealt with this subject. It dominated the message of John the Baptist, the forerunner of Christ (Matthew 3:2). It defines Jesus' response in coming to be baptized by John (Matthew 3:13-17). The Greek word (metanoeo) translated *repent* is a combination of two ideas. The first (meta) denotes a change of place or condition; the second (noeo) is to exercise the mind, to think, or to comprehend. It simply means "to change your mind." We have defined repentance as "giving up a former thought to embrace a second thought."

I fear many of us focuses the act of repentance simply on the deeds of sin. However, the former thought could be anything. In the lives of the Pharisees, it was their traditions and laws. Christ, the New Covenant, came; but they will not give up the former thought to embrace the second thought. They finally crucified "the second thought" in order to maintain the "former thought." This is how these Jews of the Dispersion got involved. For two or three months every year they came to Jerusalem from their homes in foreign lands. They expected God to do something new. They followed the leadership of Israel and became guilty of the crucifixion of Jesus. As the chief priests and elders explained it, it seemed the right thing to do. These Jews of the Dispersion were not leaders at the heart of the political activity. Should they not follow the direction of those who know?

Now the Spirit of God moved on their hearts. They are cut to the very core of their living with what they have done. They are called to *repent*, give up a former thought to embrace a new thought. There is much more for us to learn.

Cut to the Heart

The Jews of the Dispersion are simply to respond to what is going on in their hearts. It is essential to place yourself into this passage. You must identify with these particular Jews. Their emotions and feelings must become yours if you are to understand this repentance. What gripped their hearts is far beyond making a mistake. It exceeds even a bad mistake. We have all made mistakes and will do so again. When you make a mistake, you do the best you can to correct it and continue moving forward.

Part Five: I Promise You

This was not the situation with the Jews of the Dispersion.

They have been waiting all of this time for the coming of the Messiah. What this would actually mean was not fully known. It would be like our belief in the second coming of Christ. What will it actually change? How will it actually take place? What will it be like? We do not know the details. How long had they been waiting for the Messiah to come? It was thousands of years. Their forefathers prophesied concerning it; their traditions pointed to it. It is the peak of their expectation. Every day the first words pronounced in a Jewish home were "Could this be the day?" It was a reference to the coming Messiah.

As these Jews of the Dispersion traveled to Jerusalem every year, they came with the expectation that God was going to do a new thing. They did not want to miss it. Obviously they felt the new thing would be the fulfillment of their dreams of the Messiah. Could it be in their lifetime? Now they are **cut to the heart**. The movement of the Spirit of God through Peter revealed the truth to them. The Messiah has come; the new thing has happened. They did not recognize it. But it is much worse than that. Not only did they not recognize it; they actually interfered with it. They crucified the very Messiah God sent to them.

Can you imagine the sickening feeling they had in their hearts? It would be like having the breath knocked out of you. Can you imagine how you would feel? After waiting for the second coming of Jesus, after hearing about it repeatedly, He comes and you do not know it. Worse than missing it, what if you actually interfered or hindered His coming? Would not hopelessness and absolute despair grip the depths of your heart? Would you not sink to your knees in a paralyzed state of dismay?

John Wesley called these kinds of moments "an awakening." Charles Wesley wrote it in his great holiness song, **And Can It Be.**

Long my imprisoned spirit lay
Fast bound in sin and darkest night

*Thine eye diffused a quickening ray
rose, went forth, and followed Thee.*

Does this not parallel the testimony of the Apostle Paul? Saul was **breathing threats and murder against the disciples of the Lord** (Acts 9:1). He received permission from the high priest to search for those disciples in Damascus in order that he **might bring them bound to Jerusalem** (Acts 9:2). *As he journeyed he came near Damascus, and suddenly a light shone around him from heaven. Then he fell to the ground, and heard a voice saying to him, "Saul, Saul, why are you persecuting Me?"* (Acts 9:3-4). When he discovered it was Jesus speaking to him, he *trembling and astonished, said, "Lord, what do You want me to do?"* (Acts 9:6). It was an awakening. Saul was **cut to the heart**. What he thought was right was wrong. What he was doing with religious zeal was destroying the very dream he pursued.

What if I never have such moments? This is not a proper concern at all; I will have an awakening. The great question is not "if" you will have an awakening, but "how" will you respond to such a moment? Will you *repent*? Let's admit it may not be as dramatic as Saul of Tarsus' experience, but it will be as clear. Will you give up a former thought to embrace a second thought?

Let me emphasize that true repentance coming from a genuine awakening is not a CONVENIENCE. It is not that this is the best solution to a bad situation. Often we find ourselves having gone down the wrong path and Jesus is the convenient way to reverse our direction. There is forgiveness found in repentance and the acceptance of the body of Christ for support. Repentance can be a light response to an emotional moment. It can be the easiest way to relieve the pressure of a bad situation. But true repentance can only come from being **cut to the heart**. Truly embracing a second thought only happens when the first thought is seen in the light of Christ. One does not try the second thought to see if it works. Repentance is not one of many things we attempt to eliminate our problems. It must come from the deep disruption of our very inner being. We are captured with truth.

We must also highlight that the desired repentance is not a CHOICE. It is not "it is the thing to do." Many of us were taught the standard ethics of the church. We understand the doctrines of heaven and hell. We realize the necessity of repentance and forgiveness. The need to repent has been impressed on our lives. It is our obligation, duty, and responsibility. We can calculate the time we will finally do it. It would be best to pick a service which has the smallest crowd. We need to get it over. Real repentance is not experienced in this manner. It only comes from being *cut to the heart*. There must be a desperation; a realization of the hopelessness of our state. The attitude of repentance requires that we are awakened to the responsibility for our choices.

Let it be known that repentance does not result from being CAUGHT. Many times we have not been broken by what we have done but have simply been sorry we were caught. I realize that often the awfulness of the former thought may not be realized until we have been caught. God may use this fact to *cut to the heart*. But being caught has nothing to do with the depth of repentance.

Therefore, repentance is a response to being cut to the heart. Would you set aside everything that resists this? Push aside your pride which will not allow you to admit you are wrong. Set aside your traditions which may have been good at the time, but have now become stale. Boldly take sides with God against yourself. Give up a former thought to embrace a second thought.

The Name of Jesus Christ

There is a second focus found in our verse which is at the heart of repentance. It is the name of Jesus Christ. This is so fundamental to all repentance, it may not be necessary to mention. Jesus is at the heart of it all. When you give up a former thought to embrace a second thought, the second thought is Jesus. In the context of our passage, Jesus is the focus. He is the explanation of Pentecost. The Jews of the Dispersion are desperately wrong about Him. The single error in their thinking is about Him. Crucifying Christ is the worst action of their lives. They moved away from Him when they should have been running towards Him. The sin of their lives is about their lack of relationship with Jesus.

The moment Peter mentions *repent*, he links Jesus with it. It is very pronounced! ***Then Peter said to them, "Repent, and let every one of you be baptized in the name of Jesus Christ for the remission of sins; and you shall receive the gift of the Holy Spirit,*** (Acts 2:38). While the verb *"repent"* is in the active voice, we understand it is a response to the movement of the Spirit. It is not an activity they can accomplish, but a response they must make. The active voice means the Jews of the Dispersion are responsible for responding to the movement of the Holy Spirit bringing them to repentance. However, the verb ***be baptized*** is in the passive voice. Throughout the Book of Acts this verb is never in the active voice. The passive voice means the subject is receiving the action of the verb. Again Peter calls on the Jews of the Dispersion to respond. They are not responsible for the action of the baptism but are to respond by placing themselves in the position to be acted upon by baptism.

The phrase ***in the name of Jesus Christ*** does not denote a formula which is to be said over the person being baptized. This statement indicates a confession of faith from the person receiving baptism (Acts 2:21; 22:16). In other words, the person being baptized is giving up a former thought to embrace a new thought. Being baptized in His name is not a formula but a focus. Throughout this explanation of Pentecost, Peter calls them to embrace Jesus. It is in Jesus God proved Pentecost (Acts 2:22). It is in Jesus God conquered sin through the cross (Acts 2:23).

Part Five: I Promise You

It is in Jesus God overcame death by raising Jesus from the dead (Acts 2:24). It is in Jesus God gave the fullness of His presence (Acts 2:33). It is in Jesus God provided remission of sins (Acts 2:38). It is in Jesus God provides the gift of the Holy Spirit (Acts 2:38).

Peter's entire message is a call to respond to Jesus. Could I extend this message to you? Would you increase your response to Jesus? Would you seek Him with a new intensity? Would you allow Him to come to the center of your life in a new way? Would you ask Him to eliminate all distractions so your eye is single? Would you allow your passion to be for Jesus alone?

Acts 2:38

CONTENT OF RESPONDING

The moment Christianity is a series of activities it becomes more religion than redemption. "Doing" Christianity results in the re-establishment of the Old Testament covenant. This covenant was created by God as a step to the height of the New Testament covenant. In this sense it was right and good. However, in full view of the new, to cling to the old is trampling on the sacred heart of God. When it is done they **crucify again for themselves the Son of God, and put Him to an open shame** (Hebrews 6:6).

This paints again the picture of the Jews of the Dispersion and the message Peter delivers to them. God did a new thing in their midst. In their openness and seeking they sought to understand its significance. Peter preached a powerful sermon under the sourcing of the Spirit of God. He reveals Jesus as the total explanation of Pentecost. The very revelation of this new thing (Pentecost) reveals the devastation of their present position. They crucified Jesus.

How easy it is to excuse ourselves as those who were not present at that event. It is far removed from us; we would not be so cruel. While this may be true in the physical realm, it is certainly not true in the spiritual reality. If the physical event of the cross was a result of a spiritual reality, we are guilty. The interaction of the physical and the spiritual is inescapable. The spiritual war in the unseen world will play itself out on the physical stage of

Part Five: I Promise You

our lives. The marvel of the crucifixion was the fact that Jesus yielded His physical being to the activity of the spiritual realm. The spiritual war revealed itself in the physical crucifixion. This physical expression is only the brief "cross" section of the depth of what was accomplished in Christ. The generations both past and future were redeemed. Both worlds were altered forever. The spiritual war taking place then is present today. When we yield to the demonic activity of our day we participate in the very thing which crucifies Christ all over again. We are without excuse; *we* have crucified Jesus.

We stand side by side with the Jews of the Dispersion. What they heard, we are now hearing. As they were cut to the heart, we also should be. If we are open and seeking as they were, we will feel what they felt. The same cry, **"What shall we do?"** must come from our lips. We are not seeking a list of activities to accomplish in order to pay back. It is not an attempt to make things right by doing more good than bad. It is desperation from awareness that there is nothing we can do. All that is good and right for our lives is violated. We aggressively crucified the only answer for our dilemma. We are without hope; we are lost.

In the midst of the dismay of the Jews of the Dispersion, Peter comes forth with an answer. It is almost too good to be true! God has taken our rejection of Jesus as demonstrated in the crucifixion and used it to bring redemption to our rejection. The very thing which brings us to dismay and hopelessness is now the basis for our salvation. God sourced Jesus in the acts of the crucifixion, resurrection, ascension, and exaltation. God supplied Jesus with the Promise of the Father. By the greatness of His love He reversed the entire situation. We are forgiven and redeemed. There is nothing to do but respond to what God is already doing in Christ!

Listen to Peter's instruction. ***"Repent, and let every one of you be baptized in the name of Jesus Christ for the remission of sins; and you shall receive the gift of the Holy Spirit"*** (Acts 2:38).

Content of Responding | **Acts 2:38**

What is involved in this response? There are three verbs contained in his instructions. These verbs give content to the response.

Positive Response

The first one is a call to *repent*. This verb is in the imperative mood which is a command. This is not to be discussed or questioned, but obeyed. It is in the active voice which places the responsibility of the action of repentance upon the subject, the Jews of the Dispersion. At first this may appear to be a required action. However, as discussed in a previous study, repentance is a response to the action God has already taken. In the context of this passage, this group has is cut to the heart. The Spirit of Christ moved on them in a great awakening. Repentance is a response to this movement of God. The call is not for them to act and God will move on them; but God has already moved on them and is calling them to respond. This response is called "repentance."

Repent is a translation of the Greek word "metanoeo." It is a compound word. It consists of "meta" (denoting change of place or condition) and "noeo" (to exercise the mind, think, or comprehend). Thus it is to change your mind. We have defined repentance as giving up a former thought to embrace a second thought. This call to repentance must be interpreted in light of the context of Peter's sermon. Peter confronted them with their involvement in the crucifixion of Jesus. Jesus is the explanation of what is happening in the Pentecost event. These Jews must give up the former thought of crucifying Jesus and now embrace Him as ***both Lord and Christ***.

The issue of our passage focuses on the phrase *for the remission of sins*. Is this phrase connected with the act of repentance or the act of being baptized? Some propose it is during the act of water baptism where our sins are actually forgiven. This greatly

389

highlights the physical act of this sacrament. Others have strongly resisted this thought. They suggest it is a spiritual matter of the heart where reconciliation between God and man takes place. Thus the real issue is the spiritual response of repentance. The act of baptism becomes a physical response to the forgiveness already received. Therefore, it becomes very important whether this phrase is linked to repentance or baptism.

The Greek word (metanoeo) translated **repent** is plural. In the Greek text there is an article (toon) which is not translated in the English. It is a definite article (the or this). It is in the plural. There is also the Greek word (humon) which should be translated "your." This Greek word is not translated in our passage. It is also in the plural form. The Greek word (hamartia) translated **sins** is also in the plural form. This is contrasted with the Greek word (baptizo) translated **be baptized**. It is in the singular form which sets it apart from the rest of the sentence. There is a definite break in the thought of the sentence. Peter is saying that the Jews must repent for the remission of their sins and then each one of them must be baptized. It is the response of repentance (giving up a former thought and embracing a second thought) which is the condition for experiencing forgiveness of sins.

The linkage between repentance and forgiveness is highlighted in a variety of other Scriptures. The resurrected Jesus opened the Scriptures to His disciples prior to His ascension. He proposed, **"That repentance and remission of sins should be preached in His name to all nations, beginning at Jerusalem"** (Luke 24:47). Peter and the other apostles testified before the high priest. **"The God of our fathers raised up Jesus whom you murdered by hanging on a tree. Him God has exalted to His right hand to be Prince and Savior, to give repentance to Israel and forgiveness of sins"** (Acts 5:30-31).

Peter calls the Jews of the Dispersion to **repent** (give up a former thought to embrace a second thought). This response has to do with ***the remission of sins***. The Greek word translated ***remission*** is "aphiemi." When this word appears, it does not just focus on the result of a consequence or an action. It always includes the action itself. There is an action of repelling, releasing, or putting away as in deliverance. The response of repentance releases the full energy of Christ's sacrificial love to repel guilt from our lives. Sin with all of its multifaceted fingers which would imprison us is literally pushed from us. We are released, delivered, or "aphiemi" from our sins.

The content of our ***sins*** must be clearly understood. The Greek word (hamartia) translated ***sin*** means "missing the true end and scope of our lives." In the context of our passage, what is the true end and scope of our lives? Peter hasn't spoken of anything but Jesus! Everything God desires for our lives is in Jesus. Everything intended in the eternal plan for our very creation is Jesus! Intimacy found in the Spirit of Jesus fulfills the love of God for us! Anything outside of Jesus is sin. Sin is not defined in the context of a deed, but is found in how that deed relates to Jesus. If Jesus does not source it, if it is not saturated with Him, it is sin. The goodness of the deed does not justify it. The sincerity expressed within the deed does not make it righteous. The heart of the entire matter is Jesus.

The Jews of the Dispersion were ***cut to the heart***. They were not bad; they missed Jesus. They missed the true end and scope of their lives and crucified Him. Peter is calling them to repent (give up a former thought to embrace a second thought). This is a second chance!

Positional Result

This brings us to the second verb in our passage. It is ***be baptized***. This verb is also in the imperative mood which means it is a command. It is in the aorist tense, and it is the non-tense.

It does not focus on when the action takes place, but on the action itself. This verb differs from *repent*, in voice. It is in the passive voice. This means the subject is receiving the action of this verb. **Repent** is in the active voice placing the responsibility of this response on the Jews of the Dispersion. When they *repent* they will be acted upon by baptism.

I certainly do not want to mislead you regarding baptism. It is definitely a physical act which involves water. Paul likened the physical aspect of being covered with water to Jesus burial. The act of coming out from this covering was likened to the resurrection of Christ. Therefore, we are buried with Jesus and resurrected with Jesus in newness of life (Romans 6:4). Even in this discussion, there is a mystical aspect which can only be accomplished by the action of God on the individual. While an individual may be responsible for the physical action of water baptism, the spiritual reality of this baptism can only be received as the Spirit of Christ acts upon the individual. Thus it is stated in the passive voice.

Peter clearly says this in his instruction to the Jews of the Dispersion. They are to *be baptized in the name of Jesus Christ*. The usual form of baptism is *into* (eis) *the name of the Father and of the Son and of the Holy Spirit* (Matthew 28:19). However, Peter changed the approach to in (epi) the name of Jesus Christ. This does not indicate the formula to be said over the individual who is being baptized. The debate between two formulas misses the point of the passage. The *name of Jesus Christ* is simply an expression referring to the person Himself. It is not a reference to something attached to Him but to the entirety of what is contained in His person. This is not a baptism by the authority of Jesus Christ, but a baptism based on the foundation of His very person.

"Baptism" means to immerse, submerge, to overwhelm, or saturate. Peter calls the Jews of the Dispersion to give up a former thought concerning Jesus to the actual embracing of

Jesus. They are to be submerged and saturated into and upon the very person of Jesus Himself. They are devout men; the law has been the foundation of their lives. Jesus is the fulfillment of the law. He now will be the foundation of their lives. As the law dictated their actions, schedule, and perspective of life, they will be saturated in the Spirit of Jesus who will shape and form their lives.

Let it be noted again *be baptized* is singular. Strength is added to this factor with the Greek word (hekastos) translated *everyone*. It is the idea of "each" or "separating" or "singling out." In other words, Peter calls all of the Jews of the Dispersion to *repent*. If they give up a former thought to embrace Jesus, the second thought, they will be moved upon by the saturating presence of Jesus. The focus is on each individual being singled out by Christ. They will experience intimacy with His Person as He personally becomes the foundation of their lives. They will be baptized upon Him.

The call to repent is to embrace Jesus even though they crucified Him. The baptism is to be "upon" His name. They will be saturated in and upon Him. He will become the foundation of each individual life. The entire focus is on Jesus.

Provision Received

This brings us to the third verb contained in Peter's instructions. He says, *"And you shall receive the gift of the Holy Spirit"* (Acts 2:38). The Greek word (lambano) is translated *you shall receive*. It is in the indicative mood which means a simple statement of fact. It is in the future tense meaning this is the result of the response of "repentance." It is in the middle voice which has to do with personal preference and benefit. The usage of this word by Peter is significant to the passage. Lambano can be used in two different applications. It expresses the emphasis of to take, seize, lay hold of, even with the idea of force or violence. In our passage this word expresses an attitude present within the new believer. He is aggressively wanting, desiring, seeking, and longing to receive everything they witnessed in the Pentecost event. By this point, there is absolutely no resistance or hesitation. If one is *cut to the heart*, repented, and placed upon the new foundation of Jesus (baptized), would he not be aggressively taking in every aspect possible in this new relationship with Jesus?

A second application of this word (lambano) means to receive what is given or imparted, imposed, or to obtain. The focus of this application is not as aggressive. It is more passive with an emphasis on receptivity and openness. We are not forced to choose between these two applications, but we can accept both of them as true in our passage. The gift of the Holy Spirit is definitely given to us by Jesus. He received the Promise from the Father and immediately *poured out* this gift. The Greek word (ekcheo) translated *poured out* means to gush or extravagantly give. It is the picture of a full bucket of water being turned upside down. There is no doubt about our receiving. He lavished Himself upon us. This is an expression of how aggressive He is in His desire to be intimate with us. Let's link this with our own personal aggressive desire to know Him and receive all He wants to give to us. How can we not receive the fullness of the Spirit? He aggressively pours out and we aggressively receive. There is nothing that can hinder us from knowing Him.

The gift of the Holy Spirit has already been given. Peter's instructions are very important here. We must not misunderstand. He is not saying that God will give us the Holy Spirit after we have repented and been baptized. Repentance (giving up a former thought to embrace a second thought) is a response. Baptism is a response. This means God already acted and we simply respond to what He already did. This is Peter's answer to the question coming from the Jews of the Dispersion, *"What shall we do?"* He does not give a list of activities but calls them to respond to what Jesus already ***poured out***. It is a call to an open response to the movement of God upon our lives! Nothing can hinder what God already did. Let's respond!!

Acts 2:38-39

THE PROMISE

The Jews of the Dispersion just experienced an explosion in their lives. They are *cut to the heart*. It is an amazing awakening. They suddenly see the reality of truth. The Spirit went to the depths of their minds and revealed Jesus. They participated in the crucifixion; their voices joined in the jeering. They had thwarted the dreams of their forefathers as well as the hope of their lives. They crucified their own "Messiah." In desperation they cry out, *"What shall we do?"* (Acts 2:37). They are aware that there is nothing they can do. Their cry is overwhelming.

Peter will not leave them in this condition. He has nothing but encouragement to offer them. The purpose of an awakening is to bring us to new life. Peter calls these Jews of the Dispersion to *repent, be baptized*, and *receive* (Acts 2:38). He does not give them a list of things to accomplish. There are no good activities which will offset their bad deeds. He does not call them to do anything, but he does call them to respond to Jesus. Repentance is a response to the movement of God upon our lives. It is giving up a former thought to embrace a second thought. They have changed their minds. Their rejection of Jesus has now become a total acceptance of Jesus. The act of baptism is a total saturation or immersion into Jesus. The physical act is a statement of the aligning of their lives with Christ. Peter highlights the focus by calling them to *be baptized in the name of Jesus Christ* (Acts 2:38). It not a formula to be spoken, but a focus

The Promise | Acts 2:38-39

to be embraced. Jesus is now their life. The natural byproduct of this will be receiving the Spirit of Christ. What happened to the one hundred and twenty disciples at Pentecost will now be their experience as well.

In the Greek text the important issues are placed at the very beginning of the sentence. In our passage the opening Greek word is "humin." It is translated ***to you***. It is in the dative case. This means those who receive the action of the ***promise*** are these Jews. Peter begins by waving his hands and crying to them that they are included. God has not tossed them aside. He begins with reassurance. There is not any condemnation, probation, suspicion, or hesitation in the message. God made a way for you. I am speaking ***to you***. After crucifying Christ, what chance do they have? How can they possibly be included? One opportunity came their way and they completely missed it. Is all lost? NO! There is a second chance. It is a promise of God. This is a message of hope.

The second Greek word (gar) in our text is translated ***for***. It is an explanatory coordinating conjunction. This Greek word is used to assign a reason for what Peter has just said. The Jews of the Dispersion were ***cut to the heart***. In this new awakening, they respond in repentance. They see the new revelation of Jesus and they embrace it. In this acceptance they are ***baptized***, immersed, or saturated with Jesus. He is now their focus. The indwelt Spirit of Jesus within them reinforces this in their lives. Peter explains all of this to the Jews of the Dispersion when they cry out in despair (Acts 2:37). How can Peter be so certain of this acceptance? Isn't it presumptuous to boldly proclaim what God will do?

Peter does not slip from the truth in his bold announcement! It is a ***promise***! He says, ***"For the promise is to you and to your children, and to all who are afar off, as many as the Lord our God will call,"*** (Acts 2:39).

Part Five: I Promise You

Promise of the Past

This is a significant promise which we need to examine. Peter gives no explanation concerning this promise. The third Greek word (eimi) in our passage is a verb of being translated "is." God is not producing this promise at the moment. It is certainly not something we hope will come to pass if we work hard enough. This is not wishful thinking on the part of Peter. We will certainly not talk God into making this promise and keeping it. The promise is a state of being. It is already in place. If God is creative in His thought process, then doesn't He create the promise by simply thinking about it? The promise has a life of its own. It is the life of the Holy Spirit. There are several things which verify this truth.

This is a CERTIFIED promise! The fourth word in our Greek text (ho) is a definite article which is placed just before "promise." In other words, it is *the promise*. This definitely indicates that Peter has a specific promise in mind. It is also significant that Peter makes no attempt to give any details concerning the content of the promise. Evidently he knew that the Jews of the Dispersion were very familiar with the wonder of *the promise*.

This is the second time Peter refers to this promise in his sermon. In this explanation of Pentecost he proposed this promise as the climax of all God is doing in and through Jesus. God not only raised Him from the dead, but exalted Him *to the right hand of God, and having received from the Father the promise of the Holy Spirit, He poured out this which you now see and hear* (Acts 2:33). The definite article (*the*) is placed before the word *promise* in this statement as well. This certainly indicates that Peter is referring to a specific promise with specific content.

Luke also highlights this in a statement made by Jesus. Jesus was with His disciples for forty days after His resurrection. What a glorious time it must have been for them! This time became for them the *infallible proofs* of His resurrection (Acts 1:3). It was the consistency of His being with them that convinced them. They would never forget their day after day interaction with Jesus. They lived with Him, ate with Him, and traveled with Him. He taught them *of the things pertaining to the kingdom of God* (Acts 1:3). On the final day of this great appearance He gathered them together. They were on the brink of the fulfillment of all God dreamed from the beginning of creation. He instructed them *to wait for the Promise of the Father* (Acts 1:4). Evidently this was not the first time He used this phrase. In this passage, Luke quickly quotes Jesus as saying, *"Which you have heard from Me"* (Acts 1:4).

This promise also has CONTENT. This is verified by the Greek word (gar) translated "for" which we have already discussed. The reason Peter could boldly proclaim *"and you shall receive the gift of the Holy Spirit"* is because this is the content of the promise (Acts 1:38). Jesus said this same thing as He shared this vision with the disciples. Having reminded them He had spoken often to them about the Promise of the Father, He gave them content. He said, *"For John truly baptized with water, but you shall be baptized with the Holy Spirit not many days from now"* (Acts 1:5).

This content is not described in quantity such as quarts or gallons. It is the wonder of the relationship with a Person. In the discourse before His death, Jesus highlighted this content (John 14, 15, 16). In His discourse, Jesus said, *"And I will pray the Father, and He will give you another Helper, that He may abide with you forever -"* (John 14:16). All of this is part of the content of *the promise*. Jesus designates the Holy Spirit as the Helper or Paraclete. The disciples must have been greatly encouraged when Jesus said, *"another Helper."* There are two contrasting Greek words which can be translated *another*. The

Greek word (allos) as used here means another of equal quality while the Greek word (heretos) means another of a different quality. Therefore, the Holy Spirit is designated by Jesus as equal with Himself. The Holy Spirit would be Christ in us, ***the hope of glory*** (Colossians 1:27).

Another element is the CONTINUATION of the promise. As Peter boldly proclaims the wonder of ***the promise*** to the Jews, he is definitely referring to the prophecy with which he began his sermon (Acts 2:16-21). This is a quotation from the prophet Joel (Joel 2:28-32). This is but a sample of the many prophecies which validate this great promise. The very fact that ***the promise*** is found in a multitude of prophecies testifies of its long standing history. God planted this dream in the hearts of men who could not help but verbalize its truth. It shines forth as a beacon of hope for generations of time to keep us focused on the eternal plan of God. We are living ***the promise***.

Promise of Passion

This promise is also a promise of passion. The Greek word (epangelia) translated promise in our passage comes from the Greek word (epangello) meaning "to announce." It is used only for the promises of God in the New Testament with only one exception (Acts 23:21) where it means order or mandate. It has to do with "the thing promised or a gift graciously given." It is not a pledge secured by negotiation. Therefore it is contrasted with the Greek word (omnuo) which is an oath or pledge. These words are both seen in one verse of the Book of Hebrews. ***For when God made a promise*** (epaggellia) ***to Abraham, because He could swear*** (omnuo) ***by no one greater, He swore*** (omnuo) ***by Himself*** (Hebrews 6:13).

The swearing of an oath in Jesus' day was greatly abused. An oath had to do with the authenticity of the promise being made. Often they would state, "I do not have to keep my promise (oath) because I did not swear by God; I swore by the earth." In the Sermon on the Mount, Jesus absolutely eliminates any such word games (Matthew 5:33-37). In fact, He said that we should not swear at all, but simply keep our promises. If you swear by the earth, it is God's footstool. If you swear by Jerusalem, it is the city of the King. If you swear by heaven, it is the throne of God. So do not swear at all but keep your word. The attitude of an oath is that the authority which causes me to keep my promise is something greater than I am. Therefore, I have to fulfill the promise. It is the fulfillment of the promise based on the threat of the power which is greater than I am. The promise is not based on the inner love and desire of the person but the pressure of the power beyond us.

A great example of this is the oath made by Herod Antipas. At his birthday party, he was greatly pleased at the dancing of Herodias' teenage daughter. In his drunken state *he also swore to her, "Whatever you ask me, I will give you, up to half my kingdom"* (Mark 6:23). Upon the prompting of her mother she requested, *"I want you to give me at once the head of John the Baptist on a platter"* (Mark 6:25). Mark records, *"And the king was exceedingly sorry; yet, because of the oaths and because of those who sat with him, he did not want to refuse her"* (Mark 6:26). Peer pressure and powers beyond Herod Antipas forced him to do what he did not want to do.

Peter is not proposing that God made rash promises backed up by an oath. He is not forced into a situation where He must do something He really does not want to do. The Greek word (epaggello) is used fifty-two times in the New Testament. Every time it is in reference to what God promised to us. In the verb form it is always used in the middle voice. Therefore, it is an expression of personal preference. In other words, God desperately wants to fulfill this promise. Everything God has done from the start of the Old Testament is to fulfill *the promise*. In fact, we do not have a record of anything God ever did which is not about ***the promise***. His total focus of wisdom, energy, and exceedingly great power is about ***the promise***. He is driven by His love. This is the impact of what the Hebrew author was saying in the quotation above (Hebrews 6:13). God willingly based His promise on an oath. But He could find no power greater than Himself to swear by. His own heart became the very security of ***the promise***. ***The promise*** is a fulfillment of God's love for us. He removed every obstacle which might keep us from intimacy with Him. He is waiting on our response. ***The promise*** is ours.

Promise of Purpose

The final element of the great promise is the promise of purpose. The Greek word (epangelia) is translated promise in our text (Acts 2:39). The root Greek word (angelia) means something announced. The Greek word "angelos" is the announcer or messenger. This is the root word for our English word "angel." The Greek word "evangelia" is the message of good things or the Gospel. You can see this entire cluster of words all has to do with the message of truth found in the Person of Jesus. It is the "good news" of the Gospel.

In the New Testament, the usage of this Greek word (epangelia) can be gathered into three groups. The first group is the frequent references to God's promise to Abraham concerning his heir. By faith Abraham accepted these promises involved in this covenant promise; they were repeated to his sons Isaac and Jacob, through whom the promised seed should come. There are a variety of New Testament verses you should study on this subject (Romans 4:13-16, 20; 9:8-9; 15:8; Galatians 3:16-22; 4:23; Hebrews 6:13-17; 7:6; 11:9, 11,17).

A second group is the usage of this word (epangelia) used in reference to David's seed. Paul had an opportunity to preach in the synagogue at Antioch on the Sabbath day. In highlighting David he said, *"From this man's seed, according to the promise, God raised up for Israel a Savior – Jesus,"* (Acts 13:23). He restated it again, *"And we declare to you glad tidings – that promise which was made to the fathers,"* (Acts 13:32). He goes on to say that this promise was confirmed in Christ. Stephen, while preaching to the Hellenistic Jews spoke of this promise (Acts 7:17). There are numerous other Scriptures for your consideration (Romans 9:4; 8-9; 15:8; Galatians 3:22; 2 Timothy 1:1; Hebrews 9:15; 1John 2:25).

The third group is the one in which our text is located. It is *the promise* concerning the gift of the Holy Spirit. We have no reference in the New Testament referring to this great outpouring of the Holy Spirit as a promise until after the resurrection (Luke 24:49; Acts 1:4; 2:33; Ephesians 1:13). However, as already mentioned above we do have the words of Jesus saying that He often talked to them about this *promise* (Acts 1:4)

Let there be no confusion. These are not three different pictures. These are aspects of the same promise. It again highlights the great truth that the supreme goal of all God has been actively accomplishing from Abraham to King David is all focused on the intimacy of the indwelling Spirit of Jesus in our lives. The purpose of the birth, death, resurrection, and exaltation of Jesus Christ is that He might pour His Spirit into our lives. We are to be sourced by Him in the intimacy of oneness with His Presence. To miss this is to miss all that God designed for us. This sourcing is not a minor issue or an addition which is optional. This is the heart of God's purpose. It is ***the promise!***

PART SIX
ACTS 2:40-47

EARLY CHURCH MATHEMATICS

Acts 2:40-47
EARLY CHURCH MATHEMATICS

Luke structures the paragraph in our study (Acts 2:40-47) in a very simple manner. He begins by using a strong emphasis on subtraction. Then just as quickly his focus becomes one of addition. He removes one group of people and adds another group. He carefully defines each group; however, he describes in greater detail the group to which he adds. This language of subtraction and addition is used consistently by the authors of the New Testament. Paul declared, **"He has delivered us from the power of darkness and conveyed us into the kingdom of the Son of His love"** (Colossians 1:13). The Scriptures use the contrast of "light" and "darkness" to describe the quality of the two groups. "Love and hate," "Kingdom of God and kingdoms of this world," and "truth and deceit" are additional descriptions the authors use. We are to be subtracted from one group and added to another. There are no third or fourth groups. There is also no "half in one and half in another group." There are only two groups. We are either in the Kingdom of God or the Kingdom of Satan. We either walk in light or we walk in darkness.

One hundred and twenty disciples experienced Pentecost (outside God coming inside). More than three thousand Jews of the Dispersion were greatly moved by this event. They desperately desired an explanation of how this would apply to their lives (Acts 2:13). Peter, moved upon by the Holy Spirit, delivered the answer in the form of a sermon. The entire explanation is

Jesus of Nazareth, a Man whom they crucified. As the reality of this truth was deeply applied by the Holy Spirit, one can only imagine the upset and dismay gripping this group of Jews. They immediately began to cry out **to Peter and the rest of the apostles, "Men and brethren, what shall we do?"** (Acts 2:37). This is an expression of the depths of their despair; there was nothing they could do that would undo what they had done.

Peter enters into a dialogue with them. What is recorded in the Scriptures is a summary of many questions and answers which must have been proposed. **And with many other words** (Acts 2:40) is the beginning of this summary. In the Greek text, the first word of this sentence is the Greek word (heteros) translated *other*. This highlights the emphasis on the additional discussion. There is contained in this phrase the consistent urging, insisting, and calling of the Gospel. Peter did not preach and walk away from them. He answered their questions and constantly brought them back to Jesus whom they crucified. It must have been a rather lengthy time.

Peter **testified** during this dialogue (Acts 2:40). The Greek word (diemarturato) is the normal word for "testify" with a prefix (dia). This intensifies the normal word with the idea of "solemnly" or "earnestly." It has the atmosphere of pleading with them. Can you imagine the content of Peter's testimony? Did he relate his own guilt in denying Jesus three times? Did He express how he felt in the depths of his heart when he thought he could never be forgiven? Yet, Christ forgave him and gave him the fullness of His Spirit! Would Jesus not do the same for the Jews of the Dispersion?

Peter **exhorted** during this dialogue (Acts 2:40). The Greek word (parakaleo) translated **exhorted** comes from "para" (to the side of) and "kaleo" (to call). It means to aid, help, comfort, or encourage. It is used to beseech with a stronger force than the normal Greek word (aiteo) used for asking or begging. Luke uses the imperfect tense to express this exhorting. This indicates something which took place in the past but continues into the present. It could be translated "kept on exhorting." Luke emphasizes that Peter warned the Jews of the Dispersion to examine carefully the evidence he presented. Peter appealed to his listeners repeatedly.

These three statements emphasize the strength and duration of the time Peter spent with the Jews of the Dispersion. There were many additional words; Peter testified about his own personal experience with Jesus; he appealed to them time and time again. The call of truth compelled them to respond to what they were experiencing in their inner hearts. The Holy Spirit was revealing Christ to their hearts. They were to respond to the instruction of Peter, **"Repent, and let every one of you be baptized in the name of Jesus Christ for the remission of sins; and you shall receive the gift of the Holy Spirit"** (Acts 2:38).

The content of this repentance and baptism is found in our passage (Acts 2:40-47). This is the heart of the subtraction and addition.

Subtraction

And with many other words he testified and exhorted them, saying, "Be saved from this perverse generation," (Acts 2:40). Eugene Peterson renders this verse in The Message; ***He went on in this vein for a long time, urging them over and over, "Get out while you can; get out of this sick and stupid culture!"*** The actual Greek text displays the simplicity and strong emphasis of this statement. The order of the words must be noted. It would actually read as *"Save from the generation the untoward this."* Let's examine this statement.

Peter urges the Jews of the Dispersion to experience salvation. His cry is that they might "be saved." The Greek word (sozo) translated *be saved* is used fifty-four times in the Gospels.

Part Six: Early Church Mathematics

This word can be used in a variety of ways. For instance, fourteen times it is used to describe deliverance from disease or demon possession (Matthew 9:21-22; Mark 3:4; 5:23, 28, 34; 6:56; 10:52; Luke 6:9; 8:36, 48, 50; 17:19; 18:42; John 11:12). Twenty times this word is used in connection with the rescue of physical life from some impending peril or instant death (Matthew 8:25; 14:30; 16:25; 27:40, 42, 49; Mark 8:35; 15:30-31; Luke 9:24, 56; 23:35, 37, 39; John 12:27). Spiritual salvation is the emphasis of the remaining twenty times this word is used (Matthew 1:21; 10:22; 19:25; 24:13, 22; Mark 8:35; 10:26; 13:13, 20; 16:16; Luke 7:50; 8:12; 9:24; 13:23; 18:26; 19:10; John 3:17; 5:34; 10:9; 12:47). These varieties of context in the Gospels give us the tone of the usage of the word. The atmosphere of serious peril seems to hover around each of these usages. Demon possession, crippling disease, instant death, and spiritual damnation are all pending. As these monsters draw close, one must escape in order to survive. This Greek word (sozo) translated *be saved* is the act of the escape.

This same urgency and peril is present in our passage. For this reason several translations focus on the punishment which they will experience if they do not escape. The Good News Translation says, "*Peter made his appeal to them and with many other words he urged them, saying, "Save yourselves from the punishment coming on this wicked people!*" The Contemporary English Version states, "*Peter told them many other things as well. Then he said, "I beg you to save yourselves from what will happen to all these evil people.*"

This is emphasized in the Greek text with the Greek word (apo) translated *from*. This Greek word expresses motion and change of location. It indicates the separation of a person or an object from another person or an object with which it was formerly united but is now separated. The Message paraphrase has the correct emphasis. It says, "*Get out while you can; get out of this sick and stupid culture!*" There is overwhelming danger; damnation is inevitable. Peter urges them to escape, flee, or separate themselves from the group to which they have been attached.

There is a very important factor that is missed by several of the most popular translations. The New International Version translated, **with many other words he warned them; and he pleaded with them, "Save yourselves from this corrupt generation."** Note the above translation from The Good News Translation and The Contemporary English Version. In Peter's call for the people to escape (**be saved**), these translations insert the word **yourselves**. This needs to be questioned due to the grammar structure of the Greek word (sozo). This word is in the imperative mood which gives it the urgency of a command. Therefore, it has an assumed subject of "you." But it is in the passive voice; thus the subject is not responsible for the action of the verb, but is receiving the action from another source. This is what is called a "Divine action." It is not stated in the verse, but is assumed. There is no emphasis in the verse for the Jews of the Dispersion to save themselves.

The Jews of the Dispersion have no ability to reprogram their thought process. They cannot resist the culture in which they have been raised. Their family connections and relatives are all linked with this group of Jews. Their entire religious training has been saturated in the traditions of the elders. The religious practices are done so often they have become natural. They are **devout men**. Their recognition of Christ as the Messiah must be a Divine revelation. Embracing Jesus as their only salvation must be a Divine empowerment. The only possibility of repentance (giving up a former thought to embrace a second thought) demands the power of the Holy Spirit.

In our culture, we have difficulty understanding the mental agony these Jews of the Dispersion experienced. Embracing Christ would mean being subtracted from the power and authority of their spiritual leaders. They come to Jerusalem every year for the religious feasts. They trust the leadership of the priests and

Part Six: Early Church Mathematics

scribes. No doubt they were a part of the crowd who followed the urging of these leaders who at Jesus' trial incited the crowd to shout, "***Crucify Him; crucify Him!***" (Luke 23:21). Now they are being challenged to escape from the influence of that leadership. Peter calls this leadership "***this perverse generation.***" This phrase is an echo of a line in the song of Moses which would be familiar to the audience. It was used in the synagogue worship services (Deuteronomy 32:5).

The Greek word (skolios) translated *perverse* is sometimes translated crooked, bent, wicked, or warped from dryness. The old English word was "untoward." Peter's words echo the words Jesus used to describe that generation. ***But He*** (Jesus) ***answered and said to them, "An evil and adulterous generation seeks after a sign,"*** (Matthew 12:39; 16:4). He told a parable of the evil spirits returning to possess an empty individual. Jesus said, ***"And the last state of that man is worse than the first. So shall it also be with this wicked generation"*** (Matthew 12:45). Exactly who are the people to whom Jesus refers? Those who were seeking signs were the Pharisees, Sadducees, and scribes (Matthew 12:38; 16:1). Peter's reference is to the same group.

Why would Peter refer to this group as ***this perverse generation***? They were the best educated people of their time. The Sadducees were the wealthy who fostered the cultural traditions of their time. The Pharisees were those dedicated and faithful to the law, the temple, and the traditions. How are they crooked and bent? The English dictionary defines perverse as "directed away from what is right or good; perverted." It is being "obstinate and persisting in an error or a fault." It has to do with being "wrongly self-willed or stubborn."

The leaders of Israel were perverse concerning Jesus. Their rejection of Him is where they missed their direction. They were crooked and self-willed from the beginning. Peter's sermon explaining Pentecost was about Jesus. Jesus is the total focus of the Father. Everything the Father planned for redemption

Early Church Mathematics | **Acts 2:40-47**

and the new Kingdom flowed in and through Jesus. Jesus is the sacrifice bringing redemption. Jesus is the One used to conquer death and the grave. Jesus is the Man who reached the throne of the Father and is seated on the right hand. Jesus is the individual who became the King of the new Kingdom. He became both Lord and Christ (Acts 2:36). There is no other issue presented.

The Jews of the Dispersion stand guilty before the truth about Jesus. They are a part of ***this perverse generation*** because they crucified Christ. There is only one issue; it is Jesus. The content of Peter's sermon tells us that the ***many more words*** he shared with them were about Jesus. When Peter ***testified*** it was about Jesus. He ***exhorted*** them about Jesus. His call to ***repent*** (give up a former thought to embrace a second thought) was to embrace Jesus. They were to be baptized into Jesus. They were to be subtracted from the group who crucified Jesus and added to the group that embraced Jesus. This is all about Jesus.

Could I make a feeble attempt to fill the shoes of Peter? Could I urge you to respond to the Holy Spirit who wants to enable you to escape from the group, the culture, the influence which masters and dominates you? I would cry out to you, "Get out while you can; get out of this sick and stupid culture!" It may be a drug culture, an alcoholic culture, a materialistic culture, or even a religious culture. The call of the Gospel is to be subtracted from that influence and be added to another influence. Come from the Kingdom of Darkness and enter the Kingdom of Light.

What is wrong with the culture? It has to do with how the culture relates to Jesus. There were Jews of the Dispersion who defended themselves. They undoubtedly spoke of their positions in their local synagogue and their knowledge of the Old Testament. Remember these are ***devout men from every nation under heaven*** (Acts 2:5). The problem is they have missed Jesus. They have no more defense or excuses. It is time to embrace Jesus and be filled with His person. We must become His people. His mind must be ours. Everything that is not Him must be set aside whether it looks right or not. *"Get out while you can; get out of this sick and stupid culture!"*

Addition

But this is only half of the story. These Jews were not simply subtracted from one group, but they were added to another. Luke immediately says, **Then those who gladly received his word were baptized; and that day about three thousand souls were added to them** (Acts 2:41). Eugene Peterson in The Message states, *that day about three thousand took him at his word and were baptized and were signed up.* What it meant for them to be *signed up* is quickly described in the following verses of the paragraph. They immediately became disciples for there was a consistency in their involvement in **the apostles' doctrine** (Acts 2:42). They were consistent in their fellowship with the believers (Acts 2:42), and they began to link financially with them (Acts 2:45). They were subtracted from one group; but they were added to another group.

I fear many evangelical Christians are subtracted from **the perverse generation**. They see their mistake concerning Jesus. They recognize Him as their Savior. But they have not been added. The linkage to the believers is not complete. The same involvement they had with evil is not the same involvement they have with Christ. The dominating influence of the former group does not characterize the influence of the new group. They are not adequately added. They have not really *signed up*.

Christianity is not a mere correction of some activities in our life. It is way beyond a token attendance to a different organization. There is a *signing up* which takes place. It is a change in location from one group to another. Life cannot continue as it has in the past. One must learn the ways of the believers as the mind of Christ is experienced. Are you *signed up*?

Acts 2:41

A CHANGE IN LOCATION

A clear picture of Peter's explanation of Pentecost is established in this final paragraph of chapter two. Luke presents us with a summary of Peter's sermon in the first verse (Acts 2:40). Obviously the message was much longer than he recorded. The next verse indicates the immediate response of the people who were listening (Acts 2:41). The remainder of the paragraph introduces the results of their immediate response (Acts 2:42-47). At the same time he gives insight into the activities of the community of believers. In these three sections he shifts from Peter (Acts 2:40), to the persons who responded (Acts 2:41), to the group who shares in the life of the Christian community (Acts 2:42-47).

Peter calls for the Jews of the Dispersion to be subtracted from the group with whom they have identified all of their lives. The call is this, *"Be saved from this perverse generation,"* (Acts 2:40). The Message by Eugene Peterson translates it as, *"Get out while you can; get out of this sick and stupid culture!"* As we begin to study the second verse of this paragraph, the response to Peter's call will reveal the radical nature of that call. This is not a slight alteration in doctrinal belief. It is certainly not an addition to the numerous religious activities already observed. It is surprising anyone responds to such a radical call.

Then those who gladly received his word were baptized; and that day about three thousand souls were added to them (Acts 2:41). There is much here for us to consider.

Part Six: Early Church Mathematics

The Response

The sentence begins with a Greek phrase (men oun) translated **then**. There is more happening in this phrase than is indicated by this translation. The Greek word "men" has an intensifying effect in this phrase and it points ahead to another clause. Peter gives a strong challenge to the Jews of the Dispersion. Get ready! Let the drums roll as we anticipate what will happen. We leap with faith and confidence into the response of three thousand Jews.

Just prior to the Greek phrase described above there is a definite article (oi). It is actually attached to the Greek word (apodechomai) translated *those who gladly received*. This Greek word (apodechomai) is a participle in the nominative case. The subject of the sentence is **those**. This participle gives content to that subject. The subject of the sentence becomes ***those who gladly received***. The focus is on the act of receiving. The prefix of the word is "apo" which can be translated "from." The root Greek word (dechomai) means to take or receive. It is in the middle voice giving the verb the meaning of personal preference. This verb is used only seven times in Luke's Gospel account (8:40; 9:11) and five times in the Book of Acts (2:41; 18:27; 21:17; 24:3; 28:30). It often has to do with hospitality which gives it the flavor of "to welcome." The crowd welcomes Jesus (Luke 8:40) and Jesus welcomes the crowd (Luke 9:11). Paul is received by believers (Acts 18:27; 21:17). Paul also welcomes all who come to him (Acts 28:30).

However, our passage is the only place in the New Testament where this Greek word (apodechomai) does not involve the receiving or welcoming a person or a group of persons. In this passage the focus is on the receiving of ***his word***. Of course, this relates to everything Peter spoke in his explanation of Pentecost. The difficult circumstance here is the Jews of the Dispersion's involvement in the crucifixion of Jesus. It is a factor they cannot deny. But the wonder of forgiveness and the fullness of the Holy Spirit bring them out of despair into excitement and they gladly receive this message. It is important to state again that this verb is in the middle voice. This focuses on the choice of the individual as his personal preference. The highlight for them is the atmosphere of welcome and gladness as they embrace the truth.

Contained within our verse (Acts 2:41) is a rejection of ***his word*** as well. Peter indicates that some reject his word though he is not bold in this declaration. When he states the number of individuals who received the word he indicates that some did not. This is a crucial moment in the lives of the Jews of the Dispersion. From this point on everything changes and they alter their approach to life. They even change their group attachment. This is radical!

These Jews of the Dispersion do not gradually or progressively come into the Christian experience. They are confronted with the truth of their spiritual position. There is no way for them to hide in the crowd of decision makers. No one can make a decision begrudgingly. None of this crowd dares to be baptized without the full welcome of ***his word***. The implications of the baptism are far too severe.

We must not lose sight of Peter's empowerment by the Holy Spirit in regard to the delivery and revelation of this word. We discovered this at the outset of Peter's sermon. ***But Peter standing up with the eleven, raised his voice and said to them*** (Acts 2:14). It is amazing! The Greek word (histemi) translated ***standing up*** is a verb in the passive voice. Peter is acted upon by someone greater than himself. This sermon is the Biblical picture of what preaching is to be. It is saturated with Scripture; it is an explanation of Biblical passages. It is anointed and empowered by the Holy Spirit who goes to the heart of those who hear. It is interactive with those listening for they are compelled to respond and participate in these words.

Part Six: Early Church Mathematics

Although this great crowd is in a festive mood, they cannot be easily swayed by a clever speaker. Their response is not emotionally based; although, they express strong emotions. There is an eager response to *his word*. In the Greek text the order of the words are "*the* (ton) *word* (logos) *his* (autos). The article (the) is just before *word*. It strengthens the focus on the sermon and interaction of Peter with this crowd. There are some who propose that all the apostles were preaching at this time in a variety of locations throughout Jerusalem. The *three thousand* converts were an accumulation of all of these services. But this idea is not within the limits of this passage.

The Greek word (logos) translated *word* is very suggestive. It is the Greek word which is strongly used for Jesus (John 1:1). Whether or not Luke had this in mind as he wrote this verse could be debated. However, there is absolutely no doubt that the content of everything Peter preaches is Jesus. Every detail describes Jesus. The call of the message demands a response to the person of Jesus. The recognizable guilt of the listeners was on how they treated Jesus. The connection between the *word* (logos) and Jesus is clear.

This brings us back to a contrast of two Greek words. The Greek word (phone) is translated *voice* (Matthew 3:3), *sound* (John 3:8), and *noise* (Revelation 6:1). The Greek word (logos) is translated *word*. Logos is the rational thought of the mind. Biblical scholars from the earliest days contrasted the "phone" and the "word" when speaking of John the Baptist (phone) and Jesus (Word). John claimed only to be *the voice of one crying in the wilderness* (John 1:23), but Christ is emphatically declared to be *the Word was with God, and the Word was God* (John 1:1).

A "word" is something even without a "voice." A "word" in the heart is truly a word before it is spoken, but it continues to be a word after it is spoken. A "voice" is nothing. It is meaningless sound, an empty cry, unless it also is the vehicle of a "word." When they are united, there is a sense in which the "voice" precedes the "word," for the sound strikes the ear before the sense is conveyed to the mind. Although the "voice" precedes the "word," the "voice" is not really before the "word." The "word" is always before the "voice." When we speak, the "word" in our hearts must precede the "voice" on our lips. The "voice" is the vehicle by which the "word" in us is transferred to and becomes a "word" in others. In the act of accomplishing this, the "voice" passes away, but the "word" planted in the hearts of others and in the heart of the speaker remains.

This is what is happening in our passage. Peter is filled with the **Word** (logos). He becomes the "voice" (phone) of that **Word**. The response of the Jews of the Dispersion is not to a new doctrine. This is not a new religious movement. Those things may develop over time, but the call is to respond to the **Word**. The call of repentance (giving up a former thought to embrace a second thought) is to move from "crucifying Christ" to embracing Him as **both Lord and Christ**.

The Releasing

Our passage states that they **were baptized** (Acts 2:41). The ceremonial aspects of this baptism are stated in verse thirty-eight of this chapter. Then Peter said to them, **"Repent, and let every one of you be baptized in the name of Jesus Christ for the remission of sins:** (Acts 2:38). Many Biblical scholars believe that the baptism experience for the Gentiles who became Christians was different than for Jews. Gentiles were baptized in the name of the Father, Son, and Holy Spirit, while Jewish converts were baptized **in the name of Jesus Christ**. Whether this was actually true in practice or not is immaterial. In the Great Commission (Matthew 28:18-20), Jesus focused the disciples on all nations. They were to baptize **them in the name of the Father and of the Son and of the Holy Spirit**.

However, here in our passage the cultural issue is extremely different. This is not a conversion from many gods to the one God, Jehovah. It is not the acknowledgment of the promise of the coming Messiah. The issue in this setting has to do with their rejection of Jesus as the Messiah. They crucified Him. Peter calls them to *be baptized in the name of Jesus Christ* (Acts 2:38). This was the criteria of a Jew's conversion. If a Jew received baptism in this Name, he was excluded from all communication with his countrymen. No one would forfeit such privileges unless he was fully and clearly convicted. It would mean renouncing Judaism, and all the political advantages connected with it. The Jewish family life revolved around the local synagogue. They would no longer be welcome in such a gathering. Their decision even affected their jobs. Undoubtedly this contributed to the selling of *their possessions and goods, and divided them among all, as anyone had need* (Acts 2:44).

Peter makes the cost of coming to Christ very high. How can he expect them to publicly turn their backs on their culture? How can he ask them to risk becoming outcasts among their families and society? How can he demand that they accept as Messiah the very One their leaders rejected and they helped execute? Evidently Peter believed that *the remission of sins* and receiving *the gift of the Holy Spirit* was worth more than any of those things. There was no sacrifice involved!

This parallels the call of John the Baptist to the Jews of his time, *"Repent, for the kingdom of heaven is at hand!"* (Matthew 3:2). The Jews believed in a baptism which was a once-for-all turning from the old way of life to the new. This was such a radical baptism of change that it referred mostly to Gentiles converting to Judaism. There were rare conditions in which a Jew might experience this radical baptism. It applied to a traitor such as a tax collector or an impure Jewish harlot. But this radical baptism was never required of a normal Jew. Only the baptism of Gentiles into Judaism paralleled the kind of radical, once-for-all change John demanded. In other words, John treated Jewish people as if they were Gentiles, tax collectors, traitors, or harlots, calling them to turn to God on the same terms they believed God demanded of these groups.

This was radical. To call Jewish people to be baptized or repent the same way non-Jews did was offensive. This challenged the accepted, prevalent Jewish belief about salvation. In the cultural setting of Jesus' day, most Jewish people thought that if they were born into a Jewish family and did not reject God's law, they would be saved. John the Baptist preached that they had to come to God the same way that a non-Jew did. This meant that everyone came to God on the same terms. This was radical!

Our passage says, **and that day about three thousand souls were added to them** (Acts 2:41). The Greek word (prosetetheesan) translated **were added** is very strong. This word is used to signify that act by which cities, towns, or provinces changed their masters, and put themselves under another government. Peter called these Jews to go from one party to another. Three thousand people left the scribes and Pharisees and put themselves under the teaching of the apostles. They embraced Christ as the promised and only Messiah. They were baptized into this faith.

You must thoroughly grasp what this suggests. This is not about making some improvements. It is certainly not stopping certain deeds and beginning others, although this may be involved. I do not mind coming to church and working on adjusting some of my attitudes. I could use some help in my family relationships. I know I am not perfect and I am willing to receive instruction. The call of Christ is far beyond this procedure. It is a line drawn in the sand. It is a stepping stone from one group to another. It is the changing of Kingdoms. It is about being added (prosetetheesan).

This easily applies to my life. I am open to minor adjustments. I am willing to consider some correction in a few minor areas of my life. Everyone needs fine tuning in their relationships and activities. Certainly seminars on self-improvement are needed. I will attend them. I can always become a better husband and father. But Peter's demand is completely beyond this consideration. He calls for radical change at the very core of my living. This will alter who I am. This is about changing the direction of my life. Specific interests will change. I have worked a long time to become who I am. I have developed my ministry, my theology, my mind set, and my attitudes. Am I interested in anything so abrupt and radical? I do not think so.

Peter calls us to ***"Get out while you can; get out of this sick and stupid culture!"*** This is subtraction! But there is also an addition. You must be added to the new group. The involvement within this new group will be highlighted in the following verses of this paragraph. But it was a shift in the center point of all their activities (Acts 2:42-47). Have you been timid and hesitant? The Gospel is calling!

Acts 2:42

APOSTLES' DOCTRINE

Luke uses the first two verses of our study to set the tone for the entire paragraph (Acts 2:40-47). Since the Jews of the Dispersion are the first converts of the church, does is not set the tone for the rest of the church age? The tone is an emphasis we readily accept and appreciate in other aspects of our lives, but we are somewhat repelled by it in Christian experience. We refer to it in this study as "subtraction and addition." The "subtraction" is strongly presented by Peter in the opening statement of this paragraph. <u>The Message</u> by Eugene Peterson translates it as, **"Get out while you can; get out of this sick and stupid culture!"** (Acts 2:40). The spiritual location in which they dwell must be abandoned. They must do it quickly without hesitation. It is not a change in physical location; they live in a spiritual state. The spiritual location is supported by their traditions and patterns of the past. It is strongly influenced by the leadership of the Jewish nation. Their relationship to all of these influences will be altered with a change of spiritual location.

The radical nature of this relocation cannot be overstated. The doctors are attending to a patient. His heart stops beating. Immediately everyone goes into action. The entire focus is suddenly transferred to one thing. The patient is dead and must be brought back to life. The moments are critical. No one says, "Let's take a break and come back in an hour." Nothing else matters as the electrical shock is applied to the heart. Will it start beating? Will the patient change locations from the realm of the dead to the realm of the living? There is a parallel to this in the spiritual realm. Peter feels the anxiety of the matter. It is expressed in his call.

Just quitting is not all that matters. Something needs to be added. There may be subtraction; but there must be addition. Leaving one location necessitates going to a second location. In the closing verse of our paragraph (Acts 2:47) Luke says, ***and the Lord added to the church daily those who were being saved.*** Three fourths of this paragraph is dedicated to his description of what this means. In our paragraph there is the possibility of becoming focused on the activities. Is it a simple matter of not going to the synagogue but going to the church services? Or do they simply join a different group or have a different set of traditions?

Peter makes this abundantly clear in his message which brings the Jews of the Dispersion to their place of decision. The issue deals with Jesus! We cannot highlight this too often or too much. This was not about the traditions of their elders or the political structure of Judaism. Those things only matter as they relate to the person of Jesus. These Jews crucified Christ! Everything they did and all they thought was contrary to Him. Their direction was away from Christ. They lived in rebellion and rejection of Him. ***"Get out while you can; get out of this sick and stupid culture!"*** The leadership of Judaism influenced them against Jesus. Their traditions became more binding on them than Jesus. This is not about theology or religious practices; this is about Jesus. No religious ceremony will bring life back into their being. They must embrace Jesus. He is the central issue of the location change.

What will be the appearance of this new location? How will it affect their schedules, their activities, and their involvement? The rest of the paragraph answers these questions. Let's begin with this verse. ***And they continued steadfastly in the apostles'*** *doctrine and fellowship, in the breaking of bread, and in prayers* (Acts 2:42).

The structure of this verse is very enlightening. The first word in the Greek text is the Greek word (eimi) which can be translated "they were." This verb is in the third person plural; therefore it is translated "they." It is the first word of the sentence which means it is the focus of the statement. It is in the imperfect tense which refers to something happening in the past with continual action into the present. It is the indicative mood which is a simple statement of fact. If this verb was in the first person singular it would be translated "I am." It is a state of being rather than a state of action. Luke again tells us that these Jews changed locations. They have moved from one state of being to another. This indicates a radical spiritual change in their lives. Everything they do reflects on this new state of being. It is the result of their repentance (giving up a former thought to embrace a second thought). They are now living in the second thought. It is not a passing state, but it happened in the past and continues into the present moment. This must be clearly understood as this paragraph begins to unfold. The focus is not on a series of activities but upon a new spiritual location, a state of being, which results in new activities. There is absolutely no need to attempt the activities without the state of being. They would be superficial and extremely hypocritical. These activities are going to be driven by this inward motivation which is the state of being.

The second word in the Greek text is a conjunction. It is a Greek word (de) which is translated *and*. It is a coordinating, continuative conjunction. This conjunction most often establishes a contrast, but in this case it has the focus of adding on information to what has been established. Peter now highlights and expands (Acts 2:42-47) the change in location, subtraction and addition, in the lives of three thousand Jews (Acts 2:40-41). He will reveal the content.

The third word in the Greek text adds to the subject *they*.

The Greek word (proskartereo) is translated *they continued steadfastly*. This Greek word is a verb in the participle form (a verb acting as an adjective). It is in the nominative case which makes it a part of the subject of the sentence. It is a root word with a prefix. The prefix is "pros." This can be translated "to" and implies motion toward something. The root word is "kartereo." It means to be strong, steadfast, firm, to endure, hold out, or to bear the burden. It is significant to note that the same grammar structure is used for the disciples as they tarried for the outpouring of the Holy Spirit (Acts 1:14). The subject of the sentence is the action of this group persisting, enduring, and never wavering. The verb is a state of being. They absolutely would not wander from this state of being.

Both the verb and the subject are in the active voice. This tells you the Jews are responsible for responding to the change of location which is now their state of being. They are not responsible for getting into this state of being; the Holy Spirit moved upon them and brought them into a new location. Now without reservation they respond to this new place; Jesus is their place.

How does their response appear in this new place? In our verse, there are four words which are in the dative case. There are several different kinds of dative in the Greek language; however, one of them is a locative dative. It indicates a location in which the verb's action takes place. It is often translated as a prepositional phrase beginning with "in." In other words, the action of enduring, holding on steadfastly is a state of being which takes place in four locations.

Belief in Jesus

Luke writes, ***And they continued steadfastly in the apostles' doctrine*** (Acts 2:42). The Greek word (didache) translated doctrine can better be translated "teachings." There was a strong emphasis in the early church concerning the authority of the apostles. They were the eye witnesses of the life and teachings of Christ. They were the closest to the actual truth as seen through Jesus.

It appears the ***apostles' doctrine*** is twofold. First they had to be authentic witnesses of Jesus' resurrection which is about the validity of His being. Luke describes the ministry of the apostles. He writes, **And with great power the apostles gave witness to the resurrection of the Lord Jesus. And great grace was upon them all** (Acts 4:33). The Book of Acts consistently records the emphasis of the apostles' message. It was always the resurrection. It was the very first message after the Promise of the Father was poured out. Peter was preaching. The heart of his message is a quotation from David (Psalms 16:8-11). As Peter interprets this statement, he says, ***"He, foreseeing this, spoke concerning the resurrection of the Christ, that His soul was not left in Hades, nor did His flesh see corruption. This Jesus God has raised up, of which we are all witnesses,"*** (Acts 2:31-32).

Peter and John were involved in a miracle at the Gate Beautiful. The surrounding crowds were greatly moved, giving Peter a wonderful opportunity to preach to them. **Now as they spoke to the people, the priests, the captain of the temple, and the Sadducees came upon them, being greatly disturbed that they taught the people and preached in Jesus the resurrection from the dead,** (Acts 4:1-2). Thus, the leaders of Israel testified that the apostles preached that Jesus was resurrected from the dead.

As the Book of Acts unfolds into the evangelism of the Apostle Paul, we see the message of the resurrection being strongly delivered to the Gentiles. ***Then certain Epicurean and Stoic philosophers encountered him. And some said, "What does this babbler want to say?" Others said, "He seems to be a proclaimer of foreign gods," because he preached to them Jesus and the resurrection"*** (Acts 17:18; see 17:32). Paul's message

Part Six: Early Church Mathematics

before the council was the resurrection. *But when Paul perceived that one part were Sadducees and the other Pharisees, he cried out in the council, "Men and brethren, I am a Pharisee, the son of a Pharisee; concerning the hope and resurrection of the dead I am being judged!"* (Acts 23:6). As Paul was before Felix, the governor, giving his defense against the accusations of the leaders of Israel, he said, *"I have hope in God, which they themselves also accept, that there will be a resurrection of the dead, both of the just and the unjust"* (Acts 24:15). At the close of his defense he boldly proclaimed, *"They ought to have been here before you to object if they had anything against me. Or else let those who are here themselves say if they found any wrongdoing in me while I stood before the council, unless it is for this one statement which I cried out, standing among them, 'Concerning the resurrection of the dead I am being judged by you this day"* (Acts 24:19-21). Paul was then presented before King Agrippa who wanted to hear his defense. Paul told him of his heavenly vision and *that the Christ would suffer, that He would be the first to rise from the dead, and would proclaim light to the Jewish people and to the Gentiles,"* (Acts 26:23).

The one hundred and twenty disciples had to select an individual to take the place of Judas. They established the criteria for choosing this new apostle. They determined this new individual must have accompanied them *all the time that the Lord Jesus went in and out among us, beginning from the baptism of John to that day when He was taken up from us,"* (Acts 1:21-22). The driving purpose of these criteria is that they *must become a witness with us of His resurrection"* (Acts 1:22). It was not enough to experience the resurrection appearances of Jesus in order to be a proper witness of His resurrection. It was absolutely necessary to experience all the events of His life from His baptism by John the Baptist through the ascension. The content of the resurrected life is the content of the events of the life of Christ. No one can testify correctly about the resurrection of Christ unless they experienced His crucifixion. The content of His crucifixion is only understood in the events in which He poured out His life on a daily basis. Washing the disciples' feet is the style of the crucifixion. The resurrection was more than a mere event to be remembered or celebrated. It was the continuation of the redemptive ministry of Christ which expanded at His baptism by John. In other words, the content of the resurrection is the entire life of Christ.

Do you see that the message or teaching of the apostles is a focus on the person of Jesus? The Jews of the Dispersion were guilty of crucifying Jesus (Acts 2:23; 36). They have repented (given up a former thought to embrace a second thought). They now spend their time in the unfolding revelation of His Person. The indwelt Spirit of Jesus, through the revealed teaching of the apostles, bombards their lives with who He is. It would be safe to say that they saturate in the Person of Christ. They seek and hunger after Him. He is their curriculum. They are students after Him. They join Paul in crying out, "Oh, *that I may know Him and the power of His resurrection, and the fellowship of His sufferings, being conformed to His death,*" (Philippians 3:10).

The apostles' doctrine is not only saturation in Jesus, but it is saturation in the Word. The emphasis of saturation is contained in the Greek verb (proskartereo) translated **they continued steadfastly**. This was not a special three day conference or revival meeting. This was not that they met together every Thursday night for class. This search to know Him became their passion. This was the daily routine of their lives. You will remember they were described as ***devout men***. In other words, they have been saturating in the law. Their structure of life was the Old Testament law. Now their framework of reference has changed. It is Jesus. Up to this time they saw everything in their lives through the law; now Jesus is their lens. The determining fact of all decisions was the law. Now their determination is Jesus.

The Living Word brought new life to the Written Word.

The law which once had destroyed them is now bringing life to them. They saturated in the Scriptures in days gone by, but had not found Jesus (John 5:39). Now they found Jesus and the Word is alive to them. Often we attempt to describe the interaction of the Living Word in the Written Word. The Written Word is lifeless; it is simply an academic study without the Living Word. Think of the startling possibility of being filled with the Author of the Written Word and allowing Him to reveal Himself to you.

This is why we are determined to have a church which is focused on the Word. If it is just a focus on the Bible, the Written Word, it becomes doctrine, rules and concepts. It must be saturation in Jesus through His Word. It is amazing! The moment you discover Him, you find Him everywhere in His Word. The revelation of His person becomes consistent. This is our discipleship program. Here is our curriculum. In every service we will go after Jesus through His Word. In every sermon we must expose Him through His Word.

What happened to these Jews of the Dispersion? They were subtracted from their previous setting. The religious mindset that trapped them in law and ceremony has been removed. They experience the admonition of Peter. *"Get out while you can; get out of this sick and stupid culture!"* (Acts 2:40).

They now recognize that their traditions and laws caused them to participate in the crucifixion of Christ. These Jews were lifted from that environment and transported to a new dwelling place. They were added to Christ. They became a people of the Word, Living and Written!

What about their forgiveness? It was found in Jesus, the Living and Written Word. What about deliverance from the old mindset? It was found in Jesus, the Living and Written Word. What about the adjustment in their living experience? Though they come from foreign dwelling places with businesses and families, they will now saturate in the Living and Written Word. He is their answer!

Acts 2:42

BUSINESS WITH JESUS

Interpretation is determined by the context of our passage. Peter has exhorted the Jews of the Dispersion concerning their spiritual status. The Holy Spirit revealed such truth to them that they were shaken to the core. They were wrong in crucifying Christ. How earth shaking this was for them. They came to Jerusalem year after year looking for God to do something new. Who would have dreamed it would center in Jesus, the crucified One? Once this revelation came, Peter spent a considerable amount of time exhorting them and answering their questions. He calls them to a radical break from their dwelling place. The Message by Eugene Peterson translates it this way. *"Get out while you can; get out of this sick and stupid culture!"* (Acts 2:40). They must make an immediate and complete break with where they are. This is subtraction. It is not a physical location. It is not even about a religious dwelling place. It all has to do with Jesus. They are to immediately leave the place that crucifies Christ.

But it is not just a subtraction; it is also an addition. You must be added to Christ (Acts 2:41). What a change in location! It is described as light and darkness (1 John 1:5-7). The imprisonment of death is contrasted with the freedom of life (Acts 2:24). Enemies against God become intimate friends with God (Acts 2:35). They are dwelling in a new place. Our verse begins with the attitude they are to maintain in this new location. *And they continued steadfastly* is the attitude. The Greek word (proskartereo) is a root word with a prefix. The prefix is "pros," which can be translated "to" and implies motion toward something. The root word is "kartereo." It means to be strong, steadfast, firm, to endure, hold out, or to bear the burden. There is a new focus on Jesus to which they must consistently respond.

There are four words which follow in the verse. They are in the dative case. This indicates the location or setting in which this action of enduring takes place. It must be very clear the listed activities are not the focus. The consistent, enduring, focus is on Jesus. He has been and is the central issue of Peter's sermon and discussion with them. This focus and endurance takes place in the setting of *doctrine, fellowship, breaking of bread*, and *prayer*.

Belief in Jesus

The first setting has to do with **they continued steadfastly in the apostles' doctrine** (Acts 2:42). The immediate context of the **apostles' doctrine** is found in Peter's sermon explaining Pentecost. It is a total focus on Jesus. As you begin to walk through the Book of Acts listening to the message of the apostles, they are all about Jesus. These new converts are saturating in the person of Jesus. All of the apostles have experiences with the living Christ, both in three years of ministry and in the resurrection appearances. These experiences are the content. These new converts must thoroughly know and understand the One who has come to indwell them.

Business with Jesus

There is a second setting for their new focus on Jesus. In this study, the setting is *fellowship* (Acts 2:41). The Greek word (koinonia) translated *fellowship* was very significant in the early church. It is a word which is used often +by the Apostle Paul in his epistles. I am not sure "fellowship" gives us the correct picture to which Luke refers. He is not discussing the activity of "hanging out," "potluck suppers," or "an evening in the new gym." Involved in this Greek word is *fellowship* with a purpose. The idea of "partner" quickly comes to the forefront. For instance, Luke gives us insight into the linkage between Peter, James and John. He refers to James and John as *partners* (koinonos) **with Simon** (Luke 5:10). These men were *partners* in fishing. Together they had several boats, nets and equipment. They shared the work and the profits. They were business partners.

In writing to the Church at Corinth Paul says, *If anyone inquires about Titus, he is my partner* (koinonos) *and fellow worker concerning you* (2 Corinthians 8:23). This is the same Greek word used by Luke for the business involvement of Peter, James and John. Paul takes the concept from the secular business world and brings it into the spiritual linkage of ministry between himself and Titus. No one can speak against Titus without speaking against Paul. They are linked together as partners in ministry.

This Greek word is only used ten times in the New Testament, but is used numerous other times with a prefix on it. It is the word which gives expression to the body of believers. I am afraid there is no way to give the proper depth to this concept. It is translated *fellowship* in our passage. But in our thinking there are various levels of involvement in *fellowship*. We have casual fellowship with many people at church. But we are not linked with them. We certainly are not a part of their daily lives. We feel no "business" involvement as if we are linked in a great enterprise. These new converts were being called to a deeper and more complete *fellowship* than this.

There were difficult issues creating divisions among the members of the church at Corinth. One such issue was that of eating meat which had been offered to idols in pagan worship. Most Christians were poor and meat was very expensive. The meat used in the sacrificial offerings to pagan gods was offered for sale at a discounted price. The pagan temples would often sponsor entire meals at an affordable cost. Any family could come, but they would be eating the meat which had been offered to a pagan idol. What should be a Christian's proper response?

Paul makes it very plain that idols are nothing (1 Corinthians 10:19). There is no life in them; they have no effect at all. This is also true with the meat which is offered to them. It is simply meat. The issue is far beyond the idol and the meat. The Gentiles are making *sacrifice to demons and not to God* (1 Corinthians 10:20). He then pronounces the crucial issue: *I do not want you to have fellowship* (koinonia) *with demons. You cannot drink the cup of the Lord and the cup of demons; you cannot partake* (synonym of koinonia) *of the Lord's table and of the table of demons* (1 Corinthians 10:20-21).

When man lives in sin, he thinks he is in charge. After all, it is his life. He responds to his body drives and what pleases his spirit. All the time he enters into "partnership" with demons! He is a part of the Satanic enterprise. He is an aggressive business partner with the devil, working to fulfill demonic dreams and desires. In his self-centered will, he is drawn into intimate fellowship with the demonic person. It is horrifying to consider.

The Apostle Peter gives us the very opposite picture of "partnership." He begins his second epistle by speaking of the great Divine power of God. This power is the author of all things *that pertain to life and godliness* (2 Peter 1:3). God put these *precious promises* in place through His mighty power. These promises are the expression of God's heart's desire, and operating in those promises *you may be partakers* (koinonia) *of the divine nature, having escaped the corruption that is in the world through lust* (2 Peter 1:4). Every Christian enters into a partnership with the very heart of God. God's burning heart enterprise becomes ours. We are in intimate *fellowship* with what makes Him who He is!

The author of the Book of Hebrews details this possibility for us. He gives an illustration of a Christian's union with God. He tells us of Christ. ***Inasmuch then as the children have partaken*** (form of koinonia) ***of flesh and blood, He Himself likewise shared in the same, that through death He might destroy him who had the power of death, that is, the devil*** (Hebrews 2:14). A son becomes a partner with the very nature of his father. He joins the family's enterprise. His father's heritage becomes his. In fact, the father of the son's father becomes his grandfather. The son assumes the skeletons in the family closet. So Jesus became a partner with our humanity. The Greek word translated ***shared*** is a synonym of "koinonia." God became flesh. Thus the incarnation is an illustration of the kind of partnership God offers us. In fact, the Hebrew author explains God's reasoning for doing this. He is destroying the devil ***who had the power of death***. One partnership is being eliminated for the sake of a new partnership.

Do you see the Bible only considers two kinds of partnerships? There are only two possibilities for your life. You are either going to be a partner with Satan, fulfilling his dreams and engaged in his enterprise, or you will be in partnership with Christ. Either you will be filled with His nature, involved in His plans, knowing His heart or you will be possessed with the devil's demonic nature, accomplishing his ends, and embracing his heart. There is no third category. The concept of neutrality does not exist. There is no half and half.

God is pulling us into His very nature. We are not workers on the assembly line. We are sons in the main office. We are not errand boys assigned to accomplish tasks. We are business partners in the enterprise of God. Has the awesomeness of this gripped your heart? You can be a partaker (partner) in the nature of God. We have taken on the status of sons and daughters. We are next of kin to the Trinity. We are heirs of God. Beyond all of the benefits of this position is the greatness of joining God in His

Part Six: Early Church Mathematics

heart's desire. He shares His vision with us. We are resourced by His Spirit to join Him in the highest level of His dream.

Paul used the concept of grafting to express this. *And if some of the branches were broken off, and you, being a wild olive tree, were grafted in among them, and with them became a partaker* (form of koinonia) *of the root and fatness of the olive tree,* (Romans 11:17). Paul emphasizes the close participation of the engrafted branch in the total life of the cultivated olive tree. It is a partnership in a great enterprise. It is far beyond just being "a part" or receiving benefits. The grafted branch actually experiences the life giving sap of the tree. It is a vital part of the business of the tree. Without the branch the tree cannot fulfill its natural desire. Oh, to be grafted into Christ in such a way. Is it possible to become such a partner to the Divine? We become the fulfillment of His very heart's desire!

Paul is very strong when he speaks about this mystical union with Christ. He says, *God is faithful, by whom you were called into the fellowship* (form of koinonia) *of his Son, Jesus Christ our Lord* (1 Corinthians 1:9). Our life is identified with Christ. We become partners in His death and resurrection. *I have been crucified with Christ; it is no longer I who live, but Christ lives in me; and the life which I now live in the flesh I live by faith in the Son of God, who loved me and gave Himself for me* (Galatians 2:20). The danger for us is in not understanding the union of this partnership. Paul consistently clarifies the issue. *And our hope for you is steadfast, because we know that as you are partakers* (koinonia) *of the sufferings, so also you will partake of the consolation* (2 Corinthians 1:7). He clearly states the content of this suffering. *For as the sufferings of Christ abound in us, so our consolation also abounds through Christ* (2 Corinthians 1:5). The Greek word (paraklesis) translated *consolation* means "to beseech." It is the act of exhortation, encouragement, or comfort. We must exhibit through our lives, by exhortation and encouragement,

Business with Jesus | **Acts 2:42**

the very style of the cross and its redemptive force.

To become a partner with Christ is to join Him in His lifestyle. It is the lifestyle of the cross! It is His enterprise, His business. But how else can it be? If we are grafted into the root, if we are partakers of the Divine nature, will not the fruit be His? If we are business partners in the enterprise of His heart, will we not be an extension of that redemption? To join Him in His resurrection is to join Him in the fellowship of His suffering. To join Him on the deepest level of His heart's concern is to partner with Him in the accomplishment of that concern.

I want to share with Jesus on this level. I want to join my heart together with His. I surrender the right to live my own life. I want Him to live His life through me. Wherever this takes me, it will be fine. I must know intimacy with Him!

In our study so far, we have focused on partnership with Jesus. This involves my intimacy with Him and sharing the enterprise of His heart. As this emphasis expands into the context of our passage, we see the practical expression of this "business." ***Now all who believed were together, and had all things in common, and sold their possessions and goods, and divided them among all, as anyone had need. So continuing daily with one accord in the temple,*** (Acts 2:44-46). The believers displayed their tremendous unity. Their unity was not because they eliminated their differences. Jesus became so great in their lives that their differences did not matter. The dominate enterprise of Christ brought their differences into unity.

It is not uncommon for the unity of the believers to become the dominate concern in the church. That is natural because of the tangible element of human relationship. But unity of the believers is always a byproduct of unity with Jesus. These new believers moved into (koinonia) ***fellowship*** with Jesus, causing new enterprise to bring them into oneness with each other.

There are three areas to this unity. The first is "identical with all." ***Now all who believed were together*** (Acts 2:44). The

Part Six: Early Church Mathematics

Greek words (epi, to, auto) translated *together* are preceded by the Greek word (en) translated *were*. It is a verb of being. The disciples were in a state of being which placed them in a location. They were constantly coming together. This message is not meant to create guilt because you do not come to the services of the church. The issue is not "if" you come; the issue is "why" don't you want to come? Why are you not desperate to worship with the corporate body? Why do you not crave sharing with others in the corporate moving of the Spirit, linking with other believers, and receiving the revelation of the Word? Why would this not be a high priority? Why is this not your first choice? The issue is not about physical activity; the issue is about a spiritual *fellowship* (koinonia) with Jesus.

Our second issue is "identical for all." ***Now all who believed were together, and had all things in common*** (Acts 2:44). The Greek word (koinos) translated *common* is used here in the sense of what concerns all. The believers were together in a community whose attitude and practice was not based on economic theory. There was no legal socialization. Their partnership in the enterprise of Christ expressed their loving fellowship and their renouncement of ownership, all with the purpose of helping others. No one gives without relinquishing the right to keep. Only one thing can break the bondage of ownership in any area of our lives. We must experience His enterprise.

The third factor is "identical in all." ***The believers were together, and had all things in common, and sold their possessions and goods, and divided them among all, as anyone had need. So continuing daily with one accord in the temple*** (Acts 2:44-46). The Greek word (homothumadon) translated *with one accord* is a combination of two Greek words. The first Greek word (homou) means "together." The second Greek word (thumos) means "passion" or "heavy breathing." There was an attitude of passion and enthusiasm for Jesus which permeated all of their personal relationships.

What a church this must have been! But the focus is not on these things; they are a byproduct of their involvement in Jesus. We must come back to Him! He must capture us! He is our new location!

Acts 2:42

EATING AT THE CROSS

There were four very important activities in which the new Jewish converts participated. One of these activities was **the breaking of bread** (Acts 2:42). This phrase refers to a firmly fixed rite which always opened a Jewish meal. At every meal's beginning, the head of the household would rise, take a flat loaf of bread designed to be broken instead of sliced, and pronounce a blessing. The blessing went something like this. "Blessed are you, Lord, our God, King of the world, who has brought forth bread from the earth." All those gathered for the meal would then respond, "Amen." The head of the household would then break off enough pieces of the loaf for everyone, and pass the pieces to each person beginning with those seated furthest away. Then he would break off a piece for himself, and eat it, thus signifying for all that they were ready to eat what was set before them.

The Gospels record at least four times when Jesus followed this practice. On the occasion of feeding the five thousand, Matthew writes, ***Then He commanded the multitudes to sit down on the grass. And he took the five loaves and the two fish, and looking up to heaven, He blessed and broke and gave the loaves to the disciples; and the disciples gave to the multitudes*** (Matthew 14:19). This same ritual was practiced again by Jesus at the feeding of the four thousand (Matthew 15:36). During the Last Supper the eleven disciples were gripped by confusion over the issue of a betrayer. Each disciple wondered about his

Eating at the Cross | **Acts 2:42**

personal involvement in such an act. *And as they were eating, Jesus took bread, blessed and broke it, and gave it to the disciples and said, "Take eat: this is My body,"* (Matthew 26:26). Two disciples encountered the risen Lord on the Emmaus Road. They were overwhelmed with discouragement and did not recognize Jesus. As the journey came to an end, He was going further, but they convinced Him to stay. *Now it came to pass, as He sat at the table with them, that He took bread, blessed and broke it, and gave it to them* (Luke 24:30).

In our passage (Acts 2:42) we must decide if **breaking of bread** is a reference to a full meal or the Lord's Supper. In the context of our study this event is in the midst of three other activities practiced in the early church. The **breaking of bread** was done in the normal routine of family life and in the business world. Everyone in the community of believers practiced this as a regular activity. After Jesus established the Lord's Supper, the phrase **breaking of bread**, developed into a reference to this event. In addition, in the Greek text, the English word *in* is not present; there is a definite article (**the**) placed just before **breaking of bread**. This takes it from the general to the specific. It is generally accepted that the early church gathered together for a full meal; the Lord's Supper followed immediately as the conclusion of the meal.

Therefore, it appears this phrase is distinctly connected to the Lord's Supper. Everyone would agree the Lord's Supper is completely focused on the crucifixion of Jesus. This is what He commanded us to remember. As He broke bread and gave it to His disciples, He said, "Take eat, this is My body." Then He took the cup, gave thanks, and gave it to them, saying, "Drink from it, all of you. *For this is My blood of the new covenant, which is shed for many for the remission of sins,"* (Matthew 26:28). The very fact that Jesus instituted this with all of the disciples present bespeaks the community of believers. The Lord's Supper was not only experienced by the individual but by the body of Christ. The cross of Christ is planted in the middle of my personal life and in the middle of my relationship with you. The early converts were saturating in the teachings of the Scriptures (*in the apostles' doctrine*) and involved in business with the Father and each other (*fellowship*/koinonia). They were always viewing their lives and their relationships in light of the cross (*in the breaking of bread*).

A Meal Together in Light of the Cross

We need to consider a meal together in light of the cross. This is a determining truth. My relationship with you (***breaking of bread*** at the table) must always be experienced in light of His death *for me*. This involves my *pardon*. I must forgive you in the same manner and depth that He forgives me!

In the middle of the Sermon on the Mount, Jesus teaches the disciples how to pray. In the midst of this model prayer, He prays, **"And forgive us our debts, as we forgive our debtors"** (Matthew 6:12). Jesus gives a clear explanation of this statement. He says, *"For if you forgive men their trespasses, your heavenly Father will also forgive you. But if you do not forgive men their trespasses, neither will your Father forgive your trespasses,"* (Matthew 6:14-15). How has the Father forgiven me? His forgiveness is without condition or reservation. It is lavish, extravagant, and in abundance. It is forgiveness before I even ask. There is no hesitation in the Father forgiving me. If I do not forgive my brother in the same manner, I erect a blockage which stops me from receiving the flow of forgiveness. If I do not accept the Father's forgiveness, I create a blockage, and I do not experience His forgiveness. In the same manner, when I am not a channel for the flow of the Father's forgiveness to my fellowman, I create a blockage. I block my ability to receive His forgiveness. I experience the Father's forgiveness in the same manner I forgive my fellowman.

The disciples were always expressing their self-sourcing. Their bickering among themselves was focused on *"Who then is greatest in the kingdom of heaven?"* (Matthew 18:1). This statement gave evidence to their self-centeredness. This self-centeredness always determines how an individual relates to his fellowman. The example of the Father is that of a good shepherd who seeks one straying sheep at the risk of his own life (Matthew 18:12-14). Jesus immediately encourages His disciples to express this same forgiveness to their fellowmen (Matthew 18:15-20). Peter expresses concern by asking, *"Lord, how often shall my brother sin against me, and I forgive Him?"* (Matthew 18:21). Then Jesus tells "The Parable of the Unforgiving Servant," (Matthew 18:22-35). It is the story of a King who leaves a servant in charge of his finances. The servant embezzles the equivalent of $2,350,000. The servant could never pay back such an amount and begs for compassion. The King forgives his total debt. He is free; he owes nothing. He leaves the place of forgiveness and meets a fellow servant who owes him the equivalent of $16.69. He demands payment and throws the man in jail. The end of the story is a picture of how God feels about our response to His lavish, extravagant, and abundant forgiveness. The King *was angry, and delivered him to the torturers, until he should pay all that was due to him* (Matthew 18:34). In other words, when we refuse to live in the flow of the abundance of forgiveness received, our forgiveness is nullified. Jesus strongly states the principle when He says, *"So My heavenly Father also will do to you if each of you, from his heart, does not forgive his brother his trespasses,"* (Matthew 18:35).

This meal together (*in the breaking of bread*) also involves PROVISION. I must meet your needs in the same manner Jesus met my needs on the cross. *Blessed be the God and Father of our Lord Jesus Christ, who has blessed us with every spiritual blessing in the heavenly places in Christ* (Ephesians 1:3). *For*

Part Six: Early Church Mathematics

in Him dwells all the fullness of the Godhead bodily; and you are complete in Him, who is the head of all principality and power (Colossians 2:9-10). Such thoughts nearly take our breath away. We are stunned with amazement. The description of the provision is found in ***every*** and ***complete***. In fact, Jesus is the provision. There is absolutely nothing I need outside of Him. The very God who created me to fulfill His plan provided everything for me in the plan. What a plan!

We must constantly proclaim that Jesus is the provision. He does not supply us apart from Himself. He is the supply. He does not tell us about solutions because He is very wise. Can we enjoy these solutions apart from Him? Can we visit Him every Sunday and express our gratitude and that be enough? NO! He is the solution. He cannot be the provision for the important aspects of my life and I find the answers for other areas elsewhere. He is the answer to my marriage, my sex life, my financial life, my business life, my parenting, my religious life, my physical life, my emotional life, my anxiety, my depression, and my every need. We cannot fathom this truth unless we see it in the context of the fullness of the Spirit. He indwells us and in the sourcing of the Spirit of God we find all we need.

I am to meet your needs in the same manner He meets my needs. How can this be possible? I cannot indwell you; I am not the resource, He is. The statement, "I must meet your needs" must not be viewed from the perspective of self-sourcing; if it is, I become the solution to the problems of your life, not Him. I must meet your needs in the same manner He has met my needs because I am an extension of His presence in your life. I am the visible image of His invisible presence. He wants to flow through me that He might meet the needs of your life. I must abide in your presence with the same attitude He has for He is my attitude. The manner in which He views you, I must view you.

Self-sourcing asks, "How can I use you?" Spirit-sourcing asks, "How can I minister to you?" Self-sourcing sees inconvenience.

Spirit-sourcing sees opportunities. Self-sourcing protects and guards. Spirit-sourcing flows and gives. Self-sourcing is demanding; Spirit sourcing is giving. I become the answer to the needs of your life, because He is the answer to the needs of my life. It became evident among those first converts as they **had all things in common, and sold their possessions and goods, and divided them among all, as anyone had need** (Acts 2:44-45).

Eating together in the midst of the cross also involves PROSCRIPTION. This is the act of proscribing which means to denounce or condemn. I must judge you as He judged me at the at the cross. He assumed all my judgment within Himself that I might experience all His righteousness. Jesus exchanged all my judgment for His righteousness. **For He made Him who knew no sin to be sin for us, that we might become the righteousness of God in Him** (2 Corinthians 5:21). Knowing the depth of all I deserved, Jesus embraced it in its completion. Without hesitation, evaluation, condemnation, or conditions He joined me in my need that I might embrace His solution.

How quick am I to condemn you? It is as if I am just waiting to find something in your life to judge you. Paul thundered through Romans chapter one uniting the depth of man's sin with prevenient grace. We knew better and yet continued in our self-will. **Therefore you are inexcusable, O man, whoever you are who judge, for in whatever you judge another you condemn yourself;** (Romans 2:1). Paul echoed Jesus. Jesus said, **"Judge not, that you be not judged. For with what judgment you judge, you will be judged; and with the measure you use, it will be measured back to you** (Matthew 7:1-2). I am sourced by His Spirit; how He sees you is how I see you. There is no judgment.

The community of believers lives at the table. In the **breaking of bread** I see you in light of His death for me. However, there is a second thought. My relationship with you (**breaking of bread** at the table) must always be in light of His death *for you*. This immediately involves PARDON. I must forgive you in relationship to how He has forgiven you. Our self-sourcing always inspires the question, "How far do you take this? How often or how much am I required to forgive?" Earlier in this study we noted this very question asked by Peter. In the pagan world the philosophy was to do to others before they do to you. And you were never to forgive. In the Jewish world the philosophy was to do to others exactly what they do to you. An eye for an eye was the correct procedure. If you forgive, it is only after you have had your revenge. Peter considers himself very generous in proposing, *"Lord, how often shall my brother sin against me, and I forgive him? Up to seven times?"* (Matthew 18:21). Forgiving seven times is very extravagant. However, there is a limit. There are those who will always push the limit and one must withdraw their forgiveness. Jesus' answer was, *"I do not say to you, up to seven times, but up to seventy times seven,"* (Matthew 18:22). In the Old Testament context *seventy times seven* means infinity.

"*But whoever slaps you on your right cheek, turn the other to him also. If anyone wants to sue you and take away your tunic, let him have your cloak also. And whoever compels you to go one mile, go with him two. Give to him who asks you, and from him who wants to borrow from you do not turn away*" (Matthew 5:39-42). All Christians agree with these statements in principle. But the nagging issue is "how much" and "how far." As you turn the other cheek, what if they just keep hitting you? As you go the second mile, what if they just keep demanding the third and fourth?

The answer is "Jesus!" I am to go for you as far as He went for me. He went all the way to the cross. Evidently there is no limit; He never said, "It is enough." In light of the cross I must forgive you in the same manner He forgives you.

This meal together (*in breaking of bread*) also involves PROVISION. I must meet your needs in the same manner He meets your needs on the cross. Jesus displayed an indisputable

Eating at the Cross | **Acts 2:42**

principle from the cross. Your needs had priority over His needs. Your concerns took priority over His concerns. The difficulty in embracing the cross is the lack of personal advantage. There is no angle, no hidden agenda. There is no sales pitch. It is a call to lose your life as He did. In fact, it is His call. *"If anyone desires to come after Me, let him deny himself, and take up his cross, and follow Me"* (Matthew 16:24).

Another difficulty in embracing the cross is there is nothing beyond it. Isn't there resurrection? Yes, but only as you stay on the cross. In other words, the cross is not something to go through and endure until it is over. Eventually you will get to the other side of the cross and it will be finished. Biblically, I must take exception to a favorite song of the Evangelical Church, "The Old Rugged Cross." We will not exchange the cross for a crown. The cross is the fundamental principle of the eternal Kingdom of God. We do not go beyond it. It is only as I come to the cross and stay there, I live. Heaven will be heaven because of this. The needs of everyone else will have priority over your personal needs. This will make heaven on earth. It is the style of the cross.

As I join you in the meal at the cross (*in breaking of bread*) I also experience PROSCRIPTION. Here at the cross, I must judge you as He has judged you. We all marvel at the crucifixion event. Many details are not known by the non-Christian. But it appears from experience that everyone seems to know about the one who was crucified next to Jesus. While one of the criminals was criticizing Jesus, the man rebuked him. He said, *"Do you not even fear God, seeing you are under the same condemnation? And we indeed justify, for we receive the due reward of our deeds; but this Man has done nothing wrong." Then he said to Jesus, "Lord, remember me when You come into Your kingdom"* (Luke 23:40-42). This is a perfect time for Jesus to condemn, judge, and testify for law keeping. He simply says, *"Assuredly, I say to you, today you will be with Me in Paradise,"* (Luke 23:43).

Part Six: Early Church Mathematics

There was a woman who was caught in the act of adultery. The law was very clear, she should be stoned to death. The crowd gathered eagerly to fulfill the law. Stones were raised. Jesus was consulted. This was a perfect opportunity to set the record straight. Homes must be protected. Such activity cannot be tolerated. She should be an example to everyone. No doubt, Jesus will preach a strong three point sermon on the evils of adultery and highlighted the subject of "hell." Here is His comment, *"He who is without sin among you, let him throw a stone at her first"* (John 8:7).

Zacchaeus was a chief tax collector; he was very rich. He betrayed his own people in order to make himself rich. He dwelt at the bottom of all Jewish society. He made his way through the crowd to see Jesus. He was of short stature so he ran ahead and climbed up into a sycamore tree to see Jesus. Jesus looked up and saw him. It is a great opportunity to speak on the evils of riches. Surely He will condemn. Jesus will highlight the law; the crowd will join Jesus in condemning this evil man. Here are the words Jesus speaks to him. *"Zacchaeus, make haste and come down, for today I must stay at your house,"* (Luke 19:5).

When is it proper to condemn? In the Gospels, the only time Jesus offered words of judgment and condemnation was to condemn and judge religious people. Evidently condemnation must only be given to condemnation; judgment must only be pronounced toward judgment.

Am I willing to eat at His table?

Acts 2:42

BESEECHING GOD

The verse we are studying is a verse which introduces us to the daily life of the early believers. I want to remind you of the Greek words and grammar of this powerful verse. There are important insights which may be missed if only seen in the English translations. The main verb of the sentence is the Greek word "eesan" which is not translated into the English. It is the imperfect, third person, plural of "eimi." This Greek word (eimi) is a verb of being, a state of being. It is translated, "I am." Since it is the third person plural, it becomes "they were." This also gives us the subject which refers to the **three thousand souls were added to them** (Acts 2:41). The subject is expanded further by the Greek word (proskartereo) which is translated **they continued steadfastly**. This Greek word is a participle which is a verb acting as an adjective. It is in the nominative case which causes it to modify the subject. Therefore, the subject of the sentence has to do with those in a state of being which are "continuing steadfastly."

There are four words which follow in the dative case. This case indicates something of the location or setting in which the action of enduring takes place. They are **doctrine, fellowship, breaking of bread**, and **prayer**. The emphasis is not on these four activities. The important thing here is the **continued steadfastly** which happened to take place within these activities. Do not focus on the activities as if "doing" the activity is the success of the early Christians. Their success was in their spiritual state of being.

I am greatly intrigued by this. The reason for my intrigue is that it parallels another very descriptive verse. Just before the ascension of Jesus, He reminds the disciples of the Promise of the Father. He also encourages them to wait for the Promise in Jerusalem. He insists they should not depart from there (Acts 1:4). Luke gives us a description of their time in Jerusalem before the Pentecost event. He writes, **These all continued with one accord in prayer, with the women and Mary the mother of Jesus, and with His brothers** (Acts 1:14). This is the same grammar and sentence structure. The same Greek word (eesan) is used; it is not translated into English. It is the imperfect, third person, plural of "eimi." This makes it a verb of being, a state of being. Since it is the third person plural it would be translated "they were." The subject of the sentence is expanded with the Greek word (proskartereo) translated **continued**. It is a participle which is a verb acting as an adjective. It is in the nominative case which causes it to modify the subject. Therefore, the subject of the sentence is "those who are in a state of being which is **continued**." In our text (Acts 2:24) there are four datives, while in this parallel verse (Acts 1:14) there is only one. It gives the location or setting in which this state of continuing takes place. It is **in prayer**. In the Greek text the word *in* is not there; however, it is preceded by the definite article, "the."

This is the state of the early believers *before* the Pentecost event. It is also the state of the early believers *after* the Pentecost event. I investigated further and made a startling discovery. The same Greek word (proskartereo) translated **continued steadfastly** in our text is used six times in the Book of Acts. In three of those cases, it is in reference to prayer (Acts 1:14; 2:42; 6:4). We have already given you the first two references. We find the third reference in the intent of the twelve apostles. They request the selection of seven men to care for the serving of tables. The apostles said, *"But we will give ourselves continually to prayer and to the ministry of the word,"* (Acts 6:4). The grammar is different in this verse since the Greek word (proskartereo) is the main verb of the sentence. But the intent is the same.

This brings to mind Paul's focus on prayer. He said, *"Pray without ceasing,"* (1 Thessalonians 5:17). The Greek word (proseuchomai) translated *pray* is the same Greek word in our text. The Greek word (adialeiptos) translated **without ceasing** is an unusual word. It is only used four times in the New Testament. It does not mean continually in the sense of every day, before each meal, or every morning, it means uninterrupted, without intermission. It is what we call "practicing His presence." It is a Divine awareness. Intimacy with Jesus captures your mind and heart until you live moment by moment in union with Him. His influence is constantly guiding your decisions, thoughts, and attitudes. Is this possible?

He highlights the disturbing issue of exactly what these early Christians did when there is a reference to prayer. What does "praying" mean in their context? The Greek word translated *prayer* in our verse, (Acts 1:14), is in the noun form. It is used thirty-seven times in the New Testament and nine of those are found in the Book of Acts. The verb form of this same word is used sixteen times in the Book of Acts. As we read through the Book of Acts it appears they are always in a state of prayer. This Greek word is only found eight times in the Gospels as a noun. Each of these occurrences is related to Jesus. Even more amazing, the verb form of this word is used forty-seven times in the Gospel accounts. Each time it refers to what Jesus does or is used in the words Jesus speaks to others. In other words, in the Gospels the disciples never participate in the act of "prayer."

If this is true, the early church entered into a new experience. For the first time they participated in what Jesus taught them in the Sermon on the Mount (Matthew 6:5-15). Jesus ascended to the right hand of the Father and they are now praying in His name. Opening before them is a new era of communication between God and man. Were they aware as they prayed that Jesus went behind the veil for them in the Holy tabernacle not made with hands? He at that moment made intercession for them (Hebrews 7:25). I wonder who was the first one who stopped and cried out, "Let us ask the Father in His name," (John 16:23-24).

This must have amazed the angels. They had often rejoiced over the prayers of a repentant sinner, but now for the first time they were hearing prayers which were authorized and accredited by the name of the only begotten of the Father. They were prayers based on the name which recently became a *name which is above every name* (Philippians 2:9). Can you imagine the joy of that first hour of praying in the name of Christ? Something new is happening! There is a new access and interaction between heaven and earth. Something is happening which was not possible before the arrival of the new High Priest.

What was the reaction of the disciples themselves? It was not business as usual. Surely they felt and sensed the newness of the activity of prayer. It had been ritual and chants before and now it was life and power.

What a privilege to enter into discourse with the heavenly realm which they had observed in the person of Christ. What exactly was the prayer in which they participated? How long did it last? What sacrifices did they make to do it? God was preparing them for something and this was vital to the experience. Let's begin by looking at the three basic words for prayer which Paul lists for Timothy. They give us the best picture of the distinction between the ideas suggested in the three words. *Therefore I exhort first of all that supplications, prayers, intercessions, and giving of thanks be made for all men,* (1Timothy 2:1). **Supplications** (deesis) is a word which focuses on the expression of a need. It is the statement of a petition. It is possible for this word not only to be used in relationship to God but also to your fellow man. **Prayers** (proseuche) is the word in our study in Acts. It is used exclusively toward God and no one or anything else. It is a word of sacred character. It has the idea of devotion and fellowship. Then the word *intercessions* (enteuxis) expresses childlike confidence as the heart is expressed to God. There is a boldness about this word; it is entreating.

In our passage, the focus is not on intercessions or supplication; it is on prayer. We gain understanding of the word used here (Acts 2:42) as we view its usage in other places in the Scriptures. For instance, Matthew quotes Jesus as saying, **"It is written, 'My house shall be called a house of prayer,' but you have made it a 'den of thieves,'"** (Matthew 21:13). Notice the temple was not called a house of "intercession" nor was it called a house of "supplication." It is a house of prayer which meant far more than just a place to ask for something. It was a place of sacrificial offering, worship, cleansing, and the fulfillment of activities related to relationship with God. It would be like calling your home a house of marriage, meaning everything connected with marriage is contained within that house. Eating, crying, laughing, resting, planning, dreaming, and loving are all a part of what takes place in this house. It is a place where two lives intersect.

If this is the correct picture, then prayer is not about the position of your body or the tone of your voice. It is all about the activities and aspects of your life which relate to intimacy with God. It includes all conversations about Him and with Him. It is worship and singing. It is eating and knowing He provided it for you. In fact, we label this interaction "practicing His presence."

"What did you do today?"

"I spent the whole day in prayer."

"Did you work today?

"Yes, I went to work, picked the kids up after school, and ate supper with my family, but it was all prayer. I have interaction with Him in everything I do; He and I are focused on each other and nothing can break it. I feel and experience His influence.

Part Six: Early Church Mathematics

I find myself worshipping Him and moment by moment we interact in sweet fellowship."

Well, you say, this really sounds spiritual, but is it practical? Is it possible to do this? How can you maintain such a strong discipline? Even when I get on my knees to pray, with everything around me quiet, my mind seems to wander. If I cannot concentrate on Him when I have my eyes closed and my head bowed, how can I completely focus on Him when there are activities rushing around me? I easily get distracted! How can I do this?

You asked the wrong question! Luke explains in our passage why this question does not address the issue at hand. Let's look at it again: ***And they continued steadfastly in the apostles' doctrine and fellowship, in the breaking of bread, and in prayers*** (Acts 2:42). The main verb of the sentence is the Greek word "eesan" which is not translated into the English. It is the imperfect, third person, plural of "eimi." This Greek word (eimi) is a verb of being, a state of being. It is translated "I am." Since it is the third person plural, it becomes "they were." This also gives us the subject which refers to **three thousand souls were added to them** (Acts 2:41). The subject is further expanded with the Greek word (proskartereo) which is translated ***they continued steadfastly***. This Greek word is a participle which is a verb acting as an adjective. It is in the nominative case which causes it to modify the subject. Therefore, the subject of the sentence has to do with those in a state of being which are "***continuing steadfastly.***"

In the remainder of the verse, there are four descriptive words, ***apostle's doctrine, fellowship, breaking of bread,*** and ***prayer***. In the Greek language, these are in the dative case; which corresponds to the indirect object. However, in English grammar there should not be an indirect object in this sentence. An indirect object requires a direct object which requires a verb of action. In this sentence there is neither. However, there are four kinds of datives; one of them is a locative dative which is the case of these four activities.

These early disciples are filled with the Holy Spirit. Three thousand Jews who crucified Jesus encountered the Spirit of Jesus in forgiveness and intimacy. They are consumed with Him. He becomes their focus. He is not one piece of their life; He *is* their life. He is not a part of their daily schedule; He *is* their schedule. They are not tithing their income; they are giving all to Him. Yes, they experienced the teaching of the ***apostles' doctrine***; however, it was really about Him. They experienced great fellowship; but they were in business together with Him. They participated in the ***breaking of bread***; but it was about eating of Him. They gave themselves to ***prayer***; but it was not an activity. They probably had corporate prayer meetings (Acts 4:31), but prayer was no longer an activity, ritual, or ceremony. It was true life experience of interacting and living with the indwelt Jesus. Prayer was the indirect object of the state of being.

Prayer was the activity to which their focus or concentration was done or given. The action of the verb of being was on Jesus and given to the state of prayer. The disciples worshipped, praised, blessed God, fellowshipped, and ate together. It was all in the context of a state of being called prayer; because Jesus was the object of it all.

Prayer in this sense ceases to be an activity or something you do and becomes what you are. When it is something you do it creates guilt. How many hours should you pray? Is one hour a day enough to dedicate to the Christ who died for you? No wonder we feel guilty when we pray an hour or less. Would two hours relieve the guilt? Calculate all He has done for you! Will three hours be sufficient? Will I have to devote all of my time to prayer? How can I do this? Prayer must cease being an activity; I must "be" prayer. I must be so consumed with Him that nothing takes place which does not include Him. But my mind wanders and I get distracted. This does not matter if you allow Jesus to be in the middle of your distraction. The issue is Him.

We certainly understand this reality in relationship to ourselves. We have lived with ourselves for years. We totally involve ourselves in all we are doing. We are constantly fellowshipping with ourselves. We never make a decision without involving our own opinion. One man said, "Everywhere I go, I go too, and spoil everything." I never have a moment when I am not aware of "me." Is this the state of experience Jesus wants to have with me? Oh, if He could become the source of my life until the same involvement I have with myself, I now have with Him. Make it so, Jesus!

Acts 2:43

FEAR / AWE

Luke paints a glorious picture of the early church. The three thousand Jews of the Dispersion are remarkably open and accepting. They are subtracted from their old stale traditions and are added to this new Way. They are uprooted from the Old Covenant and experience the wonders of the New Covenant. They move from crucifying Jesus to embracing Him as **both Lord and Christ.** They ***gladly receive*** Peter's message. They are baptized and give themselves continually to learning, fellowship, sharing together, and practicing His presence. What a positive, thrilling picture this is.

However, Luke establishes a contrast to this picture. It is not in the sense of opposites, but in addition. He adds a key factor to what they have already experienced. This contrast is found in the Greek word (de) translated ***then*** (Acts 2:43). It is the second word in the Greek text. The verb of our sentence is the first word introducing this statement. It receives the primary focus. It is the Greek word (ginomai) translated ***came.*** It means to "come into existence." It also proposes the emphasis of a state of being, "to be." It is in the imperfect tense which emphasizes that it began in the past and is building into the present. There is a state of being which seems to have captured the group.

The group is delineated for us in the next two words of the Greek text. The Greek word (pas) translated ***upon every*** gives the scope of the involvement. It expresses the idea of oneness, totality,

Part Six: Early Church Mathematics

or the whole. The Greek word (psuche) translated *soul* limits the group to which this refers. Every individual was affected with the emphasis on the inward person. Among Bible scholars there is some disagreement as to those who are included. Some propose this refers to the Jews who are not Christians. The **wonders and signs** frightened the Jews of Jerusalem and their leaders. I do not embrace this perspective. This group of three thousand Jews and the one hundred and twenty disciples came together in such unity that the Spirit of God literally amazed them all with His presence.

One element for the basis of this thought is the limitation of the discussion of our paragraph. Nowhere in this section are the Jews of Jerusalem mentioned. The focus of the discussion is on the newly formed body of believers who participate in the wonder of His presence through teaching, fellowship, breaking of bread, and prayer. Think of the transformation in their lives. The more they learn and experience the more amazed they are!

Another important factor in this discussion is the meaning of fear. There is a major difficulty with this word. The actual Greek word is "phobos." It is the basis for our English word "phobia." The difficulty is the usage of this word in the New Testament where it is used forty-seven times as a noun. It is only used fourteen times in the Gospel accounts. It is used in the Gospels to highlight panic-stricken terror. When the disciples see Jesus walking on the Sea of Galilee in the night hour, they experience this emotion (Matthew 14:26). This is also the emotion of the soldiers who guard the tomb of Christ (Matthew 28:4). The difficulty with the word is compounded in light of the Old Testament teaching. There is an abundance of emphasis on "fearing" God in the Old Testament. There is a small amount of emphasis on "loving" God. However, in the New Testament it is entirely the opposite. Jesus never taught us to fear God. In fact, His consistent emphasis was always on loving God.

However, there is a usage of this Greek word (phobos) which can be translated "awe." Our English word "reverence" does not quite match the meaning. We must take the strong emotion found in terror and extreme fright and place it in this awe. It becomes a positive instead of a negative. This is something of the meaning in our passage (Acts 2:43). The newly formed body of Christ experiences the fullness of the Holy Spirit. They grow in the teachings and understanding of this experience. As they experience the wonder of a new intimacy with God and the demonstration of this in and through their lives, they are absolutely awestruck. Remember the verb which describes the coming of this *fear* is present tense. This means it is now with continual action. We do not know the entire span of time to which Luke refers. However, this is not just a moment in time; he refers to the beginning months of the early church.

Amiss, Afield, Astray

Three thousand of the Jews of the Dispersion were added to the one hundred and twenty disciples. They came to Jerusalem that year with the expectation that God would do something new. There was definitely a stir in the general atmosphere of Jerusalem. There seemed to be upset and tension everywhere. The elders, scribes and priests had more meetings than usual. There were small groups of these leaders gathering to speak in whispers. Things had not settled down from three years earlier when John the Baptist led a great revival among the people. Even though John was beheaded by Herod the King, Jesus took up the cause. The focus of His leadership was in Galilee, yet strong ripples of His miracles and message continually reached Jerusalem. Perhaps if He had stayed away from Jerusalem, things would have settled down. But when He rode into Jerusalem on a donkey, the people went crazy. You could see it on the faces of the leaders of Israel; they would not tolerate this any longer.

The Jews of the Dispersion were only in Jerusalem for a brief period of time. When the leaders asked them to help in an important matter that needed correction, how could they refuse? They always followed their leaders. Rome had something to do with it because Pilate was involved. The politics were always uncertain, especially to visitors. The Jews of the Dispersion were anxious to lend their support. Sure they participated in the crucifixion of Jesus. They formed the crowd which yelled at Pilate and made the demands. It seemed to be the right thing at the time. The way the leaders of Israel explained it, it seemed to make sense.

But when it was all over it was hollow and empty. There were so many unanswered questions. The whole experience of the darkness at midday was eerie. Were the rumors true about the graves of the great saints being opened? The sight of those saints walking around scared some people beyond measure. What happened to the veil in the temple certainly indicates something strange! Then the Pentecost event took place. They could not ignore all of it. There was a movement of God during Peter's sermon and conviction fell upon the Jews of the Dispersion. It became very certain that the Jesus they had crucified was now their Lord and Christ.

Can you grasp their inside feelings? How had they missed it? They were experiencing the presence of the indwelt resurrected Christ whom they had crucified. Wow! What do you call those kinds of feelings? It is not terror or fright. When you couple this with the tremendous awareness of God's forgiveness, there is an emotion which no word describes. It is the deep awareness of one's own guilt overshadowed with the wonder of the embrace of God's forgiveness. This must be seen against the backdrop of four hundred years of God's silence. These Jews had heard about the glory of God descending on the temple, but they had never experienced it. God broke the silence with Jesus, and they had crucified Him. But God would not allow that to stop Him; He forgives them and fills them with this same Jesus. They live in the awareness of this thrill.

Think of your own life. Many of us live in depression, anxiety, or discouragement. We are plagued with the physical reminders of our failures; we crucified Jesus. All of our broken relationships, physical circumstances, and memories haunt us. They point to our guilt. But He has come; He has forgiven us; He has filled us with Jesus. Doesn't something inside of you whelm up to capture your very being? If it is not terror or fright; what do you call such a feeling?

Adventure

The Jews of the Dispersion were thoroughly trained in the Jewish traditions. They observed the weekly routine of the sacrificial ceremonies for years. Even their annual spiritual pilgrimage to Jerusalem during the feast days became routine. The thrill of the holy city filled with the thousands of worshippers became ordinary. It was not a lack of belief on their part; it is the natural flow of duty. The necessity of these ceremonies pressed them to continue. God had established them; they were His commands. There was no way to quit. Duty demanded it.

The complications of life also enter into the picture. Family situations and business difficulties all complicate the emotions as well as the schedules. It is hard to work everything into a week which is already over extended. When the pressure of a business appointment crowds the scheduled duty of the synagogue, how can you not attend to business? It is not a matter of believing in the religious duty, but one has to put food on the table. There is a practical side to life which we must face.

In addition, there is this nagging question of relevance. I am sure all the ceremonies have some significance in the eternal realm, but sometimes it is hard to see in the daily routine of the activity. This is not an argument or the expression of a desire to eliminate the ceremonies. The temple must continue; the teachings must be given to our children; we must maintain the traditions.

Can you fathom the change which takes place in the lives of the Jews of the Dispersion? All routine ceremonies of the Old Testament begin to vibrate with His presence. Every one of the ceremonies brings them deeper into what He is doing in their lives. What was routine becomes intimate relationship. The God to whom they offered sacrifices is now living within them. What is the content of the ***apostle's doctrine***? The movement of the Spirit of God awakens them to the meaning of all God taught in the Old Testament. It all begins to make sense! There are no more routine ceremonies; there is intimate fellowship with God. They are not just meeting for fellowship meals; they were eating of His presence. They are not just quoting selected prayers from a book; they are actually communicating with God. How do you express this? What is the word into which this experience fits?

Have you known the duty of routine? In the fast paced culture in which we live, religious routine is quickly set aside. We just do not have time. We all admit we should read the Bible; we know we should pray; church attendance is desired. But life gets complicated. Most of us are not looking for something to do; we want to trim our schedules. The first thing to go is the routine. It isn't that we don't believe; it is a matter of relevance. The religious duties just do not seem to have any connection with my pressured schedule.

Oh, if we could only experience what the Jews of the Dispersion embraced. Suddenly there was a connection between daily life and religious ceremonies. God became real in Jesus. They were not just attending instructional classes and going to prayer meetings. It was not just an opportunity to gather with friends in the fellowship hall. The outside God came to be inside of them. They did not need to be encouraged to get involved; they burned in their hearts. They were not simply reading the Bible; the Word of God blazed in their hands. The Author lived within them and gave unending revelations. They did not simply come to church; they basked in His presence as the body of Christ ministered to their community. What word could describe this? It is not terror or fright. They are captured by Him.

Above

The Jews of the Dispersion are directed and united by the law of God as found in the Old Testament. It is so important to their existence; they develop oral traditions which give insight into its meaning and application. The difficulty between the Jews and Jesus is His acceptance of this oral tradition. He seems to think they place more value on this oral tradition than they do the laws of God (Matthew 15:3). Jesus continually speaks of something beyond the law. It is not that the law is worthless and should be discarded. The law is fulfilled. It is as if the seeds of redemption are contained within the law.

The wonderful aspect about the law is the settling aspect it brings to one's life. This only happens when it becomes mastered. Not mastered in its totality, but mastered in the sense of what is acceptable in society or the religious community. There is a sense in which they gained control of their lives through the law. Once the religious patterns were achieved, there were no surprises. The boundaries were drawn. Everything was in its place. They know what to expect. This gave each individual time to develop excuses or rationalizations for certain circumstances when the law is not upheld. Once these were experienced several times, they became routine.

The Jews of the Dispersion were ***devout men, from every nation under heaven*** (Acts 2:5). This refers to their relationship with the law. They were dedicated to the level of law which kept them acceptable to their Jewish tradition. They measured how well they performed based upon the comparison of their living with the acceptable standard of their Jewish culture. They could easily judge others by this same standard. Law keeping produced certain self-satisfaction. After all one needed personal self-sufficiency, self-security, and self-confidence.

What happens to the Jews of the Dispersion? They move from the self-sourcing to Christ-sourcing. A new realm from above descends on them. There is a flow of resource; it takes them beyond all the law can produce. Resource for living, love for embracing, and generosity for giving is sourced by the Spirit of God who comes to indwell them. Indwelling them is something above and beyond them. Now they know what Pentecost is! What is the word which expresses this awareness? It is not terror or fright.

When one walks or is pulled through the door going from self-sourcing to Spirit-sourcing, life moves to a different level. Look at the scenery. Everything is different. How can I express it? What are the words?

Acts 2:43

MINOR / MAJOR

Jesus healed all who came to Him. The Scriptures reveal this message repeatedly. Why do we not see those kinds of miracles today? Isn't the power of God the same as it was then? The early church experienced **many wonders and signs**. It is in our passage (Acts 2:43). Such miracles would revolutionize our churches today. Are we lacking something?

I am not willing to say, "This is our denomination." If we lack something I would willingly break out of the bounds of denomination, theology, church tradition, and patterns to experience whatever He desires. In the name of Jesus, I refuse to be limited by what I have always been or believed. Jesus, do a new thing in and among us. That is my heart's desire! Isn't this dangerous? I would be opening myself to every kind of doctrine and belief. The devil might move in and demonstrate his ability without my knowing it. Are there limits? Yes, there is a definite limit! It is the Scriptures. I want the Living Word to communicate the Truth through the Written Word. I refuse to step outside the boundaries of the Scriptures. Traditions do not establish the boundaries and neither does denominational theology. I will not trust my visions or my dreams. I don't even trust "the way I have experienced it." The limit is not established by my feelings or what I like. Jesus, revealed through the Word, is my revelation.

Staying focused on the major issue is one of the most difficult things. We are so easily distracted. What sparkles quickly gets our attention. The fact that we are so focused on ourselves is proven when miracles and the spectacular command our attention. We fixate on the temporary rather than the eternal issue. Being healed from cancer is more important than intimacy with Him. We desire a financial miracle much more than a salvation miracle. We welcome God's correction of our physical ailment, but refuse His Divine instruction to change our attitude. Something isn't right about this!

Minor

There are two emphases in our passage which we need to carefully examine. When reading this paragraph (Acts 2:40-47), many select this fact of ***wonders and signs*** as the major statement of the passage. They ask, "Why don't we see ***wonders and signs*** in our church? No one ever asks, "Why don't we see people selling ***their possessions and goods, and dividing them among all, as anyone had need***," (Acts 2:45)? We gravitate to the ***wonders and signs*** while selling our ***possessions and goods*** is not very appealing. ***Wonders and signs*** are likely to be more self-serving than selling our ***possessions and goods***.

Some may answer, "But it was the ***wonders and signs*** which brought about the ***fear*** which came ***upon every soul***." When people see the great power of God demonstrated, they get converted. Are you open to the truth of the Scriptures? Do you crave the mind and heart of Christ in all matters? Are you willing for Him to teach you from His Word? ***Wonders and signs*** are minor issues in our passage. There is no major focus on them; there is no attempt by Luke to highlight them as absolutely necessary for the growth of the church. He does not make them the basis of evangelism. He does not hold them up as a standard by which to measure the movement of God in our midst. The major cause of the ***fear*** was not the ***wonders and signs***.

How can we prove these statements? The first proof is found in the grammar structure of our verse. There is a conjunction connecting the two sections of our verse. ***Then fear came upon every soul*** is the first part of the statement. ***Many wonders and signs were done through the apostles*** is the second statement. The normal connecting conjunction in the Greek language would be "kai." Usually "kai" is used to couple ideas which follow directly. In other words, "kai" is used when one statement precedes another statement and the second statement naturally follows directly after this first statement. If this were the case, ***many wonders and signs*** being done would be mentioned first. ***Fear*** would follow immediately afterward because it is preceded by the ***wonders and signs***. Our verse states exactly the opposite.

The conjunction in our passage is not "kai" but "te." This conjunction is used when the opposite is true. When one statement is subjoined but does not directly or necessarily follow, "te" is used. "Kai" connects and "te" annexes. "Te" is the most general of all the conjunctions. It serves merely to show that the word or words preceding it has some connection with the one or ones following it. We must conclude from this that ***many wonders and signs*** were only one minor factor among many factors which resulted in ***fear.***

Another important factor is the occurrence of this phrase, ***wonders and signs***. Peter speaks of these manifestations in connection with Jesus. God proved Pentecost through ***Jesus of Nazareth, a Man***. He did it by producing ***miracles, wonders, and signs*** through Him (Acts 2:22). There are numerous times the Gospel writers tell us that Jesus healed everyone who was sick (Matthew 8:16; 14:35; Mark 1:32). They were a vital part of the demonstration of the Father through Jesus. In our passage, ***wonders and signs*** is connected directly to the apostles (Acts 2:43). In this reference, none of the three thousand souls who were added participated in such events. As the early church continued to grow, Luke writes, **and through the hands of the apostles many signs and wonders were done among the people** (Acts 5:12). However, one cannot state that **wonders and signs** were only connected to the apostles. **And Stephen, full of faith and power, did great wonders and signs among the people** (Acts 6:8). In Stephen's sermon, he repeated the history of Israel. He said, "**He** (Moses) **brought them out, after he had shown wonders and signs in the land of Egypt, and in the Red sea, and in the wilderness forty years**," (Acts 7:36). This phrase is attributed to Paul and Barnabas while they were staying in Iconium (Acts 14:3). After this statement, no reference is made to **wonders and signs** in the Book of Acts. We know for sure there were more miracles done than are recorded in this book, but they are not highlighted.

These two words, **wonders** and **signs**, do not refer to different categories of miracles. They do highlight different aspects of one miracle. In other words, every miracle consists of these two aspects. The "wonder" of a miracle is a translation of the Greek word "teras." It means to keep or watch. It is the aspect due to its extraordinary character that will be observed and kept in the memory. It is the startling, imposing, or amazing element of the miracle. The sign of a miracle is the translation of the Greek word "semeion." It is the aspect of the miracle which leads to something out of and beyond itself. It acts as a gigantic finger pointing beyond itself. It tells everyone that the value of this miracle is not in the miracle itself. Its value lies in what the miracle indicates about the grace and power of God. These aspects of a miracle dictate that we must not focus on the miracle. **Wonders and signs** are minor; they are instruments to bring us to the major. What then is the major?

Major

Jesus is the major issue! Everything we studied in this chapter points to this! Jesus is the explanation of Pentecost. God proved Pentecost in and through Jesus. Jesus was brought to the cross by the Father. God raised Jesus from the dead. Jesus is exalted to the right hand of the Father. Jesus received the Promise of the Father. Jesus is both Lord and Christ. The great spiritual issue of the Jews of the Dispersion is their relationship with Jesus. Their response must be "repentance." This means giving up a former thought to embrace a second thought. Jesus is the second thought. They crucified Jesus; now they must embrace Jesus! They are baptized in the name of Jesus. They are to be subtracted from one spiritual location to another. Their new location is Jesus. They continued steadfastly in a state of being; this state of being is Jesus. They saturated in the apostles' doctrine which was all focused on Jesus. They participated in fellowship which united them in business with Jesus. They broke bread which had to do with Jesus. They practiced the presence of Jesus in prayer. It was all about Jesus!

Our passage proves this in several ways. Notice that Luke says, **and many wonders and signs were done through the apostles**. The Greek word (dia) translated **through** implies motion taking place through an instrument. In our passage, the obvious instrument used by the Spirit is the apostles. The emphasis is not upon the apostles but upon what is happening in and through them. It is Jesus. He **poured out** His Spirit upon them and through them. This is the entire emphasis in the Book of Acts. Luke makes a strong attempt to down play everything but the wonder of Jesus demonstrating Himself through the lives of men. The **rulers, elders, and scribes, as well as Annas the high priest, Caiaphas, John, and Alexander, and as many as were of the family of the high priest,** (Acts 4:5-6) reported that the apostles were **uneducated and untrained men** (Acts 2:14). Education, training, and skill were not the explanation for what was taking place through them. It was Jesus! There is absolutely no emphasis on talent, charismatic personalities, or entertainment. It is all about Jesus. He is the only explanation. Jesus did **wonders and signs through the apostles.**

The *signs* are another aspect to convince us; the major emphasis is on Jesus. The Spirit of Jesus did **wonders and signs** which pointed to Jesus. This was the prediction of Jesus, **"But you shall receive power when the Holy Spirit has come upon you; and you shall be witnesses to Me in Jerusalem, and in all Judea and Samaria, and to the end of the earth,"** (Acts 1:8). A "sign" is the aspect of a miracle which points beyond the miracle event. The focus is not on the miracle but on the grace and power of Jesus working through the apostles. Every miracle the apostles did amazed the crowds and pointed them to Jesus, the source of the miracle. Jesus is the major focus.

We discover this repeatedly in the Book of Acts. Peter participates in the healing of a lame man at the gate of the temple (Acts 3:2). As the lame man was **walking, leaping, and praising God,** the people were amazed (Acts 3:10). Peter immediately **responded to the people** (Acts 3:12). His entire sermon was focused on Jesus. The **priests, the captain of the temple, and the Sadducees came upon them, being greatly disturbed that they taught the people and preached in Jesus the resurrection from the dead** (Acts 4:1-2). The miracle was a "sign" which pointed to Jesus. He was the major; the miracle was the minor. Every miracle simply established the opportunity for the apostles to declare Jesus. The miracle caused amazement (**wonders**) which pointed in the direction (**signs**) of Jesus. This is the unfolding story in the Book of Acts.

Our passage states that **wonders and signs were done** (Acts 2:43). This is another aspect which points us to Jesus as the major issue. The Greek word (ginomai) translated **were** *done* is also used in the previous sentence. This establishes a parallel. ***Then fear came*** (ginomai) ***upon every soul and many wonders and signs were done*** (ginomai) ***through the apostles***. The indication is simple. The source of the ***wonders and signs*** is the same source of the *fear*. The apostles were not responsible for either one. It was the Spirit of Jesus. He is the major focus.

The Greek word "ginomai" means to cause to be which is to generate. It means to begin to be, to come into existence as implying origin. This entire meaning focuses us on the source from which the origin takes place. The grammar of this word as used in the sentence is significant. It is in the middle voice. This speaks to the personal preference of the one who is the source of the action. It reflects the heart of Jesus who desperately, passionately wants to demonstrate His greatness to and through our lives. There are no barriers; there is no hesitation. This is an expression of His nature.

The Greek word "ginomai" is also in the imperfect tense. This indicates that something happened in the past which continues into the present. It can actually be translated "kept on." The *fear* kept on coming; the ***wonder and signs*** kept being done. Jesus kept on being the emphasis. He kept demonstrating Himself through the apostles. Again, this becomes the constant theme and emphasis of the Book of Acts. Saturating in the Book of Acts will bring you to amazement in Jesus, not in miracles. He is the major.

How does this apply to our lives? We began this study with these statements. Jesus healed all who came to Him. The Scriptures reveal this message repeatedly. Why do we not see those kinds of miracles today? Isn't the power of God the same as it was then? The early church experienced ***many wonders and signs***. It is in our passage (Acts 2:43). Such miracles would revolutionize our churches today. Are we lacking something?

All of these questions are focused on ***wonders and signs***. These are the minor issues. Our concern should not be about the lack of miracles, but about the missing reality of Jesus. Why are so few people captured by Jesus? Why is there so little emphasis on Jesus? Why is He the last resort in our lives? Why do we not proclaim Him as King in all we do? Jesus is the major. Why are we not Jesus pushers?

We all have experienced the Devil's distractions. He does not care if we are bad or evil as much as He cares about getting us distracted from Jesus. Legalism is devastating and the practice of it distracts us from Jesus. Our focus is the law instead of Jesus. We become focused on performance. Law becomes the drug addiction of our lives. Traditions are not bad unless they become the focus instead of Jesus. Church activities are not evil unless they become the focus instead of Jesus. Everything is to be an instrument to bring us to Jesus.

You and I know whether or not we are focused on Jesus. Is He the central cry of our hearts? Are we possessed with minors or with the major? The major is Jesus and everything else is minor.

Acts 2:44

BEING TOGETHER

Now all who believed were together, and had all things in common, (Acts 2:44). Our sentence begins with the Greek word (pas) translated *all*. There is an article (the) in connection with this word which means it is to be understood in a limited sense. It is not everyone in Jerusalem. It is limited to everyone within the group of believers. The number was *about three thousand souls* plus the one hundred and twenty disciples.

The second word in the sentence is the Greek word (de) translated *now*. Its primary translation is the conjunction "but." In this case, Luke establishes a contrast to give us more information about the group being discussed. We know the number of people involved and we have discovered their activities. What we now need to know concerns their attitude both personally and corporately.

As the sentence continues, we recognize the same sentence structure as in our study of verse forty-two. The subject and the verb of the sentence are given in one Greek word (en) translated *were*. It is the third person plural imperfect of "eimi." This is a state of being; when in the first person singular, it is translated "I am." In our verse, it would be translated "they" *were*. Thus the action of the sentence does not describe an activity they were doing; it is a state of being in which they were dwelling. It is in the imperfect tense. This means it can be translated as "kept on." It happened in the past and continues into the present. This seems to be emphasized repeatedly in our passage. We recognize from a previous verse, they were in a state of being which flowed into four locations (Acts 2:42). They were participating in **the apostles' doctrine, fellowship, breaking of bread,** and **prayer**. The focus is not on these activities, but on the state of being which is characterized by a continual, constant focus. The activities are incidental compared to the state of being. So it is in our present verse. What is stated in the rest of the verse is not the main focus. The issue is the state of being in which they were dwelling.

The Greek word (pisteuo) translated **believed** is a verb in the participle form. It is an adjective in the nominative case. Therefore, it modifies the subject, "they." It describes their state of being. The early church was absolutely focused on Jesus. They kept on in this state of being. They expressed it by saturating in the **apostles' doctrine**. They were also constantly aware of the business at hand, because they were in business with Jesus. They lived in fellowship with each other through the **breaking of bread**. They consistently practiced His presence as they prayed without ceasing. Now we add another element to this state of being. It is "belief."

The heart of faith is "invoking the activity of the second party." It is a sourcing issue. Believing in myself causes me to invoke my own activity to source my living. Believing in Christ is a shift in the source which allows Him to constantly enable my life. The basic reference point of their life changed. Three thousand Jews were subtracted from a self-sourced culture and added to a Christ-sourced culture. Their reference point for living had been the law, ceremonies, and their traditions. This self-sourcing caused them to crucify Christ. Now they embrace Jesus as the sole source of their living.

It is very important to grasp this concept in the passage. Those to whom this verse applies are in a state of being. Their focus is not on activities or performance. They did not all wear a Christian uniform or conform to the same likes and dislikes, but everyone in their group had this state of being. This state of being was characterized by a continual steadfastness (Acts 2:42). They "kept on" in this state of being, which is one of "faith" in Jesus. It was a radical shift to be subtracted from crucifying Christ to being added to Him. The Jewish culture, with all of its traditions, ceremonies, and laws, is their life. Now Jesus becomes their life. They practice His presence. Everything not a part of Jesus no longer interests them. They consistently invoke His activity in their behalf, and they live in His sourcing.

There is a direct object to this state of being. In the English language a "being" verb never has a direct object. In the Greek language it is called an "accusative." This state of being (*believing*) naturally flows into an activity. It is not really an activity; it is a state of being. It might be described as an attitude. In our passage it is described as **together**.

The three Greek words (epi to auto) translated **together** have an interesting usage. The first Greek word is "epi." The leading ideas of its usage is "to rest upon, on, in" and "motion upon, to, toward." The second Greek word is "to" which is a definite article (the). The third Greek word is "autos." With the definite article, this word means "the same." This phrase is used five times in the Book of Acts. It appears in the explanatory statement of the disciples who are gathered together in anticipation of Pentecost. Peter calls everyone together for a business meeting **(altogether the number of names was about a hundred and twenty)** (Acts 1:15). Our Greek phrase is translated **altogether**. This phrase is also used to describe the group when Pentecost came. **When the Day of Pentecost had fully come, they were all with one accord in one place** (Acts 2:1). Our Greek phrase is translated **in one place**. Immediately following our passage it appears in the statement: **And the Lord added to the church daily those who were being saved** (Acts 2:47). In this statement our Greek phrase is translated **to the church**. It is also used in a quotation from the Psalms when David wrote, ***and the rulers were gathered together*** (Acts 4:26). Here our Greek phrase is translated ***together***.

Concerning our passage, ***Now all who believed were together, and had all things in common,*** (Acts 2:44), you would be hard pressed to think this Greek phrase has to do with location. This large group of people (approximately three thousand one hundred and twenty) was not living together. Luke is not proposing communal living. He uses this same emphasis in chapter four. ***Now the multitude of those who believed were of one heart and one soul*** (Acts 4:32). Using the same grammar structure, Luke highlights the state of being with the use of the same Greek verb. It is the third person, plural, imperfect of "eimi." The Greek word (pisteuo) translated ***believed*** is a participle which gives content to this state of being and modifies the subject. What they believed brought them into harmony and unity. Think of the diversity in this group of believers. They were from fifteen different nations (Acts 2:9-11), all speaking different languages. They all set the diversity among them aside and focused on Jesus.

Now we need to take a closer look at the three aspects of this attitude.

Presence

Luke does not indicate that there was a removal of differences. Think of the variety of personalities within this large group of believers. Let me again remind you of the list of fifteen different nationalities and cultures represented in this group (Acts 2:9-11). The three thousand individuals added to the church were scattered among fifteen nations. They were all Jews, but necessity caused them to acquire the various cultural environments of their surroundings.

Think of the differences between the one hundred and

twenty who experienced Pentecost. The Gospel accounts are filled with the conflicts between the eleven disciples who were from Galilee and came from the same culture. They had their own opinions and preferences. They each sought power and position and they were constantly in conflict and disagreement. This group of eleven was multiplied to one hundred and twenty. Yet, something happened to them before Pentecost which brought them into one focus. Now the group was multiplied again by three thousand new people, overwhelming the potential for conflict. Yet, these believers **were together**.

There was an element within the group that overcame all their differences. These differences were not removed. They did not all dress alike or all have the same favorite color. They became involved in something so great that these differences did not matter anymore. It overshadowed the racial barriers, the cultural differences, their backgrounds, and even the economy. What could be that powerful in their lives? It was Jesus. Our verse gives us the key to understanding; **Now all who believed were together,** (Acts 2:44). Everyone within the group had the quality of belief. They were all "invoking the activity of the second party." Jesus is the Second Party! They were captured by Him. They were crucified to their self-sourcing; they were living in the sourcing of Jesus. With the Spirit of Jesus sourcing each of them, He brought them together in harmony.

Each person having the same economic level is not what unites the church. It is not the color of our skin, common backgrounds, equal educational status, or the same hobbies. We are drawn together by Jesus. He is our one common factor. He overrides our differences in theology, our differences in opinions, and our differences in cultural practices. We are united in Him. We are captured by His presence. He is sourcing us. What burns in His heart, burns in my heart; I see it burning in your heart as well. Our focus shifts from our differences to Him! His presence is our unity!

Part Six: Early Church Mathematics

Passion

Now all who believed were together (Acts 2:44). Their unity was not the absence of strife. Unity is not produced by the absence of those who disagree with us. We can have the absence of strife but not have unity. We stated this truth three different ways in order to emphasize this truth. Whenever there is strife, there is passion, and we must not live without passion. It is the emotional fuel which moves us into action.

No one can accuse the early church of existing without passion. They were gripped by a spirit of awe (Acts 2:43). Their passion compelled their finances (Acts 2:45). It drove them into evangelism and they moved their world. As the Book of Acts unfolds persecution begins. Their passion so dominates them that they would not bend even under the threat of death. A person does not experience being eaten by lions, or dipped in oil and set afire, without passion.

This group had one passion; it was Jesus! The Spirit of Jesus moved upon their lives. They saw the truth of what they had done and been. The One they crucified in order to eliminate had returned to them in powerful revelation. They encountered the Living Christ. This was not the passion of a cause or a movement. This was not a project or the latest thrill. This was the living person of Jesus. He had not returned to set on the throne in Rome. He had come to reign within the inner heart of every believer. Their passion changed. It became a passion about Jesus and what He wanted to accomplish. They were no longer thrilled about the government leadership of a new dictator or a new Kingdom which would be of benefit to them.

He indwelt them with His very presence. What burned in Him was now burning in them. This was beyond loyalty. Jesus' passion became their passion. This was intimacy with the person of Jesus. All that was in Him was now in them. Jesus was sourcing them. They *received the gift of the Holy Spirit* (Acts 2:38). How desperately we need this for our hour! Is our conversion about a new way of life? Do we talk about an organization or new club? Have we simply entered into a new cause? Have we become fascinated with a new hero? Or have we actually been captured by Jesus? Has His mind become our mind? Do we burn with His heart? Has His passion become ours?

Penetration

This is not a superficial, emotional high which will soon become secondary. A common phrase of the older saints about new converts is "They will get over it." I was seventeen years of age and was assigned to my first pastorate. It was not much. The building was an old wood framed sanctuary out in the country. On a good Sunday, twenty to thirty people attended. It still had an "outhouse" for a bathroom. The pastor who preceded me had been retired for years, but had filled in as their pastor. He continued to attend as I attempted to move into his role. After several months, we planned a revival. It was the first revival meeting in my first pastorate. Wow! I was so excited. I preached in preparation for this time with great enthusiasm. I tried to cast a vision of the potential in our families and community when the Spirit of Jesus moved among us. It was the Sunday before the revival began. With great passion I challenged the people to prayer and attendance. At the close of the service I rushed to the back to shake hands with each one of them as they departed. My predecessor waited until everyone had left. He shook my hand in friendship. As he did, he leaned back and looked down his long nose into my face. He said, "You'll get over it." At first I did not understand what he meant. I asked him to repeat it and he did. It was evident to me that he had "gotten over it."

In the church, we often speak of the need for motivation,

Part Six: Early Church Mathematics

momentum, and an increase in involvement. We create programs to aid us in this struggle. Luke reports on the early church: ***Now all who believed were together.*** They were filled with the Spirit of Jesus. He penetrated the depth of their lives. They invoked the activity of His presence in their behalf. They were Spirit-sourced. This was not an emotional high that they would get over. They did not need motivational speakers or pep rallies to keep them stimulated. They were driven from within. What drove the heart of God now drove them. They were captured with the mind of Christ.

This was the state of being in which the early church dwelt. Evangelism came from this state, and the New Testament emerged from it. It is the state of Jesus indwelling the believer. He is the source of our existence. It is Jesus and more Jesus.

Acts 2:44-45

A RELIGION OF HAVING

Now all who believed were together, and had all things in common, and sold their possessions and goods, and divided them among all, as anyone had need (Acts 2:44-45). In the Greek text this verse is stated in two complete sentences. ***Now all who believed were together*** is the first one, and the second one is ***had all things in common***. The subject and verb of the second sentence is translated from the Greek word "echo." The subject is "they" (third person plural). The verb is translated ***had*** which is imperfect active indicative. It is a simple statement of fact. This verb presents the idea of "kept on." It refers to what happened in the past and it continues into the present.

The Greek word (echo), translated ***had,*** plays a dominate role in Christian understanding. It is thoroughly and distinctively Christian. The basic meaning of this word is "to possess or own." It is used seven hundred times in the New Testament in connection with a variety of things. The use of this Greek word in the New Testament indicates that Christianity can be characterized positively as a "religion of having."

There is a long list of Scriptural references which describe the various spiritual aspects we can have. In John's account of the Gospel, it is stressed repeatedly that we have (echo) eternal life even here and now. This elevates the richness of the Christian life from the realm of hope to the realm of present possession. We have God's love (John 5:42), peace (John 16:33), grace

Part Six: Early Church Mathematics

(John17:13), light (John 8:12), and life (John 3:15). However, most startling of all is that we have (echo) God. Jesus is the very heart of this possession. There are two verses in John's epistles which are paramount. *Whoever denies the Son does not have* (echo) *the Father either; he who acknowledges the Son has* (echo) *the Father also* (1 John 2:23). *Whoever transgresses and does not abide in the doctrine of Christ does not have* (echo) *God. He who abides in the doctrine of Christ has* (echo) *both the Father and the Son* (2 John 9).

This possession of the Father and the Son is an amazing thought. We are told we belong to God often in the Scriptures. He owns and possesses us. The Old Testament refers to Israel as God's possession (Jeremiah 10:16). The prophecy of Israel was based upon this great truth. *But now, thus says the Lord, who created you, O Jacob, and He who formed you, O Israel: "Fear not, for I have redeemed you; I have called you by your name; You are mine,"* (Isaiah 43:1). This great prophecy begins with God expressing His heart to Israel, His rebellious children. God says, *"I have nourished and brought up children, and they have rebelled against Me; the ox knows its owner and the donkey its master's crib; But Israel does not know,"* (Isaiah 1:2-3).

This is the New Testament's vital truth. Paul wrote, *"Or do you not know that your body is the temple of the Holy Spirit who is in you, whom you have* (echo) *from God, and you are not your own? For you were bought at a price; therefore glorify God in your body and in your spirit, which are God's"* (1 Corinthians 6:19-20). All of us readily accept the truth that God possesses us. We are owned by God. He created us and then He redeemed us. Both give adequate evidence of this great truth. We are His!

I would like to share with you one of my favorite stories from children's church. A young boy named Tommy made a sailboat with his father's help. Carefully following his father's instructions Tommy spent hours shaping and sanding the hull. He had to make the mast just right; his sail design was very

A Religion of Having | **Acts 2:44-45**

important. He had to have a name for his beautiful ship. The day finally came when his vessel was completed and he set out to launch it. He was so excited when the wind caught the sail. He always kept a string tied to his craft as to not have trouble bringing it back. There were many wonderful times sailing this boat he had created. But one day while sailing his ship the string broke. In great horror Tommy watched as his vessel disappeared from sight. Broken hearted, he returned home in tears. A few weeks passed by when one day he walked by the local pawn shop. To his amazement in the store window was his boat. The owner of the pawn shop explained to Tommy how a fisherman had found it. The owner bought the boat from the fisherman. Tommy had no money to buy back his boat. He went home determined to raise the money. He raked leaves, washed cars, and did odd jobs. Every day he stood in front of the store window relieved that no one had purchased his boat. Finally, the day came when Tommy had the exact amount he needed. It was a proud day as he laid the money on the counter and reached for his boat. He was heard to say as he exited the store, "You are mine twice; first because I made you and second because I bought you back!"

We can easily understand how we belong to God. He has us! However, it is incomprehensible to us that we can possess God. I can grasp the reality of His ownership of me. He is the great creator and rightfully owns my life. Through my willful disobedience and rebellion, I am kidnapped by the evil one. My willfulness caused me to rebel against the ownership of God in my life. Jesus bought me back; He ransomed me. I am His twice. I can understand Jesus owning me, but how can I possibly understand that I possess and own Him? It is too much!

In the Old Testament, Israel is God's possession (Jeremiah 10:16). But it is also true that the Levites were to have God as their possession. They were not given land as the other tribes. God was their inheritance (Deuteronomy 10:9). The Book of Psalms constantly proposes this truth! *O Lord, You are the portion of my*

Part Six: Early Church Mathematics

inheritance and my cup, (Psalms 16:5). ***My flesh and my heart fail; but God is the strength of my heart and my portion forever*** (Psalms 73:26). ***You are my portion, O Lord,*** (Psalms 119:57). ***I cried out to You, O Lord: I said, "You are my refuge, My portion in the land of the living"*** (Psalms 142:5). The Hebrew word (chelqiy) translated *portion* refers to a piece of territory such as property.

In the New Testament, Jesus debates with the Jews about their Father. They insist ***"we have*** (echo) ***one Father – God,"*** (John 8:41). The great criticism of the wicked is ***and even as they did not like to retain*** (echo) ***God in their knowledge*** (Romans 1:28). Let me remind you of the Scriptures we quoted at the beginning of this study: ***Whoever denies the Son does not have*** (echo) ***the Father either; he who acknowledges the Son has*** (echo) ***the Father also*** (1John 2:23). ***Whoever transgresses and does not abide in the doctrine of Christ does not have*** (echo) ***God. He who abides in the doctrine of Christ has*** (echo) ***both the Father and the Son*** (2 John 9).

Peter confronts the lame man at the Gate Beautiful with these words, ***"Silver and gold I do not have, but what I do have*** (echo) ***I give you: In the name of Jesus Christ of Nazareth, rise up and walk"*** (Acts 3:6). Paul listed some of the "marks of ministry." The climax of his statement is ***as sorrowful, yet always rejoicing; as poor, yet making many rich; as having*** (echo) ***nothing, and yet possessing all things*** (2 Corinthians 6:10).

If God owns or possesses us because He made us and bought us back, how can we possibly claim that we own or possess Him? This is the wonder of the truth. It is not what we have done or merited; He gave Himself to us! This is so completely New Testament; there is no argument against it. Chapter two of the Book of Acts is filled with this reality. While the Greek word (echo) is not used the concept is everywhere. The "pouring out" of the Spirit of Jesus is a gift. He gave Himself to us. The promise is ***"and you shall receive the gift of the Holy Spirit,"*** (Acts 2:38).

How can we describe the dual reality of not only being owned and possessed by Jesus, but owning and possessing Jesus?

We must note in contrast, the devil and his demons are real. While in the New Testament English translations it appears as though an individual has (echo) demons (Luke 8:27), the opposite is true. The New Testament consistently presents the idea that an individual is possessed and owned by demons. No individual has (echo) demons in the sense that he owns, possesses, and has authority over them. Demons always possess him. The "having" (echo) in each case is a possession by the demons.

God owns and possesses us; we can own and possess Him. The reason is because He gives Himself to us. But the devil always owns and possesses the individual; he never gives himself to us. When has the devil ever sacrificed in your behalf? When has He ever poured himself out for you? ***And we know that all things work together for good to those who love God, to those who are called according to His purpose*** (Roman 8:28). Has the devil ever made such a promise to you? The heart of the very nature of the Father is the cross. He constantly bleeds, suffers, and dies for you. Has the Devil even for one moment made such a jester? Jesus has! I was raised on the song which says, "Now I belong to Jesus; Jesus belongs to me. Not for the years of time alone, but for eternity."

With a thorough understanding of this Greek word (echo) we must come back to our passage. ***Now all who believed were together, and had*** (echo) ***all things in common,*** (Acts 2:44). Those who crucified Christ are now forgiven. They are subtracted from the "sick and stupid culture" which bound them in traditions and self-centeredness. They are added to a completely new body. They receive the fullness of the Spirit of Christ. He possesses them and they now possess Him. How does this affect their finances and materialism?

Part Six: Early Church Mathematics

All is His

If He has (echo) me, then everything I have is His. The crucial issue in Christian stewardship is ownership. It amazes me how cunning the devil is (Genesis 3:1). He never tries to get us to quit giving our materialism to God. How can he convince us that we do not owe God anything? He simply shifts the focus from "ownership" to "amount." At the moment of this shift the approach is drastically changed. If God has (echo) everything (ownership), the question is "How does He want me to distribute it?" If the focus is on the amount, the question is "How much do I need to give?"

The underlying assumption of the last question is that I own everything I have (echo). God is worthy and requires a set amount for Himself. How much do I need to give? From the Old Testament standard a tithe (ten percent) is the bare minimum required by the law. If I give more, I certainly feel very generous. I am able to compare myself to others who do not give as much as I do. This also makes me feel very generous. If I am very wealthy, I might even give less than a tithe and still feel very generous for I give way beyond what other people give. The entire focus is on "amount."

Jesus finished preaching His last public message (Matthew 23). He was leaving the temple with His disciples. He suddenly stopped short before they reached the front exit of the temple. He quickly told the disciples to hide as if something great was about to happen. Suddenly a little old lady came waddling into the temple. She was humped shouldered and had her robes wrapped tightly about her. She went to the offering box and looked around to see if anyone was watching. Convinced she was alone; she reached into her robe and pulled out a small coin purse. She snapped it open; she turned it upside down and hit it on the bottom. All the money fell out; it was two coins. After tucking the coin purse away, she rushed out of the temple. Jesus exploded with excitement. He exclaimed, "Did you see that? That was great!" The disciples were confused. They were amazed when they saw Sadducees float several hundred dollar bills into the offering box. This old woman gave only two coins. Jesus explained, "You missed the truth. It is not the amount she gave that is important; it is what she kept!" (Luke 21:1-4).

Jesus' confrontation with the Rich Young Ruler has bothered most of us. We wrestle with His command to this young man, *"If you want to be perfect, go, sell what you have and give to the poor, and you will have* (echo) *treasure in heaven: and come, follow me"* (Matthew 19:21). Again, our concern is from the view of "amount." Is He requiring the young man to give everything? Jesus struck a blow at the very heart of the young man's spiritual condition. He had an ownership problem. He owned his possessions until they now own him. He must give up ownership. If everything belongs to Jesus everything else becomes natural.

All is Ours

In our passage, there is no suggestion toward communal living. In the context of our verse this idea would be practically impossible. There were over three thousand individuals who were added to the church (Acts 2:41). These individuals did not all live in the same house. Some suggest they may have moved into the same area or neighborhood, but that is not even stated in the passage. The Bible never suggests communal property. There was an amazing generosity among the believers, but not everyone sold everything, though some Bible scholars proposed that is what happened. The scholars further state that it did not work and the early church corrected their mistake. I do not believe this to be true. Commanal property was never proposed and no one acted upon that concept.

Jesus was now their possession; they were now His possession. This greatly affected how they treated their material possessions. They realized everything was now under His control. They responded to the direction of the One who owned all things. An example is a story from the great revival in Korea. Jesus moved in a startling way in the church there. Several families, without consulting each other, came to their pastor and one by one expressed the same idea. Each believed that Jesus wanted them to give their house to the church. This sounded like a marvelous idea at first, but it presented some immediate problems. What would the church do with these properties? How could they maintain them all? Who would pay the utilities? Where would each of these families live if they gave up their homes? After much prayer, the pastor spoke to each family about their generous offer. He told each that the church accepted their gift. However, he requested an additional favor from each family. He asked if they would be willing to continue to live in the house that God now owned. Would they pay the utilities and maintain God's property? He also told them that they must realize that anytime God sent someone their way they should invite them to stay; after all it is God's house.

All is Needed

If I am owned by Jesus and I have Him, the heart of God becomes my heart. I must meet the needs of others. It is the focus of **as anyone had** (echo) **need** (Acts 2:45). The Greek word (chreia) translated **need** most often expresses the idea of necessity. In this passage the generous heart of the Father is expressed to those who are believers. Jesus expresses this same generosity in the Sermon on the Mount to those who are evil. His expression is contrasted with the Old Testament requirements. ***"You have*** *heard that it was said, 'An eye for an eye and a tooth for a tooth.' But I tell you not to resist an evil person. But whoever slaps you on your right cheek, turn the other to him also. If anyone wants to sue you and take away your tunic, let him have your cloak also. And whoever compels you to go one mile, go with him two. Give to him who asks you, and from him who wants to borrow from you do not turn away"* (Matthew 5:38-42).

It is extremely significant that in both statements, there is no hint of meeting certain requirements to qualify. There seems to be no hesitation due to the danger of enablement. It is a simple statement of the heart of God within the believer. It is not a statement of requirement or a goal to reach. It is about the heart of God living in the believer; this is how the believer responds. Would we not be shocked if a believer responded any other way? Since all is His and all is ours, is it not true all is needed?

Acts 2:46

UNITY OF THE BELIEVERS

So continuing daily with one accord in the temple, and breaking bread from house to house, they ate their food with gladness and simplicity of heart, (Acts 2:46). There are some details concerning this verse which are not immediately apparent in translation. The subject and verb, **they ate**, is a translation of one Greek word. "Meta" is used as a prefix; it means "with" and denotes association. "Lambano" is the root word meaning "to take, or receive." It is only used seven times in the New Testament. In our translation it is translated **ate** because of the emphasis on food within the statement. It is in the imperfect tense which gives the action of this verb the thrust of continually or "kept on." It is in the indicative mood which is a simple statement of fact. Everything in the verse modifies or gives content to this activity of receiving or taking.

The opening words in the Greek text are two words (kata and hemera) translated **daily**. They are in the accusative; they are direct objects receiving the action of the main verb. Since they are the opening words of the text, they become the most important emphasis of the passage. All through this paragraph (Acts 2:40-47) the emphasis is on "keeping on, continuing." In fact, the third Greek word in our text (proskartereo) is translated **continuing**. It is in the nominative "subjective case" and is a participle (verb acting as an adjective).

The second Greek word in the text (te) is translated **so**. It

Unity of the Believers | **Acts 2:46**

is a conjunction used similarly to "and." However, it is not used as a linking conjunction but as an annexing conjunction. Luke is not linking additional activities of these believers to what he has already stated; rather he is detailing the atmosphere in which the activities were carried out. According to Luke these early believers were in a state of being (Acts 2:42). The state of being is characterized by **continued steadfastly** which is again emphasized in our text. Once this is established, Luke introduces four activities in which they participated. However, the emphasis is not on the activities but on the state of being.

They were in the *apostles' doctrine*. The teachings of the apostles throughout the Book of Acts were entirely about the resurrected Christ. This was not a focus on an event but upon Jesus who is alive. Their emphasis was on embracing the living person of Jesus. It was not about a code for living or a new set of rules, but about a relationship with a living Person. This automatically flowed into *fellowship* (koinonia) which is doing business with Jesus. This involves intimacy and sharing the enterprise of His heart. They were "business partners" with Jesus. This enterprise focused entirely on redemption. The cross was in the midst of all the activities and relationships. They participated *in the breaking of bread* which no doubt involved "the Lord's supper." They saw everything through the lens of the cross. They "practiced the presence" of the crucified/resurrected Christ. *Prayer* was their style of life.

Luke begins to give content to the life lived in these four activities. ***Now all who believed were together, and had all things in common, and sold their possessions and goods, and divided them among all, as anyone had need. So continuing daily with one accord in the temple, and breaking bread from house to house, they ate their food with gladness and simplicity of heart,*** (Acts 2:44-46). The phrase *with one accord* seems to describe an important aspect of the state of being in which the believers lived.

Often the unity of the believers becomes the dominate

concern in the church. It is natural this would happen because of the tangible element of human relationship. But this unity is always a byproduct of unity with Jesus. The unity under discussion is unlike any other unity among any other groups. The Greek word (homothumadon) translated **with one accord** is actually a compound word. The first word is "homo" which means "one and the same." The second word is "thumadon" which is temperament or mind. It has to do with passion or heavy breathing. In other words, this is not a unity which is casual. They are not just going along with an idea. There is intensity involved in this unity. There is something going on which is so gigantic it has captured them all. This word occurs ten times in the Book of Acts.

This same emphasis is made before the Pentecost event. While they waited together in Jerusalem for the coming Promise, they **all continued with one accord in prayer and supplication, with the women and Mary the mother of Jesus, and with His brothers** (Acts 1:14). This was created by the resurrected Lord. He was with them for forty days in **infallible proofs** (Acts 1:3). He captured them; He spent this time **speaking of the things pertaining to the kingdom of God** (Acts 1:3). Their imaginations were filled with the wonder of what it would be like to be filled with the same life that Jesus possessed. Jesus must have restated all the parables of the Kingdom. They saw the truth through the eyes of the resurrection. This was so huge everything else became secondary. They were mastered by this resurrected Jesus. They were "together with heavy breathing" as they waited for the fullness of the Spirit.

Now Pentecost explodes into their lives. They are filled with the Spirit of Jesus. If they were in unity before, it is intensified and increased now. They are absolutely riveted to Him. They can speak of nothing else. He is the center point of their thinking. They have time for nothing else. All other issues become non-essential in comparison. Their minor differences do not matter. They have one drive and one passion. They are "together with heavy breathing" in Jesus.

It is important to understand how this passion/unity flowed into the four key areas. *The apostles' doctrine* is all focused on the resurrected Jesus. It is not the event of the resurrection but the fact that Jesus is alive. The apostles taught the embracing of a living Christ. The *fellowship* brought the early disciples into an enterprise. They did business with Jesus. The heart of Christ became their heart. They burned with His desires. In ***the breaking of bread*** the cross was erected in all their relationships. They poured out their lives in cross style.

This unity appears to be in three areas. We want to look at them together.

Identical with All

Now all who believed were together (Acts 2:44). The Greek words (epi, to, auto) translated *together* is preceded by the Greek word (en) translated *were*. It is a verb of being. This verb is the imperfect, third person plural of "eimi" which Luke emphasizes consistently throughout the passage. The disciples were in a state of being which placed them in a location. They were constantly coming together. They were not drawn to a religious service of entertainment or to a series of fun activities. It was not organizational loyalty; they did not come together out of tradition or family upbringing.

This is not a message to create guilt because you do not come to the services of the church. The issue is not "if" you come; the issue is "why" don't you want to come? What is lacking within you? Why don't you crave worship with the body, the corporate moving of the Spirit of God, linking with other believers, and the revelation of the Word? Why would this not be a high priority? Why would this not be your first choice? It is not an issue of physical activity; it is a spiritual issue of *fellowship* (koinonia) with Jesus.

Keep the focus. This is a state of being and because it is a state of being they are drawn together. They link together and seek the revelation of the resurrected Lord. They focus their energies on the enterprise of the heart of Christ. They pour out their lives through their relationship in the cross style. They continually practice His presence. Why am I not drawn to this?

This is the truth of the beautiful illustration the apostle Paul gives. He describes the linkage of the believers as the body of Christ (1 Corinthians 12:12-31; Ephesians 4:1-16). One member of the body does not reject another member of the body. The foot does not say that it is not of the body because it is not a hand. The ear is not rejected from the body because it is not an eye. Paul cries, *"That there should be no schism in the body, but that the members should have the same care for one another. And if one member suffers, all the members suffer with it; or if one member is honored, all the members rejoice with it. Now you are a body of Christ, and members individually"* (1 Corinthians 12:25-27).

The reason behind this illustration is to show that the oneness of each member of the body is under the control of the head. Jesus is our head. The unity, enterprise, and passion all come from Him. Because I am intimate with Him and you are intimate with Him, we are intimate with each other. This draws us together (Acts 2:44).

Identical for All

This is the second area of unity. *Now all who believed were together, and had all things in common,* (Acts 2:44). The Greek word (koinos) translated common is used here in the sense of what concerns all. The believers were together in a community.

Unity of the Believers | **Acts 2:46**

Their attitude and practice was not based on economic theory. There was no legal socialization. Their partnership in the enterprise of Christ expressed the loving fellowship which renounced ownership in order to help others. No one can give without relinquishing the right to keep. Only one thing can break the bondage of ownership in any area of our lives. We must experience His enterprise.

It was the last week of Jesus' life. He and His disciples were in Jerusalem. It was on Thursday of the passion week when Jesus preached His final public message to the multitudes. The leaders of Israel had bombarded Him all day with trick questions. They were desperate to trap and discredit Him. But it backfired on them. He pronounced the "woes to the Scribes and Pharisees" (Matthew 23). After this day, Jesus was undoubtedly exhausted. He turned to leave the temple and stopped abruptly. The disciples ran into Him and each other. He must have whispered as He said, "Something great is about to happen!" He motioned for them to crouch down behind the temple pillars and wait. They probably thought some great dignitary was about to appear.

Then an old woman made her way very slowly into the temple. She had her robes wrapped around her. She was hunched shouldered and waddled as she walked. She went over to the offering box along the wall. She looked carefully to be sure no one was watching her. She quickly reached into her folded robes and brought out a small coin purse. She snapped it open, turned it upside down, and hit it on the end. All the coins fell out into the offering box. There were only two coins. She snapped the coin purse shut, tucked it away in her robes, and waddled out of the temple. Jesus stood up and exclaimed, "Wasn't that great?" The disciples starred at each other in confusion. There was nothing great about an old lady giving two small coins. They had been amazed by a wealthy Sadducee who with great style flipped out his expensive leather wallet and let a series of hundred dollar bills float into the offering box, one at a time.

Part Six: Early Church Mathematics

Jesus patiently turned to His disciples and said, "You missed it again!" *So He said, "Truly I say to you that this poor widow has put in more than all; for all these out of their abundance have put in offering to God, but she out of her poverty put in all the livelihood that she had"* (Luke 21:3-4). The issue was not the amount given; the issue was the amount which each kept. The rich gave a little and kept a lot. The old woman gave all and kept nothing. This is not about how much you give; this is about how much you keep.

Perhaps you think I am getting old and forgetful. In the study just prior to this one, I told this same story. Is it worth repeating? Is it a truth which must grip our hearts? Does it have to do with the heart of unity? Church history reveals that all division within the church has always been over money and power. This can only be because Jesus ceased to be at the core. Somehow something inferior becomes more important than the superior Christ.

Identical in All

Now all who believed were together, and had all things in common, and sold their possessions and goods, and divided them among all, as anyone had need. So continuing daily with one accord in the temple, (Acts 2:44-46). Let me remind you of the Greek word (homothumadon) translated **with one accord**. It is a combination of two Greek words. The first Greek word (homou) means "together." The second Greek word (thumos) means "passion" or "heavy breathing." There was an attitude of passion and enthusiasm for Jesus which permeated all of their personal relationships.

What a church this must have been! But their focus was not on activities; they are a byproduct of their involvement in Jesus. It is not about a financial approach or how they handled their money. All of the activities of the early church were about their passion for the heart of Christ. Or was it the very heart of Christ who gave them this passion? We must come back to Him! He must capture us! He is our new location!

Acts 2:46-47

THE LORD'S ADDITION

A middle aged couple began attending a local church. They enjoyed the services and were growing in their spiritual experience. For several months they never missed a service or any fellowship gathering. Then just as suddenly as they had starting coming to church, they abruptly ceased to attend. Their absence continued for quite some time; it was obvious they were no longer interested. What happened? Why did they stop coming? The pastor of the church needed these questions answered. He made a pastoral call to their home, and he kindly requested that they be honest with him regarding their change. Somewhat embarrassed, and with encouragement from the pastor, they gave their honest answer: "Pastor, we do not fit in with your church. Your members are mostly professional people in management positions. At the fellowship gatherings they talk about their work; they report their golf scores. We just do not fit. We do not work in management and we do not play golf."

Who was at fault? Perhaps there is no blame; it is just the way it is. "The homogeneous principle" is a common church growth principle. This concept proclaims a simple observation from growing churches: a church will grow faster if they minister to their own kind. Let's apply this concept to our passage. Think of the diversity of people represented in the first century group of believers. There were women (Acts 1:14). This included Mary, the mother of Jesus, and undoubtedly at least one former

The Lord's Addition | Acts 2:46-47

prostitute (Mary Magdalene). Many of the original one hundred and twenty were from Galilee. They were uneducated fisherman. The apostles were in this category (Acts 4:13). The three thousand Jews of the Dispersion were from fifteen different cultures and nationalities (Acts 2:9-11). These people were very diverse in their customs, food and education.

In the midst of this diversity you would think there would be clicks, divisions, and power struggles. Yet, our passage reports rejoicing, praises, and unity. *So continuing daily with one accord in the temple; and breaking of bread from house to house; they ate their food with gladness and simplicity of heart, praising God and having favor with all the people* (Acts 2:46-47). They were together with heavy breathing which bespeaks their passion (*with one accord*). Jesus was the underlying factor of their lives. They did not forsake their Jewish heritage, but utilized it. In Jerusalem the temple was the primary place where crowds would be found. In this setting they became the demonstration of Jesus (Acts 3:11-12: 5:21, 42). This large group of over three thousand Christians had a tremendous impact on the temple. This was especially true as many **wonders and signs were done through the apostles** (Acts 2:43).

While the temple was their place of worship, their homes were the place of fellowship. Obviously they could not all eat in one home. In the Greek text, Luke writes, ***down*** (kata) ***house*** (pikos) ***they received*** (metalambano) ***food*** (trophe). When they sold their possessions, it was to meet the needs of those among them. It was not communal living for they maintained their homes. In the intimacy of the home setting a common meal was shared together. No doubt they closed this time by including the Lord's Supper as well.

Luke describes the atmosphere expressed in the fellowship and unity of these believers. When you think of the increasing numbers involved, this atmosphere is compounded significantly. They went from one hundred and twenty (Acts 1:15) to three thousand one hundred and twenty (Acts 2:41) to an abundance of more than eight thousand (Acts 4:4). It is a marvelous testimony to the power of Jesus within the believers. ***They ate their food with gladness and simplicity of heart, praising God and having favor with all the people*** (Acts 2:46-47). These words only appear in the language of the Church and the Bible. Luke describes a joy which encompasses the whole person and radiates from that person. The Greek word (eggaliasis) translated **gladness** is a forceful word. It contains the idea of inner joy, but also carries with it the outward expression. It might be translated "exultation" which is "to rejoice greatly" or "to be jubilant." The Greek word (aphelotes) translated **simplicity** is only used one time in the New Testament. It carries the emphasis of "smooth." It is the picture of a plowed field which has no rocks or obstacles in it. In our passage, this description is connected to the hearts of the believers. There were no obstacles in the inner lives of these believers. It has to do with purity of intention and sincerity.

These characteristics were a strong element in the evangelism of their day. Luke records *"and having favor with all the people"* (Acts 2:47). Persecution would come soon enough. However, the ordinarily normal Jewish people found the lives of the believers attractive and a blessing. The Greek word (charis) translated *favor* means "grace." These believers experienced the abundant grace of Jesus and they shared this with all their community. Yes, they stood guilty of crucifying Christ, but the resurrected Jesus now filled them. Total forgiveness was theirs and their lives were fulfilled. Their daily lives expressed the grace they received, affecting everyone and everything around them.

In the Greek language there are two different Greek words which are translated "good." One Greek word (agathos) describes a thing as good. However, the Greek word (kalos) found in our passage, means that a thing is not only good, but it also looks good. It has a winsome attractiveness about it. The indwelt presence of Jesus brought loveliness to the lives of the believers.

The Lord's Addition | Acts 2:46-47

There are many people who are very good but they are hard. They would never do wrong or hurt you, but you are not drawn to them. The presence of the Spirit of Jesus drew the community to this new body of Christ as it was formed.

Prime Mover

These believers were filled with the Spirit of Jesus, and this set the stage or foundation for the final statement of our passage. Luke writes, **and the Lord added to the church daily those who were being saved** (Acts 2:47). The first Greek word (ho) in this sentence is translated *the*. It moves our attention from the general to the specific and is attached to **Lord**. There must be no misunderstanding as to who is responsible for the addition to the early church. The second Greek word (de) is translated *and*. It is more than just a linking conjunction, but establishes a contrast. In this case, it is a contrast between the activities of the believers, the response of the Jewish community around them, and what Jesus is doing in their midst. The third Greek word (kyrios) is translated **Lord**. This is the subject of the sentence. He is the Prime Mover of the action of this sentence. Everything is traceable back to Him. Nothing takes place but what His resource instigates it. From the beginning to the end, we see His fingerprints on everything. He has handled it! What is taking shape in the formations of this new body of believers is a direct result of the dreams of Jesus.

Peter spoke his great confession concerning Jesus. It was one of his finest moments for he received his information from the heart of God, the Father. He declared Jesus to be **the Christ, the Son of the living God** (Matthew 16:16). Jesus was amazed at his response and said, **"And I also say to you that you are Peter, and on this rock I will build My church, and the gates of Hades shall not prevail against it"** (Matthew 16:18). This is the first time in the New Testament the word *church* appears. Perhaps the most important factor in this statement is the declaration of the owner of the church. "It is ***My church***," Jesus said. The church must always be seen as His. He is also the builder of the church. The moment we deviate even slightly from this reality we divide and destroy. He is the Prime Mover of the church.

Present Tense

The action of the Prime Mover is addition. The Greek word (prostithemi) translated ***added*** is the main verb of the sentence. It is in the indicative mood which is a simple statement of fact. This action is in the imperfect tense which has the effect of "kept on." It is in the active voice which means the subject (the Prime Mover) is responsible for this action. Those who are receiving the glorious actions of "addition" ***are those who were being saved***. This is a translation of two Greek words. "Totus" is the definite article (the). "Sozo" refers to the ones being delivered or saved.

The significance of the statement seems to be in the "tense" of this action. The action of ***being saved*** is in the present tense. They are saved "now;" therefore, they are ***added***. The indication of the statement is not progressive. In other words, they are not taking the necessary steps to be saved and are only on the first one. If they do not complete all of the steps they will not be saved. They are saved "now." It is present tense. In the Greek language "present tense" contains the idea of continuation. They are saved now and this state of being will continue with them.

We understand the progression taking place in the maturing and growth of a believer. However, there is a difference in growing *into* salvation and growing *in* salvation. A new born baby is fully a human being. He will not be more human when he is middle age than he is as a baby. He may be more mature then. He is growing *in* his humanity rather than growing *into* his humanity.

In one moment these Jews are guilty of crucifying Christ and stand condemned. The next moment they are saved through reconciliation and relationship with the Jesus they crucified. That is an amazing thing to comprehend.

Passive Voice

The Greek word (sozo) translated *those who were being saved* is in the passive voice. This declares that those who are saved are being acted upon. They receive the action of the Lord who does the addition which is the saving. From the very start of their subtraction from their "sick and stupid culture," the Lord acted. They were quite content in the knowledge of Jesus' crucifixion. They followed the leadership of the high priest who was the religious authority of their hour. They did the right thing. But then Pentecost happened. God moved in a new way. The power of His word cut them to their hearts. A sickening reality settled in upon them. They were wrong; Jesus was right. From where did this come? They are acted upon by the Spirit of Jesus.

Did they not have a part in all of this? They participated by responding to what God was doing. Their repentance was a response to the movement of the Spirit upon their lives. Their baptism was a response to the call of Christ on their lives. They continued in the *apostles' doctrine and fellowship, in the breaking of bread, and in prayers*. These are not activities to get God to move and bless. They participated in these things because they responded to the state of being of His indwelt presence. They *were being saved*; but it is quite clearly stated that they have not saved themselves. This is not something they figured out, a class they took, or a new religious commitment they made. God distinctly moved upon their lives and brought them to this place. At each point, they had a choice. They lived in response

Part Six: Early Church Mathematics

to what God was doing in their lives. Jesus was the One who added them to this new group.

In the Evangelical Church we need constant reminders of this truth. We all believe in grace. *For by grace you have been saved through faith, and that not of yourselves, it is a gift of God, not of works, lest anyone should boast* (Ephesians 2:8-9). Everyone proposes the fact that no one can earn salvation. However, grace quickly is pushed aside in favor of "works of righteousness." We do not seem to realize even "works of righteousness" are a result of grace. He initiates and I respond. My response is a choice. I can choose to "do" which is self-sourced, or can choose to "respond" which is Spirit-sourced. He delights in supplying, sourcing, and giving life.

Positive Placement

In our translation the word *church* is used. In the Greek text, we discovered this word was not present. It was placed there as a result of an interpretation of what the author was intending. The actual Greek word is "autos" which means self or the same. It can easily be interpreted to mean that the Lord, the Prime Mover, added the believer to Himself.

This certainly corresponds with the emphasis of the rest of the chapter. The Jews of the Dispersion were challenged by Peter to *be baptized in the name of Jesus Christ* (Acts 2:38). This was not a formula to be proclaimed over them as they experienced baptism. It was a spiritual reality very necessary for them. They crucified Jesus; they must now embrace Him. Peter also calls them to respond in repentance (Acts 2:38). They are *devout men, from every nation under heaven* (Acts 2:5). Indeed, Abraham was their father. Of what would they have to repent (giving up a former thought to embrace a second thought)? It has to do with Jesus. They rejected Jesus; they must now embrace Him. They gave themselves to the ***apostles' doctrine*** which focused entirely on the resurrected Jesus. He is alive. They can embrace Him. They are subtracted from their "sick and stupid culture." In this cultural condition they focused on everything but Jesus. Their culture saw Jesus as a threat to all their customs and traditions. They are now added. They are not added to an organization; they do not join a new set of traditions and customs. Their new location is Jesus.

No one should be surprised that this chapter ends with a supreme focus on Jesus. Let Jesus be the focus of your life. Everything which does not point to Him you must eliminate. You cannot tolerate any distractions which will detour you from Him. Jesus, Jesus, Jesus!

ABOUT THE AUTHOR

Stephen Manley has found through the saturation of the Word the message of the cross. It is beyond an event; it is a style. Thus, the cross is not a piece of wood or an emblem, but it is the heart of the person of Christ. Cross style is the Christ style. He must be central. As an international evangelist, Stephen has taken this message to the world.

After 41 years in itinerant evangelism, Stephen Manley felt a clear call from God to come off the road for the purpose of starting the Cross Style School of Practical Ministry. In 2009, Stephen launched and became the lead pastor of Cross Style Church in Lebanon, Tennessee to create the ministry platform for future students.

The Cross Style School of Practical Ministry was launched with a desire to not only train up men and women in the Word, but to give them practical hands-on experience in ministering to a lost and dying world.

Stephen's life, testimony, and preaching has been used throughout the last six decades to touch, influence, and transform the lives of countless people around the world. For Stephen, his life is wrapped up in a total saturation of Jesus and the Word of God. Time in the Word is more than an activity or duty to schedule in his day. It is the delight of his heart and the focus throughout his day because it draws him deeper into intimacy with Jesus Christ. He wants his "moment-by-moments" saturated with the Person of Jesus and the Word. He longs for Jesus to ever increase and expand in and through His life. As he once wrote:

"Jesus is present in every situation of my life. There is no conversation in which I do not feel His presence. He participates in all my recreation. He is everywhere I go. Who would want to be without Him? He is the protection for my life. He is the fragrance I constantly smell. He is the flow of my spiritual blood giving me life. He is my constant nutrition making me healthy. I cannot survive without Him. I am a Jesus pusher!!!!

I want to push Him on you.
I want you to join me in this obsession.
You do not have to work at it; it is not a discipline.
It is as natural as breathing.
Please let Him pull you to His heart."

Learn more about Stephen Manley and the ministry of Cross Style at: **CrossStyle.org**

www.ingramcontent.com/pod-product-compliance
Lightning Source LLC
Chambersburg PA
CBHW020938230426
43666CB00005B/75